Creating Deviance

Creating Deviance

An Interactionist Approach

DANIEL DOTTER

A Division of Rowman & Littlefield Publishers, Inc.
Walnut Creek • Lanham • New York • Toronto • Oxford

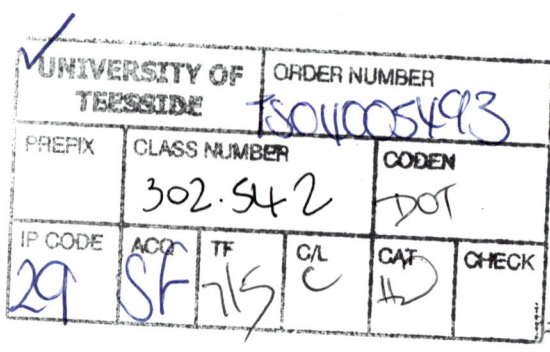

ALTAMIRA PRESS
A division of Rowman & Littlefield Publishers, Inc.
1630 North Main Street, #367
Walnut Creek, California 94596
www.altamirapress.com

Rowman & Littlefield Publishers, Inc.
A wholly owned subsidiary of The Rowman & Littlefield Publishing Group, Inc.
4501 Forbes Boulevard, Suite 200
Lanham, Maryland 20706

PO Box 317
Oxford
OX2 9RU, UK

Copyright © 2004 by ALTAMIRA PRESS

All rights reserved. No part of this publication may be reproduced, stored in a retrieval system, or transmitted in any form or by any means, electronic, mechanical, photocopying, recording, or otherwise, without the prior permission of the publisher.

British Library Cataloguing in Publication Information Available

Library of Congress Cataloging-in-Publication Data

Dotter, Daniel L. (Daniel Lee), 1952–
  Creating deviance : an interactionist approach / Daniel L. Dotter.
    p. cm.
  Includes bibliographical references and index.
  ISBN 0-7591-0503-0 (hardcover : alk. paper) — ISBN 0-7591-0504-9 (pbk. : alk. paper)
  1. Deviant behavior. 2. Symbolic interactionism. I. Title.
  HM811.D67 2004
  302.5'42—dc22   2004003945

Printed in the United States of America

∞™ The paper used in this publication meets the minimum requirements of American National Standard for Information Sciences—Permanence of Paper for Printed Library Materials, ANSI/NISO Z39.48-1992.

To Valery
Her Love Is Life's Text

CONTENTS

Acknowledgments ix

CHAPTER ONE Social Deviance, the Interactionist Tradition, and Cultural Studies 1

CHAPTER TWO The Scenario as Interpretive Strategy: An Interactionist/Cultural Studies Articulation 15

CHAPTER THREE Reading Interactionism: Pragmatism and the Problem of Meaning 53

CHAPTER FOUR The Creation of Deviance: Social Definition and the Process of Interaction 83

CHAPTER FIVE Toward a Postmodern Cultural Studies: Meaning Creation in Media Culture 135

CHAPTER SIX Rock in a Hard Place: Historical Stigmatization of Adolescent Subcultures in Popular Music 185

CHAPTER SEVEN Murder in the Media: Cultural Criminology, Constructions of Violence, and a Crime of the Early Century 225

CHAPTER EIGHT Theorizing Deviance in the Postmodern: The Turn Continues 275

CONTENTS

References 289
Author Index 333
Subject Index 339
About the Author 345

ACKNOWLEDGMENTS

One morning in November 1973 I began reading Richard Hofstadter's *Social Darwinism in American Thought* for an undergraduate independent study on historical sociology. In the background *Quadrophenia*, the brand-new Who album, played on eight-track tape. Little did I realize that this day would acquire such significant meaning over the next thirty years. Though not in a straight line, Hofstadter led to Goffman to Becker to Matza to Mead to a graduate seminar at Virginia Tech with Professor E. Gordon Ericksen, a self-described "symbolic ecologist" who was granted the Ph.D. in Sociology at the University of Chicago in the 1940s, and whose father was a student of both Mead and Dewey. A decade on, I discovered cultural studies in the work of Stanley Cohen and Norman Denzin. I got older—more mature I suppose—as Danny became first Dan and eventually Dr. Dotter. Along the way, *Quadrophenia* continued to play in the background. In fact, graduate school was my "substitute" for the typical 1960s adolescent dream of rock-and-roll stardom. By 1994 as I published my second paper on the then-emerging history of rock music, I was well aware that the rock opera was for me what I had begun to call an important cultural "text." I was becoming an aging rocker, as was its author Pete Townshend.

I offer the above as context for this book, the silent autobiographical voice informing the pages that follow. Rock music up until 1989 was literally the soundtrack of my life. As an aging rocker I gradually came to know that the 1960s and 1970s were passing into history, and that I was reinterpreting that soundtrack both in academic writing and in my wider

ACKNOWLEDGMENTS

life—overlapping textual voices taking the place of the music I had only rarely—but passionately—performed as a teen. I have replaced my drumsticks with a keyboard, but *Quadrophenia* still plays in the background.

There are many people to thank for their friendship, love, and support for me during the time it took to compose this book and beyond. All my students and colleagues at Grambling State University have been a family for years. Fred Jackson helped with the references and shared delightful conversations. Joyce Montgomery and Mary Dennis provided cheerful laughter in the morning. Shanhe Jiang and Mahendra Singh were always ready to converse between classes. Jackie Huey, Billy Williams, and Marianne Fisher-Giorlando have read various drafts and listened patiently as only friends can.

Peter Manning and Norman Denzin offered trenchant but gentle editorial comments. Paul Leslie did the same and has been a fine colleague and friend over nearly fifteen years. At AltaMira Press, I thank Mitch Allen and Rosalie Robertson for taking a chance on me. Paulette Cappel knows much about this project's development—from *Empty Glass* until now. Patti Guerriero is a marvelous artist who has taught me that art and writing are not so very different: in both we give and receive glimpses of the human condition. Jimmie and Ray Scott gladly treat me as a son, for which I am always grateful. Over the years my siblings have made unwitting contributions to this work, keeping me in their thoughts and being patient with my eccentricities. Carole and Dick have, particularly in recent years, shared family memories; David and Judy made several warm visits to Monroe; Michelle and Tom have always tried their very best to share the dream of this book—especially Tom in cheerfully enduring two Who concerts. The spirits of my parents, Chardelle and Richard Dotter, and my best friend for so long, Mike Moore, continue to watch over me. From an early age, my parents taught me a love of learning and books—and encouraged my imagination to roam. Mike and I were fellow aging rockers who took the academic turn.

At the millennium I obtained a new computer as well as a new life and someone with whom to share it. Valery and I met online and soon will marry, after a transatlantic courtship linking Scotland and America. She has indeed transformed my horizon into a richer, fuller dream than I could ever hope to imagine. Val, along with Gina and Ewan, my new family, awaits my permanent relocation. The completion of this project thus

ACKNOWLEDGMENTS

points even more to the future than the past. Borrowing a thought from Don Henley, everything is indeed different now.

My turn to the postmodern has been described—not always kindly—as one away from sociology toward philosophy. If such be true, I can take no credit for the change. Age, experience, and an epiphany or two have added flavor to my interactionism. Especially since 9/11/01, we all should revisit the enduring philosophical question of existence with renewed purpose. Now—perhaps like no other time in at least a generation—meaning, spirit, and tolerance take center stage in our personal lives and in the world. Rock music and literature, especially in the works of Pete Townshend and Theodore Dreiser, are sites of my philosophical search. Each is interwoven within my own textual biography, a three-decade narrative dance of classic rock and Chicago interactionism, especially the study of deviance. I describe Townshend as the prototypical "postmodern-punk-turned-aging-rocker." Dreiser was a journalist and novelist of American naturalism, writing roughly at the time of the first generation of Chicago sociologists. His work is an attempt to chronicle the early interface of the modern and postmodern in 1920s American culture.

As I was completing this work, Warren Zevon, a sobered aging rocker once noted for his raging party life, passed away. For me he has always been like "Randy Newman with rough edges." The wit of his songs is multifaceted: serious and comic, dark and hopeful. I like to think my life has been the better for the influence of rock; from Warren's artistry, and others' as well, I have come to realize that music is typical postmodern communication—mediated, open to endless interpretation, simultaneously mundane, liberating, sometimes dangerous. Most important, it is increasingly polyvocal, touching the lives of individuals and generations.

CHAPTER ONE
SOCIAL DEVIANCE, THE INTERACTIONIST TRADITION, AND CULTURAL STUDIES

The labeling approach represents a significant theoretical contribution to the study of deviant behavior and crime. At the same time, the perspective has generated much controversy within mainstream sociology, criticized both as a political agenda and as an empirically untestable perspective. Though it has many branches (Douglas 1984), the interactionist tradition in deviance theorizing is generally traced to its precursors, George Herbert Mead (1934) and Herbert Blumer (1969). Its classic statements continue to be the works of Edwin Lemert (1951, 1972), Howard S. Becker (1963/73), and Edwin Schur (1971). Each provides a map of the perspective, differentiating it from others. In the process several major concepts are refined and the study of deviant behavior enriched. Many of these concepts (e.g., master status, deviant career, primary and secondary deviance, retrospective interpretation, and role engulfment) have long since passed into accepted theoretical usage, regardless of orientation.

Classic works of general deviance theorizing demonstrate the compatibility of interactionism with a variety of approaches, such as functionalism or conflict theory. The work of Kai T. Erikson (1966) suggests the manner in which deviant behavior (and social responses to it) helps to shape and is itself shaped by the historical development of the community in which it occurs. Similarly, a principal thrust of Erving Goffman's (1961) *Asylums* is the constantly evolving interrelationship between staff and inmate social perceptions and the resulting social order of the total institution.

CHAPTER ONE

Still other treatises of general sociological interest are admirably informed by the interactionist tradition. The work of Jack D. Douglas (1967) on the social meanings of suicide and, more recently, the contributions of Norman K. Denzin (1987/93, 1991b) on the genesis of the alcoholic self and its connection with contemporary society illustrate the often precarious interdependence of self and social order as well as the grounding of deviant self-identity in conventional social structure.

In broad terms, then, the interactionist perspective, as applied to the study of social deviance, is very much a part of general sociological theorizing. Additionally, the above works demonstrate its adaptability to a variety of research settings and methods. Finally, the best of interactionist deviance theorizing is informed by a naturalistic appreciation for the deviant (Matza 1969) even as it illuminates the role deviant behavior and its multiple meanings play in the larger process of social change.

Interactionism and Social Deviance: Description and Context

Symbolic interactionism is concerned with the social processes through which individuals give meaning to life experiences. These dynamic processes are primarily linguistic: By means of language, written and spoken, sociocultural meaning is created, negotiated, adapted, and ultimately passed on in time and space. Individuals experience life as both intensely personal and external to themselves. Thus social norms, rules governing our behavior, of proper and improper conduct are both part of "who we are" and also of the "world out there."

Two basic concepts capture this complexity of meaningful interaction, W. I. Thomas's "definition of the situation" and Charles Horton Cooley's "looking-glass self." Stated simply, the former asserts, "If men define situations as real, they are real in their consequences" (Thomas and Thomas 1928, 572). Definition of the situation is a social process by which norms are rendered meaningful and even practical in everyday life. Furthermore, morality represents "the generally accepted definition of the situation, whether expressed in public opinion and the unwritten law, in a formal legal code, or in religious commandments and prohibitions" (Thomas 1923/71, 277).

Cooley's looking-glass self simply and effectively describes the interdependence of self-consciousness and the wider normative context: "the individual and society as opposite sides of the same coin" (Denzin 1992, 4). The self is a fluid process of communication: "the imagination of our appearance to the other person; the imagination of his judgment of that appearance, and some sort of self-feeling, such as pride or mortification" (Cooley 1902/83, 184). Cooley, as well as Thomas, recognizes that normative transgression—deviance—is a central characteristic of the self/society coin. Deviance is situated in the same communication process as conformity; one cannot exist independent of the other.

The history of the field of deviance is one of competing definitions. In his groundbreaking work on the labeling of deviant behavior, *Outsiders*, Becker (1963/73, 4–8) offers a discussion of the most common of these definitions. The simplest view is a statistical one. Deviance is conceived purely in numerical terms—how far does a person, thing, or situation depart from the average or "norm." In a sociocultural context this definition is all but useless. Statistical deviance ignores the nature and quality of social response to a person or behavior in the definition of wrongdoing.

According to Becker the second definition is the "medical analogy." Deviance is characterized as "pathological," transmuted into individual or social disease—in the latter case indicating the impending disruption of the organic normative system. The dramatically impressive metaphor of sickness obscures the importance of social processes like conflict in the study of social rules and their application. For example, drug use or sexual activity among the young may be criticized as evidence of widespread conditions of social disorganization and anomie. Also, the medical analogy suggests the existence of a higher, desirable state of consensus regarding social/psychological health.

The third perspective is more relativistic in its approach and a common sociological one. Deviance is fundamentally the failure to obey group rules or norms. This definition presents no problems as long as one assumes, once again, that norms are overwhelmingly (if not exclusively) a product of consensus and agreement across the wide spectrum of social groups. Finally, this normative definition uncritically accepts that in any given social situation all actors *understand* what the rules are, as well as the *circumstances* in which they are to be obeyed and applied by social control agents.

In Becker's judgment, the fourth definition is the most sociological and relativistic. It describes the core of the interactionist approach to deviance. According to Becker, "*social groups create deviance by making the rules whose infraction constitutes deviance,* and by applying those rules to particular people and labeling them as outsiders" (1963/73, 9). This view situates deviance or "differentness" in the social reactions of particular groups to behavior and/or actors in particular situations. Deviance-labeling may be as simple as a violation of courtesy, or as complex as a morality tale of crime and tragic fall played out in the mass media. In any case, the labeling occurs in the intersection of definitions—deviance *and* conformity. As a process, labeling connects the individual and social sides of the experience coin. Becker's formulation of this interactional definition, more than any other, prompted criticism of the approach as well as its continued importance through most of the 1970s. Presently interactionist labeling remains an influential perspective on deviance, although not necessarily occupying its earlier primacy. The calls of Becker and others to realize a dynamic symbolic interactionist approach to norm violation—as something more than statistical deviation, pathology, or simple violation of normative agreement—have been largely unheeded in recent years (Best 2004, 68–70). Still, interactionism remains fertile contemporary ground in the study of deviance.

Critiques of Interactionism

In spite of the immense contributions of deviance theorists working within the interactionist tradition, the perspective has been criticized on both conceptual and political grounds. Claims that it cannot explain the causes of deviant behavior (Gibbs 1966), or that it ignores larger socio-economic forces (with a primary focus on the subjective perceptions of individual actors), (Liazos 1972) have been commonly lodged. Similarly, countless scholars have outlined symbolic interactionism's perceived idealistic and astructural biases (Gouldner 1968, 1970; Lichtman 1970; Shaskolsky 1970; Collins 1975; Reynolds 1987, 135–57) or its general narrow focus (Maines 2001, 1–30; 2003; Ulmer 2003). From within the interactionist tradition has come the charge that the perspective has traditionally been apolitical (Hall 1972) and even today offers uneven contributions to the study of inequality (Hall 2003; Katovich 2003).

These critiques of interactionist theorizing were anticipated by the earlier work of C. Wright Mills (1964). In his analysis of American pragmatism, the philosophical antecedent of contemporary interactionism,

Mills exposes the uncritical acceptance of science and biology by John Dewey and other early proponents (Dotter 1980a). He further suggests that pragmatism ignores America's class structure, its power elite, and the consequent inequality. His own writings, especially *The New Men of Power* (1948), *White Collar* (1951), and *The Power Elite* (1956), were an attempt to emphasize the importance of social class for the contemporary study of social psychology (Denzin 1992, 58; West 1989, 128–29). At the same time he rejected Marxist theories of stratification, arguing instead for the cultural bases of power and their interpretation by the mass media and emerging occupational structures. With Hans Gerth, Mills went beyond a mere critique of interactionism's philosophical roots. The resulting *Character and Social Structure* (Gerth and Mills 1953) combines Mead, Sigmund Freud, and Max Weber into a role-based analysis of social institutions and character. Even more, the work grounds specific vocabularies of motives within the political economy of contemporary U.S. capitalism (Denzin 1992, 58). In addition to serving as a comprehensive early general critique of interactionist thought, the work of Mills also may be viewed as a precursor of contemporary cultural studies (Denzin 1989a, 1989b, 1992). With interactionism, cultural studies shares an interest in the social construction of meaning. The two traditions have much to offer the study of social deviance in late-twentieth-century America.

Cultural Studies and the Interactionist Tradition

In recent years within the social sciences and humanities (and alongside the interactionist tradition), a flexible, critical, historically informed approach has steadily taken shape. Variously known as cultural studies, postmodernism, or even poststructuralism (Sarup 1988/93), this approach seems to defy disciplinary classification or identification with any particular method. McCall and Becker characterize cultural studies as the "classically humanistic disciplines which have lately come to use their philosophical, literary, and historical approaches to study the social construction of meaning and other topics traditionally of interest to symbolic interactionists" (1990, 4).

Cultural studies, then, generally focuses on the social creation of meaning and the importance of historical context for the generation of that meaning. Cultural constructions take the form of dominant ideological narratives such as patriarchy and racism (Lerner 1972/92, 1986, 1990;

hooks 1992). The approach is most closely associated (since the mid-1960s) with scholarship at the Centre for Contemporary Cultural Studies at the University of Birmingham in Great Britain. Its adherents claim a self-conscious, critical theoretical versatility in the study of a wide variety of social phenomena (Johnson 1986/87; Hall 1980a). Included are media studies (Hall et al. 1980), communication and language (Grossberg, Nelson, and Treichler 1992), and youth subcultures (Hall and Jefferson 1975/2002b), to name several.

As it continued to emerge, cultural studies developed British and American variations. Both tended to draw (though not exclusively) from interactionism, especially concerning the social construction of meaning. According to Norman K. Denzin (1992, 75), the British variant of cultural studies originally focused on the analysis of subcultures and the study of social deviance (Willis 1978; Hall and Jefferson 1975/2002a, 1975/2002b; Hebdige 1979/2002; Cohen 1972/93). Its American counterpart pursued a model of social action in the work of C. Wright Mills (1959, 1963). In general, contemporary analyses of the production and consumption of mediated cultural forms critically focus on both their ideological bases and potential for resistance (Storey 1999). That is, interdisciplinary cultural studies evidences a political practice of myth explosion and exposure of oppressive ideological discourse (Hall 1992; Kellner 1995). Mediated constructions of social class are overlaid on those of age, gender, and race (Hebdige 1979/2002, 14–16; Aronowitz 1992, 67), what might be called "class cultures" (Clarke, Hall, Jefferson, and Roberts 1975/2002, 13) or "class movements" (Aronowitz 2003, 141).

A poststructuralist cultural studies critiques the process through which social categories (e.g., age, race, gender, and class) are created and maintained (hooks 1982; Collins 1988, 1991; Gelsthorpe and Morris 1990; Aronowitz 1992; Carlen 1994; Winant 2001, 6–10). The idea of the unified self gives way to a "proliferation of identities" (Sarup 1996, 47–49). Of particular importance is the manner in which these categories are "deviantized" (Schur 1980) across the cultural terrain (within the media, criminal justice system, or popular entertainment, and even within the generation of scientific knowledge). The production of cultural meaning and, by extension, the labeling of deviant master status is gradually commodified (Baudrillard 1988a, 1988b; Jameson 1991; Denzin 1991c, 43–46; Gottdiener 1994; Best 1994; Goldberg 1997, 90).

By contrast, interactionism itself developed in relative isolation from cultural studies until the last decade, emerging rather from the work of George Herbert Mead (1932/80, 1934, 1936, 1903/64, 1910/64, 1982) and the divergent interpretations of Herbert Blumer (1966, 1969, 1973) and Manford H. Kuhn (1964a, 1964b). The latter two scholars popularized the Chicago and Iowa schools of interactionism in the 1960s and 1970s, but to divide the perspective into two "schools" is both superficial and misleading. There was no single Chicago or Iowa variation. Furthermore, interactionists since Blumer and Kuhn have extended the perspective in countless directions, including but not limited to the dramaturgy of Erving Goffman (1959, 1961, 1963a, 1963b), the ethnomethodology of Harold Garfinkel (1967), and the existential sociology of Jack D. Douglas and John Johnson (1977).

In his intellectual history of interactionism, Denzin (1992, 13–14) correctly points out that the contemporary period (1981–1990) for interactionism is one of "diversity/new theory." He argues for the combination of "interpretive interactionism" with postmodernist concerns regarding problems of communication in a media-defined world. Fertile ground for the contemporary study of social deviance can be found on this cutting edge of interactionism and cultural studies. At the same time, sociological analyses of deviance are located in the larger historical context of meaning construction and interpretation.

The Task At Hand

My general aim is to outline convergences between the interactionist tradition and the emerging complementary field of cultural studies. The intent is to link interactionist deviance theorizing with a perspective on the social construction of cultural meaning. The labeling of social deviance includes definitions of behavior as well as status or position. Meaning resides in what people *do* and in *who* they are (Sagarin 1975, 9; Goffman 1963b). The interconnection of deviant behavior and status is particularly important with respect to the social categories of age, race, gender, and class (Schur 1984; Dotter 1987, 1994; hooks 1990; Joyce 1995; Bailey 1996; Huey and Lynch 1996; Goldberg 1997; Aronowitz 2003). Definitions of deviance are processionally realized as disvalued master status (Becker 1963/73, 32–33), incorporated along with those of conformity into and through historical self-experience. Both are central to a critical analysis of sociocultural change.

CHAPTER ONE

This book, then, has three specific purposes. First, I elaborate a layered, reflexive scenario (Dotter 1997) of deviance-generation through a review of traditional interactionist literature linked with contemporary perspectives from cultural studies. The components of the labeling process—actors, acts, rules, audiences, and societal reactions—constitute a fluid, dynamic description of stigmatization (Dotter and Roebuck 1988). The synthesis of a postmodern cultural studies interrelates four major themes: the historical crisis of meaning—what Jean-Francois Lyotard (1979/84) has termed the "postmodern condition"—as generated within media processes, especially popular culture (Connor 1989; Kellner 1995; Best and Kellner 1997; Eagleton 2000); the importance of ideological discourse for the emergence of meaning (Foucault 1970/94, 1972a, 1983; Thompson 1990; Eagleton 1991; Simons and Billig 1994); the expression of meaning in a multiplicity of social texts (Derrida 1967/73, 1967/76, 1967/78, 1972/81a; Lynn 1994; Eagleton 1996; Culler 1997; Lucy 1997); the centrality of popular culture and its consumption for meaning-creation in postmodern culture (Baudrillard 1968/96, 1970/98, 1981/94, 1988c; Kellner 1995; Storey 1999). The stigmatization of master status is generated within the mass media and frequently presented in the context of cultural consumption as entertainment.

Second, I deconstruct (Derrida 1967/76, 1977; Culler 1982; Dickens 1990; Denzin 1991a, 1994c) or provide alternative readings of specific meaning scenarios. The two scenarios each relate to the generation of deviance in twentieth-century American society: 1) the formation of youth subcultures from the 1950s to the 1970s and 2) the construction of media images of homicide and other violent crime in literature, film, and newsmaking. A postmodern cultural studies approach to deviance-generation focuses on textual biography (Mills 1959; Denzin 1989a, 1989b; Foucault 1983; Hall 1990; Steedman 1992) as commodified media stories. Textual representations, the scenarios are situated in the postmodern "turn" of meaning-creation (Best and Kellner 1997, 2001).

I treat a variety of sources (e.g., newspaper and other media accounts, and historical, literary, and social scientific interpretations) as composite texts. For each of the scenarios the basic opposition or tension animating definitions of deviance and conformity will be deconstructed as overlapping narratives: youth, gender, race, and class differences. These sociocultural discourses provide the historical context for the creation of social categories in popular culture. Additionally, the scenarios are themselves situated in the broader site of consumption and consumerism. Increasingly, the labeling process turns on media presentations of age, race, gender, and class as commodified images. The labeling scenario may be viewed as a series of "stigma contests" (Schur 1980), characterized by unpredictability of outcome and social consequence. Mediated discourses of master status are at once stigmatized and consumed.

Third, from these articulations I suggest conceptualizations for an historically informed interactionist approach to the contemporary study of social deviance and change. Combining the interactionist concern for the importance of social meaning with the cultural studies postmodernist emphasis on the historical context of that meaning places the analysis of social deviance in a proper framework: as part of the larger sociohistorical examination of meaning-generation. Interactionism generally stresses structure-as-interaction (Denzin 1992, 27–28), while cultural studies examines the critical historical importance of communication (especially the mass media) for an understanding of postmodernist culture (Hall 1990, 32–33). The two traditions merge on the critical axis of the social construction of meaning in contemporary society. Social structure is inseparable from the culture which provides its meaning context (i.e., through interaction and countless forms of communication).

The concept of scenario is imported from film studies and refers to the screenplay (Katz 1994, 1205). In two senses it represents "an interactional moment or site of meaning creation" (Dotter 1997, 252). First, the scenario is a description of meaning-generation processes. The interactive layers include deviant events, media reconstruction, and the "stigma movie." Second, as an interpretive strategy the scenario is an attempt to deconstruct or unravel (Derrida 1967/73, 1967/76, 1967/78) the textual nature of the stigmatization process, thus demonstrating the multiple interpretations given to the social generation of deviance. This practice reveals inherent ambiguities in the assignment of disvalued labels, focusing on the linguistic, ideological nature of their construction (Collins 1991; Denzin 1992, 32–33, 53–54; 1994c; Alway 1995). Rather than searching for the causes of deviance, this project treats stigmatization as a social accomplishment (Nelson, Treichler, and Grossberg 1992, 8), contextualizing deviance as various performers (e.g., actors, audiences) constructing normative definitions (i.e., rules) that link a number of joint actions.

CHAPTER ONE

The stigmatization of behavior, person, and status in particular historical circumstances (i.e., societal reactions) is the always uncertain outcome. The scenario combines a poststructuralist, postmodern theoretical synthesis with the interactional process of deviance-creation to describe and critique the assignment of disvalued labels in mediated social contexts. The strategy draws from a variety of constructionist and postmodern viewpoints, placing the analysis of deviance at the heart of the cultural studies political project (Hall 1986a, 1986b; Kellner 1995).

The social generation of deviance is thus a problematic situated process, a set of interrelated stigma contests (Schur 1980) involving numerous primary as well as secondary performers and audiences. Stigmatized definitions are structurally embodied in status designations (Goffman 1963b; Schur 1984) and are bound in a reflexive process of cultural meaning production.

Media-generated and other public representations of stigmatization—the interrelationship of acts, actors, rules, audiences, and social reactions—often confuse the layered interactive process for a more rational, causal one. The various components of the scenario, conflated or collapsed within one another, are offered for public consumption. Simultaneously, these disvaluement claims are juxtaposed with normalization counterarguments in media stories. The labeling of crime and deviance is "constitutive," involving individual actors as well as the sociohistorical context of meaning-creation (Henry and Milovanovic 1996). Cultural representations of crime and deviance, then, increasingly confuse or blur the distinction between deviant behavior and deviantized master status as scenarios are contested and consumed in legal and popular culture (Best and Kellner 2001), and political and other media spheres (Jenkins 1996, 2003a, 2003b).

As a general perspective of sociology and social psychology, symbolic interactionism (or more simply, interactionism) is uniquely American in its development. Its roots are found in the pragmatism of William James (1890/1950, 1907/91, 1909/87) and John Dewey (1981). Pragmatism developed as a *socially* liberal philosophy in contrast to the individualistic stance of classical liberalism (Dotter 1980a; Horowitz 1983, 92). The emphases of pragmatism, especially as expressed in the work of Dewey, are on the importance of naturalistic experience and the use of science for human betterment.

Emerging from pragmatic philosophy, then, the Chicago school of interactionism viewed social life as processual, the central tenet of which is the constant infusion of meaning into experience through social interaction (Dotter 1978). The application of the Chicago interactionist tradition to the study of social deviance represents the core of the so-called labeling approach (Becker 1963/73; Matza 1969; Schur 1971). Additionally, other scholars have extended the interactionist concern for the social generation of meaning in a more general manner (Ericksen 1980; Dotter 1980b). Despite constant criticism, these approaches have continued to focus on the process of meaning-generation as it relates to socially deviant behavior and status. At the same time, the process of deviance-labeling has never fully transcended the scientific, causal discourse of traditional social science. Labeling is most often viewed as the result of a pluralistic social conflict.

Changes in the nature of the communication of meaning (and, therefore, in the utilization and importance of that meaning for the labeling process) are the focus of cultural studies and postmodernist perspectives. Representing a more critical stance than interactionism, these approaches stress the role played by the mass media in the meaning-generation process (Denzin 1986a, 1986b, 1991a). The development of cultural studies is interdisciplinary, following especially symbolic interactionism, pragmatism, and to a certain extent, Marxism (Denzin 1992, 70). As stated above, in America its original inspiration is found in the work of C. Wright Mills (1959, 1963). His stance encompasses the relationship between communication and culture in the postmodern (i.e., late-twentieth-century) historical moment.

Cultural studies examines "how the history that human beings make and live spontaneously is determined by structures of meaning that they have not chosen for themselves" (Denzin 1992, 74). Human experience is a kind of grand social text, infused at every level with ideological meaning (Carey 1989). A postmodern cultural studies unmasks how taken-for-granted ideological narratives control individual and social life (Althusser 1969/96; Gramsci 1971; Hall 1980b; Eagleton 1991). At the same time, such an approach views the actor as more than simply a passive object of that control. The labeling scenario is fundamentally a semiotic process, pertaining to signs and the symbolic nature of disvaluement and negotiation (Barthes 1977; Manning 2003).

Interactionism and cultural studies are both broad perspectives on social life in the late twentieth century. Linking them through the interpretive strategy of the scenario shifts the focus from sociology as science to sociology as meaning-generation (Lemert 1992). Culture is constituted as layered ideological narratives, both product and process, inseparable from social structure in the social generation of meaning (Hebdige 1979/2002). The scenario recasts the analysis of social deviance into the broader terrain of cultural meaning-generation. Feminist perspectives, especially those emerging from social constructionist and multiracial viewpoints (Collins 1991; Lorber 1998; Daly and Maher 1998b; Barak et al. 2001), are infused into a critical reading of the otherwise gender-blind labeling process (Russell 1992; Naffine 1996; Carrington 1998).

As pointed out above, meaning emerges from the textual interconnections between and among various performers, acts, and normative definitions. Stigmatization is a process of status negotiation (i.e., age, gender, race, and class) and is constructed in particular historical circumstances (i.e., scenarios). Social structure (e.g., the creation of deviant categories) is accomplished through interaction and communication, the outcome of intense political struggles—stigma contests—among specific groups' constructions and exploitations of ideological texts. The choice of scenarios grounded in the historical subcultural experience of American youth and in the mediated images of violent crime represents a postmodernist cultural studies concern for the social creation of deviant status and identity (especially through the ideological content of the mass media). Interactionist labeling becomes a "polyvocal" (Rose 1994) narrative, incorporating age, race, and gender in a critique of media-generated meaning.

Plan of the Book

Chapter 2 combines the interactionist and cultural studies traditions in the development of the scenario of deviance-creation. The interpretive strategy draws heavily on the work of Denzin (1989a, 1989b) and Mills (1959), unmasking the textual generation of deviance, its ideological underpinnings in consumerism, and its contemporary layering within master status categories. Especially important is the articulation of multiracial feminist voices within this project (Nicholson 1990a, 1990b; Collins 1991; Lorber 1998; Butler 1990/99, 1993). Sociocultural meaning derives from a dialogue between narratives of deviance and conformity.

Chapters 3 through 5 work back from the conceptualization of the scenario. The third presents an in-depth analysis of pragmatic philosophy, connecting its roots in interactionist thought (particularly the Chicago tradition) with contemporary concerns of neopragmatism and its linguistic turn (Rorty 1967). The latter views philosophy as a narrative activity of language and history (Diggins 1994, 11). Chapter 4 develops a general review of the labeling/interactionist approach to deviance theorizing. Included are definitional issues (i.e., deviance as stigmatization process) (Goffman 1963b; Becker 1963/73; Lemert 1972), a synthesis of the various strands of interactionist theory (Douglas 1984) (i.e., Chicago School labeling, interactional conflict, sociological phenomenology, and feminist perspectives), and a presentation of the general deviance-creation process (Dotter and Roebuck 1988) grounded in these strands. Chapter 5 offers a critical take on cultural studies literature, its development of postmodern themes and its poststructuralist turn.

Chapters 6 and 7 present readings of the social generation of deviance in specific scenarios: the creation of youth subculture and its relationship to popular music in the 1950s and 1960s and the mediated construction of homicide as both information and entertainment. The first scenario is an instance of the historical construction of deviance in signature events such as the Woodstock Music and Art Fair (Spitz 1979) and in rock music's historical connection to violence (Dotter 1994). A critical part of the classic rock narrative is the inconvenient appearance of the aging rocker, an image which textually links audiences and performers over decades. Chapter 7 situates the scenario in the emerging project of "cultural criminology" (Ferrell and Sanders 1995a) and focuses on one of the first "crimes of the century." The 1906 killing of Grace Brown by Chester Gillette was novelized in Theodore Dreiser's (1925/2003) *An American Tragedy* and the 1951 film *A Place in the Sun*. Numerous texts, then, are interwoven in this reading, literary and cinematic (Lucy 1997; Denzin 1995), biographical and historical (Lingeman 1986, 1990; Brandon 1986; Brownell and Wawrzaszek 1986), and critical (Pizer 1976; Kaplan 1988; Mitchell 1989; Eby 1998). These chapters highlight the broader historical contextualization of cultural meaning production; in each case stigmatization emerges from the interplay of ideological narratives variously concerning youth, gender, race, and class differences.

CHAPTER ONE

Chapter 8 discusses the importance of the scenario for the study of social deviance in postmodern society (Sumner 1994; Best 2004). In its preliminary discussion, deviance is situated alongside the cultural politics of meaning (Jordan and Weedon 1995) and the problematic of self-as-narrative identity (Jervis 1998, 1999; Storey 1999; Holstein and Gubrium 2000; Perinbanayagam 2000). Interactionism has arguably been the most fertile American contribution to social theory. This study clarifies the centrality of cultural meaning within the perspective and reiterates the importance of the study of social deviance for a humanistic understanding of life in postmodern America.

CHAPTER TWO
THE SCENARIO AS INTERPRETIVE STRATEGY: AN INTERACTIONIST/CULTURAL STUDIES ARTICULATION

The impact of the postmodern turn (Best and Kellner 1997, 2001) on American social science has generated much controversy. The explosion, especially during the 1990s, of mediated computer technology and the implications of that technology for both knowledge and the concept of self are nothing short of overwhelming. On the other hand, the development of explanations or even descriptions of these trends is fraught with argument (Featherstone 1988; Kellner 1988; Lemert 1997, 132–46). While traditional sociological practitioners generally admit the empirical significance of changes in communication delivery and knowledge sources, they often quickly dismiss postmodern, poststructuralist theoretical characterizations as overblown or irrelevant (Bauman 1988; Ashley 1997, 46–48).

These latter characterizations have found their warmest reception among symbolic interactionists (Shalin 1993). Even within this camp, there has been widespread criticism, even rejection, of the postmodern theoretical turn (Darden, Worden, and Holyfield 1997).[1] Whatever the specifics of the argument, the general debate appears largely to be an argument "for or against" the inclusion of poststructuralist conceptions of self and culture in the interactionist canon.

As Norman K. Denzin (1996, 341) makes clear, neither interactionists nor those fully in the midst of the postmodern turn are "cut from a single cloth." There is likely as much diversity within each tradition as similarity between them. The "transdisciplinary" (Best and Kellner 2001, 12) field of cultural studies provides an hospitable intellectual meeting ground over the

CHAPTER TWO

issue of social meaning-creation (Becker and McCall 1990; McCall and Becker 1990, 5). In particular, theorizing processes of deviance creation and labeling represents fertile ground in the postmodern project.

Given the intellectual complexity of the debate and the obvious affinity of these approaches, I propose an articulation of poststructuralist cultural studies with interactionist labeling. The two traditions, selectively interwoven, illuminate the contested nature of sociocultural definitions of deviance. This chapter proceeds with the following interconnected threads. First, I present basic orienting questions that link a poststructuralist cultural studies with concerns of interactionist labeling. These questions are a general mapping for the study of stigmatized meaning generation. Second, I examine the relationship between C. Wright Mills's (1959) sociological imagination and Denzin's (1989a, 1989b) twin conceptions of interpretive interactionism and interpretive biography as a suitable context for meaning-creation. Lived experience and self are textual, layered creations.

Third, I present the concept of scenario for use in describing the process of deviance-labeling (Dotter and Roebuck 1988; Dotter 1997). The layers of the process include deviant events, media reconstruction, and the stigma movie. Finally, I frame the scenario as a postpositivist strategy for critiquing meaning-generation. Meanings of deviance are socially constructed as intertwined biographical and sociocultural narratives. Age, gender, race, and class images are primary meaning sites. The scenario's fluidity allows for a multilayered perspective on stigmatized meaning-creation. The concept refers to storytelling (Denzin 1991c; Sarup 1996) in a double sense: as a description of the mediated process of meaning-creation (Glassner 1999, 3–4) and as an interpretive strategy to transform that process (Baudrillard 1981/94, 122).

The Intersection of Deviance Labeling and Cultural Studies

The intersection of an interpretive version of deviance labeling (following Mead and Blumer) and a poststructuralist cultural studies reading is a project of cultural criticism. As Denzin (1992, 123) argues, interactionists (especially when compared to more traditional scientific sociological camps) have always been cultural critics. As I have shown, Mead and Blumer originally set the agenda of symbolic interactionism as an alternative interpretive science of communication, meaning-creation, and self-development. In the process an identifiable view of the social emerged:

> [I]nteractionists have rejected the subject-object dualism, spectator's theory of knowledge, and correspondence theory of truth, opting instead for the subject-object relativity, participant observation, and the perspectival approach to truth. (Shalin 1993, 303)

The study of deviance as a process of stigmatized labeling, especially in the 1960s and early 1970s, challenged traditional sociological conceptions of normative violation through the work of Becker (1963/73), Goffman (1963b), Schur (1971, 1980), and others. Normative meaning was viewed as situational; actors (in empirical situations of social inequality) portrayed as meaning-creators; and the response to disvalued conduct rendered problematic though not entirely unpredictable. Cultural conflict and diversity, fundamental to even early Chicago School analyses (Zorbaugh 1929/48; Park 1952; Dotter 1978, 1980b; Ericksen 1980), were embedded within a mature interactionist statement of "becoming deviant" (Matza 1969).

In the early 1980s, Jack Douglas and Frances Waksler (1982, 125) appropriately described interactionist theories of deviance as "new." In particular, this novelty arose from articulations of the various forms of interactionism with one another (e.g., labeling with phenomenology or interactional conflict). The precise differences in these emerging perspectives were not always clear. All made problematic the character of social norms and the manner in which such rules resulted in deviant labels. In their many statements, interactional theories of deviance pose the following central questions:

> What is the social context of rule (i.e., norm) creation or construction?
> How is the deviant label articulated as stigmatization in various situations (i.e., rendered representative of individual persons, groups, and social categories)?

Each of these queries assumes the processual, emergent quality of social experience (Lofland 1969). Human action and interpretation of such is not inherently linear or even meaningful. It is made so by placing rules outside of the process of interpretation (e.g., as codified, socially recognized criminal laws) and by searching for the causes of deviance, similarly suspended from the natural (i.e., interactional) creation of meaning.

Regarding the first question, the interactional process of stigmatization layers several components within and among each other in the creation of deviance as a social reality. Rules are relational constructions, differentially applied to the actor/act context. Labels, whether informal or criminal, are open to negotiation, acceptance, rejection, or compromise between enforcers and accused (Dotter and Roebuck 1988).

The second question addresses the transmutation of meaning within the labeling process from disvalued act to actor. Acts do not possess immanent stigma as sociocultural abstractions. Rather, disvaluement ultimately refers to moral judgments of individual character (Goffman 1963b; Sagarin 1969, 23–25). Such judgments are typically rendered or withheld on a case-by-case basis. The quality of stigma may also be generally applied to all members of a particular socially constructed category. Here, deviance is imputed to entire categories of persons sharing some apparent characteristic. Such sociocultural stereotypical labeling transcends matters of individual potentially deviant acts or actors, passing into the realm of "what everyone knows to be true." Thus, deviance becomes politicized relative to stigmatized status categories. As Schur (1980) points out, these political stigma contests are aimed at the institutionalization of social control. Thus, moral entrepreneurs may fight violent crime, drugs, or more generalized ills, oblivious to the constructions of status embedded in their causes. The relevance of empirical acts of deviation disappears in the rhetoric of the stigma contest.

Viewing the creation and transformation of deviance as stigma contests is inescapably a form of cultural criticism. Individual labeled events are subsumed in the wider sociocultural context of meaning-creation—a narrative of interrelated discursive acts (Perinbanayagam 1985, 20–25). Consequently, the deviance process is historicized at all levels. A poststructuralist cultural studies offers the following questions regarding the deviance problematic:

> How do the larger culture- and meaning-making institutions of society (e.g., mass and popular media, film, social science, art, religion, politics, science, and education) shape the experience of individuals in everyday interaction?

What is the historical context of cultural production and consumption in postmodern America?
How do ideological narratives (e.g., those based on gender, youth, race, and class) give structure and meaning to lived existence?

As an interpretive map, these questions suggest the wider scope of meaning-creation, of which social deviance is a particular concern. As Denzin (1992, xiii–xiv) suggests, the roots of an American version of cultural studies as criticism may be traced to the pragmatic philosophy of Dewey and others (a "philosophy of the possible"). However, the historical development of symbolic interactionism, through its links to pragmatism, portrays the forsaking of cultural criticism for a more-or-less scientific social psychology (Dotter 1980a).

Cultural studies is an interdisciplinary, self-consciously critical project. James W. Carey provides further linkage of pragmatism and the Chicago School to the cultural studies tradition:

> Cultural studies on an American terrain, has been given its most powerful expression by John Dewey and by the tradition of symbolic interactionism that developed out of American pragmatism generally. It was Dewey's student Robert Park who provided the most powerful analysis of mass culture (though he did not call it that) that was adapted to the circumstances to the country. Without attempting to do so, Dewey, Park, and others in the Chicago School transplanted Weberian sociology in American soil, though happily within the pragmatist attempt to dissolve the distinction between the natural and cultural sciences. (Carey 1989, 96)

The emergence of British cultural studies through the 1960s and 1970s (Grossberg, Nelson, and Treichler 1992; Hall et al. 1980) brought a cross-fertilization with interactionist labeling as applied to youth subculture in post–World War II Britain (Hall and Jefferson 1975/2002b; Hebdige 1979/2002). Simultaneously, British attempts articulated a theory of hegemonic culture as commodity through the work of Althusser (1969/96) and Gramsci (1971). All media, especially popular culture, become part of the commoditization process. Forms of cultural expression are increasingly ideological, circulated through the mass media (Eagleton 1991; Jameson 2002). Embedded in consumption patterns, narratives of youth, gender,

CHAPTER TWO

race, and class resistance are both deviantized and celebrated in media culture (Storey 1999); as cultural representations, these narratives become mediated mechanisms of social control. Such control is ambiguous, overlapping, and opaque, and thereby it is ideological. As Hebdige argues:

> [W]hen we come to look beneath the level of "ideology-in-general" at the way in which specific ideologies work, how some gain dominance and others remain marginal, we can see that in advanced Western democracies the ideological field is by no means neutral. To return to the "connotative" codes to which Stuart Hall refers we can see that these "maps of meaning" are charged with a potentially explosive significance because they are traced and re-traced along the lines laid down by the *dominant* discourses about reality, the *dominant* ideologies. They thus tend to represent, in however obscure and contradictory a fashion, the interests of the *dominant* groups in society. [*italics* in the original] (Hebdige 1979/2002, 14–15)

Postmodern concerns, especially the poststructuralist linguistic turn (Rorty 1967), situate ideological meaning and its consumption only within the textual play of *différance* (Derrida 1972/81b). The shape and form of texts proliferate in a widening array of media (Lyotard 1979/84). The historical subject is itself an ideologized myth. Narrative discourse serves as a mechanism of social control (Foucault 1972a), as a text to be deconstructed (Derrida 1972/81b; Culler 1982), or as a postmodern imploded, simulated hyperreality (Baudrillard 1981/94).

Denzin (1992) has drawn from both British cultural studies and French poststructuralism in his work *Symbolic Interactionism and Cultural Studies*. An engaged interactionist cultural studies must critique the process of cultural meaning production and consumption in postmodern media culture:

> An oppositional cultural aesthetic aims to always subvert the meanings of a text, to show how its dominant and negotiated meanings can be opposed. It presumes that such readings can expose the ideological and political meanings that circulate within the text, particularly those which hide or displace racial, class, ethnic and gender biases. Such readings . . . analyze how texts address the problems of presence, lived experience, the real and its representations, and the issues of subjects, authors, and their intentionalities. In the unhinging of a text there is an attempt to illuminate the dominant code and its workings. Such readings then show how the mythologies

of the culture work their way into the popular and the artistic expressions that cultural members appear to value. (Denzin 1992, 151)

In formulating an interactionist cultural criticism Denzin juxtaposes the neopragmatic vision of Richard Rorty (1979, 1982, 1989) and Cornel West's (1989) "prophetic pragmatism." For Denzin, interactionist criticism must thoroughly examine the creation of meaning in postmodern popular culture, especially its impact on gender and race images.[2] In his words:

But there is a vocabulary right now which attempts to be final, and it is the language of the media, the language of the popular. This is a language with a shifting code that subsumes everything; a language of the new which reworks the old. This language takes many forms. It can speak of resistance and protest. It can also be a deterministic, patriarchal, sexist, violent, homophobic, racist final language of social difference. It is a language which is changed and challenged daily, as it is reified in the popular. (Denzin 1992, 130)

I contend that an important aspect of this popular narrative is the labeling of social deviance, especially characterizations of immorality and violent crime. In mediated images of deviance, biographies of actors (e.g., perpetrators, victims, and spectators) and their deeds are continually offered for consumption. In postmodern culture the line between subject and history, information and entertainment, private and public, is constantly shifting—when it can be discerned at all.

From Mills to Denzin: Discovering Textual Subjects

The work of Norman K. Denzin (1989a, 1989b, 1990a, 1992) constitutes an interdisciplinary synthesis of symbolic interactionism and cultural studies. His task is to create a postmodern sociology which focuses on social meaning and the historical situation of that meaning in textual critique. This interpretive synthesis combines the sociological imagination of C. Wright Mills (1959) with a poststructuralist reading of textual biography. In Denzin's (1990a, 1) words, his project seeks "to dismantle and then recast two concepts: the sociological imagination, and lived, biographical experience. These terms are apparently indispensable to the new interpretive sociologies and anthropologies." Mills, then, is cast as an important

CHAPTER TWO

critic of mainstream, midcentury, scientific sociology, and his concept of the sociological imagination becomes part of a postmodern reading.

The Sociological Imagination: A Postmodern Reading

For Denzin, Mills's elaboration of the sociological imagination, despite its criticism of sociological method, is fundamentally modernist. The presumed existence of the sociological imagination (i.e., "the quality of mind essential to grasp the interplay of man and society, of biography and history, of self and world"), allows Mills to detail the disintegrating state of affairs for contemporary culture and the related failed promise of scientific sociology (Mills 1959, 4–5).

Denzin's postmodern rendering of Mills is an important discursive critique. Accordingly, Mills's argument is "carefully molded by the language of classical social theory: alienation; anomie; totalitarian, capitalist, and feudal societies; class; status; power; key variables; quantifiable indices" (Denzin 1990a, 3–4). At the same time Mills is identified as having introduced the term "postmodern" into American sociology (Denzin 1990a, 2). Facing an apparent dilemma (i.e., the use of modernist theoretical concepts unsuited to critical framework), Mills chooses to portray himself as the critical anti-empiricist. Furthermore, he forsakes his sociological imagination for all but rhetorical use by erasing real people with real problems from his narrative. In Denzin's view:

> But nowhere in the pages of his work(s) do these little people and their personal troubles speak. Mills speaks for them; or he quotes others who have written about them, usually novelists, like Sinclair Lewis, Booth Tarkington, Christopher Morley, or James Cain. . . . It cannot be that he writes of his own sense of being trapped and without meaning, for Mills the intellectual craftsman finds meaning in his theorizing about these lives his texts neither touch nor allow to speak. (Denzin 1990a, 4)

The theoretical potential of the sociological imagination is thereby unrealized, awaiting articulation into a developing postmodern sociology. Denzin describes this task:

> [C]an our texts capture biography, lived history, and lived experience? That is, can we ever get to the personal troubles and epiphanic experi-

ences that fundamentally alter people's lives? I conclude no. Society and its members, as they are known, exist primarily in the texts we write about them. The historical truthfulness of texts (especially those of biographical or autobiographical design) is open to question, difficult to finally determine. Textual characteristics such as reliability and validity represent only "meanings brought to them by observers who believe in an objective world that can be accurately recorded." (Denzin 1990a, 2)

The unfulfilled promise of the sociological imagination represents the cornerstone of a postmodern sociology, combined with Denzin's (1989a) concept of interpretive biography.[3] Interpretive biography, conceptualizing all lives as socially constructed in the texts written about them, is part of the larger perspective of interpretive interactionism. Thus, Denzin (1989b, 14) links traditional symbolic interactionism with phenomenological approaches and a critical biographical method to portray human experience in the postmodern epoch.

Interpretive Interactionism and Textual Biography

Interpretive interactionism has several characteristics (Denzin 1989b, 19–34). First, interpretive interactionism is existential, interactional, and biographical. As previously noted, its textual, critical biographical stance is paramount. The broader context of the biography site is Mills's sociological imagination: the relationship between personal problems and public issues.

Second, interpretive interactionism is naturalistic, a rigorous pure and applied perspective. The approach is both *ideographic* and *emic*. In Denzin's words:

> Ideographic research assumes that each individual case is unique. This means that every interactional text is unique and shaped by the individuals who create it. This requires that the voices and actions of individuals must be heard and seen in the texts that are reported. Emic studies are also ideographic. They seek to study experience from within, through the use of thick description or accounts which attempt to capture the meanings and experiences of interacting individuals in problematic situations. They seek to uncover the conceptual categories persons use when they interact with one another and create meaningful experience. (Denzin 1989b, 20–21)

CHAPTER TWO

Interpretive interactionism (and by extension, interpretive biography) illuminates the intersubjectivity of meaning-construction.

Finally, the perspective may be described as postpositivist, linked to feminist critiques of science. Especially important is the social construction of status categories, situating them in a nexus of knowledge, power, and emotion. Thus, all experience is contextualized and historically rooted in the continuous creation of status categories (Denzin 1989b, 27). Additionally, power is connected to emotional expression in contemporary society, critical to an understanding of the process whereby individuals are created as or transformed into subjects by themselves and others. Following Foucault (1983), power is rooted in subjectification and its discursive practices of transformation. Situated in the interconnection of Mills's sociological imagination, the intersubjectivity of meaning-creation, and a postpositivist critique founded on gender, knowledge, power, and emotion, interpretive interactionism develops a biographical method based on textual analysis.

Grounded in interpretive interactionism, interpretive biography locates Mills's sociological imagination in a postmodern context: *Individual lives and their siting within the sociocultural processes of meaning-creation are textual, undergoing continuous interpretation, even transformation.* In this regard, interpretive biography focuses on the narrative creation of the subject's lives (and thereby selves) as a continuous process of storytelling (Dotter and Fisher-Giorlando 1997).

Following Denzin, interpretive biography is best summarized as "making sense of an individual's life." As he further explains:

> [This approach] assumes the existence of a pivotal event in a person's life. It also assumes that this event will be a pivotal meaning structure that organizes the other activities in a person's life. This strategy involves studying how this event comes to occupy a central place in a person's life. It then examines how the meanings of this event change over time. It attempts to anchor the meanings of this event in larger cultural settings, including the mass media, the popular culture, and interacting groups. (Denzin 1989a, 66)

Interpretive biography maintains that the individual life of the actor is only fleetingly glimpsed in the texts written about that life. Moreover, no single life can be known from the text, no single self buried and awaiting revelation. The "real" life of the individual cannot be recaptured. Textual biography, layered in the tenuous connections among life events and sociocultural contexts, is a site of constant ambiguity and transformation (Turner 1990/2003). The narrative text is *defined as interpretation,* much like a literary product. Textual ambiguity represents the process of *differance* (Derrida 1972/81b), whereby differences of biographical meaning are made apparent, negotiated, and recast. *Differance,* the continual transformation of textual and intertextual meaning, undermines the phonocentric bias of contemporary thought—the primacy of speech over writing as a linguistic form (Dickens 1990, 149).

Additionally, Derrida's characterization of shifting textual meanings exposes the related logocentric bias (i.e., the assumption that the text possesses an inherent structure, and that a real subject can be unequivocally located there). Language (i.e., words as signs) has no singular meaning, but is forever relational, even incomplete, in its meaning. Texts are decentered, lacking in specific structure. Furthermore, there is no ultimate foundational meaning of a subject's biography, as the text is "open," marked both by things stated and unstated (Turner 1990/2003). Logocentric, subject-centered texts are a fallacy of the *metaphysics of presence,* whereby "authors and readers believe that real subjects can be found in the real world and then relocated in texts" (Denzin 1989a, 45).

By contrast, interpretive biography deconstructs biographical experience into a multitude of textual self-narratives in which traces of the subject can be glimpsed. The incomplete, relational character of these narratives, despite the actual events, personages, and outcomes they describe, render them fictional creations, taking the form of stories which reveal a multilayered, decentered subject. Derrida (1972/81b, 88) makes clear that the subject does not disappear in the text, but is a relational element therein (Derrida 1967/78, 226–27; Howells 1992, 347).

Interpretive biography portrays the indeterminate, interactive quality of self. Traditional symbolic interactionist approaches stress the self as emerging from and transformed through a social process of spoken and internalized communication (Mead 1934; Blumer 1969). Locating meaning and communication within social texts, interpretive biography posits the creation of multiple selves. These emergent selves are layered and provide the text a quality of constant dialogue, emerging from "the ruling myths of a society" (Perinbanayagam 1985, 93). Meaning arises from the dialectical play of textual selves, each in relation to the other (Dotter forthcoming).

CHAPTER TWO

Denzin (1989a, 31–32) offers several interpretive conceptions of self: the phenomenological, the linguistic, the material, the self-as-desire, and the self-as-ideological subject. None has an inherent structure. Each is relative to the other, and in a complex nonlinear manner all are expressed only as texts, the essence of the multilayered self.

The phenomenological self represents the thoughts and images a person has as a unique individual in relation to others. This experiential, interactional self acquires expression as the linguistic self, which supplies personal biographical meaning to lived social experience, particularly an emotional context. The internalized linguistic narrative of private conversation (Blumer 1969, 13) is layered within the self-as-material-object. Denzin describes the textual, relational nature of the material self:

> Self-as-material-object consists of all the person calls his or hers at a particular moment in time. At the same time, self-as-object is commodified in the exchange relations that exist in the person's life. In its literary, sociological, biographical form the material self is transformed into ... a book. It must be noted, however, that any written or graphic display of the self in a text (biography, autobiography) always erases or displaces the self as it is written about. The self is only in the words that are attached to it. (Denzin 1989a, 32)

Realization of the material self extends into the related self-as-desire (Holstein and Gubrium 2000, 187–88). While expressions of desire are grounded primarily in constructions of sexuality and gender, they also take form through age, race, and class socialization.

The process by which individuals are transformed into coherent textual subjects constitutes the ideological self. This narrative situates the actor in the wider sociohistorical circumstances of cultural meaning-generation and is largely unconscious in its impact (Althusser 1971; Denzin 1989a, 32). Of particular importance is the mediated quality of experience and meaning-creation (Baudrillard 1981/94). The ideological self-narrative connects the imaginary relations of individuals to their life circumstances, clouding its effects on the individual to act independently or in opposition to it. The unconscious quality of ideology represents a taken-for-granted natural order (Hebdige 1979/2002, 11–12); as narrative, the ideological self is portrayed as a centered and coherent linear product. The ideological self-narrative is uniquely postmodern, emerging in a sociocultural terrain which privileges media representations of meaning. It assumes a seemingly independent existence, communicating the myth of the coherent acting subject. As a semiological system (Barthes 1957/72, 132), myth embodies "stolen language" through which meaning is transmuted into form. In short, the linguistic expression of the ideological self masks its textual, nonlinear, layered qualities.

In individual experience, the ideological self-narrative thus appears separated from the other textual self layers (Dotter forthcoming). This oppositional character emerges because the ideologized subject is created by others who provide a distinct textual voice to the narrative. This transformation-as-subject gives a dialectical quality to lived experience (Foucault 1983). The phenomenological, linguistic, material, self-as-desire, what may be termed the creative self, enters into a continuous textual (auto)biographical dialogue with the ideological. The textual voice of the creative self, however loudly or faintly, represents the subject's attempt to transform and recapture the ideological myth. Thus, the creative self is realized as a public textual presentation of the phenomenological, linguistic, material, and self-as-desire narratives by the subject (Dotter forthcoming).

The creative and ideological selves are in constant opposition, yet dependent on one another for meaning-creation; both are fictional, literary (i.e., textual) constructions of biographical and autobiographical experience (Lucy 1997). Their semiotic positionings represent a dialectic of self-narratives (Holstein and Gubrium 2000, 79–80), through which creative expression of the subject is transmuted into an ideological narrative biography (story or myth) in the mass media. Commoditized in this way, the ideological narrative is further embedded in the subject's creative autobiographical storyline (Jervis 1998, 29–33).

Traditional biographical methods assume that selves are conscious, intentional, connected, and unified. Conversely, interpretive biography deconstructs and decenters selves-as-texts, laying bare their indeterminacy of meaning. Life narratives reveal only traces of the selves assumed to be unified therein. Textual life is a blending of opposing biographical (ideological) and autobiographical (creative) voices. Denzin reveals the indeterminacy and constant shifting of textual meaning in the dialectical narrative selves:

> Language always entails a process of deferral and delay. Language does not permit speakers or writers to ever have full access to the meaning

they are attempting to convey. Nor can they ever be fully present to themselves. As they reach forward or backward to catch a thought, that thought blurs with another, and that other thought (or word) blurs with another, until what they attempt to write or speak becomes something that bears the traces and meanings of everything that has come before. (Denzin 1994c, 189)

Self-narratives lack a center and the appearance of meaning emerges through *différance* (Derrida 1972/81b). Interpretive biography unravels bits and pieces of the self-narrative, revealing how "[t]he various multiplicities that constitute the self at a given time are involved in play and dance with each other" (Hollinger 1994, 113).

Mills's critical but modernist sociological imagination is relocated in the postmodern linguistic turn. As a literary construction, the text uncertainly links reader and writer: "Even if the author's aim is to give the fullest possible representation of his object, there is never any question as to whether he is telling *everything*. He knows far more than he tells. This is so because language is elliptical" (Sartre 1988, 70–71) [*italics* in original]. In the postmodern epoch, the text maps "a rhetorically United States of nonetheless mainly unresolved borders—between class and race, race and generation, generation and region, region and religion, religous and ethnic and national heritage—and a constantly shifting array of cultural crossings" (Bercovitch 1993, 27). The scenario is a poststructuralist rendering of meaning-creation. It frames the self-dialogue described above within and emitting from the wider sociocultural context of media culture. Definitions of deviance intermingle with those of conformity, clustering around narrative constructions of social status.

The Postmodern Scenario as Media Culture: The Stigma Movie and the Creation of Deviance

Scenario Defined

The postmodern condition (Lyotard 1979/84) is defined in the transformation of knowledge forms: from totalizing narratives (especially science) to ever-changing, mediated storylines of the moment. The concept of the postmodern scenario illustrates the situational quality of these storylines in the creation of contemporary meaning. The postmodern breakdown of narratives has resulted in a "permanent" crisis of meaning in the institutional spheres of social life. The scenario captures and characterizes this meaning crisis:

> The postmodern scenario may be broadly defined as *an interactional moment or site of meaning-creation.* As such, it is fundamentally interpretive, a multilayered presentation of a social event or historical situation. It focuses on the level and quality of social expression rather than on a specific mode of analysis. The scenario highlights the mass-mediated nature of meaning-creation. (Dotter 1997, 252)

In early filmmaking, the term "scenario" referred to the screenplay (Katz 1994, 1205). As a cinematic metaphor the scenario highlights the boundary between modern and postmodern knowledge; film itself is a transitional form of technology and art (Denzin 1995), visual images underscored by the written narrative. Film historian Neal Gabler maintains that life has *become* art in postmodern America, best exemplified as a continuous sociocultural movie, a show "far richer, more complex and more compelling than anything conceived for the more conventional media." Furthermore, as life becomes its own medium, "books and every other imaginative form exist to end in a world" (Gabler 1998, 4).

As an interpretive strategy (concerned not with causal analysis but the nature and legitimation of meaning), the scenario articulates Mills's (1959) sociological imagination and Denzin's (1989a) interpretive biography. The cutting edge of the postmodern meaning crisis marks the appearance of the sociological imagination. Narrative modernity, slowly dissolving, leads to fundamental sociocultural questions of identity and politics (Jervis 1998; Storey 1999). The scenario is closely related to literary theory (Eagleton 1996; Culler 1975, 1997; Lucy 1997), especially new historical criticism. As Steven Lynn writes:

> Historical events, new historicists observe, are nothing more than texts now. Any event has meaning because of its place within a system of meaning. Rather than moving through time, showing us how one thing led to another, new historicists are more likely to take a slice of time and analyze it as a system, studying the relationship of one thing to another. (Lynn 1994, 13)

CHAPTER TWO

As a sensitizing metaphor for the construction of postmodern sociocultural meaning, the scenario has several theoretical characteristics:

- Meaning is never fully accomplished; it is constantly negotiated and reworked as a textual process of *differance*.
- Mass media are primary agents of meaning-generation. Much of what we take as "truth" at a given moment is filtered through the lenses of television, newspapers, films and so on. In this complicated process media serve as agents of both information *and* entertainment.
- Meaning is thus problematic or complicated, ambiguous, even contradictory. Increasingly, its emergence from consumer culture obscures its ideological function of social control.
- The social creation of deviance, including its labeling, is embedded in the postmodern meaning crisis. As process, meanings of deviance are mediated and commoditized in stigma contests. The normative boundaries between deviance and conformity shift, even disappear, in the postmodern terrain of communication as consumption.

I shall examine each of these characteristics in turn, briefly framing their significance for the contemporary construction of deviance and crime.

Meaning As Text

Postmodern meaning processes are textual and "open." Jacques Derrida's (1972/81b; G. Turner 1990/2003) concepts of *differance* and deconstruction serve as descriptions of these processes. The former simply emphasizes the indeterminacy of textual meaning, its circumstantial location in the ebb and flow of signs (Culler 1982, 98–102; 1988, 224). Rather than a conventionally described method, the latter is best seen as "an attitude, a way of working with culture in order to reconstrue it" (Lemert 1997, 44). The textuality of meaning refers to its linguistic context, calling into question its presumed centered agreement; the intent of deconstruction is not some deliberate attempt to destroy meaning, and by implication, self or history (Appleby et al. 1994, 223–24; Windschuttle 1997, 4). Rather, the deconstructive attitude criticizes "modern culture's inability to tolerate or even to recognize actual social differences" (Lemert 1997, 45).

The use of the term "scenario" to describe the process of deviance generation is meant to highlight these differences, to locate stigmatization in the broader sociocultural terrain. As such, it is a form of "strategic postmodernism." According to Charles Lemert:

> Strategic postmodernists differ from radical ones in the way they attack the totalizing aspects of modernist essentialism—that is the way they wage war on totality. They are far less inclined to take for granted that the world is yet changed. They might, in fact, be properly accused of wishing the world were changed or acting as though it had. But in their writings, they take a more modest attitude toward culture and world reality than radical postmodernists. Like the radical modernists, strategic postmodernists are less concerned to imagine the new world, than to rethink and rewrite modernity itself. (Lemert 1997, 44)

Forms of deviance in the postmodern turn are textually represented, historically grounded in the relatively recent past. As a description of media process the scenario suggests the continual play of construction/reconstruction of meaning.

Meaning-Generation in Media Culture

As an interpretive strategy, the scenario focuses on the mass media, especially popular culture, as a primary terrain of meaning-creation. Truth is of a given historical moment or frame, filtered through the technologies of newspaper, television, film, and, increasingly, virtual reality. In the process through which "entertainment conquered reality" (Gabler 1998), media serve as firsthand sources of information *and* entertainment. Increasingly, media representations are experiential alternatives for "being there" or "doing that." In large measure, "TV obliterates the very distinction, the very line, between reality and unreality" (Mitroff and Bennis 1989/93, xxi). Moreover, the sociocultural importance of place has been radically altered by all forms of electronic media: "One can now be an audience to a social performance without being physically present; one can communicate 'directly' with others without meeting in the same place" (Meyrowitz 1985, vii).[4]

CHAPTER TWO

Finally, definitions of self are formed through both interpersonal acts and interpretations of media communication (Gumpert and Cathcart 1986, 13; Denzin 1988a). The mediated self does not disappear; it is situated in a process of reconstitution. The importance of popular culture for this process is evident:

> Entertainment—movies, rock music, pulp novels, comic books, television, computer games—sinks its talons into us and pulls us in, holding us captive, taking us both deeper into the work itself and deeper into ourselves, or at least into our own emotions and senses, before releasing us. (Gabler 1998, 18)

Furthermore, Denzin (1991c, 8) relates "visual literacy" or the new language of the visual to the communication of images as both entertainment and information: "The new information technologies turn everyday life into a theatrical spectacle; into sites where the dramas that surround the decisive performances of race, ethnicity, gender, sexuality and age are staged." In the postmodern turn audiences are not entirely passive receptacles of media meaning processes. For example, suspending the distinction between entertainment and truthful information involves a creative transmutation of meaning, resistance, and interpretation (Jervis 1998, 330–31). As Douglas Kellner observes:

> Yet, audiences may resist the dominant meanings and messages, create their own readings and appropriations of mass-produced culture, and use their culture as resources to empower themselves and to invent their own meanings, identities, and forms of life. Moreover, media culture itself provides resources which individuals can appropriate, or reject, in forming their own identities against dominant models. Media culture thus induces individuals to conform to the established organization of society, but it also provides resources that can empower individuals against that society. (Kellner 1995, 3)

This articulation of the popular culture scenario with the biographical life of consumers is rarely experienced directly. Rather, bits and pieces of the script are lifted as needed, resonating with and framing the life experience of the individual.

This textual interplay of audience and media is particularly apparent in media portrayals of deviance and crime. Representations of violence simultaneously titillate and frighten. The fear of crime, contextualized through both reality-based and entertainment programs (Fishman and Cavender 1998; Ferrell and Websdale 1999a), is frequently a virtual one. That is, the individual often cannot distinguish the generalized anxiety over potential victimization from a reasonable response based on its statistical likelihood. Barry Glassner (1999) locates this disquieting response in the so-called "culture of fear." In its media saturation crime becomes a singular postmodern terrain of meaning-creation.

The Consumption of Sociocultural Meaning

The continual positionings of audiences and mediated popular culture texts assures that meaning is complicated, ambiguous, and often contradictory (Turner 1990/2003). Increasingly, media culture shapes and is shaped by the logic of consumerism. Consumption of postmodern culture represents a kind of renewal of modernist forms of production (Storey 1999; Jameson 2002). The postmodern distinction is that culture itself becomes a commodity. As Fredric Jameson writes:

> So, in postmodern culture, "culture" has become a product in its own right; the market has become a substitute for itself and fully as much a commodity as any of the items it includes within itself: modernism was still minimally and tendentially the critique of the commodity and the effort to make it transcend itself. Postmodernism is the consumption of sheer commodification as a process. (Jameson 1991, x)

This "cultural logic of late capitalism" is distinct from a radical breakdown of economic productivity. Rather, it signals a fundamental transformation of meaning:

> [A] prodigious expansion of culture throughout the social realm, to the point at which everything in our social life—from economic value and state power to practices and to the very structure of the psyche itself—can be said to have become cultural in some original and yet untheorized sense. This proposition, however, is substantially quite consistent with the previous diagnosis of a society of the image or the simulacrum and the transformation of the "real" into so many pseudoevents. (Jameson 1991, 48)

CHAPTER TWO

The reproduction of culture represents the inevitable displacement of modernist productive forces. In particular, ideas, significations, and images are the most suitable commodities of the postmodern electronic media. Implosion of the event into the process that created it is the dynamic of meaning-creation in the scenario. Events are packaged and presented as images (visual, aural, virtual) *as if* they continue to represent counterfeit or modernist forms of experience (Baudrillard 1981/94; Kellner 2003b).

Rapidly expanding popular culture discourse floats freely—truthfulness is textual, largely momentary—in what Guy Debord has called the "society of the spectacle" (Debord 1967/94). In his view:

> Understood in its totality, the spectacle is both the outcome and the goal of the dominant mode of production. It is not something *added* to the real world—not a decorative element, so to speak. On the contrary, it is the very heart of society's real unreality. In all of its specific manifestations—news or propaganda, advertising or the actual consumption of entertainment—the spectacle epitomizes the prevailing model of social life. It is the omnipresent celebration of a choice *already made* in the sphere of production, and the consummate result of that choice. In form as in content the spectacle serves as total justification for the conditions and aims of the existing system. It further ensures the *permanent presence* of that justification, for it governs almost all time spent outside the production process itself. (Debord 1967/94, 13) [*italics* in the original]

The spectacle, then, defines mediated production as consumption so that "[a]ll that once was directly lived has become mere representation" (Debord 1967/94, 12).

The commodification of culture, if Jameson and Debord are correct, rationalizes consumption as a choice in everyday life, even as such choice is fundamentally precluded. In the consumption of popular culture, social values, beliefs, even worldview, are inseparable from the utility of physical objects with which they are associated (Twitchell 1999, 11–12). Cars, houses, clothing, firearms, and so on are laden with unspoken yet symbolic meaning. Even more so, sociocultural abstractions such as family, health, leisure, education, or spirituality are commodified in the postmodern terrain.[5] The range of social meanings relevant to consumption has proliferated, largely unconnected to actual patterns (Storey 1999). As Mike Featherstone observes, "Today's consumer culture represents neither a lapse of control nor the institution of more rigid controls, but rather their underpinning by a flexible underlying generative structure which can both handle formal control and de-control and facilitate an easy change of gears between them" (Featherstone 1991, 27).

Popular culture scenarios of deviance are located in this logic of consumption. Especially in electronic media culture, deviance and crime become ubiquitous commodities for both knowledge communication and entertainment (Barak 1994a; Surette 1998). The ideological content of such constructions is no less potent given their value as one or the other. Such content includes embedded age, gender, race, and class stereotypes (Stanfield 1994; Krzycki 1996; Goldberg 1997, 162–63; Potter and Kappeler 1998, 13; Doob 1999; Barak et al. 2001) and the assumption that crime has meaning only (or even primarily) as a matter of individual choice. In "only reporting what's news," media culture is little more than a reflection of popular crime narratives, especially in the lack of sociocultural context offered (Fishman 1996). Constructions of predatory street violence and crimes of morality (i.e., drug and sex offenses) are the most newsworthy of events, continuing to generate concern, anxiety, and political rhetoric (Benedict 1992; Surette 1994). Concerning ideologized journalistic constructions of drug addiction, Craig Reinarman and Ceres Duskin argue:

> Unfortunately, the nonfictional lives of African Americans in our inner cities and of growing numbers of other poor Americans are sufficiently harsh that some of them seek solace, comfort and meaning in drugs. But editors seem to believe that readers don't like to be reminded that there is something fundamentally wrong with the social system from which most of them benefit. Editors and readers alike, it seems, feel more comfortable believing that the worsening horrors of our inner cities are caused by evil individuals from a different gene pool—"addicts." Thus, a story about how crushing poverty and racism gave rise to despair that sometimes leads to drug use, abuse or addiction is not considered "newsworthy." Stories that simply depict addicts as complicated, troubled human beings would be neither comforting enough for readers nor dramatic enough for prizes. (Reinarman and Duskin 1996, 329)

Mediated images of corporate wrongdoing, when reported, are most often placed in an organizational context so that the ideology of social

CHAPTER TWO

control and responsibility of the individual is absent. In fact, aside from the morally questionable (if not illegal) sexual escapades of President Bill Clinton—themselves emergent from questionable financial activities of the Clintons—media coverage of white-collar crime has decreased (Lofquist 1996, 256).

Media constructions of crime and deviance, whether aimed at informing or entertaining audiences, largely reinforce commonsense notions about offenders, their motivations, and their actions. As commodities these constructions are rarely contextualized. Instead they are most often packaged as electronic elements of the postmodern spectacle (Kellner 2003b). In framing the concept of "newsmaking criminology," Gregg Barak observes, "Understanding the construction of newsmaking requires an examination of the conscious and unconscious processes involved in the mass dissemination of symbolic consumer goods" (Barak 1994b, 3). Constructions of crime emerge from complex institutional activities involving media sources, criminal justice organizations and agents, medical and health professionals, political groups, and various public audiences (Jenkins 1996, 2003a, 2003b).

Since interactions involving these groups occur over time and are often truncated, the "whole story" is rarely reconstructed. Most often the narrative is significantly circumscribed, ideologically situated as personal choices and issues of social control and embedded in a web of facts known largely in hindsight and subject to reinterpretation. Many mediated stories may emerge from the same set of facts, juxtaposing images of deviance and conformity:

> Symbolic rewarding is accomplished primarily by identifying heroes, villains, and neutral characters and associating them with specific traits, beliefs, or kinds of behavior. Symbolic punishment is achieved through labeling or stigmatizing certain activities or traits as antisocial, deviant or undesirable. Sometimes this rewarding and punishing is done explicitly, sometimes it is accomplished by way of unspoken assumptions, or by the framing of news accounts. (Barak 1994b, 13)

Regardless of the particular contents of rewards and punishments, the assumed context is that audiences know and share some degree of commitment to existing social arrangements (e.g., the legitimacy of norms protecting private property and defining acceptable sexual conduct or the expression of violence). Media are not the only constructors of crime and deviance in society. But it is through media representations that most people organize their knowledge about crime and other situations of stigmatization.

Creating Deviance: The Scenario as Stigma Contest

Constructions of deviance in the scenario are textual (Dotter and Fisher-Giorlando 1997), organized in three interactive layers. The first layer is that of the *deviant event*. In commonsense terms the deviant event refers to the spatial/temporal occurrence of behavior (Clinard and Meier 2004, 28–34). The event includes the primary components of acts and actors, normative definitions, and societal reaction (Dotter and Roebuck 1988). The act may relate the participants as perpetrator and victim (e.g., violence) or as coactors (e.g., theft).

Vincent F. Sacco and Leslie W. Kennedy propose a similar conceptualization of the "criminal event." Its episodic nature is of particular theoretical significance, unfolding in three stages:

> (1) the *precursors* of the event, including the locational and situational factors that bring people together in time and space, (2) the *transactions* that indicate how the interactions among participants define the outcomes of their actions, and (3) the *aftermath* of the event, including the report to the police, their response, the harm done and the redress required, and the long-term consequences of the event in terms of public reactions and the changing of laws. (Sacco and Kennedy 2002, 10–11) [*italics* added for emphasis]

For Sacco and Kennedy, the three-stage criminal event details complexity over time and space. Traditional conceptions of crime and deviance tend to emphasize one stage at the expense of others in searching for causal connections.

My theorizing of the deviant event expands Sacco and Kennedy's concept in three ways. First, the deviant event problematizes the relationship between laws and other norms. Thus, societal reaction as criminal stigmatization is only one possibility. While informal reactions define more general constructions of deviance, these same situational nonlegal responses are embedded in criminal punishment as well. Second, the processual movement of the criminal event in time and space is supplemented by similar symbolic transformations of meaning. That is, meaning layers continuously overlap with one another as the event evidences spatial and temporal change. The deviant event is only one layer or emergent frame in the process of stigma creation; it is textual, "not conceivable in an originary or modified form of presence" (Derrida 1967/78, 211). Finally, multiple deviant events may be situated in time and space, although linkages among them are frequently unclear. In particular, actors may be associated across events in a wider organizational context. The deviant event is generally unmediated in traditional labeling perspectives, and it typically includes acts and actors, rule enforcers, and perhaps an immediate audience (particularly if the act is carried out in a public place). Societal reaction is emergent from behavior of the participants (including potential audiences), linked by situational normative definitions. The abstraction of the deviant event represents the primary subject for traditional studies of deviant behavior. Criticism of interactionist labeling focusing on knowledgeability and so-called "secret deviance" is framed by the presumptive character of the deviant event. Becker's (1963/73) formulation of "secret deviance" and its potential for stigmatized labeling addresses the interactive dynamics of the event. Meaning may be quite clear to the participants, or it may be marked by ambiguity, even misunderstanding and ignorance. In any case, the deviant event describes real people, their putative actions, situational normative constructions, and reactions flowing from them.

The second layer is that of *media reconstruction*. It is bounded by the expanded activities of media, law enforcement, and other audiences in offering interpretations of the deviant event. These audiences, individuals and especially organizations (i.e., moral entrepreneurs), often become primary actors in a second-layer drama of meaning-generation. All electronic media may be represented, although today television retains primacy of image and its transmission.

Reconstructive interpretations are contested in at least two senses. The "facts" of the event are reviewed for consistency and completeness. This process may generate a logical chain of explanation from the event or lead to a certain amount of speculation. By no means is the clarity of the deviant event assured. Also, the media reconstruction moves to a kind of social typing of the event, rendering its description or explanation as exemplary of broader sociocultural images (Klapp 1962). Interpretations likely link the event to others of its kind. Mark Fishman describes this process of typing crime as news:

> News judgments continuously overlap in space and time. Editors of afternoon and evening media look for, and are oriented by, the news in the morning media. Editors of the morning media derive their sense of news from afternoon and evening media. Since these media may be in different regions and different cities, news judgments spread throughout an indefinite expanse of territory. The wire services and a few nationally-read newspapers, *The New York Times* and *Washington Post*, increase the diffusion of news judgments throughout the United States. (Fishman 1996, 61)

As coverage of the event continues, typing can lead to its thematic anchoring in a broader discourse. For example, a homicide may become identified as part of a crime wave (Fishman 1996) or a possible instance of serial murder (Jenkins 1994).

The actions of moral entrepreneurs are relevant to the layer of media reconstruction. Activities of such individuals or groups aim at legitimizing the power to act within a legitimate moral universe. As Nachman Ben-Yehuda observes, "[W]e may view many different centers enveloped by corresponding symbolic-moral universes, which confront, conflict, and negotiate with one another" (Ben-Yehuda 1990, 13). The power to label thus defines a stigma contest (Schur 1980), in which the media are principal, but not unique, participants. The origins of moral panics likewise are tied to the politics of deviance on contested moral grounds. According to Goode and Ben-Yehuda: "[T]he key ingredient in the emergence of a moral panic is creation or intensification of hostility toward and denunciation of a particular group, category, or cast of characters" (Goode and Ben-Yehuda 1994, 74). The appearance of moral panics in the deviance generation process is the point at which media reconstruction overlaps with the final layer of the scenario.

Extending Denzin's (1995) conception of the "cinematic society," I call this third layer the *stigma movie*. It represents the point (never identifiable in any final sense) at which mediated reconstructions of deviant events become ideologized as social control narratives. The nature of ideology in this layer can be described as a "political 'double bind,'" which is the simultaneous individualization and totalization of modern power structures" (Foucault 1983, 216). Deviance becomes dramatized knowledge and entertainment, drawn from events in everyday life. The boundary between the moral content of knowledge (i.e., normative relations) and its function to inform or afford pleasure is erased or at least rendered irrelevant. Stigmatizing discourse is interweaved with that of conformity. Increasingly, institutional sources of social control (actors in the criminal justice system, family, school, and church) must locate their voice in this layer as deviance becomes more sensational and politicized.

The stigma movie refers to the implosion (Baudrillard 1981/94) of the mediated deviance-generation process. The commodification of deviance as a cultural representation becomes its own experience. For example, while most Americans have neither perpetrated nor been the victim of a serious act of violence, fear of crime remains a primary topic of media culture. According to Alison Young:

> The trauma of identification through subjectification in the image can be read as a series of symptoms which always displace the pleasure in pain onto something else. The issues which are commonly taken as contemporary crises for the crimino-legal complex function as symptoms of the anxiety that lies at the heart of the economy of representation of crime. (Young 1996, 19)

The stigma movie also refers to the fact that popular culture is a primary terrain for representations of deviance. Jeff Ferrell and Clinton R. Sanders mark the reflexive dynamic of crime and popular culture: "In the same way that everyday crime and criminalization operate as cultural enterprises, everyday popular culture undertakings—those social activities organized around art, music, and fashion—are regularly recast as crime" (Ferrell and Sanders 1995b, 7).

The implosion of deviance-generation rests on two related sociocultural developments. The first is the spread of what Orrin Klapp (1991) calls "social inflation." The term refers to a generalized diluting of symbolic meaning. Klapp (1991, 4) identifies four types of social magnifiers which contribute to symbols' loss of value: overstatement, crusading, contagious communication (i.e., hysterias), and emotional hitchhiking (self-expansion by identification with others).[6]

In particular, the last of these, emotional hitchhiking, is tied in with the second development: mediated cultural heroism (Dotter 1987, 1994, forthcoming). Postmodern celebrity is a significant terrain of meaning-creation in consumer society. Overlapping with the traditional media avenues to fame (including film, television, sports, and popular music) is the increasingly important and visible criminal/deviant celebrity. While many of these are persons with fame apart from their misdeeds (e.g., President Bill Clinton, O. J. Simpson, Clarence Thomas), others (e.g., Monica Lewinsky, Amy Fisher, Anita Hill) were spontaneously celebrated as parts of mediated, reconstructed deviant events transformed into a movie. While much if not most of celebrity deviance deals with sexual behaviors, its theoretical importance as a type of symbolic inflation should not be underestimated. Universally communicated, if not admired, such celebrated textual selves are more and more often the terrain of meaning/deviance generation in postmodern America.

Scenario as Storytelling and Social Theory: The Voices of the Text

The Layering of Event, Reconstruction, and Stigma Movie

The scenario links the deviant event, media reconstructions, and the stigma movie. As a text, meaning emerges from the interplay of the three layers. Once the initial event is set into motion, ambiguity becomes possible if not certain. Many events (perhaps the majority) are short-lived, consisting only of the actions of perpetrators and victims; they are never reported to law enforcement or other amplifying audiences.

A substantial number of events are interpreted in media reconstructions of various sorts. Most "local" deviant and crime events reported in newspapers and even through electronic media are of this type. The circulation of informational crime knowledge is concentrated in the relationship of events to reconstruction. This connection of event and reconstruction is problematic. As pointed out above, traditional studies of deviance view the event as unmediated, involving only principal actors and audiences. In the postmodern scenario, the event itself is from the beginning arguably a media representation. At the very least the particulars of the event—actors, audiences, and so on—are established through media processes, especially reporting. Of necessity, media reconstruction relates the history of a deviant event as an ever-growing number of related events linked to the first. Audience participation in the history of events is expanded to include criminal justice officials and additional media, once reporting is accomplished. Media reconstruction is not always transmuted into the stigma movie, even in the face of a criminal trial, conviction, and imprisonment. However, when even a minimum of media reconstruction occurs, meaning of the event becomes problematic not only for actors (especially victims), but any mass audience as well. Normative/legal relations, definitions of acts, and societal reaction are all negotiable in the process of reconstruction.

The movie represents the layer in which the stigma contest (Schur 1980) is thoroughly sited and deviance is most highly commodified. It often includes celebrity actors, though not always. The production of the stigma movie is in its exhibition. Once play begins, the event and reconstruction are subsumed in presentation. The stigma movie, then, is most often scripted around the master statuses of age, gender, race, and class. Not infrequently, this layer may interrelate any combination of these in a complex narrative (Aronowitz 1992, 2003; Goldberg 1997, 8). Sarup separates narrative into its components of story and discourse: "Each narrative has two parts: a story (*histoire*) and a discourse (*discourse*). The story is the content, or the chain of events. The story is the 'what' in a narrative, the discourse is the 'how'" [*italics* in the original] (Sarup 1996, 17). In the stigma movie, story is emergent from deviant events and, most importantly, their media reconstructions. All elements—acts, actors, normative relations, audiences, and societal reactions—are situated in a dramatic, continuing (and therefore transformative) storyline. Narrative, the dramatic thrust of the story, is never complete.[7] As Sarup observes, "An interesting point about narrative existence (the characters) in the drama is that they must remain the same from one event to the next. If they do not, some explanation (overt or covert) must occur. In drama, it seems that some principle of coherence must operate, there must be some sense that the identity of existents is fixed and continuing" (Sarup 1996, 17).

In the narrative of the commodified scenario, Denzin's (1989a) concept of epiphany is an important discursive element. It represents an interactional frame having great effect on and significance for a person's life. Commencing from the epiphany, the meaning of life is radically altered (Denzin 1989a, 70–71; 1989b, 15). The epiphany is a life event (positive or negative) during which character and self are defined and redefined, often abruptly. Denzin (1989a, 70–71; 1989b, 129–30) distinguishes four types:

the major epiphany (touching the entire fabric of the person's life); the cumulative epiphany (describing eruptions or reactions occurring over a long time period); the illuminative or minor epiphany (representing a problematic moment in the individual's biography); and the relived epiphany (in which meaning emerges through reexperience of life events).

Particular examples are endless: birth and death of family members, marriage and divorce, the onset or progression of physical disability, murder, wife-battering, and so on. The impact of such events as life-turning epiphanies depends on the individual actor's circumstances (i.e., the organization of events in the biographical narrative). As a textual production and reproduction, the epiphany is interactional, located within social relationships. Furthermore, its interpretation, and thereby its significance, is situated in a broader sociocultural narrative. Thus, biographical texts are produced in sociocultural processes of communication. Within the scenario, deviance or criminal labeling can represent any or all of these types of life-turns. As a major epiphany, biographical stigma is located in the space between deviant events and media reconstruction. The creation of deviance as master status is enmeshed between the reconstruction and stigma movie layers. Thus, biographical meaning is situated in sociocultural context.

As a process of deviance-generation the scenario may be characterized as documentary, dramatic, or, most often, a layering of both as its storyline unfolds. For example, scenarios based on newsmaking criminology (Barak 1994b) emerge from an event having occurred in space and time. Media reconstructions will include interpretation and elaboration of what is known of the event at a given point, as well as the insertion of opinion, speculation, and so on. Implosion occurs with the appearance of the stigma movie, which assumes an apparently independent existence. The scenario, then, *contextualizes* event, reconstructions, and the stigma movie in time and space. Even the occurrence of the event is a textual, literary product, an articulation of language communicated in mass media forms (Hall 1986a). Derrida argues, "This condensation of history, of language, of the encyclopedia, remains here indissociable from an *absolutely* singular event, an *absolutely* singular signature, and therefore also of a date, of a language, of an autobiographical inscription" [*italics* in the original] (Derrida 1992, 43). The event is rendered meaningful in its mediated reconstruction and production as a stigma movie. Its "reality" in time and space is constantly interpreted and reinterpreted: "No context can entirely enclose it. Nor any code, the code here being both the possibility and impossibility of writing, of its essential iterablilty (repetition/alterity)" (Derrida 1977, 182). Finally, "undecidables are terms which mean both one thing and its opposite; neither one thing nor its opposite" (Howells 1999, 79).

Scenarios may also be based on purely fictional narratives or some combination of historical events and their embellishment. Novels and other literary texts, "in their singularity, decline to explore what they are exemplary *of* at the same tine that they invite their readers to become involved in their predicaments and the consciousness of narrators and character who are in some sense posited as exemplary" (Culler 2000, 282) [*italics* in the original]. Such is particularly the case in popular culture scenarios with the primary aim of entertainment. Sources may include novels, films, and musical texts, to list a few. In dramatic, fictional scenarios, meaning is no less real as a cultural representation. The stigma movie may emerge from a fictional event and storyline and also carry lasting imagery and meaning. Denzin highlights the play of the dramatic and the documentary: "The new information technologies turn everyday life into a theatrical spectacle; into sites where the dramas that surround the decisive performances of race, ethnicity, gender, sexuality, and age are staged. These dramas are staged against the backdrop of compelling newsworthy events which are shaped by uncertainty, unpredictability, and natural disaster" (Denzin 1991c, 8). Postmodern knowledge and meaning are technologically organized and controlled. They are consumed, particularly but not exclusively, as video, cinematic, and, increasingly, virtual images (Denzin 1995). Especially in mediated popular culture, these images blend in the stigma movie.

The Scenario as Interpretive Strategy

In addition to describing the process of mediated meaning-creation, the concept of scenario also serves as a strategy for deconstructing that process (Dotter and Fisher-Giorlando 1997). It is an interpretive stance or attiude tentatively situated in the "seventh moment" of qualitative research (Denzin 2002a, 484). The fluid history of interpretive ethnography can be reviewed as a series of such moments, overlapping in time, space, and perspective (Denzin and Lincoln 1994; Lincoln and Denzin 1994).[8]

THE SCENARIO AS INTERPRETIVE STRATEGY

A "crisis of meaning" has been textually unfolding since the late 1980s and continues today. More specifically, this crisis has three themes: representation, legitimation, and praxis (Denzin 2002a, 482–83). Representation is problematized in the textual nature of sociocultural life, and legitimation calls into question traditional models of verification such as reliability, validity, and generalizability. Praxis involves the critical task of locating the lost voices in texts and as such is intimately concerned with historical interpretation and reinterpretation. As Lincoln and Denzin frame the project: "The move is toward pluralism, and many social scientists now recognize that no picture is ever complete, that what is needed is many perspectives, many voices, before we can achieve deep understandings of social phenomena, and before we can assert that a narrative is complete" (Lincoln and Denzin 1994, 581–82). I assert that the lost voices—of the young, women, minorities, and poor—are, by their silence in the texts, stigmatized and thereby controlled.

Overall, this meaning crisis evidences in contradictory ways both ruptures and turns in knowledge and its use. Manning's observation speaks to this point:

> The term "crisis" of representation implies some generalized dissatisfaction with modern social science, but it has meaning only in fields in which notation and theory are qualitative. Marginal subfields within social science, for example, symbolic interactionism, social psychology, ethnography, literature (especially literary criticism, an elaborate mirror job—a critique of critiques), and to a lesser degree, social history are being reshaped. (Manning 2002, 581–82)

The scenario's poststructuralist stance is a fluid one and its relation to deconstruction open to debate. Dictionary definitions of the term notwithstanding, "deconstruction is not a method and cannot be transformed into one" (Derrida 1991, 273). Despite its identification as a literary method, the term is grounded in philosophy, in the phenomenology of consciousness as well as the problematic of science and knowledge generally:

> As a unique attempt to approach cultural phenomena and disciplinary fields in terms of the relation between being and knowledge, deconstruction still has much to tell us even (and particularly) after the current paradigm shift to cultural studies, which itself emerges from a continuation

CHAPTER TWO

of the epistemic crisis that first saw the reconfiguration of philosophy as deconstruction. (Rajan 2002, xi)

Furthermore, deconstruction is most often considered more or less identical with poststructuralism. With the currency of the linguistic turn, deconstruction was expropriated as a device for textual, rather than philosophical criticism (Rajan 2002, 1–4).

Derrida's (1994, 175–76) sense of deconstruction is opaque and yet glimpses a transformative quality; it may be described as "an art of interruption" (Bennington 2000, 3). My own reading of the term focuses on the liberating quality of textual meaning, allowing incorporation of many "new," heretofore unheard, voices: women, the young, people of color. Put simply, deconstruction represents "a questioning of the 'is,' a concern with what remains to be thought, with what cannot be thought within the present" (Royle 2000, 7). Deconstruction, then, is not a tool for the obliteration of meaning. Rather, in the scenario it represents an appreciation for the multiplicity of meanings text may offer—"reconstruction with a difference" (Lemert 2002, 225). Narrative represents the totality of the storyline and also its open-ended character of meaning (Punday 2003, 4–5).

Similarly, Michel Foucault's (1977) concept of transgression describes the complexity of social meaning-creation and the transformative processes in textual reading, and it helps situate deviance labeling in the textual linguistic turn. The creation of stigmatizing meaning (Dotter and Roebuck 1988) is a continuous process, occurring on many different levels, in response both to events and to hypothetical situations, across time as well as physical and social space. Transgression captures its problematic contested framings, even as it suggests its fluid character:

> Transgression is an action which involves the limit, that narrow zone of a line where it displays the flash of its passage, but perhaps also its entire trajectory, even its origin; it is likely that transgression has its entire space in the line it crosses. (Foucault 1977, 33–34)

While Foucault's (1970/94, 236–43; 1972a, 184–86) emphasis on the ideological content of knowledge and its use for social control is central to the scenario, it cannot be accepted uncritically. His reification of discourse renders the subject with no voice whatsoever—an untenable perspective for any interactionist theorizing. My location of Foucault follows that of West:

"Like Foucault, prophetic pragmatists criticize and resist forms of subjection, as well as types of economic exploitation, state repression, and bureaucratic domination. But these critiques and resistances, unlike his, are unashamedly guided by moral ideals of creative democracy and individuality"[9] (West 1989, 226). While the textual subject is decentered in the meaning crisis, its reconstruction is a constant process of discovery and reinterpretation. In concluding "that a constitutive criminological vision of a human subject must be open to both human diversity and specificity, as well as being contingently formed so as to adjust to emerging renditions of subjectivity," Stuart Henry and Dragan Milovanovic (1996, 12) coin the term "recovering subject." Their point is that the subject can never be fully recaptured. At the same time, human subjectivity and the meaning processes flowing therefrom are revisable and pliant.

Self is located in this process to recover, to reconstitute, the decentered subject; it becomes "a site, a point where various social, cultural, economic, linguistic, and psychological forces [happen] to intersect" (Lilla 1998, 37). Deviance-labeling is a valued terrain to observe such siting and recovery of the subject. In the words of Anthony Giddens, "A self identity has to be created and more or less continually reordered against the backdrop of shifting experiences of day-to-day life and the fragmenting tendencies of modern institutions"[10] (Giddens 1991, 186).

In its layered, interactive presentation, the scenario is a form of radical constructivism, wherein a knowledge claim "is thought to be valid if it is viable or if it provides functional fit, that is, if it works to achieve a goal" (Schwandt 1994, 127). Values, norms, and concepts of good and evil are necessarily relativized in the culture of consumption (for Baudrillard, imploded). With Derrida (1997), I believe that a reconstituted concept of justice may emerge from thoroughgoing deconstructive transformation. In viewing the generation of stigma as continually emergent in the web of deviant events, media reconstruction, and the production of the stigma movie, the scenario "turns attention to the margins and reverses the usual adherence to dominant cultural values" (Manning and Cullum-Swan 1994, 468). This marginalization of voice represents the ideological character of all texts, calling into question "the very idea of a modernist discourse of deviance" (Lyman 1997d, 241).

In the scenario, deviance shifts back and forth between biographical images and the broader context of cultural meaning framed in master status.

CHAPTER TWO

The labeled self, embedded in master status, is both a momentary commodity and a creative subject. As discourse, conformity and deviance are defined in relation to one another, in the boundaries between situational societal reaction and resistance to such, in the interplay of normative interpretation and representation of those stigmatized (Halley 2000, 45). Mills's sociological imagination is radicalized into a kind of "political semiotics of selfhood" (Brown 1987). The creation of deviance and stigmatized status is necessarily discursive and negotiated (Perinbanayagam 1985, 20–21).

In the stigma movie, demarcation of deviant events, normative negotiation, and societal reaction are realized as the terrain of identity politics. The scenario offers a textual critique of this process, whereby identity becomes "a multidimensional space in which a variety of writings blend and clash. These writings consist of many quotations from the innumerable centres of culture, ideological state apparatus, and practices." Finally, identity, and thereby sociocultural meaning, is constructed from biographical differences in an historical context, creating "the space in which the human subject exercises a measure of interpretive freedom" (Sarup 1996, 25).

A deconstructive stance, the scenario seeks tentative answers to issues of identity and deviance labeling. Denzin (1994c, 190) suggests several questions framing a deconstructive attitude: How are the biographical subject's presence and voice evidenced in the text? How is the subject's life animated in time and space (i.e., given a linear presentation)? How is the textual life given structure? What is the nature of intertextuality (i.e., the presence of one text in another and vice versa)? To these I add only two: What is left unstated in a text? and, How is the subject's voice silenced or excluded from the text? Textual meaning is a blend of what is stated in a text and what is left unsaid. The latter can be inferred or implied. Also, not all voices are equally accessible in a text (Turner 1990/2003).

As a cinematic metaphor the scenario represents a form of storytelling (and retelling). For Denzin (1991c, 156) the principal cinematic story is that of the cultural logics of late capitalism (Jameson 1991), contextualized by a new "universal norm" of cultural diversity. Simultaneously, there are traces of patriarchal and racist narratives to subvert the main storyline. As he concludes:

> Our most powerful effects as storytellers come when we expose the cultural plot and the cultural practices that guide our writing hands. The story

THE SCENARIO AS INTERPRETIVE STRATEGY

> I have been trying to tell argues that we have all fallen victims to a cultural plot which says we can capture postmodernism within a single interpretive framework. Having captured this moment, in all its complexities, we can do better sociology, or even write a postmodern sociology of postmodernism. Perhaps this is an impossibility. (Denzin 1991c, 156–57)

For Denzin, postmodern reality, so exemplified in cinematic discourse, is fluid, changing, and defined by multiple interpretations. In the scenario these interpretations represent the voices of the labeled Other (Connor 1989, 234), embodied in labeled master statuses. The voices are located, often contradictorily and only briefly, in media representations and stigma movies based on deviant events.

I view the scenario as a theoretical project of the postmodern moment. Best and Kellner (2001, 13–15) persuasively argue for creative interpretive strategies aimed at understanding meaning-creation at multiple levels and not simply at its destruction. In confronting the postmodern crisis of meaning, I propose the scenario as a guide to the expansion of social theory as interpretation (Denzin 1994a; Marcus 1994). Best and Kellner (2001, 15) offer a concise description of this task: "Together, social maps and historical narratives study the points of intersection between individuals and their cultures, between power and knowledge. To the fullest degree possible, they seek to lift the veils of ideology and expose supposed givens as contingent and the present as a social construct, while providing visions of alternative futures."

As a sensitizing concept (Blumer 1969) the scenario attempts to locate meaning in the widest variety of mediated contexts. For example, events may be interlinked in a broad historical scenario of deviance creation, as I will show with youth subculture formation in chapter 6. Conversely, the traditional labeling of discrete episodes of deviant behavior may be its focus, allowing for contextualization and interpretation—the aim of chapter 7. In the first instance, historical description is the goal, and in the second, a critique of the labeling process leading to stigmatization. Having outlined the contours of the scenario, in the next chapter I will work backward, dissecting the philosophical roots of the concept in detail. These include the peculiarly American perspective of pragmatism, its familiar convergence with interactionism, and the linguistic turn of contemporary neopragmatism.

CHAPTER TWO

Notes

An earlier composition of this chapter was published as "Creating Deviance: Scenarios of Stigmatization in Postmodern Culture" in *Deviant Behavior: An Interdisciplinary Journal* 23: 419–48, 2002 (Taylor and Francis).

1. For a more complete discussion of the critical reception of postmodern social theory within interactionism, see dialogue between David R. Maines (1996a, 1996b) and Norman K. Denzin (1996) in Volume 19 of *Symbolic Interaction*.

2. Charlene Haddock Seigfried (1996, 31–32) offers a reading on the convergences of pragmatism and feminism. She suggests that the former's linking of the philosophical project with explicit value judgments and its emphasis on experience and human action lead to the view that gender is not primarily a biological category but a culturally mediated assumption of identity.

3. Goffman (1963b, 62–72) acknowledges that traditional sociology has neglected the concept and method of biography, aside from its use as career life history.

4. Meyrowitz (1985) cites the murder of Lee Harvey Oswald, suspected assassin of President John F. Kennedy, by Jack Ruby as a prototypical example of witnessing-through-media.

5. William Leach (1993) provides a critical historical account of the rise of consumer culture in America from the 1890s to 1932. He argues that individual choice had little to do with its creation as a sociocultural entity. Rather, it was created from above by business elites, and it served to effectively mute competing sociocultural narratives of the "good life." Related histories of the early century chart the rise of nightlife (Erenberg 1981) and public amusements (Nasaw 1993). Lizabeth Cohen (2003) dissects the interface of politics and consumption as it developed following World War II, and James B. Twitchell (1999) offers a celebratory take on contemporary consumerism.

6. Elaine Showalter (1997) outlines the prevalence of hysterical epidemics (i.e., "hystories") in contemporary media, and Barry Glassner (1999) the mediated culture of fear.

7. In his critique of postmodernism as an invalidation of traditional narrative, Michael Roemer (1995) argues conversely that stories are preclusive, over before they begin.

8. The seven moments of ethnographic inquiry, all of which have traces in the present, include the traditional (1900–1950), the modernist (1950–1970), blurred genres (1970–1986), the crisis of representation (1986–1990), the postmodern or experimental (1990–1995), the postexperimental (1995–2000), and the future (2000–?) (Denzin and Lincoln 2000, 2–3).

9. Denzin (1991a, 32–34) offers a similar reading of the intersection of pragmatism and poststructuralism.

10. Charles Lemert (1994) differentiates self and identity in the historical processes of their conceptual usage. He contends that "self" is largely a white male construction, while "identity" more often flows from the works of feminists and people of color. While his distinction may be historically accurate, I see no reason why the two cannot be practically equated. The self refers to the process by which identity is created. Simultaneously, the product of identity is transmuted into self-signification.

CHAPTER THREE
READING INTERACTIONISM: PRAGMATISM AND THE PROBLEM OF MEANING

The intellectual tradition of symbolic interactionism represents the most important American contribution to sociological theory. Through the years its various branches have reflected the institutional and political concerns of academic culture and the larger society (Bulmer 1984; Carey 1975; Faris 1970). In doing so, the perspective has been plagued by a "double-edged specter" (Denzin 1992, 2). Thus interactionism has been the central interpretive, subjective approach toward human social conduct to emerge in contemporary mainstream sociology. At the same time, its proponents have traditionally championed the search for objective, scientific principles to explain such conduct.

Despite this dilemma (or perhaps because of it), interactionism in its multiple varieties has remained remarkably fluid in its application to diverse research settings and problems (Rock 1979). Most important of these is its historical approach to the study of crime and social deviance. Stressing the social meaning attached to misconduct and resulting consequences, the labeling approach has arguably dominated the field for some four decades (Douglas and Waksler 1982, 125–26).

This chapter has three aims. First, the philosophical roots of interactionism in the pragmatic philosophies of William James, Charles S. Peirce, John Dewey, and especially George Herbert Mead are explored. The interpretive/scientific turns of interactionism are thereby traced to this historical context of pragmatism's early development and its diffuse influence on the development of the original Chicago School of Sociology (Joas 1993, 26–28; Rock 1979, 59–101).

CHAPTER THREE

Second, the work of Herbert Blumer (as a disciple of Mead) is examined. Especially critical is his movement of the generation of social meaning through symbolic interaction to center stage (Blumer 1969). While a comprehensive survey of the various branches of interactionism is beyond my scope,[1] the interactionist influence on the study of social deviance is most pronounced in the writings of the so-called Chicago School. Certainly, this tradition includes much scholarship that is neither interactionist in viewpoint nor strictly concerned with the study of disvalued behavior. Still, the theoretical intersection of interactionism and perspectives on deviance is apparent in the Chicago tradition. The work of Blumer as an interpreter of Mead for Chicago interactionism is paramount.[2]

Third, I present a brief reading of pragmatism's revival in the interdisciplinary debates of cultural studies (West 1989; Denzin 1992; Dickstein 1998b). Of particular importance is the neopragmatic emphasis on the linguistic turn and the problem of meaning (Rorty 1967, 1989; Mouffe 1996). For over a century the philosophy has informed debates over the context of modern—and now postmodern—narratives (Hildebrand 2003; Stuhr 2003).

The Philosophical Roots of Interactionism

The intellectual history of symbolic interactionism is firmly linked to the emergence of pragmatism, the uniquely American contribution to philosophical thought (Dotter 1980a). From the early work of C. Wright Mills (1964) to contemporary analyses (Joas 1993; West 1989; Diggins 1994), the development of pragmatism has been amply chronicled. Likewise, its influence on generations of early Chicago sociologists (from W. I. Thomas and Herbert Blumer through Everett C. Hughes to Howard S. Becker and others)[3] has been established (Kuklick 1973; Kurtz 1984; Joas 1993, 14–51).

Pragmatism itself may be viewed through innumerable lenses, "developed as a theory of meaning and then as a theory of truth" (Hook 1974, ix). As Morris Dickstein (1998a, 3) writes, "Within the American tradition, this practical, result-oriented side of Peirce, James, and Dewey places their work in a line that goes back at least to Benjamin Franklin, while the pragmatists' commitment to creative self-transformation shows the influence of Emerson." The tradition, then, is thoroughly American in outlook, emerging after the Civil War. It is rooted as well in the changing institutional arrangements wrought by industrialization and urbanization as the twentieth century unfolded.

In *The Metaphysical Club,* Louis Menand (2001) combines biography and intellectual history to create his narrative retelling of pragmatism as "a story of ideas in America." To the triad of James, Peirce, and Dewey, he adds the jurist Oliver Wendell Holmes. These four thinkers shared what Menand calls an "attitude toward ideas." In his words:

> What was that attitude? If we strain out the differences, personal and philosophical, they had with one another, we can say that what these four thinkers had in common was not a group of ideas, but a single idea—an idea about ideas. They all believed that ideas are not "out there" waiting to be discovered, but are tools—like forks, knives and microchips—that people devise to cope with the world in which they find themselves. They believed that ideas are produced not by individuals, but by groups of individuals—that ideas are social. They believed that ideas do not develop according to some inner logic of their own, but are entirely dependent, like germs, on their human carriers and the environment. And they believed that since ideas are provisional responses to particular and unreproducible circumstances, their survival depends not on their immutability but on their adaptability. (Menand 2001, xi–xii)

Ideas, then, are based on contingency and therefore are less useful as ideology or even as an essentialist, abstract philosophical system. From its beginning, pragmatism was fraught with contradictions and ambivalence: self-expression and social context, logic and feeling, theory and empirical reality, science and moral faith. What emerged was a fluid method of "critical common-sensism" (Peirce 1940/55, 290–301). Henry Steele Commager succinctly summarizes its practical, empirical thrust:

> Pragmatism was a philosophy of expedience. It put ideas to work and judged them by their results. It accepted "any idea upon which we can ride" as "true instrumentally," and instrumentalism came to be its preferred name. It rejected theories and abstractions and established the single standard of workability. It was as practical as the patent office—or the Declaration of Independence. Its expediency was individual; it came, increasingly, to be social, to require that men work together to establish the truth of their hopes. (Commager 1950, 96)

CHAPTER THREE

Arguably the most famous of American philosophers, William James was also the popular champion of pragmatism outside of academia. In a lecture delivered at the University of California at Berkeley in 1898, James makes the first public mention of "pragmatism," appropriately acknowledging Charles Sanders Peirce as originator of the term (West 1989, 54–55).

William James

William James's contribution to the pragmatist canon is sketched in his *Principles of Psychology* (1890/1950). His belief that the organism possesses the ability to choose alternative courses of action provided the basis for functional psychology (Joas, 1993, 5). James was a nominalist concerned with individual morality, and his rendering of the "philosophy of the possible" related to individual, not collective, choice. Individual experience gives rise to beliefs and ideas relevant first and foremost to the individual. In fact, his psychology is based not on social action, but on individual stream of consciousness (Dotter 1980a; Joas 1993, 20).

Still, James recognized the conflict of ideas characterized by pragmatism. In particular, he addresses the ambiguity for religion engendered by the advance of scientific knowledge. He sets the two in opposition in his commonsensical discussion of "tender-minded" rationalistic traits and "tough-minded" empiricist ones. The resolution of this opposition for the philosophical layman is to be found in what James calls "pluralistic monism." In short, everything "is necessarily determined, and yet of course our wills are free: a sort of free-will determinism is the true philosophy" (James 1907/91, 9–10). For James (1907/91, 18) pragmatism represented the framing of such problems of experience, "a philosophy that can satisfy both kinds of demands. It can remain religious like the rationalisms, but at the same time, like the empiricisms, it can preserve the richest intimacy with facts." The result is a compromising middle ground that does little to upset the status quo (West 1989, 57).

James viewed pragmatism as a method for seeking instrumental truth through concrete individual experience. In his own words:

> It is astonishing to see how many philosophical disputes collapse into insignificance the moment you subject them to this simple test of tracing a concrete consequence. There can *be* no difference anywhere that doesn't *make* a difference elsewhere—no difference in abstract truth that

doesn't express itself in a difference in concrete fact and in conduct consequent upon that fact, imposed on somebody, somehow, somewhere, and somewhen. The whole function of philosophy ought to be to find out what definite difference it will make to you and me, at definite instants of our life, if this world-formula or that world-formula be the true one. [*italics* in the original] (James 1907/91, 25)

Truth is *made* through experience. Meaning arises in relation to its use by the individual (James 1907/91, 36–38, 96).[4] James, then, helped to develop and popularize the pragmatic tenets of instrumentalism and the relational perspective on meaning, albeit in an individualized context. It remained for Peirce to combine a pragmatism of the social with the logic of scientific inquiry.

Charles S. Peirce

Peirce (1940/55, 254–55), the originator of the term "pragmatism," later coined the term "pragmaticism" to differentiate his version of the narrative from that of James. Peirce argued that his pragmatic method was concerned with the social construction of meaning and thereby knowledge. His task was to examine the logic and empirical grounding of this process. Furthermore, the study of meaning described what Peirce (1940/55, 27–273) called *intellectual concepts*, those ideas related to the determination of objective fact. Meaning is thus of social origin and unconcerned with feeling. As Menand observes, "For Peirce, there was much more at stake than a theory about knowledge. Nominalism, he believed was a philosophy in aid of selfishness. This was not simply because nominalism denies knowledge its social character; it was because by acknowledging the reality only of individuals, nominalism denies the social altogether" (Menand 2001, 229).

Peirce's realism was a constructed and conditional one: "For possibility being the denial of a necessity, which is a kind of generality, is vague like any other contradiction of a general. Indeed it is the reality of some possibilities that pragmaticism is most concerned to insist upon" (Peirce 1958/66, 215). This logical realism (Brent 1993/98, 299) was Peirce's take on the centrality of science for pragmatism. Similarly, Peirce rejected a mechanical version of determinism: "Try to verify any law of nature, and you will find that the more precise your observations, the more certain they will be to show irregular departure from the law" (Peirce 1958/66, 170).

Peirce's (1940/55, 98–119; 1991) logical-empirical pragmatism, based on the social character of knowledge, is given its fullest treatment in his theory of signs. According to Peirce, every sign is "connected with three things, the ground, the object, and the interpretant" (Peirce 1940/55, 99–100). The subject areas of semiotics, the process by which signs are rendered meaningful, correspond to each of these in turn: pure grammar (the characteristics of the sign which give rise to meaning); logic proper (the conditions of representational truth, relating the sign to its object); and pure rhetoric (the rules by which one sign and/or idea gives rise to another). For Peirce, semiotics is the study and discovery of logical rules for meaning-creation. Meaning is neither wholly arbitrary nor entirely predictable. The sign attains meaning only in subsequent thought or action, by way of the interpretant. Peirce thus provides a phenomenological framing of the meaning process: "Not only will meaning always, more or less, in the long run, mould reactions to itself, but it is only in doing so that its own being exists. For this reason I call this element of the phenomenon or object of thought the element of Thirdness" (1940/55, 91). The generation of meaning is relational, expressed always as a triad: "an interpretation of the thought as a sign of a determining object" (Hoopes 1991, 7).

Peirce developed pragmatism as a logical semiotic system, open but not overcome by diversity in meaning. He recognized the connection of thought and social action. I turn now to Dewey, whose rendering of pragmatism focused on social action in the relationship of the individual to modern society.

John Dewey

The influence of John Dewey is crucial to the development of pragmatism for two related reasons. First, in 1894 Dewey was appointed Professor of Philosophy and Chair of the Department of Philosophy, Psychology and Education at the University of Chicago, positions he held until his departure in 1904. In this decade he became the founder and principal intellectual leader of the Chicago School of Pragmatism. Interestingly, it was William James who bestowed the title on the department after a group publication in 1903 entitled *Studies in Logical Theory* (McDermott 1981, xvii).[5] Second, in his strategic position of influence at Chicago (with the aid of his long-term friend and colleague George Herbert Mead), Dewey guided pragmatic thought to an interdisciplinary synthesis of sociology, psychology, and biology (Rucker 1969, vi). This articulation reflected the influence not only of Mead, but also of William James, as well as the pervasiveness of Darwinism in late-nineteenth-century American thought (Ryan 1995, 130; Degler 1991, 113; Hofstadter 1944/55).

In Dewey's hands, then, pragmatism became an instrumental science of knowing, based upon human experience in a social context. Dewey articulates the interactive relationship of human experience to nature:

> It is not experience which is experienced, but nature—stones, plants, animals, diseases, health, temperature, electricity, and so on. Things interacting in certain ways *are* experience; they are what is experienced. Linked in certain other ways with another natural object—the human organism—they are *how* things are experienced as well. Experience thus reaches down into nature; it has depth. It also has breadth and to an infinitely elastic extent. It stretches. That stretch constitutes inference. [*italics* in the original] (Dewey 1929/81, 252)

According to the relational perspective of truth and meaning, human experience (and thereby instrumental, creative action) becomes embedded in situations. This grounding underscores the meaningfulness experienced through such action (Joas 1993, 4–5). Pragmatism thus becomes a liberating, interactive philosophy of social action, at once indeterminate and rendered meaningful by the human organism's interaction with its environment. The relational, "experimental" character of knowledge stands in sharp contrast to earlier philosophical conceptions of truth (Dewey 1910/81).[6]

The social basis of experience becomes even more complex, considering the movement into the new economic and industrial order of twentieth-century America. Writing at the beginning of the Great Depression, Dewey elegantly captures the confusion experienced by the individual caught in an historical period of great social upheaval:

> The shift that makes the older individualism a dying echo is more marked as well as more rapid in this country. Where is the wilderness which now beckons creative energy and affords untold opportunity to initiative and vigor? Where is the pioneer who goes forth rejoicing, even in the midst of privation, to its conquest? The wilderness exists in the movie and the novel; and the children of the pioneers, who live in the

midst of surroundings artificially made over by the machine, enjoy pioneer life idly in the vicarious film. I see little social unrest which is the straining of energy for outlet in action; I find rather the protest against a weakening of vigor and a sapping of energy that emanate from the absence of constructive opportunity; and I see a confusion that is an expression of the inability to find a secure and morally rewarding place in a troubled and tangled economic scene. (Dewey 1930/81, 611–12)

The problem of social meaning in modern, industrialized society may be seen as a crisis of values and ideology. However, with his instrumental, creative, and indeterminate pragmatic method, Dewey does not envision an inevitable choice between the individual and the social, but a new individualism based on the application of science and technology to the problems of modern society:

Our problems grow out of social conditions: they concern human relations rather than man's direct relationship to physical nature. The adventure of the individual, if there is to be any venturing of individuality and not a relapse into the deadness of complacency or of despairing discontent, is an unsubdued social frontier. The issues cannot be met with ideas improvised for the occasion. The problems to be solved are general, not local. They concern complex forces that are at work throughout the whole country, not those limited to an immediate and almost face-to-face environment. Traditional ideas are more than irrelevant. They are an encumbrance; they are the chief obstacle to the formation of a new individuality integrated within itself and with a liberated function in the society wherein it exists. A new individualism can be achieved through the controlled use of all the resources of the science and technology that have mastered the physical forces of nature. (Dewey 1930/81, 617)

In Dewey's instrumentalism (i.e., the creative application of thinking to problem solution), the construction of knowledge is related to that of authority. Meaningful thought is directed at "problematic situations" for the achievement of individual emotional stability *and* intellectual control. Furthermore, in modern scientific methodology he sees the possibility of a permanently valid standard of knowledge, applied as a socially responsible reform-minded plan (Diggins 1994, 227). In effect, then, Dewey's pragmatism may be seen as a modernist response to the ever-present duality of mind and spirit (Diggins 1994, 3–7). The individual, in a socially interactive environment, creatively solves problems through the application of human experience. Simultaneously, experience and environment are transformed by creative, meaning-generating actors. Darwinism and science preclude the return to any previous *a priori*, given philosophical systems through the very fact that they offer liberation from those systems (Ryan 1995, 231). At the same time science is subjected to the same instrumental pragmatic test as other forms of knowledge: Does it offer creative solutions to problems?

Finally, history, like philosophy and science, must meet the instrumental standard of practicality. Its limited usefulness in providing meaning to present situations and circumstances outweighs concerns about history as human destiny, as a vehicle for moral judgment, or as a system for establishing laws of social relations (Diggins 1994, 251). At the same time, history can be known scientifically, stripped of romantic, nostalgic elements. Dewey espoused a naturalism in which "philosophy must learn to live with the approach to the world that the natural sciences have developed" (Ryan 1995, 231). Herein ideas are open and fluid, subject to the test of experience.

Pragmatism in the thought of John Dewey is simultaneously American and modernist with its emphasis on verifiable scientific knowledge. Although science promises liberation from religion and other forms of absolutism, its assumption of value-neutrality (i.e., that science, in and of itself, is neither good nor bad) creates a substantial dilemma for the development of an interpretive style of sociological theorizing. With his pragmatic, instrumental method, John Dewey and his disciples recast the philosophical discourse in America, and his pragmatic vision through decades evolved from a psychological to substantially a sociological narrative (Ryan 1995, 126–27). More than a philosopher in the traditional sense, Dewey was a social critic, participating in cultural debate throughout a long life (West 1989, 71). His friend and colleague George Herbert Mead extended Dewey's social philosophy more directly into an interpretive model of self-development and meaningful experience.

George Herbert Mead

George Herbert Mead is likely the most enigmatic intellectual figure in American sociology at the turn of the twentieth century. In spite of the fact he published no book-length elaborations of his work, Mead's influence on

CHAPTER THREE

the development of interactionism is profound. Compared to that of his contemporaries William James and John Dewey, then, Mead's thought is presented in fragmented, overlapping pieces.[7] This work exists in two forms: 1) numerous journal articles published during his lifetime and 2) four books published posthumously, edited from transcriptions of student lecture notes. Mead's books include *The Philosophy of the Present* (1932/80), *Mind, Self, and Society from the Standpoint of a Social Behaviorist* (1934), *Movements of Thought in the Nineteenth Century* (1936), and *The Philosophy of the Act* (1938).[8] Of these, only *Mind, Self, and Society* is seriously studied, even by interactionists themselves. My discussion will draw from all four of the books as well as from other sources.[9]

Four important points organize Mead's thought as a pragmatist and early interactionist. First, the influence of Darwinian evolution is evident throughout. For Mead, the roots of pragmatism are to be found in the interrelationship of behaviorist psychology and the scientific method. Mind is constantly evolving, realized in instrumental creative action, the organism coping with its environment (Mead 1936, 345; Reck 1964, xvi). At the same time, science represents "the evolutionary process grown self-conscious" (Mead 1936, 364), organized for problem-solving activity.

Second, human use of complex language systems is a precondition for the appearance of cultural (i.e., symbolic) normative standards and therefore self-development (Mead 1934, 78–79). Language, then, is the mechanism for the social constitution of the individual: the ability to view our own actions, thoughts, and feelings as objects. This reflexive, object-taking character of the self leads to a third important organizing principle in Mead's thought: the primacy of social consciousness over individual experience. As Mead states in his pathbreaking article, "What Social Objects Must Psychology Presuppose?":

> Objective consciousness of selves must precede subjective consciousness, and must continually condition it, if consciousness of meaning itself presupposes the selves as there. Subjective self-consciousness must appear *within* experience, must have a function in the development of that experience, and must be studied from the point of view of that function, not as that in which self-consciousness arises and by which through analogical bridges and self-projections we slowly construct a hypothetically objective social world in which to live. [*italics* in the original] (Mead 1910/64, 112)

Reynolds observes, "Mead insists on deriving both mind and self from society rather than the other way around. Social experience, behavior in association with others, is a precondition for the emergence of both selves and minds" (Reynolds 1987, 52). The logical order of emergence, then, is apparently society, self, and mind.

If mind is grounded in creative social action, language (through role-taking and symbolization) provides the social basis for both mind and self, and social consciousness precedes individual experience; the act serves as the reflexive translator of social consciousness and individual experience. In reference to the manipulation stage of the act, Mead discusses the relationship between the two:

> The process of identifying the object and correcting our attitudes in the presence of unsuccessful conduct through the use of significant symbols (social in origin) in inner conversation is itself only a form of conduct, and as conduct is as immediate as any other type. In its reference to the object which is being analyzed and reconstructed it is mediate, and in its imagery of past and future conduct it sets up a field of experience which is in sharp contrast with that of the surrounding world of perceptual objects. (Mead 1938, 17)

In this sense social action *is* the path to self-consciousness. The instrumental method of pragmatism thus serves both individual and social ends. Comparing pragmatism to other philosophical conceptualizations of action, Joas writes:

> Even before he had unequivocally assigned himself to the school of pragmatism, the problem of the relationship between action and consciousness was a central concern for Mead; the interpretation of consciousness as a phase of action that is functional for the successful continuation of the action made it possible for him to link his ideas to Darwin's insights and also to entertain the hope of transcending the Cartesian dualisms. It was not the relationship between the utility-oriented or moral individual action and social order, but rather the relation between action and consciousness, that moved Mead's thought forward. (Joas 1993, 248)

From a contemporary interactionist standpoint, the importance of the relationship between meaningful action and consciousness is summarized in

CHAPTER THREE

Mead's views on self-development. The major conceptualizations here are the stages of that development and the processual nature of the self. According to Mead (1934, 152–60) the self develops in two primary stages, each related to the role-taking ability of the individual and the associated importance of language as well as the social context of experience. The central character of Mead's reflexive self is the ability to view one's own actions as objects. For purposes of illustration, then, his discussion focuses particularly on the activities of younger children.

In the *play* stage the child is capable of assuming one role at a time. Thus the child "plays" at being mother, father, sibling, and so on. In such imaginative construction, the individual roles of significant others may be amplified and expanded over time as the child assumes each. In the *game* stage the actor is able to assume several roles simultaneously. This construction is considerably more complex than that associated with the play stage. The viewpoints and activities of numerous other social selves must be accounted for, and the actor's own meaningful behavior emerges from this multiple role-taking. The social primacy of role-taking and its link with language is summarized in the familiar concept of the "generalized other." In Mead's own words:

> It is in the form of the generalized other that the social process influences the behavior of the individuals involved in it and carrying it on, i.e., that the community exercises control over the conduct of its individual members; for it is in this form that the social process or community enters as a determining factor into the individual's thinking. In abstract thought the individual takes the attitude of the generalized other toward himself, without reference to its expression in any particular other individuals; and in concrete thought he takes that attitude in so far as it is expressed in the attitudes toward his behavior of those individuals with whom he is involved in the given social situation or act. But only by taking the attitude of the generalized other toward himself, in one or another of these ways, can he think at all; for only thus can thinking—or the internalized conversation of gestures which constitutes thinking—occur. And only through the taking by individuals of the attitude or attitudes of the generalized other toward themselves is the existence of a universe of discourse, as that system of common or social meanings which thinking presupposes at its context, rendered possible. (Mead 1934, 155–56)

The creation of self-consciousness through the internalization of the generalized other in the game stage is possible only through language. Mind (and thereby meaningful action) is socially grounded in the cultural context of society. In discussing both the play and game stages Mead emphasizes the part played by rules or normative definitions in self-development. Mind is expressed through conduct even as the self emerges as process through that same conduct.

The self-as-process evolves from the interplay of the "I" and the "me" (Mead 1934, 173–78; Perinbanayagam 1985, 88–93). In a sense these interdependent perspectives are different aspects of self. The "I" is the creative, spontaneous perspective which is always present in the "me" of the following moment. The "me" provides social context and is constituted through the role-taking discussed previously. While we may subjectively identify the self as the "I," its presence is known only objectively and historically through the role-taking of the "me."

In *The Philosophy of the Present* Mead further elaborates the relativity of perspectives in the processual nature of the self. Emergence is defined as "the presence of things in two or more different systems, in such a fashion that its presence in a later system changes its character in the earlier system or systems to which it belongs" (Mead 1932/80, 69). This simultaneous and interdependent quality situates consciousness in a present, part of the social development of mind and self. While the self-as-process is grounded in the emergent character of role-taking, in the fluidity of the "I" and "me," behavior always exhibits some degree of indeterminance.

Past and future are significant only in relationship to a present. We can make reference to historical pasts through conceptions which are thereby only represented in a present. The same relativity holds for future events. New experience ensures that the future will never be fully known. The past is not irrevocable, and the future represents pragmatic possibility (Miller 1973/80, 175).[10]

As stated earlier, the act links social consciousness and individual experience and thereby is important to an understanding of the temporal relativity of self. The act is in the present, "but a present that a discursive mind constitutes, a constitution in which the signifying traces and residues of past acts, just as the anticipation of a future, play a part" (Perinbanayagam 2000, 8). The principle of sociality refers to the adjustment of temporal perspectives, culminating in the present and in social action.

CHAPTER THREE

For Mead, then, sociality is both the principle and the form of emergence (Mead 1932/80, 85; Miller 1973/80, 190). Sociality and emergence are the mechanisms for role-taking and the constant interplay between the "I" and "me," relating mind to the reflexive social self. As David L. Miller observes:

> It is because of the social component of the mind of an individual that he can be aware or conscious of that past out of which a present problem has arisen, and, in the solution of that problem, or during the process of adjustment that takes place by reflective intelligence, the individual must occupy two systems at once—the old system, the world that was there and taken for granted, the generalized other or the Me, and that new order constructed by virtue of the activity of the creative I, an order which will lead to adjustment and enable the individual to continue in a new system, a system (or order) to which the old must make an adjustment inasmuch as the Me and the generalized other are changed in the new order. (Miller 1973/80, 203–04)

In such a manner mind and self are historically situated, and thought as well as action evolves from them.

According to Hans Joas (1985, 64), Mead's related concerns of self-development and the self-as-process are linked in an earlier, little-known article entitled "The Definition of the Psychical." Originally published in a 1903 University of Chicago commemorative volume, the work has never been fully reprinted. An excerpt is found in Andrew J. Reck's edited anthology of Mead's writings (Mead 1903/64). Reck summarizes the importance of this article for Mead's later concerns with self-development and self-as-process:

> The psychical is itself a particular phase in the evolutionary development of reality. Mind or consciousness comes into existence when an intelligent organism has its ongoing activity interrupted by a problem. It is a special kind of instrument for the intelligent organism to deal with its problem and find the appropriate solution in order to resume its ongoing activity. (Reck 1964, xviii)

Mind, then, becomes integral to an understanding of meaningful human conduct even as it is woven into Mead's later analyses of self and society.

In his treatment of the psychical, Mead extends Dewey's concept of the reflex arc and attempts to solve three problems (Joas 1985, 78): the dualistic nature of self and experience (subjective versus objective consciousness), formulation of a social conception of the individual, and determination of the cognitive value of individual knowledge. These three concerns represent the primary linkage between Dewey and Mead. Dewey's efforts resulted in the evolution of pragmatic philosophy, functional psychology, and social criticism, while Mead pressed the former toward a preliminary interactionist social psychology. For each, the application of knowledge by creative actors culminates in socially meaningful behavior and consciousness. Rock summarizes the pragmatic self-narrative: "Selves are built up and known in the pursuit of projects. They are objects amongst the other objects of a situation and as objects, they may be either the ends or the means of action" (Rock 1979, 46). The self is a dynamic process of communication, "a recursive sign or system of signs, constituted by the mind, a process with ups and downs, bumps and grinds, with starts and false strarts and retreats" (Perinbanayagam 2000, 45).

Following the lead of Mead, Herbert Blumer founded the contemporary school of Chicago interactionism. His work stresses the generation of social meaning through symbolic interaction and further extends the interpretive stance of the pragmatists. Like his precursors, Blumer would grapple with the role of science in an interpretive framework.

Herbert Blumer and Symbolic Interactionism

More than any other scholar, Herbert Blumer is seen as the direct intellectual descendant and proponent of the thought of George Herbert Mead.[11] In pursuing a doctorate at the University of Chicago, Blumer came into close contact with Mead and a number of other early Chicago sociologists, including Robert Ezra Park and Ellsworth Faris. As a faculty member first at Chicago and later at the University of California at Berkeley, he coined the term "symbolic interactionism" and is generally accepted as the contemporary founder of the perspective (Reynolds 1987, 76).

The intellectual development of symbolic interactionism owes more to Blumer as teacher of generations of interactionists than as a highly published interactionist. As interpreter of Mead he set the interactionist foundation for the widely identified Chicago School,[12] from which numerous

CHAPTER THREE

competing and complementing versions have since evolved. I follow the Chicago School of interactionism for two reasons: 1) its thoroughgoing interpretive stance, focusing on social meaning and action as constructed by creative actors and 2) Blumer's at-the-time unfashionable critique of quantitative scientific methodology in the social sciences. He thus advocates a naturalistic approach to the empirical world, not one focused singularly on cause and effect, but meaning-generation. Like earlier pragmatists, his critique of science did not question the basic validity and utility of empirical knowledge, but the nature of the social world.

My discussion of Blumer's work is organized along two lines. First, I examine the three basic principles of symbolic interactionism and the corresponding "root images" that give rise to them (Blumer 1969, 6). Taken collectively, these interrelated ideas stress the importance of meaning-construction in human social activity. Self-as-experience and the larger terrain of sociocultural meaning are linked. For Blumer and Mead, all actors possess a processual rather than structured self, one defined through meaningful action. Second, I outline Blumer's methodological stance for symbolic interactionism, at once critical of strictly quantitative procedures and lacking a broad-based critique of empirical science as a way of knowing. For Blumer and the pragmatists, science was a useful procedure and not a potential process of ideological control.

The Premises and "Root Images" of Blumer's Interactionism

According to Herbert Blumer (1969, 2) symbolic interactionism as a unique perspective on human social life is predicated on three basic premises. The first of these states that human beings act toward things in a meaningful way. That is, objects with which a person comes into contact are endowed with some symbolic significance. Objects may be physical things (e.g., desks, automobiles), living beings (e.g., people, animals), or abstract principles (e.g., mathematical equations, social norms). Additionally, they may be combined in a variety of ways. Thus, the broad idea of progress may in some manner interrelate human nature with technological development, the physical environment, and social institutions; or an everyday social encounter may connect leaders with subordinates, friends with enemies.

Blumer's second premise is that the meaning of objects is created from social interaction between people, individually and collectively. In this sense social interaction (i.e., communication in its myriad forms) continually generates meaning in time and space (Dotter 1980b; Ericksen 1980). In fact, the latter two concepts are themselves symbolic constructs that both arise from and govern conduct. Social meaning, then, may be simple or complex, fleeting or laden with significance. Regardless of the particular form of communication (e.g., spoken, written, visual, or aural), meaning *always* arises from and is contextualized by social interaction.

The third premise establishes the importance of interpretation as a mediating process. Actors negotiate meaning in particular interactive settings, including face-to-face-encounters, mass media accounts, and even individual imaginary conversations. Simultaneously, interpretation ensures that meaning is at once enduring and fluid. As a social product it is constantly emerging and inherently problematic, even as the interaction setting renders it lasting.

Taken together, these three premises situate meaning in the social experience of the individual and suggest what I term the "layered" quality of that meaning. The generation of meaning is interactive, subject to individual as well as collective scrutiny. Its creation is generally continuous as opposed to discrete. Finally, the layered quality of meaning-generation is fundamentally nonlinear, such that its existence does not follow a neat, predictable causal pattern. Rather, meaning is fashioned from an almost infinite variety of cultural objects in a like number of social settings.

According to Blumer (1969, 6–20), the three premises of symbolic interactionism are grounded in several "root images"—a collective framework for human social life and conduct: 1) the nature of human society and group life, 2) the quality of social interaction, 3) the importance of objects, 4) the centrality of the human being as a social actor, 5) the basis of human action, and 6) the interlinking of action. These six images are the key for understanding how meaning is created and maintained in society.

Human action, rooted in individual conduct, is the starting point for life endowed with meaning. As Blumer relates, "[H]uman groups or society *exists in action* and must be seen in terms of action" [*italics* in the original] (Blumer 1969, 46). Such action is framed in a social context, to be sure. Yet it is the meaningful behavior of individuals that, more than anything else, characterizes both cultural content (e.g., norms, values, and beliefs) and conceptions of social structure (e.g., social position, status, role, and authority). Thus, human action in its multitude of forms gives rise to the larger constituencies of culture and society.

Human action is consequently organized into group patterns: "the activities of the members occur predominately in response to one another or in relation to one another" (Blumer 1969, 7). In other words, social interaction is not some empty, taken-for-granted medium, but is important for its own sake. Culture and social structure are dependent on interaction for existence and elaboration—not the converse. Actors perform and negotiate through communication rather than as a result of preexisting structural factors (e.g., social status). Such a view certainly stresses the situational quality of interaction—fluid and changeable, though not wholly unpredictable.

The social milieu—culture and structure flowing from social interaction—is composed of objects (Blumer 1969, 10–11). These objects, created through symbolic interaction, may be physical, social, or abstract. Following Mead, the Blumerian object is anything that can be indicated or referred to. Examples include automobiles, motion pictures or other media, political philosophies, or concrete individuals with imputed motives or positions. The connecting thread for all objects—material and nonmaterial—is that they are rendered meaningful through social interaction.

In Blumer's symbolic interactionism, the human actor is not outside the interaction process or manipulated by it. Rather, the human organism is constituted through symbolic interaction, making meaningful indications to others and interpreting same. In short, the actor possesses a "self." Placed in a vocabulary of action, the person "can be an object of his own action" (Blumer 1969, 12). Certainly, the actor's objectification of conduct through self-indication is not always planned, rational, or explainable in advance. The situational nature of self-indication or objectification is the emergent quality of meaningful social interaction:

> Like other objects, the self-object emerges from the process of social interaction in which other people are defining a person to himself. Mead has traced the way in which this occurs to his process of role-taking. He points out that in order to become an object to himself a person has to see himself from the outside. (Blumer 1969, 12–13)

Through social interaction we initially take the viewpoint (i.e., role) of others toward our own conduct. This role-taking with respect to our own conduct characterizes all symbolic interaction.

At the same time, the human actor is capable of what might be termed "symbolic intra-action" or interaction with himself. As Blumer explains:

> This interaction is not in the form of interaction between two or more parts of a psychological system, as between needs, or between emotions, or between ideas, or between the id and the ego in the Freudian scheme. Instead, the interaction is social—a form of communication, with the person addressing himself as a person and responding thereto. (Blumer 1969, 13)

The human actor, constantly creating a self, is defined by this layered quality of social communication. With symbolic intra-action, the actor becomes a role maker in contradistinction to traditional portraits of a role player (Dotter 1980a). The physiological capacity for memory obviates the need for daily (or even more frequent) self-re-creation. Still, although memory may have a physiological basis, its importance for self-creation is as a symbolic, necessarily transmuting, narrative. The behavior of the creative self-actor is fundamentally interpretive, not dependent on a reified system of causal explanation, psychological or sociocultural. Rather, these latter two contexts are constituted *through* biographical, lived self-as-experience.

Finally, Blumer's conception of "joint action" captures the layered quality of social life as something more than additive self-experiences. "The joint action has a distinctive character in its own right, a character that lies in the articulation or linkage as apart from what may be articulated or linked" (Blumer 1969, 17). Symbolic interaction and self-as-process are a never-completed, always emerging narrative of communication.

Similarly, social structures and cultural knowledge do not exist independent of biographical self-experience. Such experience, when socially organized and culturally explained, is characterized as joint action—articulated and interlinked to the self-as-creative-actor. This interpretive stance has led to a methodological critique of social science causal models. Within traditional interactionism, much debate has centered on a science based on naturalistic inquiry.

CHAPTER THREE

Symbolic Interactionism as Methodological Critique

Over twenty years ago symbolic interactionism was aptly described as the "loyal opposition" to social science causal models (Mullins 1973; Fine 1993, 62). Working backward from Blumer, the interpretive thrust is apparent: A creative self-actor (through the communication medium of language) is defined by fundamentally meaningful individual and articulated joint actions. As associated with Mead, the reflexive character of the self and the relativity of perspectives suggest a processual, layered character to social life (Park 1952; Rock 1979), not an *a priori* structural one. Likewise, the instrumentalism of Dewey represents a modernist take on the mind/spirit duality. In fact, science itself can be subjected to standards of practicality. Finally, William James's emphasis on the primacy of individual choice and experience effectively links action and interpretation.

Taken collectively, these views do not so much reject the traditional scientific method (i.e., prediction, experimentation, and control) as they seek to refine or recast it. James, Dewey, and Mead transformed stimulus-response behaviorism into a more complex pragmatic psychology. Science—as an expression of individual experience and reflection—may be used to solve the modernist crisis of alienation brought on by industrialization, urbanization, and attendant social disorganization.

By the 1960s Blumer's (1969) symbolic interactionism constitutes a full-blown critique of the domination of statistical quantification within the discipline of sociology (Colomy and Brown 1995, 23–24; Fine 1995a, 8–9). On this dramatic intellectual stage, an interpretive symbolic interactionism was meant as the corrective to rampant generalizing associated with functionalist systems theory. While Blumer's critique of scientific orthodoxy exposes the quantification bias which continues to grip the discipline, his pragmatic reading of meaning flowing from social action argues for a reconstituted scientific vision (i.e., explanation without prediction and control). This instrumental stance seeks "a method that would separate the observer from the observed, so that valid, scientific observations could be made" (Denzin 1992, 7). Blumer (1969) no doubt rejects quantification and variable analysis in favor of exploration, "sensitizing concepts," and participant observation. At the same time, he argues for a methodology that yields verifiable knowledge and "meets the fundamental requirements of empirical science" (Blumer 1969, 21). His interpretive perspective is firmly grounded in a pragmatic modernist take, in which science is never adequately critiqued.

An example of this instrumental approach to science and its use in the empirical understanding of social life is Blumer's (1939/69) methodological reservations regarding Thomas and Znaniecki's (1984) *The Polish Peasant in Europe and America*. He contends that their analysis of "human documents" (i.e., life records) is inadequate to the task of representing the social reality they interpret. In his view:

> The authors have shown surprising liberality in making generalizations—generalizations which seem to be very good, but for which there are few if any data in the materials. Omitting this overload of generalization, the important question is whether the materials adequately test the generalizations (regardless of their source) which are being applied to the materials. As our previous discussion has pointed out, the answer is very inconclusive. Some interpretations, indeed, are borne out by the content of the documents, and sometimes the interpretations do not seem to be verified adequately; in both instances, of course, the materials are a test. Usually, however, one cannot say that the interpretation is either true or not true, even though it is distinctly plausible. (Blumer 1939/69, 121)

Blumer's task is to faithfully describe the empirical makeup of the sociocultural world (i.e., the process of meaningful human action and self-creation). His symbolic interactionism, while staunchly interpretive, must constantly struggle with the methodological implications of his "root images." The dilemma centers on creative actors (interpreters) and their attempts to accomplish science. Blumer goes on to reason:

> The inadequacy of human documents in testing interpretation is a primary reason why they are rejected by many as materials for scientific study. When one adds to this the fact that usually the separate document cannot very well stand evaluation according to the criteria of representativeness, adequacy, and reliability, it is easy to see why human documents become suspect as a scientific instrument. Yet to renounce their use in the scientific investigation of human life would be to commit a fatal blunder, for theoretically, they are indispensable and actually they may be of enormous value. The effective use which has been made of them by Thomas and Znaniecki is ample demonstration of this value. (Blumer 1939/69, 125)

It seems Blumer is rather unconvincingly arguing for the use of an interpretive perspective to "test" for and validate scientific generalizations.

CHAPTER THREE

Denzin describes a similar methodological debate (some fifty years later) among interactionists, with Blumer at its center. Denzin concludes, rather ironically, "Blumer is truly a man for all seasons and all people." This "Blumer circle" is "[l]ike two squirrels chasing each other around a tree, it is impossible to see who is chasing whom" (1992, 55–56). In short, his interpretive vision remains clouded by attempts to render it scientific. As Blumer has pointed out, the problem is founded in the fetish for quantification and the search for general social laws. Its solution lies in a thoroughgoing discursive critique of science that neither early pragmatists nor Mead and Blumer accomplished.

Pragmatism and Neopragmatism: From Modern to Postmodern

Meaning and Experience

Recent decades have witnessed a re-examination of pragmatism across the interdisciplinary field of cultural studies, especially in the latter's narrative turn (West 1989; Denzin 1992, 2003b; Manning 2003). This neopragmatism is rooted in a critical postmodern reading of American society and culture since World War II and extends even earlier to at least the 1920s (Douglas 1995). Cornel West's reinterpretation (1989) attempts to infuse the tradition with elements of political radicalism and thus examines a wider range of thinkers in its narrative, including W. E. B. Du Bois, Reinhold Niebuhr, Lionel Trilling, Roberto Unger, and Michel Foucault, among others. In his view:

> [pragmatism's] evasion of epistomology-centered philosophy—from Emerson to Rorty—results in a conception of philosophy as a form of cultural criticism in which the meaning of America is put forward by intellectuals in response to distinct social and cultural crises. In this sense American pragmatism is less a philosophical tradition putting forward solutions to perennial problems in the Western philosophical conversation initiated by Plato and more a continuous cultural commentary or set of interpretations that attempt to explain America to itself at a particular historical moment. (West 1989, 5)

The crisis metaphor that West identifies is likewise found in a postmodern "prophetic pragmatism"—which "calls for reinvigoration of a sane, sober, and sophisticated intellectual life in America and for regeneration of social forces empowering the disadvantaged, degraded, and dejected" (West 1989, 239). West recognizes that the language of opposition, and certainly that of stigmatization, has changed since the 1960s. Modernist conflicts over categories of social class, gender, race, and age in the mediated postmodern moment are interwoven and variously framed as narrative questions of cultural politics (Jordan and Weedon 1995; Bauman 1995; Bourdieu 1995) and as voices of subverted identities (Hebdige 1979/2002; Goldberg 1993, 1997; Butler 1990/99, 1993; Haraway 1995) and of the marginalized other (Jervis 1999). In short, early pragmatism and the natural and social sciences indeed were of a cloth in confronting the problems of modernity, which are even now contextualized in the postmodern moment. According to Lemert, "Forgotten in all the postmodern anxiety is the fact that postmodernism is merely the currently fashionable name for a complicated series of cultural and theoretical inventions, each of which were adjustments to the realities of the world in the second half of the twentieth century" (Lemert 1997, 17).

As I have outlined their emergence, pragmatism and Chicago School interactionism were the peculiarly American attempts to recast traditional problems of philosophy and meaning as modernism unfolded. Dickstein frames this context: "Pragmatism, like modernism, reflects the breakup of cultural and religious authority, the turn away from any simple or stable definition of truth, the shift from totalizing systems and unified narratives to a more fragmented plurality of perspectives" (Dickstein 1998a, 4).

Pragmatists were centrally concerned with the problems of modern experience and a philosophical conception of science that aided in explaining the natural world—including society and culture—without embedding it in unchallenged abstractions. In the hands of its founders pragmatism was cautiously optimistic, sometimes even exhilarating. Truth and certainty were cast as problems of modern experience, but the search for knowledge continued (Diggins 1994, 217–50; Hildebrand 2003). In the most general of ways, the rebirth of neopragmatism in the unfolding of the postmodern is not surprising and may be seen as an extension of pragmatism's antiformalism. Menand implies the link: "To the extent that philosophy is an effort to erect what we know about how we know into a formal system, pragmatism cannot help acting the role of termite—undermining foundations, collapsing distinctions, deflating abstractions,

CHAPTER THREE

suggesting that the real work of the world is being done somewhere other than in philosophy departments" (Menand 1997, xxxi). The overlap between early pragmatism and later versions is by no means straightforward (Hildebrand 2003), nor is postmodernism a simple historical extension of modernism. The context is found in neopragmatism's linguistic turn in contemporary mediated sociocultural processes.

Rorty in the Linguistic Turn

Neopragmatism's linguistic turn is an attempt to articulate European, especially French, narratives of meaning crisis in an American frame. The turn is also diffused across disciplines, including sociology, literature, history, and philosophy, among others. It represents a rethinking of social theory "by emphasizing the role of language, or discourse, in social life" (Lemert 1997, 66). Arguably the most influential neopragmatist of the linguistic turn is Richard Rorty (1967, 1979, 1982, 1989). He contends that descriptions of the world are not independent of the language used to convey them:

> Truth cannot be out there—cannot exist independently of the human mind—because sentences cannot so exist, or be out there. The world is out there, but descriptions of the world are not. Only descriptions of the world can be true or false. The world on its own—unaided by the describing activities of human beings—cannot. (Rorty 1989, 5)

Rorty (1999, 35) draws two major distinctions between the classical pragmatists and neopragmatists. The former focus on the problematic of experience and the usefulness of the modernist scientific method in verifying truth. The latter shift the critique to the textuality of language and abandon the primacy of science in the postmodern search for knowledge. In this process, justification and truth are relational: "There is nothing to be said on the latter subject not because truth is atemporal and justification temporal, but because *the **only** point in contrasting the true with the merely justified is to contrast a possible future with the actual present*" [italics and **bold** in the original] (1999, 38–39).

The textuality of the linguistic turn opens the possibility of dialogue between American neopragmatism and the European theories of the postmodern (Diggins 1994, 13), especially Derrida's poststructuralism.

This dialogue is critical and derives in no small part to differences in sociohistorical as well as cultural contexts. Rorty offers his neopragmatist take on what he considers to be a misreading of Derrida: "Despite his prediction that 'the Book' will be replaced by 'the text,' Derrida intensely admires the great authors who stand behind the texts he glosses; he has no doubts about his or their authorship. Although he of course has doubts about metaphysical accounts of the nature of the self and of writing, he has no interest in dissolving the books in which great human imaginations have been most fully themselves into anonymous, rootless, free-floating 'discourses'" (Rorty 1996, 13–14). In the linguistic turn of postmodern media culture, meaning is fluid, with no one method or type of knowledge privileged over others. A "post-philosophical culture" (Rorty 1982) emerges, marked by increasingly-difficult-to-sustain academic boundaries. The meaning crisis within the linguistic turn becomes a search for alternate methods of description:

> This process of coming to see other human beings as "one of us" rather than as "them" is a matter of detailed description of what unfamiliar people are like and of redescription of what we ourselves are like. This is a task not for theory but for genres such as ethnography, the journalist's report, the comic book, the docudrama, and, especially, the novel. (Rorty 1989, xvi)

The novel, as well as film and recorded music, are vital texts for the description of everyday life. They provide the opportunity to engage in philosophical contemplation, to become "readers of our own experience" (Bromwich 1998, 375).

The pragmatic tradition, literature, mass audio, and cinematic arts are situated in the linguistic turn: the narrative emergence of the postmodern within the problematics of modernity, especially the transformation of self in mediated culture. As Malcolm Bradbury observes, "[T]he novel proceeds through generational aesthetic change to conduct an ever-shifting inquiry, internal and external, into the way life is and the way it can best be perceived and expressed. Sometimes it is reportorial, sometimes psychological; sometimes it is dominantly realistic, sometimes predominantly experimental or surreal" (Bradbury 1983/94, x). The intertextuality of mediated narratives overlays written texts with audio and cinematic ones. Literature is representational, narrative telling and retelling that focuses as much on form as content. As recorded texts, music and film go beyond mere representation in constructing mediated images by offering a more immediate form of communication (Monaco 2000, 26).

Contemporary pragmatism in the linguistic turn is a genealogical philosophy (Stuhr 2003, 185–86): modern in its logic of experience and the scientific method, postmodern in contextualizing the pluralism of meaning and self-identity. The former freed pragmatists to think pragmatically about the practice of philosophy, and the latter opens the possibility of dynamic multivocal discourses. Furthermore, philosophy and literature are overlaid and also played against one another in a coupling, and "any thought of expelling philosophy from the practices of writing in the name of literary 'free play' or 'textuality' is doomed: philosophy will always come in by the back door—indeed, it will never have left the house" (Attridge 1992, 13). Mediated cultural politics is constructed as competing gender, race, age, and class identities in the postmodern scenario. As Judith Butler observes:

> Though there are clearly good historical reasons for keeping "race" and "sexuality" and "sexual difference" as separate analytic spheres, there are also quite pressing and significant historical reasons for asking how and where we might read not only their convergence, but the sites at which the one cannot be constituted save through the other. This is something other than juxtaposing distinct spheres of power, subordination, agency, historicity, and something other than a list of attributes separated by those proverbial commas (gender, sexuality, race, class), that usually mean that we have not yet figured out how to think the relations we seek to mark. (Butler 1993, 168)

Deviance does not disappear into relativism, but is "transgression understood differently, understood problematically" (Stuhr 2003, 148). As Foucault observes, "[T]ransgression forces the limit to face the fact of its imminent disappearance, to find itself in what it excludes" (Foucault 1977, 34).

In its pragmatic context Chicago interactionism created the interpretive groundwork for a naturalistic inquiry into the nature of social deviance as meaning-creation. The labeling approach, its direct offshoot, gave rise to several related perspectives less encumbered by a pragmatic past. Still, the deviant label emerges in a complex interpretive process of meaning-generation. Similarly, the self is layered in that same process. These twin concerns of meaning and its relation to narrative self are the purview of contemporary cultural studies, especially its linguistic turn. In articulating perspectives on deviance (chapter 4) with a cultural studies reading (chapter 5), I argue that contemporary interactionism, far from being theoretically exhausted, is a continually fruitful enterprise.

Notes

1. Larry T. Reynolds (1987) divides contemporary interactionism into four major varieties: the Chicago School, the Iowa School, the dramaturgical genre, and ethnomethodology. Likewise, Norman K. Denzin (1992, 1–21) offers a brief social history of the development and institutionalization of symbolic interactionism as a sociological perspective with numerous schools. Several monographs deal with the development and influence of the Chicago School generally, including its interactionist tradition (Faris 1970; Matthews 1977; Kurtz 1984; Bulmer 1984). A volume edited by Gary Alan Fine (1995b) assesses the continued significance of Chicago interactionism for contemporary American sociology. The book argues for the existence of "a second Chicago School" during the postwar years 1946–1960. This generation includes Howard S. Becker, Erving Goffman, Joseph Gusfield, and Gregory Stone, among others. Primary mentors and teachers of the group were Herbert Blumer, Everett C. Hughes, Robert Redfield, Anselm Strauss, David Riesman, Ernest Burgess, and Louis Wirth (Fine 1995a). David Maines (2001) offers an articulation of Mead, Blumer, and Park in arguing the importance of interactionism for general sociology.

2. Blumer's own research topics were varied. Consistent with his interest in social psychology and collective behavior, he articulated the work of Mead and Park in the analysis of fashion, film, race prejudice, and other topics (Lyman and Vidich 1988; Denzin 1992, 5). In the preface to *Symbolic Interactionism: Perspective and Method*, Blumer (1969, vii–viii) relates his long-standing concern for symbolic interactionism and its relationship to methodological problems (dating from his doctoral dissertation, "Method in Social Psychology"). Interestingly, Tamotsu Shibutani and Howard Becker are the two former students singled out as instrumental in his decision to publish the 1969 volume.

3. Considered part of the interactionist heritage but conspicuously lacking significant pragmatist influence (Joas 1993, 40) is the work of Erving Goffman (1959, 1961, 1963a, 1963b, 1967, 1971, 1974, 1979, 1981). In comparison to Blumer's (1969) concept of joint action, Goffman's dramaturgical theater-oriented model is highly metaphorical (Ericksen 1980; Dotter 1980b; Perinbanayagam

CHAPTER THREE

1985, 64–70), focusing more narrowly on favorable presentation of self in face-to-face encounters (Blumer 1972). Philip Manning (1992) offers a brief but comprehensive treatment of the importance of Goffman's ideas for modern sociology. Paul Rock (1979) sees the conflicting roots of symbolic interactionism in American pragmatism and the formalism of Georg Simmel. He traces the latter's influence on Goffman: In large part Goffman's work "may be read as an effort to reveal the basic logic of sociation, a logic which can be discovered in a variety of superficially diverse settings" (Rock 1979, 50). In chapter 4 I introduce Goffman's concept of stigma and its importance in the labeling process.

4. Diggins points out that in *The Meaning of Truth* (James 1909/87), "a newer James emerges, an older philosopher who, responding to pragmatism's critics, now leans more toward realism than constructivism, more toward knowledge as agreement and conforming rather than creation and transforming, more toward an object of belief with reference to the real than the activity of will that works upon the real and shapes it" (Diggins 1994, 135).

5. Darnell Rucker (1969) and Charles Morris (1970, 174–91) offer accounts of the Chicago pragmatists.

6. Diggins summarizes the manner in which, as pragmatism developed, Dewey's concept of relational truth differed even from that of James: "Dewey was more interested in establishing a valid criterion for knowing on the basis of doing rather than in developing a stance for believing on the basis of feeling. To Dewey, James's position seemed to rely on an emotional inwardness that had little reference to either public awareness or the uses of cool, reflective intelligence" (Diggins 1994, 140).

7. Norman K. Denzin (1992, 2) dates the "birth" of symbolic interactionism with the appearance of John Dewey's (1896/1981) article on the reflex arc in psychology, William James's (1890/1950) *Principles of Psychology*, Charles Horton Cooley's (1902/83) *Human Nature and the Social Order*, and George Herbert Mead's (1910/64) "What Social Objects Must Psychology Presuppose?" Cooley's (1909/62) *Social Organization: A Study of the Larger Mind* might be added to this list.

8. Two useful anthologies of published works are those edited by Anselm Strauss and Andrew J. Reck (Mead 1964a, 1964b). Additionally, one volume of previously unpublished works has been edited by David L. Miller (Mead 1982).

9. David L. Miller (1973/80) and Hans Joas (1985) offer extended treatments of Mead's work.

10. According to Miller, Mead conceptualized two kinds of presents. In the specious present there are no doubts, uncertainties, or inhibitions. The second present "has been added to because of inhibitions in action" (Miller 1973/80, 38-39). Pasts and futures are constructed, evolving backward and forward from a present.

11. J. David Lewis and Richard L. Smith (1980) offer an analysis of the principal strands of pragmatism and their relationship to the general development of Chicago sociology. Of particular import is their linking of the thought of Mead and Peirce. Denzin (1984), in turn, provides a critique of their position. He suggests they explicate how a Peirce semiotic might fit with Mead's articulation of language and symbols.

12. Stanford M. Lyman and Arthur J. Vidich (1988) present an interpretation of Blumer's work as a sociological rendering of a public philosophy.

CHAPTER FOUR
THE CREATION OF DEVIANCE: SOCIAL DEFINITION AND THE PROCESS OF INTERACTION

The labeling approach to the study of social deviance and crime has been formulated, debated, and refined for some four decades. Gaining its greatest currency in the 1960s and 1970s with the works of Howard S. Becker (1963/73, 1964, 1967) and Edwin Schur (1969a, 1969b, 1971), the perspective has been subjected to much scrutiny and critique. Its intellectual persistence (if not popularity) is evidenced by the appearance of the eighth edition of the edited text *Deviance: The Interactionist Perspective* (Rubington and Weinberg 2002).

The approach has generated research on countless topics, much of it related to esoteric "deviant worlds" outside the mainstream of intellectual discourse—at least according to both conservative and radical critics. Alexander Liazos (1972), of the latter group, had labeling squarely in his sights when lamenting "the poverty of the sociology of deviance." Labelists have conducted naturalistic studies on marijuana use (Becker 1953), mental illness (Scheff 1964, 1966; Goffman 1961), "tearoom" sexual practices (Humphreys 1970/75), nude beaches (Douglas and Rasmussen 1977), and suicide notes (Jacobs 1967). More recent research has continued this trend, dealing with the subculture of horse players (Rosecrance 1986), stigmatization of "fat admirers," men who are sexually attracted to obese women (Goode and Preissler 1983) and of obesity generally (Goode 1996b), as well as the existence of subcultures of chronic ex-mental patients (Herman 2002).

Throughout its history interactionism has developed parallel traditions dealing with the historical and political effects of labeling in a variety of

CHAPTER FOUR

settings. Included here are two landmark studies by Kai T. Erikson. *Wayward Puritans* (1966) examines the labeling process and its links to definitions of conformity in the witch trials of colonial Salem, Massachusetts; *Everything in Its Path* (1976), an ethnographic portrait of the flood disaster aftermath (during the winter of 1972) in Buffalo Creek, West Virginia, details the manner in which governmental policy fractured entire communities and contributed further to the trauma of victims. Similarly, there are interactionist-informed studies of the significance of moral entrepreneurship for the American Temperance Movement (Gusfield 1963/86) and the social construction of risk in its contemporary incarnation (Wagner 1997); the labeling dynamics of gender deviance (Schur 1984); the post–World War II moral panic regarding the emergence of juvenile delinquency as a social problem (Cohen 1972/93; Gilbert 1986; Dotter 1987, 1994); and analyses of contemporary moral panics (Ben-Yehuda 1988, 1990; Goode and Ben-Yehuda 1994).

There is also a continuously growing body of criminological literature addressing diverse interactionist concerns, including the "invention" of the gangster as the public enemy (Ruth 1996); the social construction of child abuse (Pfohl 1977; Johnson 1985, 1988, 1989) as well as serial homicide (Jenkins 1994); a processual experiential explanation of dangerous violent criminality (Athens 1989/92, 1997); and the anatomy of an interactionist sociology of crime (Hester and Eglin 1992). To be sure, much of the recent literature is interdisciplinary, written by scholars in history, criminology, communications, and other fields in addition to sociology. In its evolution the interactionist theory of social deviance and crime has remained vitally important to a broader base of interpreters than ever before.

This chapter develops several important points. First, I present a general interactionist conceptualization of deviance and crime. Included are classic statements from Becker (1963/73), Schur (1971), and Goffman (1963b), detailing the centrality of deviance as social stigma as well as the importance of naturalism for the tradition (Matza 1964, 1969). Critiques of the approach are also examined.

Second, I summarize the various theoretical strands of the approach—what Jack D. Douglas (1984) has called "special interactionist theories." Following the lead of the last chapter, the Chicago School of interactionism and its labeling offshoot are seen as the core to the tradition.

Also of note are interactional conflict and sociological phenomenology. A major point of difference among the three types of theories is the amount of individual freedom accorded the individual actor in negotiated meaningful life experiences (Dotter and Roebuck 1988, 22). To these three traditional interactionist branches, I add feminist perspectives on deviance and criminological theorizing (Daly and Maher 1998a). This latter grouping is connected to interactionist labeling (Schur 1984) even as it goes well beyond traditional androcentric male-framed interactionist theorizing (Gelsthorpe and Morris 1990; Scraton 1990).

Finally, I propose a synthesis woven from elements of all four theoretical strands, representing a contextualization of the interactive labeling process. This synthesis describes and maps the specific social process by which deviance is labeled. The layered conceptualization of the deviance- and crime-generation process includes actors, acts, rules, audiences, and societal reactions (Dotter and Roebuck 1988; Dotter 1997). Viewed as a series of "stigma contests" (Schur 1980), this process is interpretive, highlighting meaning-creation as disvalued master status.

A General Interactionist Conceptualization of Crime and Deviance

Distinctions and Definitions

Social deviance may be generally defined as transgressions of group conduct norms. Erich Goode (1996a) succinctly summarizes two general points of view to its study. These are objectivism and constructionism. The difference between them hinges on the basic question each addresses regarding the nature of disvalued conduct and resulting status.[1]

The objectivist stance (also known as positivism, determinism, or essentialism) asks, "Why do some people violate standards of conduct and others refrain from such violation?" The answer lies in some kind of causal explanation as to observed deviant behavior. These antecedent causes are varied, but fundamental, essential factors. For example, biological or psychological predispositions may explain all sorts of deviant conduct—from terrible, seemly inexplicable acts of violence to repeated, even compulsive, violations of everyday norms; or social conditions such as inequality or poverty may be studied as the explanation of crimes against property (e.g., burglary, bank robbery) or person (e.g., rape, murder, assault). In short, the

CHAPTER FOUR

causes of deviance (i.e., answers to the "why" question) have focused on personal characteristics and social situations to explain wrongdoing.

The constructionist approach poses a different query: "How does the social construction and interpretation of rules influence the judgment of disvalued conduct?" The answer lies not in antecedent prior causes, but in an analysis of how rules are created and applied. As Goode states, constructionism in fact can be broken down into a number of interrelated questions:

> Some of the questions this orientation asks include "Why are certain rules laid down in the first place?" "Which rules are laid down?" "Whose rules are they?" "Who has the power to define the norms and their violation?" "Who, and what, is designated as deviant?" "What characteristics are regarded as deviant?" "What happens to someone who is singled out as deviant?" "What is the nature of the punishment that results from a particular definition of wrongdoing?" "How do members of a society keep wrongdoing—and wrongdoers—in line?" (Goode 1996a, vii)

The second approach, then, examines the construction of rules (both everyday norms and crimino-legal ones), how they are applied (officially as well as unofficially), and the social as well as individual consequences of that application (sanctions or punishment).

The questions put forth by each approach provide two basic contexts for the study of crime and deviance. The particular question or questions make certain assumptions regarding the nature of social life, which in turn influence conceptions of wrongdoing. Objectivism stresses that social reality, not unlike the physical world, is subject to discoverable laws or generalities. Thus, patterned behavior is linked to scientific causal analysis. Constructionism assumes that the character of social life is created through social interaction. While patterned, social interaction is also unpredictable and must be constantly negotiated and agreed upon. Both points of view begin with rule violation. An objective analysis seeks to explain that violation while a constructionist one seeks to describe its complexity and the manner in which meaning is created as well as interpreted.

More specific definitions of deviance, then, depend on the initial point of view. Following constructionism, social deviance can only be understood as a process of definition. There is no act or situation that is universally condemned (although some may come very close to being so). Furthermore, even when agreement is reached regarding deviance and conformity, it is a situationally created and sustained agreement. Definitions of deviance and crime are social accomplishments, subject to interpretation and reinterpretation in particular historical circumstances.

The patterning of deviance through social interaction is dynamic and subject to change over time. It is not so much that "anything goes," but that what goes in any particular circumstance is put together by actors in concert, but also disagreement, with one another. In the words of Howard S. Becker:

> [D]eviance is *not* a quality of the act the person commits, but rather a consequence of the application by others of rules and sanctions to an "offender." The deviant is one to whom that rule has successfully been applied; deviant behavior is behavior that people so label. [*italics* in the original] (1963/73, 9)

A specific definition of deviance respects this interactive nature of its generation. This deviance-generation is not subject to the laws of nature or science; rather it is like a story or narrative, to which a pattern is *imposed* by the actors involved. According to Edwin M. Schur:

> Human behavior is deviant *to the extent that* it comes to be viewed as involving a *personally discreditable* departure from a group's normative expectations, *and* it *elicits* interpersonal or collective reactions that serve to "isolate," "treat," "correct," or "punish" *individuals* engaged in such behavior. [*italics* in the original] (Schur 1971, 24)

The interactionist approach, then, sees deviance-generation as a complex outcome, interrelating several components: actors, acts, rules, audiences, and societal reactions (Dotter and Roebuck 1988). Becker's initial formulation focusing on the deviant label served to de-emphasize the importance of the overall process and led to much criticism.

Deviance as Stigmatization and Disvaluement

Schur's attempted definitional refinement not only outlines the generation process, but explicitly states the creative quality of the deviant label. That is, the core of deviance-labeling is its transformative power for the discredited outsider, what Frank Tannenbaum (1938) has called the "dramatization of evil." The creation of social deviance represents the

CHAPTER FOUR

ultimate, if unpredictable, *stigmatization* of the individual (or even entire social categories). The view of social deviance as a process of stigmatization obviates the need to conceptualize so-called "positive deviance" (Dodge 1985; Harman 1985). Following Edward Sagarin (1985), I view the latter as an oxymoron, a self-contradicting phrase. The nature of social deviance is rooted in normative transgression and the response to such. From a definitional stance, positive functions, consequences, and so on are quite beside the point.

A stigma may be conceived as "a failing, a shortcoming, a handicap" (Goffman 1963b, 3).[2] Its meaning and consequence revolve around the discreditable nature of the label. As Schur suggests above, stigma-as-discredit cannot be objectively determined. Following Goffman further:

> The term stigma and its synonyms conceal a double perspective: does the stigmatized individual assume his differentness is known about already or is evident on the spot, or does he assume it is neither known about by those present nor immediately perceivable by them? In the first case one deals with the plight of the *discredited*, in the second with that of the *discreditable*. This is an important difference, even though a particular stigmatized individual is likely to have experience with both situations. [*italics* in the original] (Goffman 1963b, 4)

Stigmatization implies knowledge (or lack of it) that serves to taint the identity of the individual. Again, the application of this knowledge constitutes the "created" quality of deviance. The person is or may be disvalued on its basis.

In Goffman's (1959) dramaturgical take, the consequences of stigmatization are primarily related to problems associated with identity management. The stigma, revealed or secreted, is rendered meaningful through the actor's theatrical (i.e., metaphorical)[3] presentation of self and responses to it. Identity management is rooted in the wider process of social interaction, creating what might be called "disvaluement conversations" (Young 1996). Through such conversations the stigmatized actor is linked to the general process of deviance-generation (i.e., stereotyped).

As Goffman elaborates:

> The attitudes we normals have toward a person with a stigma, and the actions we take in regard to him, are well known, since these responses

> are what benevolent social action is designed to soften and ameliorate. By definition, of course, we believe the person with a stigma is not quite human. On this assumption we exercise varieties of discrimination, through which we effectively, if often unthinkingly, reduce his life chances. We construct a stigma-theory, an ideology to explain his inferiority and account for the danger he represents, sometimes rationalizing an animosity based on other differences, such as those of social class. We use specific stigma terms such as cripple, bastard, moron in our daily discourse as a source of metaphor and imagery, without giving thought to the original meaning. (Goffman 1963b, 5)

In short, stigmatization labels the individual by inclusion in a category of outsiders. The label transmutes the quality of the original "act" to suggest that the individual is somehow naturally deviant. As Goffman observes, the application of the label may go far beyond the deviant act for its justification. The stigma ideology allows for entire categories of people to be labeled if not as deviant, then as "different," "weird," or "strange." In this sense, stigmatization and its consequence take many forms and degrees, including formal and informal responses. Of the latter, a particularly neglected one in sociological study, even by Goffman, is that of shame (Scheff 2003). In whatever form, stigmatization suggests individuals may be defined as deviant more for *who* they are (Schur 1984) (e.g., based on gender or race) than for *what* they have done in any immediate sense (e.g., committed a murder or assault).[4] The linking of disvalued behavior and the accompanying stigma is found in Edwin Lemert's (1951; 1972, 63–66) distinction between primary and secondary deviation.

The meaning of deviance, then, may be found not only in behavior (i.e., violation of norms and laws); it also may take on the character of master status (Becker 1963/73, 32–33). For example, a person stigmatized as a murderer may be attributed any number of other disvalued traits as well (e.g., dishonesty, cunning, or ability to commit other crimes). As with categories such as gender, race, or physical disability, criminality and other discredited actions may become part of Goffman's stigma theory or what I have termed disvaluement conversations. As Goffman writes:

> The term stigma, then, will be used to refer to an attribute, that is deeply discrediting, but it should be seen that a language of relationships, not attributes, is really needed. An attribute that stigmatizes one type of

CHAPTER FOUR

possessor can confirm the usualness of another, and therefore is neither creditable nor discreditable as a thing in itself. (Goffman 1963b, 3)

The nature of disvaluement conversations is complex and very often ambiguous. A stigmatizing label is ultimately enmeshed with an act and actor, in any but the most abstract situations (Dotter and Roebuck 1988). Furthermore, stigmatization may apply both to behavior as well as to the labeling of entire categories of persons as discredited. Thus, race, gender, physical handicap, and so on enter into Goffman's "language of relationships" in the creation of master status. The imputation of deviance, then, may be based on *status* or social position as well as behavior. According to Sagarin, this anchoring of stigmatization in status is especially important as we make sense of the labeling process and its components: "[A]*s persons in a given status, whether or not they commit acts associated with their groups and imputed to them, they are disvalued and reacted to in a negative manner by large numbers of persons in the society*" [*italics* in the original] (Sagarin 1975, 5). Deviance as stigmatization and disvaluement reveals the interpretive quality of the interactionist approach. The search for cause is forsaken in favor of an understanding and description of social deviance as naturally occurring.

Natural Deviation

The objectivist approach generally views social deviance in strictly normative terms. Violations are more or less disvalued according to abstract categorizations of what is considered appropriate conduct. In one form or another this approach has been dominant through most of the twentieth century and became associated with mainstream scientific sociology.[5] The constructionist viewpoint, primarily informed by interactionism but also containing Marxist and conflict perspectives, gathered momentum through the 1960s and remains a viable alternative today. Stephen Pfohl offers a dramatic portrait of the intellectual and general sociocultural posturing of the objectivist stance:

> The story of deviance and social control is a battle story. It is a story of the battle to control the ways people think, feel, and behave. It is a story of winners and losers and of the strategies people use in struggles with one another. Winners in the battle to control "deviant acts" are crowned

with a halo of goodness, acceptability, normality. Losers are viewed as living outside the boundaries of social life as it ought to be, outside the "common sense" of society itself. (Pfohl 1985/94, 3)

If objectivism presents a moralist/scientific take, interactionism can be seen as naturalistic. That is, social deviance—stigmatization created through an interpretive process—is not inherently disvalued. Rather, its various forms emerge just as do those of conformity.[6]

David Matza has cogently outlined the principal conflicting philosophical conceptions of naturalism. He writes, "In the dominant conception, naturalism is equivalent to scientific philosophy, experimental method, a stress on objective, external, or observable features of phenomena, and, in general, positivism" (Matza 1969, 4). The antithetical view is of subjectivism, identified with idealism, existentialism, and the primacy of individual experience.

Undaunted by traditional philosophical discourse, Matza offers this turn of definition:

> Naturalism, as the very term implies, is the philosophical view that strives *to remain true to the nature of the phenomenon under study or scrutiny*. For naturalism, the phenomenon being scrutinized is to be considered object or subject depending on its nature—not on the philosophical preconceptions of a researcher. That specific nature commands the fidelity of naturalism. [*italics* in the original] (Matza 1969, 5)

The nature of complex sociocultural phenomena will most surely not be apparent nor particularly easy to determine. Nonetheless, Matza goes beyond even the pragmatic emphasis on the scientific method as grounded in experience. In his view, "naturalistic observation may also include experience and introspection, the methods traditionally associated with subjectivism" (Matza 1969, 5). Certainly, the general equation of naturalism with science and the objectivist view may have merit—when the objects of study are in fact objects. Thus, the physical world of nature may unfold according to "natural" laws.

However, untold numbers of social scientists have (historically and contemporarily) failed to recognize the difference between physical and human nature. That is, human nature is defined by a subjective, or if you will, intersubjective consciousness. Matza frames the difference:

CHAPTER FOUR

> The misconception of man as object oscillated between two major forms: the first radical, the second heuristic. In the first, man *was* object. In the second, scientists deemed it heuristic merely to act *as if* man were object. In both views, however, a similar consequence appeared. Irrespective of whether man was object or merely heuristically treated as object, the terms of analysis were set in a fashion that minimized man's causal capacity, his activity, his tendency to reflect on himself and his setting, and his periodic struggles to transcend rather than succumb to the circumstances that allegedly shaped and constrained him. [*italics* in the original] (Matza 1969, 7)

For Matza, an interactionist viewpoint of the deviant actor repudiates an objectivist stance. Deviance is to be viewed, even experienced, as a social accomplishment, ("natural deviation") emerging within the same process by which conformity is constructed:

> The appreciation of shift, ambiguity, and pluralism need hardly imply a wholesale repudiation of the idea of common morality. Such an inference is the mistake of a rampant and mindless relativism. Plural evaluation, shifting standards, and moral ambiguity may, and do, coexist with a phenomenal realm that is commonly sensed as deviant. The very meaning of pluralism, the very possibility of shift and ambiguity depend on a wider consensus, founded in common understandings, regarding the patently deviant nature of many nonetheless ordinary undertakings. (Matza 1969, 12)

Interactionist theorizing in social deviance has been subjected to much criticism, especially by those claiming the mantle of scientific objectivity and empiricism. As in the above debate on naturalism, sometimes the basis of criticism may not be as it seems.

The Intellectual Drama of Labeling: Criticism and Response

From the modest initial statements of Tannenbaum and Lemert, through the cogent Chicago articulation of Becker, to the syntheses of Goffman and Schur, the labeling approach to deviance has generated controversy and criticism. Indeed, it can be argued that the perspective (and continued response to it) dominated the theoretical development of deviance studies through most of the 1980s, sparking "a major industry of criticism" (Plummer 1979, 119). While not necessarily dominant, contemporary interactionist formulations remain influential in a more fractured intellectual discourse (Scull 1984; Gibbs 1995).

Initial critiques of the tradition took several interrelated objectivist paths (Dotter and Roebuck 1988; Goode 2001, 25–31). The principal thread argued that labeling could not explain the *causes* of deviant behavior, that social reaction did not account for initial acts of deviance (Gibbs 1966; Akers 1968). Traditional scientific explanations assume the concrete, observable character of norms and rules; studying deviance is a matter of identifying normative violation and searching for the etiology of such behavior in biological, psychological, or sociological predispositions. In the positivist sense, then, labeling was not a theory at all.

Becker (1963/73) and others (Kitsuse 1962; Schur 1969b, 1971; Rains 1975; Goode 1975) responded to this charge: "Labeling" was never intended to be a causative theory of deviance, but rather a perspective or approach to explain how misbehavior might be situationally defined and given context by differential application of rules. In Becker's view:

> The original proponents of the position, however, did not propose solutions to the etiological question. They had more modest aims. They wanted to enlarge the area taken into consideration in the study of deviant phenomena by including in it activities of others than the allegedly deviant actor. They supposed, of course, that when they did that, and as new sources of variance were included in the calculations, all the questions that students of deviance conventionally looked at would take on a different cast. (Becker 1963/73, 179)

In his typically restrained but direct style, Becker thus reminded early critics that their claims against the approach were specious, if not utterly contrived.

This positivist causative critique gave rise at the same time to a related debate over "falsely accused" or "secret" deviance. As framed by Jack Gibbs:

> [For the sake of consistency, labelists] would have to insist that behavior which is contrary to a norm is not deviant unless it is discovered and there is a particular kind of reaction to it. Thus, if persons engage in adultery but their act is not discovered and reacted to in a certain way (by members of the social unit), then it is not deviant! Similarly if a person is erroneously thought to have engaged in a certain type of behavior

and is reacted to "harshly" as a consequence, a deviant act has taken place! (Gibbs 1966, 13)

Again, this observation assumes the narrow positivist focus on the actor and behavior, as does Gibbs's (1966, 11) characterization of the approach as "relativistic in the extreme." His normative, objectivist stance assumes the only thing at issue is whether or not the behavior is committed.

Edwin Lemert (1972, 1974), himself identified as an early labeling proponent, has addressed problems with the relativity of societal reaction as well as the general interactionist stance of labeling. Specifically, he holds that there is an objective reality associated with the study of deviance that cannot be ignored or lost in definitional processes.

Schur has countered that relativism is indeed the strength of the labeling tradition. Furthermore,

> Gibbs is correct in his charge that no unequivocal basis for distinguishing what is deviant from what is not has been established, yet as labeling proponents would rightly insist the attempt to make such a clear-cut distinction is misguided. It is a central tenet of the labeling perspective that neither acts nor individuals are "deviant" in the sense of immutable "objective" reality without reference to processes of social definition. (Schur 1971, 14)

Moving social construction of deviance to the forefront of consideration not only refocuses debate away from causal explanations; it also broadens and renders problematic the outcome of societal reaction (including recognition of secret and falsely accused deviance). As Becker (1963/73, 185–88) maintains, the positivist critique confuses two distinct but related processes of social construction. The first concerns what reasonable persons might interpret as deviance or conformity based on their understanding of social rules, causes of behavior, and so on. The second process relates to the actual application of labels, formal and informal, to specific actors in particular situations.

Objectivism conflates these two, assuming they are identical. Viewing deviance as interactional—the outcome of concerted, often complicated, collective action—allows us to note where the two processes are distinct as well as potentially overlapping. Social definition focuses on "the drama of moral rhetoric and action in which imputations of deviance are made, accepted, rejected, and fought over" (Becker 1963/73, 186). Secret deviance and falsely applied imputations are as much a matter of social construction as labels related to "true" deviance or conformity (Becker 1963/73, 180–81).

The issue of cause, then, has represented one broad positivist criticism of labeling. Another deals with the effects of labeling itself, again betraying a narrow focus on the behavior and the application of the label (the second process described above). This argument maintains that the act of labeling does not inevitably result in a self-fulfilling prophecy of a deviant career (Goode 2001, 117–18). A number of critics (Bordua 1967; Akers 1985, 30–32; Gove 1980) point out that punishment may be an effective deterrent, and that wrongdoers often resist repeated deviation. In short, this view suggests that labeling is neither a necessary nor sufficient explanation for entrance into a prolonged deviant career and assumption of a deviant identity (Mankoff 1985).

Once again, the constructionist approach does not argue for the creation of deviant lifestyles or self-concepts as the certain outcome of labeling. However, in questioning strictly normative conceptions, interactionism makes clear that the deviant label is often ambiguous and involves the efforts of more than simply the deviant actor (Becker 1963/73, 186; Goode 2001, 113–15). As with other positivist critiques, this objection fails to accord any validity to the process of deviance labeling. Rather, actors simply choose to obey fundamentally unquestioned norms.

A recent elaboration of the positive effects of stigmatization is found in the work of John Braithwaite (1989, 1995) on reintegrative shaming. Anchored in the objectivist, scientific tradition of theory testing, the approach distinguishes between traditional stigmatization and efforts by the community to establish means for reacceptance of law-abiding members (delabeling). The latter process of reintegrative shaming, however, seems based on a simplistic conception of normative structure. By way of example, Braithwaite offers the family as the best site to observe the process at work. While such may be the case, we can hardly assume that reintegrative shaming is particularly effective in situations involving other than primary groups, especially as the complexity of the stigmatization/delabeling increases.

Criticism of the interactionist approach to deviance has also come from sources other than mainstream scientific sociology. Marxist and other radical scholars have often leveled the charge that labelists concentrate on exotic, relatively unimportant forms of wrongdoing at the expense of a thoroughgoing structural analysis of status/class differentials and the consequent crimes of the powerful (Liazos 1972; Davis and Stasz 1990, 44–46).

Thus, critical theorists argue that the labeling approach, while focusing on definitional processes, continues to take a nonstructural, ahistorical view of deviance production. The corrective for this blindness to history and structure may be a Marxist perspective, locating deviance production in the structural contradictions of twentieth-century capitalism (Taylor, Walton, and Young 1973; Spitzer 1975), or a posthumanist theory that attempts to draw from both objectivist and constructionist approaches (Thio 1995). In either case, the interactionist approach is seen as essentially microsociological, devoid of a coherent politicized concept of labeling as social control (Davis 1975, 205–8).[7] Becker (1963/73, 181–89) has addressed this perceived bias in his conceptualization of the deviant label as a process of collective action.

Closely related to the structure/history criticism is the idea that interactionism creates sympathy for those labeled, focusing on a kind of "underdog" ideology at the expense of developing a more comprehensive theoretical stance (Davis and Stasz 1990, 45–46). Much of the above critique by Liazos (1972) centers on the attempts by labelists to humanize, even "normalize," the deviant and most wrongdoing. Marxist critics argue that toleration cannot replace structural equality and attempts to make the state more accountable for its collective actions (Davis 1975, 193–95). Through its liberal bias the interactionist perspective indirectly exacerbates institutionalized patterns of oppression, racism, inequality, and so on (Gouldner 1968).

The philosophical defense of labeling to this morals charge is found in its embrace of naturalism discussed earlier. Matza relates the importance of a naturalistic stance for the study of deviance-creation:

> The growth of the sociological view of deviant phenomena involved, as major phases, the replacement of a correctional stance by an *appreciation* of the deviant subject, the tacit purging of a conception of pathology by a new stress on human *diversity*, and the erosion of a simple distinction between deviant and conventional phenomena, resulting from intimate

familiarity of the world as it is, which yielded a more sophisticated view stressing *complexity*. [*italics* in the original] (Matza 1969, 10)

Matza's articulation of appreciation, diversity, and complexity as interrelated elements of naturalism should not be construed as a dismissal of moral judgment. In fact, moral judgments are enmeshed in this same complicated natural reality. If labelists represent liberal supporters of "underdog" deviants, they usually admit the charge (though sometimes begrudgingly) (Becker 1967; Plummer 1979, 110).

Becker disentangles this charge from the agendas of both radical and conservative social thinkers:

> Scientists often wish to make it appear that some complicated combination of sociological theories, scientific evidence, and ethical judgments is really no more than a simple matter of definition. Scientists who have made strong value commitments (of whatever political or moral variety) seem especially likely to want that. Why do people want to disguise their morals as science? Most likely, they realize or intuit the contemporary rhetorical advantage of not having to admit that it is "only a moral judgment" one is making, and pretending instead that it is a scientific finding. All parties to any major social and moral controversy will attempt to gain that advantage and present their moral position as so axiomatic that it can be built into the presuppositions of their theory, research, and political dogma, without question. I suggest to the Left, whose sympathies I share, that we should attack injustice and oppression directly and openly, rather than pretend that the judgment that such things are evil is somehow deducible from sociological first principles, or warranted by empirical findings alone. (Becker 1963/73, 202–3)

The moral judgments of labelists are no less important than those of other theorists. At the same time, the constructionist approach holds (unlike the objectivist) that moral judgments are socially created in the same manner as scientific ones. The above critiques of interactionist deviance theorizing demonstrate the importance of a constructionist approach. It need not always be the dominant one, in offering many paths to follow. I now examine the intricate strands of interactionist theorizing in the study of stigmatized behavior and people.

CHAPTER FOUR

The Strands of Interactionist Deviance Theorizing

The Four Strands

Interactionist perspectives on deviance have generated much conceptual and ideological critique. Fundamental to these dialogues is the often unexamined assumption of a single interactionist "theory" to criticize or defend. Both proponents and opponents have contributed to the problem, especially in the indiscriminate identification of labeling with interactionism. In responding to critics of his ideas as found in the first edition of *Outsiders*, Becker (1963/73) provides the first real attempt to address the dilemma. He argues for the term "interactionist," replacing "labeling." The former expands the emphasis beyond the individual act of labeling to the wider context of social construction of meaning. To be sure, this reconsideration of terms did not answer all objectivist concerns. However, it represented a critical base for argument to develop *within* the perspective.

Almost a decade later Jack D. Douglas and Frances Waksler (1982) pick up the thread of Becker's definitional reformulation. With a passing nod to Tannenbaum (1938) and Lemert (1951), they summarize interactionist theoretical development, curiously calling for recognition of a "new" perspective. In their words:

> This new perspective has emerged through the work of a number of theorists and has been given a number of names: new symbolic interactionism, labeling theory, dramaturgy, phenomenology, ethnomethodology, and existential sociology. The differences of names and of specific theories must not, however, obscure for us the fundamental similarities in their views of the sociology of deviance and their fundamental dissimilarities from earlier absolutist theories of deviance. These similarities constitute the new theoretical perspective and distinguish all these theories from earlier perspectives on deviance. (Douglas and Waksler 1982, 22)

At first glance their argument for such a new perspective may seem inappropriate, given the rich interactionist tradition in sociology generally. At the same time, that tradition has hardly been developmentally static, especially in the area of social deviance. The labeling/interactionist debate did much to energize theoretical advance in both spheres.

Douglas and Waksler (1982, 126) succinctly outline the shifting edges of such a perspective. First, deviance is constructed by social actors. Everyday social interaction is the basis of these constructions. Second, meaning-creation is problematic for actors (regarding definitions of both conformity and deviance). The construction of meaning is constant, fluid, and layered in the varieties of social acts. Finally, sociologists' meaning-constructions present even more interpretive difficulty than those of lay members. Definitions of deviance are enmeshed in philosophical assumptions regarding the character of social life, and the assumptions are open to debate and question.

These three points frame the identification and exposition of "special interactionist theories" of deviance (Douglas 1984, 9–12). For purposes of discussion Douglas has sketched three broad interrelated types. Symbolic interactionism includes dramaturgical elements (Goffman 1959; Lyman and Scott 1970) and traditional Chicago School labeling. Interactional conflict combines structural elements of Marxism with a view of social action allowing some context for construction of meaning by actors (Neff 1980). Ecological and subcultural conflict are also traced to the Chicago perspectives of social disorganization and differential association (Dotter 1978; Sutherland et al. 1992). Sociological phenomenology, including existential sociology and ethnomethodology (Garfinkel 1967; Douglas and Johnson 1977; Douglas 1970), emphasizes almost exclusively the latitude of individual actors to create and react to meaning contexts in everyday life.

To update these three types, I add the emergence of an interdisciplinary feminist strand of deviance theorizing, heavily influenced by interactionist imagery (Goode 1996a, 123–28). This strand draws from critical feminist criminology (Gelsthorpe and Morris 1990; Rafter 1990; Naffine 1996; Daly and Maher 1998a) and its relationship to stigmatization based on gender as well as race (Rice 1990; hooks 1992; Carlen 1994). Ideologies of sexism and racism are viewed as dominant, exploitative modes of sociocultural control (Donovan 1985/96; Collins 1991; Doob 1999). This evolving critique of labeling based on gender and race draws freely from the widest scope of social science and humanistic literature (Douglas 1977/88; Gates 1988) and increasingly includes the intersection of social class (Andersen and Collins 2004b; Barak et al. 2001). It ties in with more traditionally interactionist theories through its constructionist stance (Schur 1984).

Interactionism is a synthesis of all four strands. From symbolic interactionism, I draw on the classic statements of Chicago School labeling;

CHAPTER FOUR

Becker's labeling reformulation outlined above remains the most substantial continuing interactionist contribution to deviance theorizing. Interactional conflict focuses on the political and subcultural context from which deviant labels emerge. Phenomenological concerns situate the actor in the process of meaning-creation. The inclusion of a feminist strand expands interactionism into a theory of deviance-as-collective-action and stigmatization. The various branches are not distinct theories, but broad overlapping conceptualizations of how social life is rendered meaningful. For example, traditional labeling bridges the conceptual gap between interactional conflict (traditionally based on enduring aspects of inequality and resulting criminal labels) and phenomenology (grounded more in actors' construction of meaning). Also, the feminist strand, in particular, is interdisciplinary, drawing even more liberally than the others from a wider range of intellectual sources (Carrington 1998; Daly and Maher 1998b).

A Synthesis of Interactionist Perspectives

The four strands of interactionist deviance theorizing—Chicago School labeling,[8] interactional conflict, sociological phenomenology, and feminism—share an emphasis on the social creation of meaning. Furthermore, all view the deviant label as a process of stigmatization. The label is not a cause of further deviance, but an interpretation of its context. In synthesizing the four perspectives, I forsake the search for causal connections, instead offering a general description of the process through which deviance is socially generated. Each strand provides important theoretical emphases and insights into the process of deviance creation. Like Blumer (1969) I seek a perspective which, constructed from several interrelated points of view, will sensitize the observer to the interactive quality of deviance.

At its most basic level, stigmatization is a process of social definition. Selectively combining concepts and themes from four strands of interactionism does not aim for logical consistency or completeness. Instead, the intent is to respect social interaction as a natural process. Deviance is not inherently bad, ill, or even sick, but the outcome of multiple lines of social construction. The process by which deviance is socially created includes a number of elements: actors, acts, rules/norms, audiences, and societal reactions (Dotter and Roebuck 1988). These elements inform the four interactionist theoretical strands with varying emphases throughout. In

THE CREATION OF DEVIANCE

synthesizing the four strands, I highlight their interconnections. My intent is to reformulate the manner in which meaning-creation (i.e., the stigmatization process) constantly shifts between different combinations of these elements. The process simultaneously encompasses individual situations of labeling as well as wider sociocultural constructions of deviance. Social deviance, like conformity, is a naturally occurring phenomenon; the process of its social definition is complex, moving from individuals to categorizations based on collective stigma.

Chicago School Labeling

Interactionist labeling is arguably the most mainstream of the strands. Its view of meaning, while not based on static normative consensus, begins with a critique of social rules which allows for a certain degree of sharedness (Becker 1963/73; Douglas 1984). Many of the criticisms already discussed flow from the nature of this shared meaning as cause and consequence of social control. It can often be a small step from agreed-upon and enforced social norms to unproblematic labeling of behavior as disvalued, and to questioning the causal logic of a self-fulfilling prophecy.

Additionally, this strand is often linked with more conventional noninteractionist theories of deviance. For example, Kai Erikson's (1964, 1966) work on the importance of social reaction and its situational quality, as well as his analysis of the labeling process in Colonial America, can easily be read from a functionalist stance. Instead of outlining the functions of deviance, his analyses make clear the functions of the deviant *label* (e.g., boundary maintenance and social cohesion for the unlabeled in the community).

Even Becker's (1963/73) original theoretical argument in *Outsiders* is built on the importance of rules (e.g., norms) and rule enforcers for an understanding of the deviant label. His criticism of consensus-oriented normative approaches was itself nominally rooted in a sharedness of the social rules which may not always exist. Thus, in the later reformulation he introduced the "potentially deviant" act (unlabeled, but likely to be so if discovered) as a counterpoint for other situations already identified ("pure" and "secret" deviance) (Becker 1963/73, 20–21, 181).

In their time, however, the works of both Erikson and Becker were viewed as anything but conventional—a time when even social science conceptions of deviance might still focus on "pathological" elements or, at

CHAPTER FOUR

most, disruption of static normative consensus. These classic statements of interactionist labeling are crucial for the characterization of deviance as process and definition (Matza 1969, 37), and for what Becker (1963/73, 181–84) later termed "deviance as collective action."

The meaning of deviance emerges from the interrelated joint actions (Blumer 1969) of individuals and groups. While the societal reaction or label summarily describes the process of stigma-creation, collective action expands that process to include several other related elements as well: actors, acts, rules, and audiences. Collective action in the defining of deviance is based upon social rules, either informal norms or law. The interactionist or constructionist approach does not equate normative definitions with certain social reaction. Nor does it ignore the naturalistic quality of joint action to punish as a means to correct or deter. Rather, it maps the social process by which deviance is rendered meaningful.

Matza refers to the process of deviance-generation as "signification." In his words, "To signify is to *stand for* in the sense of representing or exemplifying. An object that is signified, whether it be man or thing, is rendered more meaningful" [*italics* in the original] (Matza 1969, 156). Meaning emerges not simply from the label, but the entire process of creation in which that label is embedded. Furthermore, the emergent meaning of any situation (i.e., rules as well as labels) possesses no inherent finality; it may lead to other constructions and consequences.

Rules and their enforcement are the central problematic of the deviance-definition process. Societal reaction, legal or otherwise, cannot occur in the absence of a normative context. Within this context deviant acts are rendered meaningful by the labeled actor and audiences. To more fully understand the importance of rules for societal reaction, Goode has proposed a "soft reactivism"[9] (Goode 1981, 51–52). This view draws several conclusions regarding norms and their relationship to social action. First, norms do not in and of themselves cause or inhibit behavior. According to Goode (1996a), the normative (i.e., objectivist) sociologist observes and catalogues the rules and then matches them to expected societal reactions. Conversely, the soft reactive sociologist begins with the societal reactions, and then constructs normative images to describe the significance of the former.

Second, no rule is absolute. Instead, probability is central to an understanding of normative application and even wider societal reactions. In a word, rules are subject to interpretation. Blumer (1969) terms the process of meaning-interpretation through joint action symbolic interaction. Third, given the probability (or even possibility) of stigmatization by audiences, the actor's interpretation of events is crucial. This includes the individual's self-image as well as beliefs and knowledge regarding the likelihood of being labeled. Finally, while societal reactions do not "create" deviant behavior, they are part of the very process through which that behavior is rendered meaningful. As Goode observes, "[Societal reactions] impart *to* certain acts their peculiarly deviant ('criminal,' 'sick,' etc.) quality" [*italics* in the original] (Goode 1981, 51).

Increasingly, the signification of deviance extends well beyond the commission of a particular act by an identifiable actor in circumstances which are objectively perceived and evaluated. Rather, stigmatization becomes layered in its production and interpretation. The variety of circumstances attendant to behavior or persons being labeled is the contemporary character of collective action.

David Downes and Paul Rock capture the complexity of deviance-definition:

> It is not the simple presence of deviance but its quality, scale, and location which typically shape a reply. Very often, deviation will be 'normalized' and accommodated, built into the fabric of accepted life. It is only when it is inexplicable, disorganized, or threatening that a gross reaction can take place. Crisis occurs when others cannot or will not cope. Its precipitation hinges on prevailing ideas about propriety and harm, the social structure of the audience, and the appreciation of possible remedies. Some groups are tightly organized, others have a loose order, and others little apparent order at all. In turn, there is a great variation between the schemes which confer coherence on the world and between the abilities of people to monitor one another. (Downes and Rock 1982/98, 193)

This complexity surrounding deviance-generation is especially heightened in the contrast between criminal and noncriminal forms.[10] Serious criminal significations, especially relative to acts of violence, are paramount. In fact, societal reaction to crime contextualizes the broader application of noncriminal labels. According to Matza:

> Outside the context of the central part in the very conception of crime and deviation, its key role in the selection of those destined to continue

CHAPTER FOUR

> becoming deviant, and its ancient but amazingly resilient commitment to the method of penalization, the state's relation to deviation was easily conceived as *correction*—with due allowance made for deficiency of knowledge, inefficiency, corruption, or mistake. In context, as one might expect, its role has been a bit more devious and even in principle not so beneficent. So potent an apparatus as Leviathan should display its effects in manifold ways and even on those not yet patently in its grip. One need not be in prison to be affected by Leviathan; nor must Leviathan be a police-state to cast a shadow over its subjects. [*italics* in the original] (Matza 1969, 144)

The social reaction to crime, then, is unique in the state's ability to apply the label. Correction of the stigmatized is one, but by no means, the only goal of joint action on the part of the state. The institutionalized power to label through the actions of criminal justice "audiences" is the most basic political quality of the labeling process.

Interactional Conflict

Of the remaining three strands, interactional conflict is most closely linked with Chicago School labeling (Dotter 1978; Neff 1980). Initially, the perspective of social disorganization was in its broadest sense concerned with sociocultural conflict among constantly multiplying urban groups (Park, Burgess, and McKenzie 1967; Short 1971). In the city-as-social-ecology, the nature and consequence of such conflict was seen as adaptive in the long run, not disruptive or exploitative. Robert Park (1950, 1922/70; Matthews 1977, 159–60) brought an experienced journalist's eye to bear on the ecological model, as in his study of the immigrant press and the process of "americanization."

Park (1952, 145–48) offered arguably the most compelling articulation of social ecology, developing his conceptualization of community in a naturalistic Darwinian framework of competition, dominance, and succession. His rich metaphor described these interdependent processes as a "web of life" for communities; the city was seen as a "social laboratory" marked by both ecological and cultural patterns (Park 1952, 73–87; Maines 2001, 78–86). Park's (1952, 261) conservative analysis of conflict ending in accomodation parallels that of Georg Simmel (1964, 1971) as well. Conflict is a fundamental social process and also important for understanding formation of the individual personality, especially as found in the urban setting. Park's (1950, 370) concept of the marginal man—"the individual who finds himself on the margins of two cultures and not fully or permanently accommodated to either"— interrelates the social and individual layers of the ecological process. The Chicago School of interactionism thereby maintained a fluid agenda, freely mixing images of ecological process with ethnographic naturalistic detail of urban experience. As Rock observes, while symbolic interactionism "does not wholly shun the idea of social structure, its stress upon activity and process relegates structural metaphors to a most minor place. It works instead upon the limited sections of visible social life whose evolution can be rendered comprehensible. Like Simmel's own analysis, it applies the forms of change to apparently trivial areas of sociation" (Rock 1979, 50).

The social psychology of Mead gradually shifted the ecological focus of system maintenance and related character formation to an interactional concern with the viewpoints of individual actors. As Nanette J. Davis explains:

> George Herbert Mead's social psychological assumptions played a crucial role in formulating an interactional model to supplement, if not to replace, the ecological one. This tradition stimulated a concern for the shaping and structuring of interaction by the ecology of the material world. Relating natural areas to cultural traditions generated the notion of the city as a social construct or a "state of mind." This distinctive point of view led to an outpouring of naturalistic studies. (Davis 1975, 42–43)

Chicago social ecology, coupled with the influence of Mead's interactionism, led to an appreciation of deviance as a natural urban phenomenon (Matza 1969; Rock 1979, 92–96). Case studies of different forms abounded,[11] including Jewish ghetto life (Wirth 1928/62), community transition (Zorbaugh 1929/48), hobos (Anderson 1923/65), taxi-dance halls (Cressey 1932/69), delinquency (Shaw 1930/66, 1931/68), and gangs (Thrasher 1927/68; Whyte 1943/55). In this context personal disorientation was subsumed by system-level disorganization as gradual social change. The interactionally informed study of deviance examined myriad "social worlds" with their own normative frameworks (Matza 1969; Dotter 1978).

The normative conflict of these worlds with the larger social system was termed social disorganization. Such conflict was a constant element of

CHAPTER FOUR

urban life, evidence of the city's ability to foster and eventually absorb cultural diversity (Zorbaugh 1929/48). In moving beyond statements of deviance-as-pathology, social disorganization proved to be rich in theoretical complexity. As Downes and Rock write:

> On another plane, disorganization could be described as a property of the wider social structure. It would then refer to the relations *between* and not within worlds. Social differentiation, a period of excited social change, or uneven development can exaggerate the instability of those relations, leading to strain and a breakdown of local order. In turn, particular worlds can become dislocated, thrown up out of their context and exposed. They can achieve a social and moral independence which some sociologists have chosen to emphasize. [*italics* in the original] (Downes and Rock 1982/98, 72–73)

This systemic conflict between self-contained deviant worlds and the transforming larger society rests on the concept of affinity. According to Matza, its definition is simple: "Persons, either individually or in aggregates, develop predispositions to certain phenomena, say delinquency, as a result of their *circumstances*" [*italics* in the original] (Matza 1969, 90–91). The appreciation for deviant forms fostered by in-depth observation contrasted with the ecological focus on crime/delinquency rates in so-called natural areas (Shaw and McKay 1942/69). The apparent "affinity" between poverty and deviance could not be easily reconciled with the developing interactionist empathy for the deviant actor. As such, early efforts to describe deviance as a process of social definition through interactional conflict were of limited success.

Edwin Sutherland's concept of differential association expanded early interactional conflict into a more focused subcultural variety (Sutherland et al. 1992). Affinity-generated conflict was replaced by that engendered through affiliation. Affiliation is described by Matza as follows:

> the process by which the subjected is *converted* to conduct novel for him but already established for others. By providing new meanings for conduct previously regarded as outlandish or inappropriate, affiliation provides the context and process by which the neophyte *may* be turned "on" or "out." [*italics* in the original] (Matza 1969, 101–2)

The process, then, is the generic form of differential association, constituting the subcultural site for deviant behavior and supporting normative context (i.e., differential social organization). Affiliation-as-interactional-conflict connects Sutherland's differential association and differential social organization (the structuring of groups for either conventional or criminal behavior). In short, "Sutherland invented the principle of normative conflict to account for the distribution of high and low crime rates; he then tried to specify the mechanism by which this principle works to produce individual cases of criminality" (Sutherland et al. 1992, 101).

Thus, differential association goes well beyond social disorganization in establishing linkages between deviant actors, their acts, the rules violated, the enforcers challenging violations, and the societal reactions of subcultural and other audiences. Differential association relates to the social process by which rules, along with criminal and anticriminal behavior patterns, are given meaning. The affiliation is normative, subcultural, and interactional; it does not refer to association with this or that type of person. That is, criminal or conforming behavior patterns are learned from a variety of persons and shaped within the experience of the individual actor. The learning of deviant patterns through differential association is not a matter of simple "contagion" at the hands of criminals, but a complex social psychological interpretive process.

Matza frames the interactional character of affiliation:

> Conversion is mediated through a reconsideration of the self and its affinities. In the context of experience, consciousness may shift itself so as to incorporate new terms of reference, new issues of relevance. Only the context of experience can provide the terms and issues that are the very tissue with which meaning is built and disposition discovered. Though peers or other educators are part of the experience, it is a mistake to reduce the affiliative circumstance to a process in which the initiate capitulates, or does not, to the pressure of others already converted. The others are considered–but with the phenomenon they represent, practice and sponsor. (Matza 1969, 119)

Differential association recasts ecological normative conflict as a proliferation of subcultures. In the process, the ground for an interactional theory of deviance-generation is broken. The bridge between differential association and labeling is provided by the concept of deviant or criminal career.[12] Becker (1963/73) uses the term to interconnect deviant actors with their acts, and social reaction with assumption of deviant identity, as well as to designate the application of rules by formal and informal enforcers. The development of deviant career hinges on learning through differential association and subcultural formation. Becker's analyses of marijuana users (1953), the actions of drug law enforcers (1963/73, 59–78), and the jazz musician subculture (1951) represent early statements of the processual nature of deviance. The interactional conflict strand, partially developed from differential association, eventually led to the theoretical identification of criminal behavior systems (Clinard, Quinney, and Wildeman 1994).

Differential association may be summarized as a subcultural learning theory of crime and deviance. It refined the portrait of social disorganization, depicting interaction, and eventually, sociopsychological conflict, as normative (Vold, Bernard, and Snipes 1998, 185–86).[13] The former image is usually subsumed in the face-to-face interaction of actors participating in the process of differential association (Davis and Stasz 1990, 37).

Marxist and other critics have pointed out that, for Sutherland, the state is conceived benignly, as a neutral arbiter in the conflict process. Davis offers the following observation:

> Sutherland never explored the process by which crime rates are constructed. By assuming that high rates reflect basic differences in group values and modes of organization, Sutherland fell into a common sociological error. In most modern communities, crime rates may actually say more about differential power than about differential-social-organization. Sutherland was too close to the Chicago School's view of ethnic variation as the major form of social difference to see the class and caste conflict that characterize urban organization. (Davis 1975, 134)

Nonetheless, the roots of interactional conflict are apparent in the many reformulations of differential association as well as in Sutherland's conceptualization of white-collar crime (1949/83).

In its many varieties interactional conflict theory often overlaps with interactionist labeling. As pointed out earlier in this chapter, a major Marxist criticism of the latter is its lack of a central structural role for the state in the labeling process. Interactionist labeling and, to a lesser degree

THE CREATION OF DEVIANCE

all forms of interactional conflict, have often been cast as mirror images of mainstream objectivist theories (Gouldner 1968; Mullins 1973).

I contend that the two remain useful in describing the general process through which deviance is socially defined. There are countless classic examples of interactionism informed by the process of social conflict. For example, Joseph Gusfield's (1963/86) historical analysis of the American Temperance movement characterizes Prohibition and its repeal as instances of "status politics." The symbolic conflict involved the ways of life depicted by Protestant and Catholic cultures.

Prohibition (i.e, the legal/constitutional stigmatization of alcohol and those who use it) is arguably the most extreme example of the problematics of deviance-definition. The Volstead Act (i.e., the Eighteenth Amendment to the U.S. Constitution) criminalized the manufacture, sale, and transportation of alcoholic beverages on a national level. Societal reaction and enforcement became a matter of broad cultural and legal conflict. If the act was "unenforceable," it did not even technically outlaw the drinking of such beverages. The sheer volume of individual instances of deviance-labeling created a crisis reaching across actors and audiences, individual normative violations and punishments.

With repeal, the definitional focus changed radically. As Gusfield writes:

> The object of concern became the deviant drinker, the alcoholic. The substance of alcohol lost its place as the *bete noir* of the movement as attention shifted to the user. It went from abusive substance to substance abuse.... The significance of this change has been immense. It removed the alcohol problem from its role in political conflict by removing it as an attack on popular culture. [*italics* in the original] (Gusfield 1963/86, 199)

The outcome of interactional conflict, then, is social definition of deviance: the manner in which norms provide a cultural context linking acts, actors, and audiences to resulting societal reactions. In the case of Prohibition, the societal reaction was highly problematic, even a defining cultural moment.

Becker (1963/73, 135–46) presents a similar conceptual analysis of the Marijuana Tax Act and the related Harrison Act (which prohibited the use of opiate drugs for all but medical purposes). Again, the construction of rules/norms is paramount to comprehending the interrelations of acts, actors, audiences, and societal reactions.

CHAPTER FOUR

Becker details the political backdrop of the Harrison Act:

> The Harrison Act, for instance, was so drawn as to allow medical personnel to continue using morphine and other opium derivatives for the relief of pain and such other medical purposes as seemed to them appropriate. Furthermore, the law was carefully drawn in order to avoid running afoul of the constitutional provision reserving police powers to the several states. In line with this restriction the Act was presented as a revenue measure, taxing, unlicensed purveyors of opiate drugs at an exorbitant rate while permitting licensed purveyors (primarily physicians, dentists, veterinarians, and pharmacists) to pay a nominal tax. Though it was justified constitutionally as a revenue measure, the Harrison Act was in fact a police measure and was so interpreted by those to whom its enforcement was entrusted. One consequence of the passage of the Act was the establishment, in the Treasury Department, of the Federal Bureau of Narcotics in 1930. (Becker 1963/73, 137)

According to Becker's analysis of the historical record, it was the Federal Bureau of Narcotics that provided the primary impetus, throughout the 1930s, for defining marijuana as an undesirable drug. This included legal lobbying as well as media-generated activities to stigmatize usage of the drug as dangerous. In fact, prior to the agency's efforts, such usage was apparently not widely opposed or viewed with alarm. With the Harrison Act as a precedent, the Marijuana Tax Act was passed in 1937 with no organized opposition.

As with Prohibition, the above account is based on conflict as an interactional process of stigmatization. The passage of the Marijuana Tax Act interrelated a disvalued cultural definition with individual instances of violation as well as an entire apparatus for enforcement. Interactional conflict stresses that rules are not static or without political foundation. In his analysis Becker (1963/73, 129–33) demonstrates that rules pass through a kind of "natural history," rooted in generalized values and eventually moving to a stage of specific enforcement. As a consequence, the normative quality of the rule becomes increasingly situational. Additionally, it may alter the abstract value statements from which it emerged.

Later case studies and theoretical development of deviance-generation as political conflict have followed two paths. First, deviance-generation is viewed as an organizational phenomenon, arising from "criminogenic" value configurations that encourage, even broadly define situations for, widespread corruption (Gross 1978). White-collar and related corporate crime (Douglas and Johnson 1978; Denzin 1978) have increasingly been placed in such an organizational framework. At issue is the manner in which the accomplishment of organizational goals (e.g., maximization of profit) necessitates the situational application or even complete disregard for legal rules.

Second, there are more explicit attempts to combine interactional conflict with selected structural aspects of Marxism. Stephen Hester and Peter Eglin (1992) present an important synthesis for a redirected sociology of crime, combining symbolic interactionism, ethnomethodology, and interpretive-historical accounts of crime construction. Their view is that social conditions (e.g, class relations) may present constraints to actors even as these same constraints are practically created in everyday life (Hester and Eglin 1992, 24).

Ronald Neff (1980) offers a labeling/conflict articulation centering on the importance of rules and their application as the outcome of power struggles, reflective of society's stratification system. His analysis incorporates micro-, intermediate, and macro-levels. Similarly, Austin T. Turk argues that political organization of society hinges on the negotiation of legitimate normative authority and the use of power. In his words, "Political criminality becomes understandable as a socially defined reality, produced by conflict between people who claim to be authorities and people who resist or may resist being their subjects" (Turk 1982, 36).

The foregoing discussion makes clear that interactional conflict has been best utilized in the description of criminal deviance. This theoretical development concentrates on legal rules and their institutionalization in the wider culture, especially examining their interpenetration in everyday life. I now examine the third strand of interactionist deviance theorizing: phenomenology. Its focus is the intersubjective experience of actors and their behavior. Even here, the related elements of rules, enforcers, audiences, and societal reactions point to the broader interactional process of meaning-creation.

Sociological Phenomenology

The strand of sociological phenomenology is best described as "hard reactivism." Proponents of these theories view meaning as radically constructed, in specific social situations, in the consciousness of the individuals.

CHAPTER FOUR

The normative quality of deviance is more fluid and open to negotiation. As Douglas summarizes:

> Phenomenologists are much more concerned with the ways in which individuals construct the meanings of things for themselves and in their own consciousness. They see the social world as ultimately much more individual constructions than do other interactionists, though they certainly see interactionism as fundamentally important. They are much more concerned with the complex forms and problems of meaning construction. (Douglas 1984, 11)

Rules and societal reactions evidence no "objective" character; their negotiated character shifts the focus to actors and their acts. Social interaction is the communicational medium for a kind of intersubjective consciousness, emerging from the shared normative meanings of actors' everyday lives (Douglas 1971, 203–12).

The entire process of deviance as social construction is rendered problematic. The situational quality of rules and reactions turns on unexamined taken-for-granted assumptions about the enduring qualities of social life (ethnomethodology) or on the emotionality of the actor's consciousness and emergent symbol universe (existential sociology). The meanings created by actors may often be at wide variance with those of enforcers or other audiences.

In this created intersubjective reality, the meaning of normative constructions is constantly changing, open to question among the many participants. As Douglas (1971, 139) contends, a phenomenological analysis of norms is fundamentally the study of "rules in use." There is no logical relationship between abstract moral principles (e.g., the sanctity of human life) and the particular normative statements which may be developed to preserve them (e.g., laws prohibiting abortion). Similarly, the simple social existence of rules (legal or informal) does not insure a societal reaction based on probable consensus. In short, normative agreement and reactions to deviance must be described and understood on their own terms, as created, explained, rationalized accomplishments of actors. Downes and Rock offer the following elaboration:

> Social reality appears when people decipher their environment; put forward proposals and interpretations; respond to their own and others'

constructions; modify, accept, or reject what is about them; and thereby build a world for themselves. In this manner, description, describing, and described are much the same. What gives them authenticity and solidity, making them properly social, is recognition and ratification by others. The phenomena of society emerge when they are given public response. (Downes and Rock 1982/98, 215)

Entering the symbolization process by which everyday life, including definitions of deviance, is created constitutes the task of the "phenomenological observer." As embodied in a distinct "methodology," this task is fraught with ambiguity. It involves the observational interrelationships of the natural and theoretic stances (Douglas 1970, 14–16). The natural stance is that perspective utilized by actors in everyday communication. It is framed by countless commonsense assumptions about the nature and quality of human life, social and otherwise. For purposes of daily communication, most of the content of social interaction is uncritically accepted in favor of getting on with the "business at hand."

The theoretic stance is that taken by the phenomenological observer in an effort to problematize the meaning generated by actors in everyday life. As Douglas summarizes the perspective, "To take the theoretic stance toward the everyday world is to stand back from, to reflect upon, to review the experience taken for granted in the natural stance" (Douglas 1970, 15). At its most basic, the assumption of the former stance to the social world requires a recognition of the existence of the latter one. This process of phenomenological doubting places the observer in a position not usually occupied by actors in the everyday world of communication—at least not on a conscious level.

In practice the phenomenological observer describes the process of meaning-generation as faithfully as possible in terms of actors' definitions of their conduct. As a method, then, phenomenological analysis may best be termed introspective, an attempt to recreate the experience of others. Downes and Rock offer the following: "Mind is turned back on itself, examining its own processes and replies to the world" (Downes and Rock 1982/98, 216). Phenomenological introspection represents how the observer "imagines he understands his reactions to his surroundings."

Such a take on the nature of social meaning discounts any privileged, prior existence of an objective normative structure. Instead, norms are continually interpreted by creative actors, responding to particular behavior as well as the communications of audiences. Normative objectivity is reformulated in a radicalized manner, as creation and maintenance of tenuous transsituational acts-of-meaning (Douglas 1970, 31–32). Constructions of deviance are very much tied into the assumption or rejection of stigmatizing identities. That is, societal reaction provides a context for creation of the "deviant" self. In fact, in the natural stance of everyday life, the labeled actor's own symbolizations regarding his conduct are inseparable from the societal reactions to which he responds. According to Douglas, "The same individuals can and do accept 'conflicting' moral rules, yet not experience any conflicts between these different rules because they *apply them to different situations in their lives*. The rules are *situationally meaningful*" [italics in the original] (Douglas 1971, 29).

Transsituational, interactionally derived rules are not absolute pronouncements, but are phenomenologically relevant only when constructed for use in particular instances by actors and evaluated by audiences. The interrelation of rules and acts in the communication of various interpreters constitutes the natural stance. The contribution of sociological phenomenology to an interactionist perspective on deviance-generation is simple but vital: describing the conflict, pluralism, and ambiguity emerging from different meaning layers in the labeling process.

Interactionist literature on social deviance contains prime examples of this contribution. In his monograph *Deviance and Identity*, John Lofland (1969, 39–40) distinguishes two types of deviant acts, defensive and adventurous. Each is contextualized within the actor's situational perceptions and motivations. With the defensive deviant act, the actor is responding to a perceived threat to person or position. Through encapsulation and closure, the actor chooses the deviant act from a range of likely alternatives. The first constrains the actor's temporal-spatial frame of reference, and the second represents the psychosocial process by which deviance becomes an acceptable if not apparently necessary response. "The important factor here is the reflexive relationship of act to actor. The act exists initially as a kind of symbolic potential, depending on the choice of the actor" (Dotter and Roebuck 1988, 25).

The motivations of the adventurous deviant act are excitement, enjoyment, or enchantment. It is an attempt by the actor to enhance or energize the concept of self (e.g., to demonstrate social control or elevate self-esteem). For most actors the adventurous deviant act is an infrequent situational occurrence, often spontaneously enacted from perceived opportunity. As a more common indulgence it is more oriented to transsituational norms and accompanying roles.

Throughout the 1960s and 1970s, the strand of phenomenological sociology (and the related perspectives of ethnomethodology and existential sociology) expanded the understanding of the deviance-generating process. Included were studies on police peacekeeping activities (Bittner 1967); management of gender identity and stigmatization (Garfinkel 1967); the situational meanings of suicide (Douglas 1967); and the general problematics of normative construction (Douglas 1971).

Existential sociology, focusing on the importance of emotions and feelings in human consciousness, seemed especially appropriate to deviant research settings (Douglas and Johnson 1977; Douglas and Rasmussen 1977). Emotions contextualize drives and perceptions of the actor engaged in the world of everyday life. Conflict, even at the individual level, is central to the shaping of the existential self (Douglas and Waksler 1982, 148). Finally, self-knowledge is inescapably absurd or full of contradictions (Lyman and Scott 1970).

While sociological phenomenology focuses on the perceptual/cognitive link of the deviant actor to act, the perspective does not discount the role of societal reaction in the makeup of criminal consciousness. At the same time, such descriptions of crime are grounded in the everyday life experience of the actor's interpretation. Additionally, although largely individual in its consequence, conflict is an important aspect of that interactional interpretation.

I turn now to the final strand of interactionist deviance theorizing. Feminism sheds important conceptual light on the process of deviance creation. Stigmatization based on gender and other biocultural characteristics (e.g., race, age) fundamentally recasts the labeling process from disvalued behavior to entire social categories.

Feminism

Since the 1960s feminist perspectives have gradually penetrated the various social science disciplines. This is not to suggest their inclusion as part of mainstream theoretical discourse, even in sociology. Rather, feminism has faced significant obstacles to development in practically all disciplines, leading to the necessity of a thoroughly interdisciplinary critique

CHAPTER FOUR

of traditional sources of knowledge (Lerner 1976, 1986, 1993).[14] Especially relevant is the theoretical intersection of gender and race (hooks 1992; Collins 1991). The two are subject to disvalued labeling in countless sociocultural contexts. At the same time, the theoretical significance of their overlap has steadily emerged from constructionist views of gender, "multiracial" feminism, and feminist criminology (Russell 1992; Rafter and Heidensohn 1995; Lorber 1998; Mann and Zatz 1998).

It is probably more accurate to speak of "feminisms," a reflection of the term's broad usage (Gelsthorpe and Morris 1990, 1–2; Daly and Chesney-Lind 1988, 536–38). Its referents are legion and interdisciplinary, ranging from philosophy and social movements to literary criticism, psychology, and criminology. Feminism may be defined as a point of view; its focus is to examine how "women experience subordination on the basis of their sex" (Gelsthorpe and Morris 1988, 224). I offer this admittedly simplistic definition, realizing it does not cover all instances of academic or everyday application.

As might be expected, the reception of feminist perspectives within the traditional interactionist crime/deviance paradigm has been slow to develop (Millman 1975). Despite early labeling's critiques of objectivism, its proponents demonstrated no theoretical sensitivity for the importance of gender as a social construction. Ngaire Naffine characterizes Becker as "the great white *male* hunter whose romantic flirtation with deviant culture had much to do with his own style of masculinity. He described the male-dominated world of the jazz scene, which he could slide into precisely because he was a man" [*italics* in the original] (Naffine 1996, 41).

Later criticisms have identified this gender blindness in criminology as well (Daly and Chesney-Lind 1988; Messerschmidt 1993; Leonard 1995; Klein 1995a, 1995b, 1995c). Traditional perspectives on crime (again, including interactionism) have failed to appreciate the connection between ideological portrayals of women and their consequent subordination in academic discourse, what has been called "malestream criminology" (Scraton 1990; Smart 1995).

Naffine outlines the intellectual costs of gender blindness to the practice of traditional criminology:

> The costs to criminology of its failure to deal with feminist scholarship are perhaps more severe than they would be in any other discipline. The

reason is that the most consistent and prominent fact about crime is the sex of the offender. As a rule, crime is something men do, not women, so the denial of the gender question—and the dismissal of feminists who wish to tease it out—seems particularly perverse. (Naffine 1996, 5–6)

The gender blindness of deviance/criminological perspectives is both conceptual and empirical. Regarding the former, since symbolic constructions of masculinity have normally been ignored in describing the context of disvalued behavior, the patriarchal context of theorizing has undergone little challenge. Relating to empirical issues, the unquestioned predominance of male participation in serious crime and deviance (as found in official rates and statistics) has served to isolate the female experience. Female criminals become "the aberrant group even when compared with an aberrant group" (Naffine 1996, 8).

Impeding the development of a feminist criminology have been the numerous "controlling images" of women in criminal justice (Rafter and Stanko 1982, 2–3). These stereotypical portrayals (primarily based on assumptions about women in general) dominate traditional criminological literature and have done much to sabotage meaningful, gender-sensitive theoretical discourse. Included among these images are "woman as the pawn of biology," "woman as passive and weak," "woman as impulsive and nonanalytic," "woman as impressionable and in need of protection," "the active woman as masculine," and "the criminal woman as purely evil." Each of these images derives from the minority status of women in society (Rafter and Stanko 1982, 4–6).

Emerging feminist approaches are theoretical counterweights to traditional, entrenched male-dominated explanations of crime (Howe 1990; Daly and Maher 1998a). In shifting and refining the gender focus, feminist perspectives broaden the criminological enterprise to include related issues such as race in novel ways. As mentioned above, feminist scholarship represents a vital, evolving terrain, drawing on many traditions and disciplines. Its application to the study of crime and deviance arguably represents the most significant theoretical advance of the last two decades, although along a slow and sometimes uncertain path (Carrington 1998).

The theoretical relationship between gender and race in the study of stigmatization is complex and often contradictory. In a feminist constructionist view, the two cannot be separated, but are instead mutually

CHAPTER FOUR

reinforcing stigmatization processes. As Naffine (1996, 54) notes: "[W]e all have a colour which affects our lives in different ways, depending on whether our racial group is associated with privilege or disadvantage. To fail to see this is to reinstate the white woman's assumption that the problem for women is always firstly one of gender, never one of race; that race somehow comes afterward as simply another layer of disadvantage and so is not always an integral dimension of experience."

Marjorie S. Zatz and Coramae Richey Mann, writing more from the viewpoint of ethnicity, come to a similar conclusion. Failure to recognize the intersection of gender and race "has been the bane of the women's movement and of movements based on ethnicity" (Zatz and Mann 1998, 6). In short, both identities are cultural representations with broad implications of stigma and discredit for those so identified (Daly and Stephens 1995).

The voices of feminism, combined with those theorizing the significance of race, remain ill at ease with traditional white androcentric (i.e. male-centered) theorizing (Russell 1992); additionally, they run counter to an objectivist, scientific epistemology. For the latter reason, feminist theorizing on deviance/crime may be generally characterized as constructionist (Lorber 1998, 160–61). As such, I will argue momentarily that the social production of gender has much in common with and can be extended to include other important biocultural categories like race and age. The many "feminisms" represent a significant bridge from interactionism to the emerging terrain of cultural studies (Carrington 1998). As Farganis (1994b, 2) makes clear, "Any analyses of feminist theory or of the subjects of which it writes must walk a tightrope between the generalizing that tries to capture the zeitgeist, or spirit of the times, and the particularizing of events that directs attention to a specific cast of characters."

An interactionist feminism focuses on the cluster of meanings given to the biocultural category of gender. The category is overlaid with a variety of normative constellations that contextualize the behavior of women, always in relation to men. Gender exists as an individual characteristic and a social category. As an individual characteristic, its biological basis is rooted in commonsense understanding and is generally *assumed* to be deterministic in some fundamental, if unspecified, way. As a cultural construction, gender constitutes a social category, the concern of interactionist feminism. As R. W. Connell argues:

> When biological determinism is abandoned, gender is still usually seen in terms of socially produced individual character. It is a considerable leap to think of gender as being also a property of collectivities, institutions, and historical processes. . . . There are gender phenomena of major importance which simply cannot be grasped as properties of individuals, however much properties of individuals are implicated in them. (Connell 1987, 139)

Gender as a socially constructed category (Lorber 1998, 160–61; West and Zimmerman 1998), overlaid with discriminatory normative valuations, is thus fundamental to the process of deviance definition. It is a "linking concept," a process rather than a determining characteristic. Gender connects individual characteristics with joint actions of people in the process of meaning production (Connell 1987, 140).

We may extend this interactionist conception of gender-as-process to the understanding of two other important biocultural categories, age and race. As with gender, each of these is interpenetrated with unexamined normative assumptions. These assumptions, reflected in language and everyday usage of the terms, serve to differentiate ethnic groups or young from old. The outcomes of situated joint action (i.e., social process), age, race, and gender are each laden with symbolism, the purpose of which is to establish "natural" (i.e., biological) divisions within each category. For example, gender is routinely divided as male/female. As such, its commonsense understanding renders it the most deterministic of the three. In a more complex fashion, race is separated into a larger number of divisions: black, white, Hispanic, even "other." For almost four hundred years of American culture, the primary designations have been black and white. However, everyday constructions of race allow for greater variety and interpretation than do those for gender. Similarly, age is given meaning through a multiplicity of designations: "adolescence," "middle-age," "elderly," and so on. As a process of definition, these designations symbolically organize people (perhaps otherwise very dissimilar) into identifiable statuses.

The primary interactional difference between age, race, and gender lies in the mutability of the categories. Gender and race are generally viewed as lifelong designations; age is constructed as a natural biological progression from infancy to death. Age is easily socially determined and tracked (though often disguised); gender assignment may be somewhat more problematic; race even more so.

CHAPTER FOUR

Feminist criminology in recent years has begun to elaborate the relationship between race, gender, and societal reaction to the female criminal (Rafter 1990; Daly and Stephens 1995; Daly and Maher 1998b). The social creation of female criminality must be examined within the historical patriarchal context in which it arose. Race as a similarly devalued status is an integral part of that context. On a conceptual level, male domination was historically institutionalized through the "invention of hierarchy" (Lerner 1990, 108). Gender difference as deviance and domination was accompanied by a similar pattern of racial oppression.

In the latter historical instance, under U.S. slavery black women were exploited for manual labor (as were their male counterparts) as well as sexual and reproductive services (i.e., their children became a marketable commodity). Race, then, as a deviant status was and is interrelated with gender. As such, race and gender are part of a single "invention of hierarchy" in which ascribed, devalued status leads to differential treatment of the labeled and an institutionalized structure of domination. Thus, gender and race as deviant social categories have historically been inseparable (Lerner 1990, 110–11).

Age, on the other hand, is routinely incorporated in studies of crime and deviance (Schur 1973). Feminist theory has preliminarily begun to interweave conceptions of gender, race, and age (as well as class) into a more integrated constructionist description (Daly and Maher 1998a; Carrington 1998; Barak et al. 2001). As James Messerschmidt cogently argues:

> Marginalized, racial minority boys—as with white, middle-, and working class boys—produce specific configurations of behavior that can be seen by others within the same immediate social situation as "essentially male." As we have seen, these different masculinities emerge from practices that encompass different resources and are simultaneously based on different collective trajectories. (Messerschmidt 1993, 117)

Defining as deviant or criminal the actions of young men, especially young black men, has become the institutional preoccupation of the American criminal justice system (Donziger 1996). At the same time, the contemporary development of black and white youth subcultures seemingly committed to deviance, and increasingly, criminal conduct, suggests that deviance-labeling based on age, race, and gender is a complex process

(Gilbert 1986; Rose 1994). The historical blindness to gender, race, and even age constructions continues today, but less so than in earlier decades. Within mainstream deviance-theorizing, interactionism has been more amenable than most perspectives to "feminization," given its constructionist stance. Schur's (1984) monograph *Labeling Women Deviant* examines gender stigmatization (i.e., disvaluement) as a categorical sociocultural process. In his words:

> The stigmatized person is reacted to primarily as "an instance" of the [stigmatized] category. At the extreme, he or she is viewed as having no other noteworthy status or identity. When that point is reached a person becomes—in the eyes of others, for all practical purposes—*nothing but* "a delinquent," "a cripple," "a homosexual," "a black," "a woman." [*italics* in the original] (Schur 1984, 30)

The stigmatizing devaluation of gender or race subsumes all differences among the behavior of individuals, objectified within created symbolic categories (hooks 1992). Unlike Becker's (1963/73) original usage of the term master status (i.e., an overall devaluation of self or character based on labeled deviant behavior), gender stigmatization is much more transsituational and permanent. The labeled self is "engulfed" (Schur 1971) in a discredited sociocultural stereotype.

The same categorical stigmatization applies to societal reactions based on age. However, it varies in nature and quality, depending particularly on normative overlay. For example, adolescents and their activities constitute the primary object of deviance-labeling by older audiences (Dotter 1987, 1994). Simultaneously, individual characteristics are abstracted into a collectively disvalued lifestyle and stereotypically taken as evidence of personal disregard for everyday "norms in use" (Douglas 1971). As with gender and race, assignment to a specific disvalued social category constitutes master status, based on who the labeled *are* (personally and categorically discredited) and not necessarily on what they may have *done* (Goffman 1963b). In short, existential absurdity and meaning conflict surround the social creation of biocultural categories as stigmatized master statuses.

Labeling based on the problematic designations of age, race, and gender compounds the ambiguity of social definition in those instances involving specific allegations of deviance. The creation and application of

CHAPTER FOUR

such categorical normative constellations permeates the labeling experience for women, racial minorities, and youth. That is, specific rules maintaining age, race, or gender differences interpenetrate the general labeling process, increasing ambiguity and confusion of meaning. As Schur observes with respect to gender norms:

> While these norms sometimes may be buttressed by formal definitions and procedures (as in the psychiatric diagnosis and legal rulings) they operate for the most part on a level of informal interaction. Yet their pervasiveness and their continuous application to women, in various combinations, more than make up for whatever they may lack in formality. Compounding this widespread vulnerability to deviance-defining is the fact that women are often subjected to norms that contradict one another. As a consequence their efforts to conform to one standard may be treated as deviance when viewed from the standpoint of the opposing one. (Schur 1984, 51)

This normative ambiguity and conflict is illustrated in the area of sexual behavior and expressiveness of women. The problematic of societal reactions toward rape exposes the cultural schizophrenia of women-as-sex-objects. Normative expectations are that a "good" woman must be chaste, but not unapproachable. Furthermore, she must not be "overly assertive" in communicating her desires. Meanings of rape emerge from this hazy amalgam of gender norms: A woman of unchaste reputation is granted little empathy as a rape victim; overly aggressive women who claim rape risk not only personal reputation, but a charge (often within the law) of false accusation of sexual assault. As Susan Brownmiller explains:

> Male fear of the false rape charge brought by a lying woman—the old syndrome of Potiphar's wife—is written into the rape laws of various states in the form of special rules of evidence that are conspicuously absent from evidentiary rules governing other kinds of violent crime. Unless these rules of evidence can be met, a prosecutor cannot bring a case into court, even though he knows, the victim knows, and the rapist knows that a crime has been committed. (Brownmiller 1975, 370)

Normative definitions and societal reactions regarding sexual behavior of minorities and youth are similarly convoluted. Adolescents, especially black adolescents, are stereotyped (through the norms of a mainstream culture created by white adults) as oversexed and irresponsible actors—unable or unwilling to exercise even a modicum of control over carnal impulse. While laws technically protect particularly the young female from statutory rape, the recent passage of specialized sexual predator statutes reflects the fractured view of sexuality in both popular and legal culture. As with adult women, statutes designed to shield younger females may result in conflicts not dissimilar to those found in adult rape trials. Similarly, female delinquents have historically been incarcerated at higher rates than males—presumably a reflection of cultural norms protecting their innocence and "purity."

There are five categories of gender norms which overlay the process of deviance-defining for women (i.e., constellations of rules that do not apply to men): 1) presentation of self (e.g., emotions, nonverbal communication, and appearance); 2) marriage/maternity (e.g., any number of nonmarried statuses, sexual promiscuity, or voluntary childlessness); 3) sexuality (again promiscuous behavior or general sexual orientation); 4) occupational choice (e.g., pursuit of traditionally "male" careers); and 5) generalized "deviance norms" relating inappropriate acts for women, but not men (e.g., women who engage in acts of predatory violence such as homicide or armed robbery) (Schur 1984, 52–53). All but the fourth may be extended to social situations involving racial minorities and youth.

The context of these "categorical normative constellations" and their enforcement serve to circumscribe the actor in an ideological justification. In fact, regarding all forms of biocultural disvaluement, labeling as master status may be termed "inferiorization" (Schur 1984, 23). That is, if women, ethnic minorities, or adolescents are simply objects, examples of a stereotypically deserving fate, audiences tend to be indiscriminate in their reactions. Individual differences between actors are largely ignored or perhaps utilized as justification for further inferiorization. Societal reactions are linked to norms in a self-perpetuating construction of person-as-stigma.

My discussion has centered on a constructionist approach to gender and related biocultural categories. While the feminist strand of interactionist deviance-theorizing is the least developed of the four, it holds the brightest future for articulation (Daly and Maher 1998a, 1998b; Carrington 1998). Its interdisciplinary development has incorporated images of race stigmatization and may be extended to include other disvalued statuses engaged in the conflict of identity politics. Consequently, I view this strand as an indispensable bridge between interactionist perspectives and the developing cultural studies narratives. The present excursion has sought only to place feminism in the context of the interactional process of meaning-creation. Having discussed each contributing strand, I now summarize this process and its components.

Creating Deviance: The Process of Social Definition

Elements of the Process

The process of deviance-generation consists of five interrelated elements, emphasized to varying degrees in the interactionist theoretical strands. These are actor, act, rules, audiences, and societal reactions. The process, describing social deviance as meaning-creation, is not characterized by antecedent causal factors; instead, the various layers of normative definition and societal reaction, relating acts, persons, and social categories, constitute the focus. Following Blumer (1969), the process of deviance definition represents a joint action or, more appropriately, articulated joint actions. In his words:

> Such articulation of lines of action gives rise to and constitutes "joint action"—a societal organization of conduct of different acts of diverse participants. A joint action, while made up of diverse component acts that enter into its formation, is different from any one of them and from their mere aggregation. The joint action has a distinctive character in its own right, a character that lies in the articulation or linkage as apart from what may be articulated or linked. Thus the joint action may be identified as such and may be spoken of and handled without having to break it down into the separate acts that comprise it. (Blumer 1969, 17)

Rooted in social interaction, then, the joint action assumes a symbolic, transsituational character. This character must always be contextualized from the points of view of particular actors. Blumer (1969, 56) makes clear the interpretive importance of the actor (i.e., the "acting unit"): "The acting unit is lifted out of the position of being a neutral medium for the play of determining factors and is given the status of an active organizer of its action." The participants in the deviance-generation process are pragmatic, creative actors, and the meaning that emerges may be viewed as a kind of natural problematic of social interaction. It is the various participants (i.e., actor, and audiences), interlinking their actions, who create definitions of deviance both in specific situations and with respect to entire social categories.

Actor and Act

Matza (1964) paints a telling portrait of the creative delinquent actor as neither completely constrained by social milieu nor totally free to initiate individual conduct, terming the conditions to act as "soft determinism." This interactional view of "drift" may be extended from the delinquent to the deviant actor. It is the potential of the actor to create meaning (i.e., to interpret norms) that provides the links to other actors in the process. In Matza's words:

> The image of the delinquent [actor] I wish to convey is one of drift, an actor neither compelled nor committed to deeds nor freely choosing them; neither different in any simple or fundamental sense from the law abiding, nor the same; conforming to certain traditions in American life while partially unreceptive to other more conventional traditions; and finally, an actor whose motivational system may be explored along lines explicitly commended by classical criminology—his peculiar relation to legal institutions. (Matza 1964, 28)

The act is dialogic, "addressed to other and self simultaneously and answered by self and other as well" (Perinbanayagam 2000, 7).

While "harder" versions of determinism stress the actor as object of social forces, this constructionist view lays bare the *relation* of the actor to the many others in the deviance-generation process. An actor fits her own meaningful actions (not always without perhaps great difficulty) in with those of audiences. This relation, of course, is based on interpretations of rules by all participants (Perinbanayagam 1985, 20–22). Norms situate actors with respect to one another's actions and positions. In the process the problematic norms are negotiated, *often well beyond the original act in question.*

Rules as Relations: Participants in the Societal Reaction Process

Audiences, interlinked with the initiating actor, are crucial to the development of the stigmatized label. No act is inherently disvalued. Rather,

CHAPTER FOUR

the nature and quality of societal reaction depends on the interpretations of audiences, either specific or general. As Goode points out:

> It is the *audience* who determines whether something or someone is deviant; no audience, no labeling, therefore, no deviance. However, an audience need not *directly* view an act, condition, or person; audiences can witness behavior or conditions "indirectly," that is, they can hear or be told about someone's behavior or condition, or they can simply have a negative or condemnatory attitude toward a class or category of behavior. [*italics* in the original] (Goode 2001, 114)

The interrelation of actors and other participants, mediated by normative constructions, thus leads to the relative possibility or probability of the societal reactions. These reactions may be to specific instances of deviance, or to stigmatized conditions associated with the actor, abstract categories of persons, or sociocultural situations. The nature and the quality of the label depends fundamentally on participation of the audiences. As Erikson observes:

> Deviance is not a property *inherent in* certain forms of behavior; it is a property *conferred upon* these forms by the audience which directly or indirectly witness them. The critical variable in the study of deviance, then, is the social audience rather than the individual actor, since it is the audience which eventually determines whether or not any episode of behavior or any class of episodes is labeled deviant. [*italics* in the original] (Erikson 1964, 11)

There are several types of audiences, symbolic and otherwise, that may offer societal reactions (Schur 1971, 12–13). Society-at-large is an audience in two senses. First, when a deviant episode is given widespread national or international media coverage, the entire society may effectively be called to witness in the process of meaning-creation; second, when the evaluation of meaning is abstracted to categories of persons or behavior beyond the context of a single or related episodes, the label may be applied as a collective one. The society-at-large audience rarely if ever participates directly in the labeling process. In fact, the existence of this audience is primarily an outcome of the circulation of meaning relative to earlier multiple instances of deviance-defining.

A second type of audience is those persons with whom the actor has daily, routine social contact (including significant others such as friends, loved ones, coworkers, and so on, as well as strangers in contact with the initiating actor). This audience is likely to witness given acts engaged in by the "drifting" actor. Significant others need not necessarily have direct knowledge of every episode in order to have an informal but direct social-psychological impact on the actor. Their reaction is obviously tied in very closely with the actor's own self-concept and definition of the situation. In this regard, potential partners in the initiating actor's enterprise, or those who are known to him as having committed similar acts, constitute an important source of supportive meaning.

A third type of audience is official and organizational control agents, so-called "moral entrepreneurs." Becker (1963/73, 147–63) distinguishes between two types of moral entrepreneurs: rule creators and rule enforcers. Rule creators include political/legislative bodies charged with official rule-making activities as well as community and national groups unofficially involved in the sociopolitical process of deviance-generation. The creation of rules is a multifaceted activity carried out by elected and appointed governmental officials as well as moral crusaders. It involves legal as well as nonlegal forms of rule-making.

As my earlier examples of interactional conflict in rule construction suggest, legal and other forms are not isolated normative processes, but are bound in the overall sociocultural context of meaning-creation. Rule creation represents multiple, complicated, and interlinked webs of joint action. This politics of rule-making is not inherently democratic, but does generally include the participation of divergent groups with agendas that must somehow be reconciled. For example, the passage or modification of criminal law emerges from the politically legitimate legislative body. At the same time, there are countless groups of "moral crusaders" attempting to influence the official process. Becker points out that the latter is not simply a "meddling busybody," intent on controlling the behavior of others: "The crusader is not only interested in seeing to it that other people do what he thinks is right. He believes if they do what is right it will be good for them. Or he may feel that his reform will prevent certain kinds of exploitation of one person by another" (Becker 1963/73, 148).

Rule enforcers are those audiences charged with ensuring normative compliance. For Becker, the most important enforcers are the police, although in any given situation there are others as well. These include formal criminal justice and related support participants (e.g., judges, lawyers, physicians, and other experts) as well as informal agents. With respect to the latter, enforcers may in fact also be significant others for the actor.

There is a fluid relationship between enforcers and creators, as Becker points out: "With the establishment of organizations of rule enforcers, the crusade becomes institutionalized. What started out as a drive to convince the world of the moral necessity of a new rule finally becomes an organization devoted to the enforcement of the rule." (Becker 1963/73, 155–56). In short, the activities of moral entrepreneurs, creators and enforcers, are found in the normative interface connecting constructions of deviance and crime.

Goode and Ben-Yehuda aptly describe the constructions of meaning by this audience:

> Rule creators and rule enforcers should not be thought of as isolated individuals acting on their own, however. It must be emphasized that they tend to create and enforce rules and laws, either directly or indirectly, as representatives of specific categories, factions, or groups in society. Their efforts will be endorsed or supported by members of these categories *to the extent that* they reflect their sentiments, views, or interests. [*italics* in the original] (Goode and Ben-Yehuda 1994, 81)

Through the activities of creators and enforcers, then, the potential for societal reactions, formal and informal, remains dynamic. Similarly, the relational character of norms transcends the individual situation of labeling to include the symbolic audience of society-at-large.

Societal Reactions as Stigma Contests

While not necessarily unpredictable in outcome, societal reaction is best described as problematic. The joint action of actors and audiences, mediated by norm negotiation, is a layered, relative process. By layered, I mean there is no direct linear relationship among the elements leading to any particular outcome. Meaning emerges from an intermixture of elements. Relativity (Goode 2001, 114) implies that at any moment in the process of deviance-creation, participants, their acts, and the interconnecting normative context may lead to likely reactions. Furthermore, at some later time, the juxtaposition of these elements may result in similar or even quite different meaning-constructions or labels. Thus meaning is highly fluid, an outcome of interactional communication.

Compared with the objectivist approach's catalogue of causal explanations for deviance, interactionism focuses on a description of the process of stigmatization. As Goode and Ben-Yehuda state:

> Our view is that the relativistic, subjectively problematic perspective is far more fruitful in helping us to understand reality than is the objectively given approach. We take *evaluations* of behavior as our point of departure. In doing so, we insist on two points: one, that the subjectively problematic dimension is worthy of study in its own right; and two, that it is impossible to predict the subjective dimension from the objective. [*italics* in the original] (Goode and Ben-Yehuda 1994, 68)

Labels relate, often simultaneously, to individuals, social categories, or abstracted sociocultural situations. The context of their creation and enforcement through joint action produces collective rule-making, interpersonal reactions, or organizational processing (Schur 1971, 11).

The creation of deviance is a natural phenomenon. That is, definitions of stigma and their application arise from the same process as those of conformity. In fact, the relativity and interpenetration of the two characterize sociocultural change. In this wider arena, the deviance-generating process becomes a series of politicized "stigma contests." As Schur observes, "When people engage in organized political activity on deviance issues they are, in fact, intentionally attempting to influence what might otherwise seem an irreversible course of events. They are trying to ensure that a particular balance of power will tip in their favor" (Schur 1980, 8). Such contests represent ongoing cultural struggles to define right and wrong, the nature of a "good" society, as well as its critique.

The study of deviance as meaning-creation and social change represents a significant shift of perspective. As Schur elsewhere observes:

> The attribution of deviantness cuts across the enormous substantive variability of deviant situations. The defining and reacting process through which this attribution occurs is always present regardless of the particular type of behavior involved and whatever individual causes may have precipitated specific instances of that behavior. (Schur 1979, 8)

CHAPTER FOUR

The creation of deviance, its relationship to conformity, and its implications for social change are a unique contribution of interactionist theorizing. Ultimately the layered meaning process interweaves sociocultural definitions with those of self-identity.

Creating Deviance: The Intersection of Self and Culture

The social process by which deviance is rendered meaningful mirrors the interactional conception of self elaborated in chapter 3. The self, according to Mead and Blumer, emerges through social interaction and interpretation. Similarly, deviance as stigma represents the figurative instance of spoiled identity (Goffman 1963b), proceeding from the individual label to the "inferiorization" (Schur 1984, 23) of collective experience, from specific behavior to historical interpretation of circumstance (Goode and Ben-Yehuda 1994, 41–42).

The interactional nature of deviance-creation suggests that meanings of stigma are layered and reciprocally bound: from the individual event, to categorical, more abstract "deviance norms" (Schur 1984), and finally to normative constellations giving context to disvalued master status. Stereotyping of behavior, individuals, and groups constitutes the interactional flow of this layering (Goode and Ben-Yehuda 1994, 72). Furthermore, layering of meaning expands the scope of labeling to include the distinction between "situational" and "societal" deviance (Plummer 1979). Both represent deviance, the meaning context of which moves from the concrete to transsituational.[15]

"Societal" deviance is comprised of widely censured classes or categories of behavior (i.e., robbery, homosexuality, alcoholism). Conversely, "situational" deviance refers to stigmatization of persons and behavior in specific instances. Labeling is applied to given situations, even as it is abstracted beyond them. Generally accepted definitions of disvaluement are not always applied (Goode and Ben-Yehuda 1994, 71). Deviance as master status exhibits meaning on multiple levels.

Some of the most important scholarship regarding deviance creation examines the flow of meaning from one context to another. For example, in *The Construction of Homosexuality*, David F. Greenberg goes well beyond the interactionist viewpoint of "norms in use" (Douglas 1971) to incorporate an ideological component in the labeling of homosexuality: "Ideology grows out of lived experience and is thus itself a social product" (Greenberg 1988, 498). Individual instances of sexual deviance are labeled and punished, however sporadically, as unnatural and immoral. At the same time, contemporary normative definitions of heterosexuality are blind to the historical context of sexuality as commoditized self (Schur 1988).

Similarly, Norman K. Denzin's (1987/93, 362) interactionist portrait of alcoholism and recovery is based on his concept of the alcoholic self: "Narcissistic and self-centered, the alcoholic self uses alcohol as a mirror, seeking in the self-reflections that alcohol offers a truer picture of itself." However, he makes the following observation regarding the sociocultural symbol of alcoholic deviance: "The alcoholic signals a doubt about the inner, felt truth of the culture and its times. By living that doubt into existence . . . the alcoholic becomes the symbolic representation of every modern individual who also has doubts about the meaning of modern existence."

Increasingly, the social creation of deviance assumes the symbolic character of master status. At the same time, the deviant symbol is removed from its original interactional context and transmuted into an image for entertainment and information in the mass media. This latter transformation, grounded in media culture, marks a cultural studies approach to postmodern meaning generation. Chapter 5 presents a detailed reading of cultural studies literature, especially its links to labeling in the British variant and later poststructuralist readings.

Notes

1. In the sixth edition of his text on deviance, Goode (2001, 24–28) elaborates the objectivist/constructionist categorization to include the "fruitful" normative and reactive definitions. Alex Thio (2004) offers a similar distinction, grouping perspectives into the positivist and constructionist categories.

2. Goffman describes the metaphorical character of stigma in history and its relationship to contemporary conceptions:

> The Greeks, who were apparently strong on visual aids, originated the term *stigma* to refer to bodily signs designed to expose something unusual and bad about the moral status of the signifier. The signs were cut or burnt into the body and advertised that the bearer was a slave, a criminal, or a traitor—a blemished person, ritually polluted, to be avoided, especially in public places. Later, in Christian times, two layers of

CHAPTER FOUR

metaphor were added to the term: the first referred to bodily signs of holy grace that took the form of eruptive blossoms on the skin; the second, a medical allusion to this religious allusion, referred to bodily signs of physical disorder. Today the term is widely used in something like the original literal sense, but it is applied more to the disgrace itself than to the bodily evidence of it. Furthermore, shifts have occurred in the kinds of disgrace that arouse concern. [*italics* in the original] (Goffman 1963b, 1–2)

3. Ericksen (1980) offers a thorough critique of Goffman's use of dramaturgical metaphor.

4. Edward Sagarin defines marginality as "outside the pale of the culture but not condemned by others." He lists certain ethnic subcultures such as the Amish and occupational groups like jazz musicians by way of example. Furthermore, he argues that "they are outsiders who are more self-segregated than pushed out of society, and who are seen by others as different rather than evil" (Sagarin 1975, 34). Sagarin's position—that marginality is not deviant—seems rather contrived. Differentness implies some measure of social disvalue, even if not extending to the label of evil. In his work on deviant societies (e.g., dwarfs, homosexuals, mental patients), Sagarin (1969) recognizes the complexity of differentness, marginality, and deviance.

5. Hester and Eglin (1992) present a similar interpretation in their critical analysis of the sociology of crime. Their argument is originally framed as the difference between social problems and sociological ones. Social problems are politically and morally defined (Spector and Kitsuse 1987; Best 1989; Ibarra and Kitsuse 1993; Miller 1993; Miller and Holstein 1993), while sociological ones motivate theoretical inquiry. Other sources provide detailed summaries and critiques of objectivist theoretical development and its combination of moralist and scientific rhetoric (Rubington and Weinberg 1995; Davis 1975; Davis and Stasz 1990).

6. Becker (1963/73, 165–76) cogently summarizes the theoretical and accompanying methodological problems in the study of social deviance. Of particular significance are the moral questions that emerge for the researcher. Regarding the latter, Laud Humphreys, in reviewing considerations due to unknowing subjects, calls for "the need for each of us to make frequent ethical self-examinations—and this applies to research as well as business and politics" (Humphreys 1970/75, 231).

7. William Chambliss (1985) and Richard Quinney (1970, 1977) articulate a Marxist argument on the role of law in crime creation, especially the activities of the state as a control agent.

8. I do not include Goffman's dramaturgy in my synthesis as it lies outside the pragmatic development of symbolic interactionism, as pointed out in chapter 3. His (Goffman 1963b) conceptual elaboration of stigma is central to the deviance-

creation process, much closer to Blumer's (1969) take on meaning as emerging through joint action. Furthermore, Goffman's (1959) theatrical metaphor restricts meaning-generation to face-to-face encounters (Blumer 1972).

9. Goode (1981, 50) views Becker and Chicago School labeling as representative of "soft reactivism," a middle ground between traditional normative approaches which reify norms as systems and the "hard reactivism" of ethnomethodologists.

10. Edward Sagarin (1975, 24–33) distinguishes between definitions of crime and deviance. Of central importance is their overlapping character.

11. Bulmer (1984) provides an analysis of the importance of empirical research at the University of Chicago, especially during the 1920s. Kurtz (1984, 60–83) concisely summarizes Chicago School research into five categories: urban and community studies, public opinion and communications, race and ethnic studies, crime and deviance, and political sociology.

12. Everett C. Hughes (1958) provides an analysis of the term as it relates to traditional occupational activity.

13. The theoretical development of differential association as a product of the Chicago School is evident. Edwin Sutherland received his doctorate from the University of Chicago in 1913 and was influenced by W. I. Thomas, Robert Park, and Ernest Burgess, among others (Kurtz 1984, 76–77).

14. For a comprehensive review of the multiple voices of feminist theoretical development, see the following works regarding general statements: Josephine Donovan (1985/96) offers a succinct summary, including feminism's confrontations with Marxism, Freudianism, and existentialism; Nancy Hartsock (1987) synthesizes a feminist historical materialism. Sondra Farganis (1994b) examines the part played by historical forces in the development of feminist theory and practice.

15. Douglas (1971, 173–226) offers a phenomenologically informed discussion of situational/transsituational meaning construction.

CHAPTER FIVE
TOWARD A POSTMODERN CULTURAL STUDIES: MEANING CREATION IN MEDIA CULTURE

In recent years sociology and related academic disciplines have been marked by the intersection of postmodern social theory and a cultural studies approach to meaning-generation.[1] The two are often considered to be synonymous, leading to much debate over terms, emphases, and perspectives. Furthermore, a postmodern cultural studies has distinct, if inconsistent, connections with mainstream sociological theory, most evident in its convergences with interactionism (Becker and McCall 1990; Denzin 1992).

Cultural studies is not a single perspective or method, but a generalized critique of sociocultural processes of symbolization. According to Michal McCall and Howard S. Becker (1990, 4), the field represents the "classically humanistic disciplines which have lately come to use their philosophical, literary, and historical approaches to study the social construction of meaning." The roots of the field are interdisciplinary (Grossberg, Nelson, and Treichler 1992), with particular focus on gender, race, age, and class issues. The emergence of postmodern social theory, often conflated into a poststructuralist critique of language and communication, is equally convoluted. Overlapping with the above cultural studies characterization, its major concerns center on the development of media culture and its commoditization in late-twentieth-century capitalism (Denzin 1991c; Kellner 1995; Best and Kellner 1997).[2]

The aim of this chapter is to outline a postmodern cultural studies approach to meaning-creation. Specifically, I address three interrelated issues. First, I present a number of cultural studies definitional concerns, including its postmodernist and poststructuralist turns. Second, I briefly examine the field's history. Its development is roughly divided into four interrelated phases: the Frankfurt School, British cultural studies, the American tradition, and feminist voices. Finally, from these foundations I detail a postmodern cultural studies with several interconnected foci: the importance of the "postmodern condition" (Lyotard 1979/84); the centrality of ideological discourse in the creation of cultural meaning (Foucault 1970/94, 1972a, 1983); the expression of that meaning in a multiplicity of social texts (Derrida 1967/73, 1967/76, 1967/78); and the transformation of postmodern culture through creation and consumption of media images (Baudrillard 1968/96, 1970/98, 1981/94, 1988b, 1988c, 1996; Best 1994; Gottdiener 1994; Kellner 1994; Stevenson 2002). The postmodern condition marks a contemporary crisis of meaning (Eagleton 2000), the textual erosion of experience boundaries (Debord 1967/94; Denzin 1995; Kellner 2003b). Media culture gradually circumscribes communication processes at all levels of society.

Cultural Studies, Postmodernism, and Poststructuralism

An Interdisciplinary Approach to Problems of Meaning

In its broadest sense cultural studies may be described as an interdisciplinary project concerned with the problematics of cultural meaning production. Throughout its academic emergence, debates and disagreements over terminology, focus, and method have abounded.[3] The controversial, fluid reality of cultural studies is captured in the use of the term "project" as both verb and noun. The field is ever emerging, constantly shifting. It awaits portrayal in the present, on the page and screen, in music, film, and literature, projected from individual experience and opposing it.

In focusing on its objects of study, Richard Johnson asks the following question: "What is cultural studies *about*?" [*italics* in the original] (Johnson 1986/87, 43–44). His answer interrelates consciousness and subjectivity, "the historical forms of consciousness or subjectivity, or the subjective forms we live by, or, in a rather perilous compression, perhaps a reduction, the subjective side of social relations." Further, and more important, Johnson offers the basic structuralist claim "that subjectivities are produced, not given, and are therefore the objects of inquiry, not the premises or starting points."

The interweaving of consciousness and subjectivity is a sociocultural process characterized by the production, use, and transformation of cultural knowledge forms by active, interpreting subjects. As I shall argue momentarily, this process is by nature "ideologized," unconsciously engaged in by the actor who manipulates cultural objects (i.e., material and nonmaterial) as if such objects exist outside of this reflexive process (Barthes 1957/72; Althusser 1969/96, 1971; Hebdige 1979/2002). Culture and individual are inextricably bound in a textual process of communication (Carey 1989). The place of culture in such a process is multifaceted, resistant to dichotomizing or other simplifications. At the same time culture exists only through and within the experience of interacting individuals.

As an integral part of the process of communication, culture and its analysis is considerably expanded to include not only its myriad forms, but a general critique of its dominant themes and practices. Thus cultural studies may examine both "high" forms and popular mass-produced and -consumed ones. Additionally, cultural enterprises such as science or religion are self-consciously exposed as institutional spheres for the ideological control of social life (Johnson 1986/87; Agger 1992). Especially important is the social creation of status categories based on gender (Smith 1989; Nicholson 1990a; Curti 1992; Ingraham 1994; Alway 1995), age (Hall and Jefferson 1975/2002b; Willis 1978; Hebdige 1979/2002), and race (Collins 1991; hooks 1992; Wallace 1992; West 1992; Goldberg 1997; Winant 2001). The practice of cultural studies as critique is increasingly concerned with how best to describe the process of meaning-generation in postmodern society.

The historical construction of cultural studies itself mirrors the meaning ambiguity which is its subject. Much traditional critique of the field focuses on its lack of central theoretical vision or method. As an emergent interdisciplinary project, cultural studies resists rigid organization or classification.[4] According to Stuart Hall:

> Cultural studies is a discursive formation, in Foucault's sense. It has no simple origins, though some of us were present at some point when it first named itself in that way. . . . It is a whole set of formations; it has

CHAPTER FIVE

its own different conjunctures and moments in the past. It included many different kinds of work. (Hall 1992, 278)

Cultural Studies and Postmodernism

Postmodernism is a controversial, confusing term, its use often laden with emotion by defenders and opponents alike.[5] Denzin (1986b, 194) characterizes the term "as both a form of theorizing about societies and a period in social thought." In each case its definitional hallmark is the highlighting of the uncertainty of cultural meaning in everyday society as well as in attempts to theorize about that reality (McRobbie 1994, 24–27). C. Wright Mills offers this early recognition of social changes leading to postmodernity:

> We are at the ending of what is called the Modern Age. Just as Antiquity was followed by several centuries of Oriental ascendancy, which Westerners provincially call the Dark Ages, so now the Modern Age is being succeeded by a post-modern period. Perhaps we may call it: The Fourth Epoch. (Mills 1959, 165–66)

The emergence of this epoch, or time frame, has been gradual, roughly since the end of World War II (Jameson 1991, 2002; Denzin 1991c). In chapter 7, I will argue its periodization back to the first quarter of the twentieth century.

The contemporary appearance of postmodernity is historically and philosophically overlaid with Enlightenment (i.e., modernist) social thought (Gay 1966, 1969; Lyman 1997c). Modern, Enlightenment-spawned social theory institutionalized the ideas of rationality and causation (Martindale 1960). The former led to the belief in progress and perfectibility of social institutions and the latter to the search for scientific laws in all spheres of life, the discovery of which would yield control of the "natural" environment.

The disquieting character of postmodernity lies in its questioning of this modernist construction of meaning. As Mills observes:

> But definitions, like everything social, are historically specific. And now our basic definitions of society and of self are being overtaken by new realities.... [W]e find that too many of our old expectations and images are, after all, tied down historically; that too many of our standard cate-

gories of thought and of feeling as often disorient us as help to explain what is happening around us; that too many of our explanations are derived from the great historical transition from the Medieval to the Modern Age; and that when they are generalized for use today, they become unwieldy, irrelevant, not convincing. (Mills 1959, 166)

In its broadest sense, then, "postmodernism" represents a thoroughgoing critique of meaning processes as received from Enlightenment ideals, extending beyond the boundaries of social science to include all knowledge bases. This "crisis of meaning" (Dotter 1997) represents the arbitrary boundary between the modern and postmodern. The demarcation of the two is fluid and ambiguous, in a constant process of "becoming."[6] Postmodernity is the "rewriting of modernity" (Lyotard 1991, 24–36).

Denzin describes the sociocultural critique of postmodernism and its backlash:

a movement in the arts; new forms of social theory; historical transformations which have occurred since World War II; cultural life under late capitalism; life in a mass-mediated world where the symbol of reality (hyper-reality) has replaced the real; a conservative historical movement characterized by a backlash against the political activities of many marginalized voices and communities (racial minorities, gays, elderly, women). (Denzin 1996, 341)

In short, postmodernism represents an amalgam of themes and perspectives. It cannot be easily summarized in a logical fashion or by a short list of characteristics. To even attempt so requires a reversion to modernist concepts of meaning-creation (i.e., rooted in essentialist visions of philosophy and history).

The postmodern is at once academic and everyday, social and cultural, conservative and radical, political and disengaged, constraining and liberating. As Madan Sarup argues:

It is also said that in postmodernism there is: a shift of emphasis from content to form or style; a transformation of reality into images; the fragmentation of time into a series of perpetual presents. There are continual references to eclecticism, reflexivity, self-referentiality, quotation, artifice, randomness, anarchy, fragmentation, pastiche, and allegory. Moreover, with the development of postmodernism in recent years,

CHAPTER FIVE

> there has been a move to "textualize" everything: history, philosophy, jurisprudence, sociology and other disciplines are treated as so many optional "kinds of writing" or discourses. (Sarup 1988/93, 132)

The enterprise of postmodern social theory is a daunting one: to describe a sociocultural reality which resists description in traditional terms; to critique institutionalized discourses such as science and religion without replacing them with similarly deterministic ones (e.g., technology-driven change); to situate identities in the cultural context of ideology. The postmodern theoretical project must critically examine "an under-theorizing of language, the human subject, the mass media, commodity relations in the consumer society, and the legitimation crisis surrounding science, knowledge and power in the modern world" (Denzin 1986b, 194). Postmodern discourses are frequently criticized for obscuring reality much more than clearly describing it, their proponents knowingly, even irreverently, dismantling traditional cultural symbols for no apparent purpose or end. At the same time, these discourses indicate fundamental problems with traditional sociological theorizing (Best and Kellner 1997, 23).

Marxist concepts such as ideology and hegemony, central to earlier versions of cultural studies (Althusser 1971; Gramsci 1971; Hall 1980b, 1986a, 1986b; Hebdige 1979/2002, Eagleton 1991), have been articulated into a view of language, commoditization, and media culture as a reflexive process (Kellner 1995). At the same time, positivistic sociology has been roundly criticized in many quarters for being increasingly irrelevant to contemporary practical concerns (Denzin 1987; Lyman 1995). In this milieu the postmodern critique should not be dismissed as trendy, fashionable, or even elitist. Rather, the contemporary meaning crisis should continue to embolden theorists to examine the interface between modern and postmodern culture (Eagleton 2000). In the process the classical debates between mainstream scientific sociology, Marxism, and interactionism will continue (McRobbie 1992; 1994, 24–25). Especially important is the dialogue, frequently strained, critiquing the applicability of postmodernist cultural studies for feminist concerns (McRobbie 1994; Farganis 1994a; Seigfried 1996).

Postmodernism is not a dismissal of the past, the destruction of Enlightenment, or an inherently subversive movement. It addresses enduring questions regarding the nature of knowledge and social reality (Lyotard 1988, 4–7). The "postmodern turn," academically evident in cultural studies as well as in everyday life, represents fertile ground for theoretical articulation. As Steven Best and Douglas Kellner argue:

> Indeed, we choose to deploy the discourse of a postmodern "turn" or "shift" instead of "rupture" which stresses extreme breaks, discontinuities, and an apocalyptic sense of ending and completely new beginnings. Rather, for us, the notions of "shift" and "turn" signify novel developments, yet also retain continuities with modernity and modern theory, pointing to shared assumptions, presuppositions, modes of thought and discourse, practices and strategies, and vision. (Best and Kellner 1997, 25)

The crisis of meaning characterizing the turn from modernity to postmodernity has much potential for understanding the human condition (Eagleton 2000). A poststructuralist critique of meaning situates cultural studies squarely in that turn.

The Poststructuralist Critique

Poststructuralist formulations have developed in response to the crisis of meaning (Dotter 1997) of the postmodern turn. In a cultural studies framework, they represent modifications of structuralist emphases on language as a meaning system (i.e., a structured totality). Poststructuralism is an extension of semiotics, the study of signs (Barthes 1957/72; Storey 1999; Manning 2002, 2003); it emerged even as structuralism was at its height of influence in the late 1960s (Dosse 1997b, 17). The most important poststructuralist critiques are found in the writings of Michel Foucault (1972a) and Jacques Derrida (1967/76, 1967/78).

In general, the convergence of structuralism with poststructuralism[7] rests on three interrelated themes: the nature of the subject, a rejection of historicism, and the criticism of philosophy (Sarup 1988/93, 1–4). Both structuralism and poststructuralism detail the dissolution or "decentering" of the human subject (Sarup 1988/93, 2; Denzin 1994c). The focus of the former, especially in the work of Claude Levi-Strauss (1963), is "to describe culture as a system of differences, wherein the meaning of any unit is defined through a system of contrasts with other units" (Marcus and

Fisher 1986, 28). More radically, poststructuralism calls into question the entire philosophical construction of the subject:

> The term "subject" helps us to conceive of human reality as a construction, as a product of signifying activities which are both culturally specific and generally unconscious. The category of the subject calls into question the notion of the self synonymous with consciousness; it "decentres" consciousness. (Sarup 1988/93, 2)

The subject, then, is a philosophical creation, supplying meaning to Enlightenment notions such as progress and perfectibility. In particular, poststructuralism questions the idea that there is a discernible pattern in history (Appleby, Hunt, and Jacob 1994), especially a progressive one. Historical laws, then, are not naturally discoverable, but shrouded in mythmaking (Barthes 1957/72; Storey 1999). History is at once devoid of an evaluative component (Foucault 1972a) or conceived as without end (Derrida 1967/76, 1967/78).

Similarly, poststructuralism is identified as an antiphilosophical discourse. As we shall see later in this chapter, the works of Michel Foucault and Jacques Derrida exemplify a critique of received philosophical discourse, from the constitution of the subject, to the composition of historical laws, to the ideological function of philosophy as social control. Totalizing philosophy, describing "essential" characteristics of being or social existence, is nothing more than a narrative discourse. Unexamined and accepted, the potential for its abuse is apparent (Bannet 1989).

This brief summary of the poststructuralist critique of meaning illuminates the roots of a postmodern cultural studies: the problematic of meaning, especially in media and popular culture. Before presenting a detailed poststructuralist reading of this problematic, I offer a brief account of the historical development of cultural studies.

A Brief History of Cultural Studies

The development and practice of cultural studies can been traced to a number of sources. These include the Frankfurt School, British cultural studies, the American tradition, and feminist perspectives. In recent years, the latter three varieties have been heavily influenced by the poststructuralist turn already mentioned. Rather than a linear historical progression, the emergence of the field has been characterized by Douglas Kellner (1995, 20) as "theory wars." This metaphor highlights the struggle within the academy to describe and critique the post–World War II conflict of cultural development. Each of the above perspectives contributes certain common synthetic elements, including but not limited to the following: development of a consumer society which at once constrains and liberates meaningful social action (the Frankfurt School); a proliferation of subcultures, based initially on consumption, providing the symbolic terrain for identity politics and political resistance (British cultural studies); the continued emergence and exponential growth of media culture as a process of communication (the American tradition); and a comprehensive constructionist critique of gender as a social category (feminist perspectives). As an emerging field, then, cultural studies is marked by theoretical diversity, even conflict.

The Frankfurt School

The Frankfurt Institute for Social Research was founded in 1923, a school of critical theorists whose goal was to reexamine the sociocultural bases of modern society in light of the failure to secure a lasting peace following World War I. The school's critique was a reformulation of three classical thinkers: Karl Marx, Sigmund Freud, and Max Weber (Lemert 1995, 122). The synthesis was interdisciplinary, ranging from philosophy to artistic expression to popular culture in the developing consumer capitalism after World War I (Arato and Gebhardt 1982/97). Malcolm Waters describes the school's development:

> [T]he unique philosophical and theoretical orientation, known as the Frankfurt School of Sociology, only began to emerge with the appointment of Max Horkheimer to the Directorship of the Institute in 1930. Horkheimer managed to attract or retain a galaxy of the leading, mainly Jewish, intellectuals in Germany at the Institute, including Adorno, Benjamin, Fromm, Kirkheimer, Lowenthal, Marcuse, Neumann, and Pollack. With the rise of the anti-semitic and anti-liberal Nazi regime the Institute moved first to Geneva in 1933 and then to New York in 1935. (Waters 1994, 188)

CHAPTER FIVE

Culture and its process of creation were central to the modernist critique of the enslavement and oppression of humanity. Critical theory "was aimed at diagnosing the ills of modern society (the things that prevented people's fulfillment) and identifying the nature of the social changes that were necessary in order to produce a just and democratic society" (Layder 1994, 186).

In this narrative, consumption-based, technology-driven capitalism confuses an artificial affluence with human freedom. The culture of consumption thus becomes an ideology for oppression and control. Similarly, the rationalization of the scientific method (i.e., the search for causal laws) drives a wedge between the cultural as object and the subjective search for truth through emancipation. An examination of the failure of Enlightenment philosophy was central to the Frankfurt project. In *Dialectic of Enlightenment*, Max Horkheimer and Theodor Adorno write:

> The dilemma that faced us in our work proved to be the first phenomenon for investigation: the self destruction of the Enlightenment. We are wholly convinced—and therein lies our *petitio principii*—that social freedom is inseparable from enlightened thought. Nevertheless, we believe that we have just as clearly recognized that the notion of the very way of thinking, no less than the actual historic forms—the social institutions—with which it is interwoven, already contains the seeds of the reversal universally apparent today. [*italics* in the original] (Horkheimer and Adorno 1972, xiii)

The heart of the dialectic is the struggle of the individual against cultural, ideological domination. Knowledge and power are manipulated in consumer capitalism:

> The fallen nature of modern man cannot be separated from social progress. On the one hand the growth of economic productivity furnishes the conditions for a world of greater justice; on the other hand it allows the technical apparatus and the social groups which administer it a disproportionate superiority to the rest of the population. The individual is wholly devalued in relation to the economic powers, which at the same time press the control of society over nature to hitherto unsuspected heights. Even though the individual disappears before the apparatus which he serves, that apparatus provides for him as never before. (Horkheimer and Adorno 1972, xiv)

In short, cultural commodification transforms individual consciousness into a mass psychology of fabricated similarity of experience. "The flood of detailed information and candy-floss entertainment simultaneously instructs and stultifies mankind" (Horkheimer and Adorno 1972, xv).

Similarly, science, once a radical discourse to be used for human betterment, had become increasingly rationalized and bureaucratized. Once created, this culture of science serves to objectify the place of human actors in the social world. According to Stanley Aronowitz:

> These constructed objects now constitute our second nature. Reason, which became the religion of the bourgeois Enlightenment, had through its permutations within science become thoroughly instrumentalized, and could no longer provide the way to any truth beyond the propositions of science and their technological application in the work of dominating nature and humans. In effect, ethical and philosophical inquiry, now subordinated to science, had lost their critical character (critical in the sense of transcending the conditions of the given empirical world). (Aronowitz 1994, 111)

The Frankfurt critical project was to redeem the hopes of the Enlightenment by unmasking the ideological component of culture. In Kellner's words: "Its proponents coined the term 'culture industries' to signify the process of the industrialization of mass-produced culture and the commercial imperatives which drove the system" (Kellner 1995, 28–29). The accomplishment of the project, never fully realized, was sought in a thoroughgoing critique of contemporary consumer culture.

The politically engaged social theorist viewed mass popular culture and its political landscape from a privileged, enlightened position. That is, the Frankfurt critique dichotomized cultural expression into "high" authentic art and "low" ideologized forms for the masses. Truth and enlightened liberation may be found only in the former; popular culture is a debased and debasing mode of social control, foisted on passive, nondiscriminating audiences. As Aronowitz explains:

> [G]enuine high art was the last refuge of critical practice in a world completely dominated by total administration. Society was marked by a wizened lifeworld in which entertainment replaced a vital public sphere where citizens are competent to fully debate political issues and can really

CHAPTER FIVE

> control their own affairs. The degradation of art consisted in its subordination to the technological colossus which controlled nearly every aspect of social life except that of the artistic avant-garde, whose subversive content was virtually assured by its distance from art forms consonant with popular taste. (Aronowitz 1994, 124)

In this subject-object dialectic, the technological capability to reproduce copies of art and its performance alters the aesthetic experience and the very meaning of audience itself (Benjamin 1968). This fundamental transmutation erases constraints of time and space as well as the individual perception of unique meaning associated with the artistic experience.

The ideological practice of popular culture, then, accelerates the subordination of the subject in consumer capitalism. If, as classical Marxism has always contended, capitalism contains the seeds of its own destruction, how can commodification of culture continue to stave off revolutionary change? This basic contradiction between Marx and the Frankfurt theorists has never been completely resolved. Its most complete statement is found in the work of Herbert Marcuse (1964/91), *One Dimensional Man.*

Marcuse holds that the contradiction endures through the spread of a highly technologized consumer culture, promoting the evolution of capitalism in the following ways:

> It creates affluence, thus removing many of the grounds for dissent, and diverting attention from a true intererest in liberation.
>
> It focuses attention on consumption patterns which are common to all classes in society and blurs the distinctions between them.
>
> It softens working conditions as factories are automated and the labor force shifts into white collar occupations, thus reducing a sense of opposition.
>
> It allows the development of a welfare state in which people's lives are dominated by bureaucratic imperatives.
>
> It markets increased leisure that offers an illusion of freedom without offering access to critical reason.
>
> It provides for sexual permissiveness within a surface gloss of advertising and mass-mediated entertainment that also offers an illusion of freedom from sexual repression. (Waters 1994, 190)

TOWARD A POSTMODERN CULTURAL STUDIES

Technology, coupled with consumption, constitutes a powerful ideological mechanism of control. Traditional sources of social unrest, even extreme instances of poverty, violence, or inequality, are diffused in the face of profit and affluence. In short, Marxist class conflict is attenuated, if not effectively eliminated, in a sociocultural terrain of individual freedom and consumption (MacIntyre 1970, 75; Aronowitz 2003, 6–7).

Among Frankfurt theorists, Walter Benjamin (1968) maintains measured optimism in the face of consumer popular culture. The technological reproduction of culture has potentially radical implications. That is, culture is mass-produced, but by various audiences may lead to multiple meanings and cultural interpretations (Storey 1999). In Benjamin's (1968, 219–26) view, cultural reproduction, especially in film, allows audiences to actively participate in the process of cultural meaning-creation. This active role of audiences revolutionizes mass culture as an object of interpretation. As articulated by the Frankfurt School, the duality of subject and object, exemplified in state administrative bureaucracy and capitalist technological development, is the cultural dialectic that serves to both seemingly liberate and constrain humanity. Jurgen Habermas, the most well known of second-generation Frankfurt theorists, extends critical theory beyond an analysis of art, reproducibility, technology, and oppression into a defense of Enlightenment knowledge and rational social organization. Habermas suggests that the still-incomplete project of modernity must be allowed to proceed since it "provides the only normatively powerful critique of power we know" (Lemert 1995, 81).

Following Max Weber, Habermas (1993) contends that art is only one of three knowledge spheres, including also science and morality. Referring to critiques of modernity as "the false programs of the negation of culture," he observes:

> Communication processes need a cultural tradition covering all spheres—cognitive, moral-practical and expressive. A rationalized everyday life, therefore, could hardly be saved from cultural impoverishment through breaking open a single cultural sphere—art—and so providing access to just one of the specialized knowledge complexes. (Habermas 1993, 100)

Habermas posits an interactional theory of cultural communication processes, giving equal weight to each of the spheres. Political discourse and participation will thus energize and emancipate cultural debate. He concludes:

> In sum, the project of modernity has not yet been fulfilled. And the reception of art is only one of at least three of its aspects. The project aims at a differentiated relinking of modern culture with an everyday praxis that still depends on vital heritages, but would be impoverished through mere traditionalism. This new connection, however, can only be established under the condition that societal modernization will also be steered in a different direction. The life-world has to become able to develop institutions out of itself which sets limits to the internal dynamics and to the imperatives of an almost autonomous economic system and its administrative complements. (Habermas 1993, 102–3)

This "radical modernism" (Lemert 1995, 81) of Habermas veers from first-generation Frankfurt criticism to a kind of systems-approach to the rationalization of culture under the control of various experts (Waters 1994, 192–95).

The Frankfurt School represents an historically situated project, founded and developed between the two World Wars. In particular, its cultural critique of classical Marxism led to great disillusionment with the development of postmodern society. The school's contributions to the development of cultural studies are its recognition of the importance of mass media in the creation of cultural forms and the centrality of popular culture for the contemporary generation of meaning in consumer capitalism. With respect to the latter, the Frankfurt School was fundamentally pessimistic about the spread of popular culture, instead arguing for a traditional hierarchical, even elitist, view of art and its experience. Further developments of cultural studies, more profoundly influenced by postmodern media culture, have democratized its study.

British Cultural Studies

The advent and growth of British cultural studies dates from 1968, with the founding of the Centre for Contemporary Cultural Studies at the University of Birmingham. As a theoretical and political project, the school espoused a new reading of the term "culture." This critique extends through the work of the Centre's founder, Richard Hoggart (1957/98), to E. P.

Thompson (1963), and Raymond Williams (1958/66, 1961/2001, 1982, 2001).[8] The study of culture represented a self-conscious, reflexive activity of engagement with the social world. Simultaneously, there was an intense theoretical edge to the Centre's activities. Stuart Hall (1992), onetime Director of the Centre, maintains that this theoretical political tension continues to be the hallmark of a fertile cultural studies, no matter the source of its national identity.

Cultural analysis was historically contextualized, the boundaries of the term expanded and energized to include a wide array of forms (Turner 1990/2003). As Dick Hebdige notes: "In the early years, when it was being established in the Universities, Cultural Studies sat rather uncomfortably on the fence between these two conflicting definitions—culture as a standard of excellence, culture as a 'whole way of life'—unable to determine which represented the most fruitful line of enquiry" (Hebdige 1979/2002, 7). From the beginning, then, cultural studies was controversial in approach, at once identified with definitional disputes and debates concerning method and substance. Over time, this state of affairs led to the description of the field as interdisciplinary. One may argue that from its inception to the present, cultural studies is best characterized as "anti-disciplinary"—permanently ambivalent concerning the traditional boundaries of academic disciplines (Nelson et al. 1992, 1–2).

Theoretical and methodological approaches have freely mixed and mingled in this eclectic terrain. Nonetheless, two important sites of contention are evident. First, British cultural studies was animated by its continuing encounter with Marxism through the works of Louis Althusser (1969/96, 1971) and Antonio Gramsci (1971).[9] The specification of linkages between the economic infrastructure of capitalism and its cultural superstructure represents the central problematic of this encounter (as was substantially the case with Frankfurt School theorizing).

Second, in the 1990s British cultural studies has seen a "linguistic turn" (Hall 1980b, 1980c, 1992), moving away from the earlier neo-Marxist critique toward a consideration of identity politics, especially of age, gender, and race. The turn emphasizes the fragmentation of experience and reflects not only the relative decline of neo-Marxist perspectives, but the gradual articulation of postmodernist concerns into cultural studies (McRobbie 1992; 1994, 61–74).

CHAPTER FIVE

The intent of early theory work at the Centre was to formulate a neo-Marxist political critique outlining the ideological content of culture and its relation to contemporary class structure (Turner 1990/2003, 9–32). Culture is both product and process, constraining and liberating, reciprocally dependent upon and influencing the structural institutional arrangements of society. The description and critique of contemporary culture hinges on the importance of ideology for the construction of social meaning (Barthes 1957/72, 1977; Hall 1980b, 1986a; Eagleton 1991; Storey 1999).

According to Althusser (1969/96, 232–34), ideology is captured in two overlapping senses: as a 'representation' of the imaginary relationship of individuals to their real conditions of existence and as the process by which the relations of production are reproduced. As a cultural construct, ideology offers descriptions of reality and even solutions to problems (e.g., political or religious beliefs); as a social process, ideology refers to the socially organized behavior that renders life meaningful for the individual subjects so constituted—rituals, customs, norms given meaning through behavior (Althusser 1971, 162–77).

Similarly, Gramsci's (1971) treatment of hegemony has organizational and behavioral components. Hegemony represents "an accomplishment of social groups or classes which can penetrate 'private organizations' so that knowledge, values and standards can be manipulated in their own favor" (Waters 1994, 183). Characterized as both the organization of cultural knowledge for class interests as well as the civil and political behavior patterns through which it is maintained, hegemonic control evidences a "moving equilibrium." That is, it must be won, maintained, and even affirmed (Hebdige 1979/2002, 16).

Ideology-in-use is central to the concept of hegemonic control. All groups in the political process use cultural constructions to argue, justify, and expand their positions relative to others. Here, the social category of intellectuals is particularly important. As Gramsci argues:

> What we can do, for the moment, is to fix two major superstructural "levels": the one that can be called "civil society," that is the ensemble of organisms commonly called "private," and that of "political society" or "the State." These two levels correspond on the one hand to the function of "hegemony" which the dominant group exercises throughout society

and on the other hand to that of "direct domination" or command exercised through the State and "juridical" government. The functions in question are precisely organisational and connective. The intellectuals are the dominant group's "deputies" exercising the subaltern functions of social hegemony and political government. (Gramsci 1971, 12)

Hegemony is the ideological bridge between structural social relations and creation of culture. It appears as fundamentally "normal," independent of history or narrow interest (Barthes 1957/72; Hebdige 1979/2002, 9).

This neo-Marxist formulation of the active creation of culture as ideology produced a number of critical analyses of youth subculture in postwar Great Britain (Hebdige 1979/2002). These studies occasionally drew freely from non-Marxist theory (i.e., especially interactionist deviance labeling) and elevated the examination of popular culture forms to the status of serious inquiry (Cohen 1972/93; Frith 1981; Hall and Jefferson 1975/2002b). From its beginning, then, British cultural studies vacillated between a Marxist emphasis on the ideological basis of class and a subcultural critique rooted in consumption, style, and the self-conscious resistance of identity politics (Clark 1990).

The second point of contention within British cultural studies has been its so-called linguistic turn toward poststructural interpretations of meaning-creation, "the discovery of discursivity, of textuality" (Hall 1992, 283). This turn, ever so gradually, opened dialogues to the significance of gender and class construction in both popular and academic culture:

> cultural studies has long been concerned with the everyday terrain of people, and with all the ways that cultural practices speak to, of, and for their lives. In this sense, the significance of "the popular" in cultural studies involves the observation that struggles over power [hegemony] must increasingly touch base with and work through the cultural practices, languages, and logics of the people—yet "the people" cannot be defined ahead of time. There is no simple hierarchical binary system that can be taken for granted, as if "the people" are always subordinated to an elite minority and subordination can be defined along some single dimension of social difference. (Nelson et al. 1992, 11)

Cultural hegemony, then, is tentatively constructed around interpenetrating domains of social status—age, gender, race, and class (Goldberg

CHAPTER FIVE

1997; Aronowitz 2003; Andersen and Collins 2004b). Focusing on meaning, interpretation, and the nature of the subject, the linguistic turn, a consequence of communication practices in postmodern society, profoundly affected British cultural studies. As Hall relates: "Nevertheless, the refiguring of theory, made as a result of having to think questions of culture through the metaphors of language and textuality, represents a point beyond which cultural studies must now always necessarily locate itself" (Hall 1992, 283–84).

The poststructuralist linguistic turn represents the intermingling of postmodern social theory with the traditional cultural studies emphasis on meaning-creation. It presented feminism (and related perspectives based on the politics of difference and identity) with a "pathway to the postmodern." The neo-Marxist concern with the nature of ideology and hegemony is reformulated in a concern for the textual, fragmented, decentered subject. McRobbie expresses the problem in a feminist frame:

> The most important issue might be the one of who gets to be able to express their fragmentation, and who is able to put into words or images or sounds, the language of their private, broken subjectivities. In short who can contest, who can represent and who gets to be listened to? In this sense fragmentation can be linked with the politics of empowerment, with finding a way of mounting a challenge. A unity of sorts emanates from the tumult of fragmented voices. (McRobbie 1994, 29)

Even in the poststructuralist terrain, marked by multidimensional layers of meaning-creation and interpretation, feminist and other previously marginalized voices have hardly found a friendly reception (Smith 1989; Oleson 1994). The theory and politics of identity difference represents a double-edged weapon capable of cutting both ways: The theoretical space it provides feminist voices and others must be fought for, claimed, and reshaped. As we shall see momentarily, traditional cultural studies (both British and American) is only now developing an emergent form of feminist inquiry.

The American Tradition

The American tradition of cultural studies is multifaceted, although it has developed most fully around the concept of media culture (Carey 1989). Emerging from this focus is the analysis of popular culture forms as sites of meaning-creation. An analysis of postmodern media culture probes the nature of ideology and its consumption as entertainment in consumer capitalism. That is, ideology is not experienced as hegemonically enforced from above, but emerges as countless consumer-audiences adapt it to their own daily rounds of experience (Hall 1980b, 1986a). As Kellner (1995, 3) argues, media culture induces "individuals to identify with dominant social and political ideologies, positions, and representations. In general, it is not a system of rigid ideological indoctrination that induces consent to existing capitalist societies, but the pleasures of the media and consumer culture."

This argument is similar to Marcuse's view as already discussed. The ideology of consumption (i.e., the desirability of consumer culture), framed in countless images/messages from the more general media and popular culture, attenuates any structural or political differences arising within capitalism. Media culture, ubiquitous and spectacular, erases the boundaries of personal and social experience in the welter of "choices" at least hypothetically available to the consumer. Theoretically, these choices exist for all; in practice, consumption of popular culture is radically segmented by age, gender, race, and class in American society.

This interface of capitalist economy and its cultural formations may be called the "cultural logic of late capitalism" (Jameson 1991; Denzin 1991c, 25–26). In brief, the ideology of consumption is an effective agent of social control, even as actual consumption is severely limited in much of society. Furthermore, the content of postmodern media culture is increasingly characterized in popular forms, especially film and music. Consumption is an important link for experiences between subcultures, generated and spread by media culture (Aronowitz 1992, 193–95).

However, unlike Frankfurt School disdain for popular culture forms, the American cultural studies tradition holds that postmodern popular culture is extremely important in generating meaning for audiences (Kellner 2003b). There is little or no distinction between high and low forms. Either may be ideologized, packaged, and sold to potential consumers. At the same time, consumer audiences are not entirely passive categories, created and led for the economic benefits of the ruling class. As Kellner remarks:

> audiences may resist the dominant meanings and messages, create their own readings and appropriations of mass-produced culture, and use their

CHAPTER FIVE

> culture as resources to empower themselves and to invent their own meanings, identities, and forms of life. Moreover, media culture itself provides resources which individuals can appropriate, or reject, in forming their own identities against dominant models. (Kellner 1995, 3)

Media culture provides context for both the subjugation and liberation of audiences. Its popular forms are particularly important, engendering a discourse of similarity and creativity. As a postmodern form of communication, media culture embodies much ambiguity and contradiction: It highlights socially created biocultural differences such as race, gender, and age, thereby mythologizing the categories (Barthes 1957/72). At the same time, it provides a forum for the celebration of these differences and the experiences they signify.

Herein lies the backlash of postmodern cultural forms, including social theory (Denzin 1996). Differences between social categories are critiqued and shorn of myth, creating a seeming vacuum to be filled with images of past nostalgia (Jameson 1991; Denzin 1991c). These heretofore outdated, even anachronistic, sociocultural narratives are reconstructed full-blown in the present—packaged and sold as visions of contemporary society.

The media-generated debate over family values is a case in point. Media portrayals of the many familial forms in contemporary society, based on truth, half-truth, stereotyping, and downright distortion, give birth to backward-looking nostalgic views on "the family" of generations ago. Meaning is often conflated or confused, mixing historical interpretation, popular culture images, and oral tradition as well. From this discourse, historical constructions of the family emerge as a pristine alternative to nasty, brutish contemporary ones.

This dialogue will no doubt continue in the postmodern context of *differance* (Derrida 1972/81b), the ebb and flow of subject and object, of self and other. While the risk it suggests is disquieting, even frightening, so is the suggestion that society return to earlier sociocultural patterns that can hardly be described as liberating or even enlightened. Thus, postmodern analysis is often more revealing for what is left unsaid as for what is articulated. In the words of John W. Murphy (1989, 16): "Critique and interpretation are allowed to intermingle, and they produce a very potent concoction. Expectations are questioned and norms dissolve, as society expands through creative acts."

TOWARD A POSTMODERN CULTURAL STUDIES

A postmodern cultural studies focusing on the production/reproduction of popular culture knowledge must develop a critical stance. For the products of media culture are most often both "liberal" and "conservative" in message, thereby assuring the largest possible audience. As Kellner argues:

> The artifacts of media culture are thus not innocent entertainment, but are thoroughly ideological artifacts bound up with political rhetoric, struggles, agendas, and policies. Given their political significance and effects, it is important to learn to read media culture politically in order to decode its ideological messages and effects. (Kellner 1995, 93)

This reading encompasses the intersection of gender, sexuality, race, and class (Goldberg 1997; Aronowitz 1992, 2003; Andersen and Collins 2004b) and includes an examination of the theoretical assumptions and technical manner of media presentation.

Mills recognizes the importance of the sociological imagination as a counterbalance to the proliferation of media culture: "Every interest and power, every passion and bias, every hatred and hope tends to acquire an ideological apparatus with which to compete with the slogans and symbols, the doctrines and appeals of other interests. As public communications are expanded and speeded up, their effectiveness is worn out by repetition" (Mills 1959, 81). Furthermore, his analysis of the white-collar "new middle classes" goes beyond a traditional Marxist conception. Class is not only a structural, economic category, but a cultural and mediated one as well. As Mills states in *White Collar*, "The forms of political consciousness may, in the end, be relative to the means of production, but, in the beginning, they are relative to the contents of the communication media" (Mills 1951, 333).

In the postmodern moment class is intersubjectively negotiated. Though he recognizes the importance of the "mass arts" for this process, Mills had little use for them as a lasting basis of self and identity. These latter become ambiguous and problematic in the context of media proliferation. "Contents of the mass media seep into our images of self, becoming that which is taken for granted, so imperceptibly and so surely that to modify them drastically, over a generation or two, would be to change profoundly modern man's experience and character" (Mills 1951, 334). Finally, consciousness of class is most evident in the members of the

CHAPTER FIVE

"power elite." Otherwise, it is largely diffused in mediated society without clear boundaries (Mills 1956).

Media culture as a context for meaning-creation is decidedly complex. In the American tradition of cultural studies, this meaning process has been critiqued and examined at great length in three forms: film, political discourse, and popular music. Within this literature, the postmodern or linguistic turn is evident. At the same time, postmodern popular culture becomes a site of continuous meaning-creation, an industry of both entertainment and information (Dotter 1994; forthcoming).

Norman K. Denzin (1988b, 1991a, 1994b, 1994c, 2002b) has produced a body of work critiquing gender, race, and other images in contemporary film.[10] Relating "visual literacy" or the new language of the visual to the communication of images as both entertainment and information, he argues: "The new information technologies turn everyday life into a theatrical spectacle; into sites where the dramas that surround the decisive performances of race, ethnicity, gender, sexuality and age are staged" (Denzin 1991c, 8).

Arguably, Denzin's three most influential works on cinematic images are *Hollywood Shot by Shot* (1991b), *Images of Postmodern Society* (1991c), and *The Cinematic Society* (1995). The first volume deals with representations of alcoholism in Hollywood films from 1932 to 1989. Denzin describes the significance of his analysis: "I attempt to uncover the recurring symbolic and interactional meanings Hollywood has brought to the alcoholic's experiences. I assume that a project in cultural interpretive studies must examine how cultural texts, like alcoholism movies, create possibilities of experience that are then lived out in the lives of ordinary interacting individuals in the contemporary postmodern period" (Denzin 1991b, xiv). His analysis focuses on the relationship between consciousness and subjectivity (Johnson 1986/87), its cultural, ideological, and objectified existence.

The latter two volumes more systematically situate the study of film as cultural criticism and meaning-generation in a postmodern frame. The first juxtaposes Denzin's (1991c) articulation of postmodern social theory with film critiques, including *Blue Velvet* (1986), *Wall Street* (1987), *Crimes and Misdemeanors* (1989), *sex, lies and videotape* (1989), *Do the Right Thing* (1989), and *Paris, Texas* (1984). In *The Cinematic Society* Denzin (1995) argues that movie audiences in the postmodern epoch are "voyeurs" employing numerous gazes, and that film as entertainment also serves the function of surveillance. He identifies numerous interrelated specific and general gazes, including the medical, investigative, technological, informational, erotic, accidental, inquisitive, masculine, feminine, secret, and so on (Denzin 1995, 191). In particular, he contends that film structures sociocultural discourses regarding gender, race, and class.

For audiences, cinematic culture makes seeing analogous to knowing (Denzin 1995, 50). Furthermore, the voyeur's gaze, turned inward toward the self, represents a powerful form of social control; it is both cultural and biographical. In post-surveillance society the "individual has interiorized the hearing and visual gaze of an 'objectified,' external, generalized, nameless, often faceless, other. This technological other is everywhere and nowhere, in hidden cameras and recording devices, in telephone answering machines, electronic mail systems and home burglar alarm systems" (Denzin 1995, 191). Communication and control, once the exclusive purview of spoken and written language (perhaps supplemented by visual images) is now primarily accomplished through visualization in a culture dominated by the cinema as a form of popular art.

Kellner (1995) has produced important studies on the development of media culture. He expands Debord's (1967/94) concept of the "society of the spectacle" to a variety of specific sites: "Social and political conflicts are increasingly played out on the screens of media culture, which display spectacles such as sensational murder cases, terrorist bombings, celebrity and political sex scandals, and the explosive violence of everyday life" (Kellner 2003b, 1). In two case studies Kellner (2001, 2003a) frames political discourse in the context of spectacle and the role of media in creating it: the controversial, contested election of George W. Bush as President in 2000 and the 9/11 terrorist attacks leading to the subsequent expansion of the "war on terror." He is thoroughly critical of the Bush Administration's unilateral foreign policy and its doctrine of military preemption, as well as its role in domestic political events such as the Enron scandal. In each of these works Kellner infuses the concept of spectacle with an appropriately serious analysis of media complicity in its creation.

Popular music constitutes the third site of meaning-creation in contemporary society. Beginning in the 1950s rock and roll emerged as the dominant such form, its development fueled by the appearance of adolescent consumers in the postwar years of economic prosperity (Gilbert

CHAPTER FIVE

1986; Dotter 1987). Consumption-based subcultures coalesced around the music from the 1960s forward. Later work on popular music and youth identity has focused on the proliferation of subcultures through the 1970s and beyond. For example, Van M. Cagle (1995) examines the relationship between the work of Andy Warhol and the emergence of glitter rock; in particular, he details how artists of the 1960s and 1970s used the media "directly as a channel for expressing their most 'insidious,' and subsequently, their most lethal, artistic ideas and arguments" (Cagle 1995, 4).

In *Black Noise* Tricia Rose (1994) sketches the connections binding rap, contemporary black culture, and trends in mainstream society. In her words:

> Rappers and their young black constituency are the miners, they are the cultivators of communal artifacts, refining and developing the framework of alternative identities that draw on Afrodiasporic approaches to sound organization, rhythm, pleasure, style, and community. These cultivation processes are formally wedded to digital reproduction and life in an increasingly information-management-driven society. Rap is a technologically-sophisticated project in African-American recuperation and revision. African-American music and culture, inextricably tied to concrete historical and technological developments, have found yet another way to unnerve and simultaneously revitalize American culture. (Rose 1994, 185)

Similarly, there are analyses of heavy metal subcultures (Gaines 1991; Weinstein 1991), the postmodernization of rock music by heavy metal forms (Kotarba 1994), and avant-garde music as oppositional discourse (Coreno 1994). Common threads connecting these works are the relationship of the music to subcultural actors interpreting it for consumption and identity politics and to the processes of meaning-generation in the wider society (Storey 1999). In both cases, music mediates cultural representations of age, gender, race, and class. The importance of such marginalized representations is central to feminist cultural studies perspectives. The following section examines feminist voices in the postmodern cultural studies terrain. As with feminist/constructionist theorists of crime and deviance, these voices are vital to a poststructuralist take on stigmatization.

Feminist Voices

As I have preliminarily illustrated, feminist scholarship has developed as an interdisciplinary project. Since the 1960s its location in the study of crime and deviance has been at once burdened with ideological conflict and theoretically fruitful (Naffine 1996; Young 1996; Daly and Maher 1998a; Carrington 1998). A second area in which contemporary feminist voices have achieved gradual clarity is within cultural studies, especially relating to its poststructuralist, linguistic turn. Much of the poststructuralist critique of meaning has likewise been the concern of feminist scholars (Butler 1990/99, 1993, 1997a). At the same time, the affinity of the postmodern project for feminist voices is uneasy and complicated (Nicholson 1990b; Farganis 1994a; Alway 1995).

The poststructuralist critique of meaning undermines conceptions of the self, philosophical inquiry, and the nature of historical reality. In traditional, Enlightenment-based narratives of social theory, these three conceptions constitute "homocentrism" (Lemert 1979). That is, traditional social theory views man as a knowing, centered subject, philosophy as the search for essentialist, absolute Truth, and history as the patterned unfolding of that Truth in self-realization, progress and so on.

Charles Lemert defines homocentrism as *"that discursive formation which centers itself upon man as a finite subject who dominates his own history. Finitude, subjectivity, and historicism*—these nineteenth-century inventions are the marks of man as a center" [*italics* in the original] (Lemert 1979, 16). In short, man, the finite knowing subject, realizes himself through historical action. As Lemert explains homocentric man: "Thus, all of the great ideas of the nineteenth century—Kant's practical reason, the liberal theory of value, natural selection, and evolutionism—were all historicist in the sense that knowledge, value, and life were saved from the doom of finitude by *history* understood as the realm of successions and analogies in which man created a meaningful human world over against nature" [*italics* in the original] (Lemert 1979, 19).

Homocentric social theory is likewise the concern of the many feminist philosophies, epistemologies, theoretical reformulations, and critical programs. A poststructuralist feminism views theory as a discourse to be critiqued, its patriarchal assumptions exposed. Man and his subjective consciousness is transformed into multiple voices of experience. However, this discursive transformation is problematic. It is likely that "a centered

CHAPTER FIVE

theory is incapable of treating a decentered phenomenon. In other words, a homocentric sociology may not be able to talk about so dispersed and eccentric a thing as discourse." Instead of discursive pluralism, current theorizing may resemble "marginally diversified attempts to organize sociological talk homocentrically" (Lemert 1979, 14).

This state of affairs presents unique challenges and opportunities for feminist theorizing. In a self-reflexive, critical intellectual dialogue, feminist voices have begun to outline the problems and potentials of a polyvocal postmodern cultural studies (Nicholson 1990a; Collins 1991; Alway 1995; Lorber 1998). The poststructuralist turn and feminist voices converge in a critique of science and historicism. Feminism has long been generally skeptical of the scientific method as a mode of control (Harding 1990). A poststructuralist feminism extends this skepticism to broader questioning of philosophy and the historical rootedness of meaning. As Linda J. Nicholson writes:

> Therefore, the postmodern critique has come to focus on philosophy and the very idea of a possible theory of knowledge, justice, or beauty. The claim is that the pursuit itself of such theories rests upon the modernist conception of a transcendent reason, a reason able to separate itself from the body and from historical time and place. Postmodernists describe modern ideals of science, justice, and art, *as* merely modern ideals carrying with them specific political agendas and ultimately unable to legitimize themselves as universals. Thus, postmodernists urge us to recognize the highest ideals of modernity in the West as immanent to a specific historical time and geographical region and associated with certain political baggage. Such baggage includes notions of the supremacy of the West, of the legitimacy of science to tell us how to use and view our bodies, and of the distinction between art and mass culture. [*italics* in the original] (Nicholson 1990b, 4)

Feminist scholarship, then, finds common ground with postmodernist critiques of the problematic of modernity in social theory. Furthermore, Joan Alway (1995, 219–20) argues that feminism replaces this traditional problematic with one relative to gender: "Rather than being primarily concerned with the nature, limits, and possibilities of modernity, feminist theorists focus on the significance of gender, on the range of gender roles and gender symbolism found in social life, and on how they either maintain social order or promote social change."

TOWARD A POSTMODERN CULTURAL STUDIES

This "feminization" of the poststructuralist critique has radical implications for both social theory and the place of feminist perspectives within it (Farganis 1994a; McRobbie 1994). The gender question (i.e., the relative invisibility of women's voices in the narrative of general social theory) historically contextualizes knowledge and its use as traditionally patriarchal, representing the positions and viewpoints of men in the social order. At the same time, feminist voices have become self-reflexively aware that their critique should provide space for the concerns of other groups silenced in the patriarchal modernist narrative (Fraser and Nicholson 1988; Flax 1990; Baca Zinn and Dill 1996).

In short, feminized social theory must examine the embedded nature of its own assumptions and practices in resisting a marginalized voice and must become polyvocal to be ultimately emancipatory. According to Dorothy E. Smith:

> At each historical point the society objectified in sociological discourse crystallizes the invisible presences and concerns of its makers: at each historical point, it sanctifies through such objectification the institutionalized exclusions, as *subjects*, from the discourses of power, of women as a social category, of people of color, and of members of nondominant classes. [*italics* in the original] (Smith 1989, 59)

A polyvocal feminist critique of patriarchal domination recognizes multiple levels, or layers, of oppression in which constructed statuses are neither interchangeable nor equal. Arguing for a "both/and" conceptualization of domination, Patricia Hill Collins observes:

> Replacing additive models of oppression with interlocking ones creates possibilities for new paradigms. The significance of seeing race, class, and gender as interlocking systems of oppression is that such an approach fosters a paradigmatic shift of thinking inclusively about other oppression, such as age, sexual orientation, religion, and ethnicity. Race, class, and gender represent the three systems of oppression that most heavily affect African-American women. But these systems and the economic, political, and ideological conditions that support them may not be the most fundamental oppression, and they certainly affect many more groups than Black women. Other people of color, Jews, the poor, white women, and gays and lesbians have all

CHAPTER FIVE

had similar ideological justifications offered for their subordination. (Collins 1991, 225)

The layering of oppression in the sociocultural patriarchal context becomes interactive, a "matrix of domination" in which the effects of multiple statuses constantly intersect in social structure and experience (Andersen and Collins 2004a, 2004b). Furthermore, the social construction of biocultural categories such as age, race, and gender are fundamentally politicized in media presentations, espousing stereotypical viewpoints of such categories. Likewise, popular culture representations of labeled Others, even when striving for "realistic" portrayals, seldom expose the interlocking nature of cultural representations, through which all categories develop some amount of both privilege and disvaluement. For example, "white women are penalized by their gender but privileged by their race. Depending on the context, an individual may be an oppressor, a member of an oppressed group, or simultaneously oppressor and oppressed" (Collins 1991, 225). The debilitating effects of patriarchal definitions are thereby diffused throughout myriad social and cultural sites.

Simultaneously politicized and stereotyped images are presented for consumption as both information and entertainment. In addition to its normally private context, as exercised within the family and other relatively intimate situations, patriarchy becomes publicly expressed in mass cultural representations, applicable to innumerable groups. Sylvia Walby compares the two contexts relative to gender:

> Public patriarchy is a form in which women have access to both public and private arenas. They are not barred from the public arenas, but are nonetheless subordinated within them. The expropriation of women is performed more collectively, than by individual patriarchs. The household may remain a site of patriarchal oppression, but it is no longer the main place where women are present. (Walby 1990, 178)

Thus, women are routinely portrayed as emancipated, even favored, actors in popular culture images, at odds with the daily experience of continued institutionalized inequality.

Furthermore, in postmodern media culture the patriarchal narrative is extended to include groups other than women. As with gender, race and age are presented as both liberating and constraining categories. For example, youth is celebrated in American popular culture, even as it is subverted in its political effects. Race is similarly characterized in contradictory fashion. The gradual emergence of a black middle class is popularly confirmed even as constructions of street crime, especially violence, are racialized (Goldberg 1997, 161–63).

The decentered historically rooted subject of the poststructuralist critique, leading to the emergence of many voices in media culture, has produced cautionary statements of feminist scholarship. For example, Christine Di Stephano (1990, 75–76) contends that male voices benefit much more from a postmodern cultural context in which knowledge is challenged and rethought. As such, feminist inquiry is inconsistent with postmodern conceptualizations on a number of grounds. The latter represent a white, male, Western take on the decentered subject. Furthermore, mainstream postmodern social theory has been largely insensitive to matters of gender construction. Finally, and perhaps most importantly, decentered postmodern cultural criticism undermines any effective political critique of media culture that purports to speak for women as a marginalized category. Feminist political consciousness risks becoming obsolete, and gender disappears in a cacophony of claims.

While the poststructuralist critique of meaning has exposed the ideological basis of privileged claims to Truth (i.e., science and patriarchy), the danger exists that competing claims will be relativized in the extreme (Benhabib 1990). Especially as the claims of women and other marginalized categories are subsumed as commodified objects in media culture, their potential for radical change is greatly attenuated. In short, the politics of consumer culture prevent postmodern social theory from being truly liberating. Much as Marcuse argued, postmodern, technologized culture is inherently conservative, usurping the vitality of multiple voices.

Given the dangers of a sociocultural reality characterized by the politics of infinite difference, feminist perspectives remain central to the emerging postmodern terrain (Huyssen 1990; Heller 1993). Thus, identities contextualized by gender, age, and race are products of imposition and the negotiation of desire, within specific "locales," such as the home, workplace, and so on. As Elspeth Probyn explains:

> [W]e are continuously working to make sense of and articulate both place and event. Moreover, as we approach others' locales we must keep

CHAPTER FIVE

> in mind that women are never simply fixed within locale. We may live within patriarchy, but at different levels, and in different ways the struggle to rearticulate locale continues. (Probyn 1990, 182)

The poststructuralist highlighting of difference need not collapse into the anarchic relativism of experience. As feminist perspectives have amply described, sensitivity to historical context is paramount for the examination of meaning-creation (Nicholson 1990b, 9–10). A postmodern cultural studies, informed by poststructuralist elements, situates that examination within processes of media culture.

A Postmodern Cultural Studies: Media Culture as Ideological Text

Jean Lyotard: The Postmodern Context

The ambiguous nature of the term *postmodern* lies in its application to a seemingly endless variety of situations. I dispense with offering a neat catalogue of definitions or characteristics. Such a traditional approach violates the nature of postmodern reality in any case. Instead, I introduce the idea of postmodern *context*, meant to capture the complexity of contemporary sociocultural life. The decentered subject of poststructuralism is located within this context. Self is defined through symbolic knowledge, the fleeting, ever-changing, even mythical, product of linguistic communication processes (Barthes 1957/72). As these processes are mediated, and thereby increasingly complicated, the creation of meaning is transformed. As a symbol system, culture develops endless layers of knowledge, sources, and interpretations.

According to Jean-Francois Lyotard, the "postmodern condition" represents a radical transformation in the nature of knowledge and its legitimation. In his words:

> The object of this study is the condition of knowledge in the most highly developed societies. I have decided to use the term *postmodern* to describe that condition. The word is in current use on the American continent among sociologists and critics; it designates the state of our culture following the transformations which, since the end of the nineteenth century, have altered the game rules for science, literature, and the arts. The present study will place these transformations in the context of the crisis of narratives. [*italics* in the original] (Lyotard 1979/84, xxiii)

For Lyotard, postmodern forms of knowledge represent a rupture with those of the past. Modernism is marked by grand sociocultural narratives such as patriarchy, individualism, progress, and democracy. The validity of knowledge is centered in the naturalistic, objective, quantifiable character of the scientific method. As evolved from the Enlightenment, science has never been a pure, closed system; but its continued dominance requires explanation and legitimation as such. Consequently, the linguistic rules of science—describing and impacting the natural universe through cause/effect imagery, laws, technology, and prediction—have precluded serious challenges from being voiced except sporadically.

The exact nature of the modern/postmodern break is open to debate (Lyotard 1991; Best and Kellner 2001, 11–21). Anthony Giddens (1990, 1991) argues that modernity has not disappeared even as the postmodern emerges. Therefore, describing the boundary between the two as a rupture may be inaccurate. As previously noted, Best and Kellner (1997) describe the shift as the postmodern turn. The transformation from one to the other is gradual, necessarily incomplete. In their words:

> One could indeed argue that the modern itself is highly polysemous and unstable, constantly undergoing change and development. On this reading, the modern is always articulating itself in novel or radically new forms, and the "postmodern" can thus be interpreted as a form of the modern. (Best and Kellner 1997, 25–26)

Additionally, "the postmodern is a radicalization of the modern, which intensifies modern phenomena like commodification, massification, technology, and the media to a degree that generates genuine discontinuities and novelties from the modern world" (Best and Kellner 1997, 26).

Postmodern forms of knowledge represent at least the genesis of the breakup of the scientific narrative. As Lyotard observes:

> In contemporary society and culture—postindustrial society, postmodern culture—the question of the legitimation of knowledge is formulated in different terms. The grand narrative has lost its credibility, regardless of what mode of unification it uses, regardless of whether it is a speculative narrative or a narrative of emancipation. The decline of narrative can be seen as an effect of the blossoming of techniques and technologies since the Second World War, which has shifted emphasis from the

CHAPTER FIVE

>ends of action to its means: it can also be seen as an effect of a redeployment of advanced liberal capitalism after its retreat under the protection of Keynesianism during the period 1930–60, a renewal that has eliminated the communist alternative and valorized the individual enjoyment of goods and services. (Lyotard 1979/84, 37–38)

The postmodern condition, then, represents increasingly fragmented knowledge forms linked to consumer capitalism. In countless contexts, the individual actor must confront a bewildering array of choices, mass-mediated for consumption. Traditional evaluations of knowledge tend to blur or even lose their distinctiveness (Lyotard 1988, 6–7). For instance, knowledge becomes at once true and entertaining—indeed, true because it *is* entertaining. Science is politicized, and politics conflates into salacious scandal.

Increasingly, postmodern popular cultural images represent the reproduction of social life for consumption and meaning-creation (Storey 1999). Communication as "language games" replaces traditional narratives, and the self becomes an active participant in the process. According to Lyotard:

>A *self* does not amount to much, but no self is an island; each exists in a fabric of relations that is now more complex and mobile than ever before. Young or old, man or woman, rich or poor, a person is always located at "nodal points" of specific communication circuits, however tiny these may be. [*italics* in the original] (Lyotard 1979/84, 15)

In this communicative transformation of self, popular culture has become an important form of postmodern knowledge. Its consumption links the participation of both performer/creators and audiences. Finally, it competes with other knowledge sources in the postmodern terrain with vitality and validity (Storey 1999).

Lyotard's conception of the postmodern is arguably optimistic or at least neutral. His intent is to describe the undermining of grand teleological narratives and the change in the nature of cultural knowledge over the last half century (Lyotard 1997). In any event, his description of the postmodern condition stops short of a poststructuralist critique. The contextualization of knowledge and self is a process traceable from the dawn of modernism to the present day. However, its postmodern, poststructuralist manifestations assume the widest array of guises, altering contemporary cultural experience in qualitative ways. Chief among these is the discursive nature of such experience.

Michel Foucault: Knowledge, Discourse, and the Practice of Ideology

The work of Michel Foucault defies easy classification as structuralist or poststructuralist. Its poststructuralist edge can be viewed as an interwoven dialogue involving elements of structuralism, phenomenology, and hermeneutics (Dreyfus and Rabinow 1983, xix). His project decenters grand historical narratives such as progress as well as the idea of a unique knowing actor (i.e., subject). As a result his views have stimulated much controversy among Marxists, feminists, traditional historians, and other poststructuralists.

Foucault conceives of culture as historicized discourses or discursive formations:

> Whenever one can describe, between a number of statements, such a system of dispersion, whenever, between objects, types of statement, concepts, or thematic choices, one can define a regularity (an order, correlations, positions and functionings, transformations), we will say, for the sake of convenience, that we are dealing with a *discursive formation.* [*italics* in the original] (Foucault 1972a, 38)

He analyses a number of such discourses including madness (Foucault 1965/88), man as a subject of scientific knowledge (1970/94), medicine (1973/94), crime and punishment (1975/79), and sexuality (1976/90, 1984/88, 1984/90). Of particular importance are so-called rules of formation: "conditions of existence (but also of coexistence, maintenance, modification, and disappearance) in a given discursive division" (Foucault 1972a, 38). These rules of formation are not to be equated with a set of discoverable structural codes or keys to historical interpretation. Rather they represent a sort of loose analytic framework associated as much with a sensitivity to historical discontinuity as any linear interpretation. Furthermore, they "include considerations involving who may speak, on what subjects, in what contexts, with what authority, and so forth" (Surber 1998, 208). Rules of formation, then, describe the practical processes through which discursive knowledge is institutionalized

CHAPTER FIVE

and thereby legitimated as truth. Foucault maintains that the historical actor is thoroughly controlled through such ideologized constructions of knowledge, no more so than by the force of modern expert scientific opinion. His critique of the impact of such narratives on individual lives exposes the coercive nature of commonly accepted knowledge as sources of power in the hands of credentialed experts.

As a cultural critic Foucault (1972a, 1972b) develops his interrelated methods of archaeology and genealogy in order to "open the [historical] structures up to temporal discontinuity and shifts that determined the endless game of discursive practices" (Dosse 1997b, 238). Archaeology represents a method of critical description for Foucault, an attempt to problematize the emergence and transformation of discursive historical knowledge:

> the problem is no longer one of tradition, of tracing a line, but one of division, of limits; it is no longer one of lasting foundations, but one of transformations that serve as new foundations, the rebuilding of foundations. (Foucault 1972a, 5)

Conversely, genealogy is a method of prescription, the demystification of knowledge as an historical mechanism of social control. At the same time, genealogy constitutes an attempt to interweave historical subjectivity, knowledge, power, and social control into a fluid, powerful interpretive strategy—in short, a counterpoint to the controlling function of scientific discourse (Dreyfus and Rabinow 1983, 237).

Archaeology and genealogy represent Foucault's interrelated projects of historical criticism. In both cases Foucault's intent is not to rewrite history, but to decenter it:

> In short, the history of thought, of knowledge, of philosophy, of literature seems to be seeking, and discovering, more and more discontinuities, whereas history itself appears to be abandoning the irruption of events [discourses] in favor of stable structures. (Foucault 1972a, 6)

With his emphasis on discourse formations as ideological practice, Foucault equates knowledge with power. His hope is to expose their intimate connectedness in postmodern society: "Power is the suppressed and concealed other of the modern disciplines concerned with knowledge, and

Foucault's strategy is to reveal this suppressed hierarchy, reverse its terms, and reinscribe them, in a new account of both power and knowledge" (Surber 1998, 214).

This creative reversal of power and knowledge has profound implications for the nature of consciousness and the historical subject. For Foucault the traditional history of knowledge, especially since the eighteenth century, is an attempt to justify and portray as natural the movement from discourses based on reason to those founded on empirical science. Embedded in this linear narrative is the knowing historical subject. As a poststructuralist Foucault decenters not only history, but its subject as well. He offers the following critique of history and the subject as a unifying narrative:

> If the history of thought could remain the locus of uninterrupted continuities, if it could endlessly forge connexions [sic] that no analysis could undo without abstraction, if it could weave, around everything that men say and do, obscure synthesis that anticipate for him, prepare him, and lead him endlessly towards his future, it would provide a privileged shelter for the sovereignty of consciousness. (Foucault 1972a, 12)

With genealogy Foucault seeks to unravel the problematic of power in contemporary society, to "show us how our culture attempts to normalize individuals through increasingly rationalized means, by turning them into meaningful subjects and docile objects" (Dreyfus and Rabinow 1983, xxvii). Increasingly, the exercise of power in everyday life is characterized less by brutality and caprice, and more by its natural appearance—what might be called the "practice of ideology" in various scientific, political, economic, religious, and media discourses.

Foucault (1983, 208–9) details three modes by which individuals are created as or transformed into subjects by themselves and others: scientific classification, dividing practices, and subjectification.[11] Scientific classification refers to the institutionalization of science as the ascendant anthropomorphic discursive formation. Dividing practices objectify the individual as insane, sick, or criminal, always with comparison to the sane, healthy, and law-abiding. Finally, subjectification describes the ways the individual transforms her- or himself into a subject, searching for sexuality, happiness, fulfillment, and so on. Power, then, is layered into historical consciousness, finding its everyday expression with respect to the "embodied subject" (Surber 1998, 213).

CHAPTER FIVE

Creation or transformation-as-subject may take the form of three interrelated struggles. According to Foucault:

> Generally, it can be said that there are three types of struggles: either against forms of domination (ethnic, social, and religious); against forms of exploitation which separate individuals from what they produce; or against that which ties the individual to himself and submits him to others in this way (struggles against subjection, against forms of subjectivity and submission). (Foucault 1983, 212)

He maintains that these three modes may exist singularly or in combinations with one another (although one tends to dominate). Furthermore, he observes that in contemporary society the third type of transformation—struggles against subjection, forms of subjectivity and submission—has become relatively more important, if not paramount. Simultaneously, struggles against forms of domination and exploitation have not disappeared (Foucault, 1983, 212–13).

Foucault (1983, 212) distinguishes two meanings of the term *subject*: "subject to someone else by control and dependence, and tied to his own identity by a conscience or self-knowledge." Power is thus an exterior imposition and an interiorized discourse. It is layered, dependent not on conscious manipulation by subjects but on the textual quality of discursive historical knowledge. In Foucault's (1970/94, 312) words, "man appears in his ambiguous position as an object of knowledge and as a subject that knows." This modern search for the keys to the problem of self Foucault (1970/94, 303–43) summarizes as "Man and his Doubles." Discursive knowledge masks a will to power (Dreyfus and Rabinow 1983, 114).

Foucault (1997) remains deeply ambivalent about the Enlightenment as an historical and philosophical construct, refusing to submit to the "blackmail" of being "for or against" it. He summarizes the importance of genealogy as a kind of "permanent critique of ourselves" aimed at avoiding easy comparisons between humanism and Enlightenment. He states further:

> We must proceed with the analysis of ourselves as beings who are historically determined, to a certain extent, by the Enlightenment. Such an analysis implies a series of historical inquiries that are as precise as possible; and these inquiries will not be oriented retrospectively toward the

> "essential kernel of rationality" that can be found in the Enlightenment, which would have to be preserved in any event; they will be oriented toward the "contemporary limits of the necessary," that is, toward what is not or is no longer indispensable for the constitution of ourselves as autonomous subjects. (Foucault 1997, 313)

Foucault's poststructuralist critique begins with the historical text and continues to include an examination of the historical actor. Viewed from the perspective of Lyotard's postmodern condition, it would seem that the totalizing historical narratives with which Foucault is concerned have begun to break up. I now offer a reading of the "linguistic turn" in poststructuralism as found in the work of Jacques Derrida.

Jacques Derrida: The Poststructuralist "Linguistic Turn"

Derrida's poststructuralist project is a thoroughgoing critique of structural linguistics and phenomenology, calling into question the basic presuppositions of Western philosophical tradition. While his deconstructive project has been particularly influential for literary criticism (Attridge 1992; Derrida 1992; Makaryk 1993), Derrida was trained in philosophy and his thought remains best situated in terms of philosophical debate. Derrida's unraveling of structuralism and phenomenology is found in several principal works: *Of Grammatology* (1967/76); *Speech and Phenomena* (1967/73); *Writing and Difference* (1967/78); and *Positions* (1972/81b). Given my interest in the poststructuralist linguistic turn, I limit my discussion of Derrida to his critique of structural linguistics (Saussure 1986) and his alternative of deconstruction.[12]

Derrida's critique of Western philosophy proceeds from two fundamental, encompassing observations: As an historical narrative, it privileges, places above, or favors speech over writing (i.e., is *phonocentric*). At the same time traditional philosophy equates being with immediate presence (i.e., is *logocentric*). As Derrida maintains:

> *the history of* (the only) *metaphysics*, which has, in spite of all differences, not only from Plato to Hegel (even including Leibniz) but also, beyond these apparent limits, from the pre-Socratics to Heidegger, always assigned the origin of truth in general to the logos, the history of truth, of the truth of truth, has always been . . . the debasement of writing, and

CHAPTER FIVE

its repression outside full speech. [*italics* in the original] (Derrida 1967/76, 3)

While Derrida's (1967/76, 102–5; 1972) project owes much to the structuralist recasting of philosophy, he feels the latter stopped short of the radical critique needed. In particular, he believes the structural linguistics of Ferdinand de Saussure exhibits the same phonocentric and logocentric biases.

Saussure (1986, 15–16) conceptualizes linguistics as subsidiary to semiology, the latter defined as the science of signs in social life; linguistics is concerned specifically with the study of language; and language is conceived as a structured, closed system of signs (Saussure 1986, 21–22). The focus of linguistics, then, is the structure of language. For Saussure (1986, 65–71) this structure emerges from the sign, itself constituted as a *relation* between the signifier (an auditory or visual image) and the signified (a mental conceptualization) (Surber 1998, 159–60). Signs are arbitrary in that there are no natural connections which link images to concepts. At the same time, signs are sociocultural constructions dependent on the norms of the linguistic community. Finally, Saussure's (1986, 96–98) conception of language and its structure is synchronic, the study of its relational rules at a single point in time. As a result, spoken language is privileged over written: "[W]riting obscures our view of the language. Writing is not a garment, but a disguise" (Saussure 1986, 29).

Derrida (1967/76, 29) describes the traditional phonocentric/logocentric stance of linguistics: "The science of linguistics determines language—its field of objectivity—in the last instance and in the irreducible simplicity of its essence, as the unity of the *phone*, the *glossa*, and the *logos*. This determination is by rights anterior to all the eventual differentiations that could arise within the systems of terminology of the different schools" [*italics* in the original]. Speech produces language which yields reason/truth.

In Saussure's general linguistics spoken language is a closed system, the "center" of which is discoverable as a set of structural codes relating signs (i.e., words) to one another. According to Derrida (1972/81b, 25–26), by reversing the hierarchy of spoken and written language, the logocentric notion of "centered" truth is problematized. At the same time he questions why Saussure places writing "outside" of the closed linguistic system, as a kind of second-order activity (1967/76, 34). Derrida feels Saussure means to protect and restore the system against "contamination" from writing. Indeed, Saussure (1986, 30–31) acknowledges the "tyranny" of the written word, especially regarding modification of pronunciation.

Finally, Derrida (1972/81b, 27–28) questions the synchronic, cross-sectional framework of structural linguistics. That is, a synchronic structure may note difference in meaning without accounting for how those differences are produced. Derrida coined the term *differance* to describe the latter situation, the play of differences. In his words:

> Differences are neither fallen from the sky nor inscribed once and for all in a closed system, a static structure that a synchronic and taxonomic operation could exhaust. Differences are the effects of transformations, and from this vantage the theme of *differance* is incompatible with the static, synchronic, taxonomic, ahistorical motifs in the concept *structure*. [*italics* in the original] (Derrida 1972/81b, 27)

Introducing *differance* is much more than ironic wordplay. Contrasting with difference (opposing meaning contexts), Derrida's verbal invention describes the process(es) *within a text* which give rise to differences in meaning: "*Differance* is neither signs nor the differences between them but a sort of open field of play out of which both arise... [an] intersection of temporality becoming spatialized" [*italics* in the original] (Surber 1998, 205).

Derrida's "ultrastructuralism" (Dosse 1997b, 17) develops the philosophical project of deconstruction, meant to decenter or problematize the philosophical subject of traditional philosophy as well as the discoverable structure of synchronic linguistics. He seeks to reverse or rupture the phonocentric/logocentric biases, "to display the latent metaphysical structure of the text in a way that opens the possibility of understanding the text in a way different from that intended by its author" (Dickens 1990, 149).[13] Deconstruction does not destroy meaning, but recasts it as a textual process, what might be called the continuous discovery of *differance* in the text. Barbara Johnson, translator of Derrida's *Disseminations*, summarizes the problematic addressed by the play of *differance*: "The illusion of the self-presence of meaning or of consciousness is thus produced by the repression of the differential structures from which they spring" (Johnson 1981, ix).

CHAPTER FIVE

Deconstruction represents a two-step process for Derrida, involving reversal and displacement (Dickens 1990, 149). The first involves a description of oppositional meaning hierarchies. "To deconstruct the opposition is above all, at a particular moment, to reverse the hierarchy" (Derrida 1972/81b, 41). The second step is to present a critical alternative rendering of the text, a "'double reading' whereby each reading would serve as a starting point for a critique of the other" (Surber 1998, 203). Meaning is multilayered within the text and can only emerge from the play of differences. As Derrida observes, deconstruction proceeds as follows:

> through a double gesture, a double science, a double writing, put into practice a *reversal* of the classical opposition and a general *displacement* of the system. It is on that condition alone that deconstruction will provide the means of *intervening* in the field of opposition it criticizes and which is also a field of nondiscursive forces. [*italics* in the original] (Derrida 1977, 195)

Deconstruction is a radical stance insofar as it attempts to critically examine the presumed clarity of a text and thereby its meaning. The narrative text is open to endless interpretations, much like a literary product. This view of textual ambiguity is contained in Derrida's description of *differance*:

> It is a question, rather, of producing a new concept of writing. This concept can be called *gram* or *differance*. The play of differences supposes, in effect, syntheses and referrals which forbid at any moment, or in any sense, that a simple element be *present* in and of itself, referring only to itself. Whether in the order of spoken or written discourse, no element can function as a sign without referring to another element which itself is not simply present. This interweaving results in each "element"—phoneme or grapheme [spoken or written]—being constituted on the basis of the trace within it of the other elements of the chain or system. This interweaving, this textile, is the *text* produced only in the transformation of another text. Nothing, neither among the elements nor within the system, is anywhere ever simply present or absent. There are only, everywhere, differences and traces of traces. [*italics* in the original] (Derrida 1972/81b, 26)

Differance, the continuous transformation of textual and intertextual meaning, effectively counterbalances the phonocentric bias of contemporary thought—the primacy of speech over writing as a linguistic form. According to Johnson, "To mean, in other words, is automatically *not* to be. As soon as there is meaning there is difference" [*italics* in the original] (1981, ix). At the same time, Derrida's (1972, 264–65) elaboration of the shifting, changing text undermines the related logocentric bias (i.e., the belief that the text possesses an inherent structure, and that a real subject can be located there) and renders interpretation as problematic. If words, as signs, have no stable meaning, then texts are decentered, lacking in specific structure.

While textual deconstruction, emphasizing the instability of meaning, is largely considered apolitical (Lilla 1998), there has been some attempt to situate the practice in a Marxist theoretical context (Ryan 1982; Dickens 1990). Over the years Derrida has rarely discussed or drawn out the historical and political implications of his deconstructive project. Recently he has published two works in an apparent effort to do so. In *Politics of Friendship*, Derrida (1997) maintains in a typical poststructuralist guise that Western political thought is clouded by the concept of self-identity. The seeking of such identity in political groups masks individual differences for the sake of political unity. Furthermore political groupings, social classes, and nations are linguistic constructions, not natural (i.e., centered) categories. If these groupings promote unity of members, they establish hierarchies of power and privilege as well (Derrida 1997, 75–77, 276–78).

In *Specters of Marx* Derrida (1994) argues that Marx remained squarely in a logocentric dilemma, substituting a socialist narrative for a capitalistic one. He muses that we must search for a "certain experience of the emancipatory promise," found only in an "idea of justice." Such an experience is, Derrida asserts, "irreducible" and "undeconstructible." It may represent the "formality of a structural messianism, a messianism without religion, even a messianic without messianism" (Derrida 1994, 59). Ever the philosopher, Derrida may change meaning contexts to make his deconstructive project politically relevant to the new millennium. Still, it is unlikely that such quick, nimble jumps will provide a basis for political action. In fact, in Derrida's "revelation" of justice Mark Lilla (1998, 39–41) finds evidence of Derrida's "intellectual desperation." Indeed he argues that conceptions of both structuralism and deconstruction—as they have been put forward in American scholarship—"are philosophically and practically incompatible with liberal principles."

CHAPTER FIVE

As poststructuralists both Derrida and Foucault decenter consciousness and meaning (Nealon 1993, 67–71). By comparison, Derrida deconstructs all sorts of philosophical texts to probe for indeterminate meaning, while it might be argued that Foucault deconstructs history (Surber 1998, 215). Both find Saussure's structural linguistic paradigm inadequate to address sociocultural problems of contemporary society. At the same time, the removal of (wo)man from the reading of culture (substituting texts and linguistic discourses) creates the possibility of confusion and, even more, the charge of political decontextualization disguised as wordplay. The controversy about Martin Heidegger's Nazi involvement and his influence on their works (Appleby et al. 1994, 210; Derrida 1989; Lilla 1998, 38; Windschuttle 1997, 11–12) exposes a confounding postmodern conundrum: If the subject is only textual (Derrida) and knowledge masks a will to power (Foucault), how are postmodern values to be constructed? Furthermore, what standards of judgment (even textual ones) are the likely outcome of postmodern mediated political discourse? Since its spread to America, postmodern social theory has exhibited the capacity to promote liberation *and* despair. The postmodern cultural context, within which theory is embedded, is a kaleidoscope of image and meaning transformation. Indeed, the American context is marked by mediation and commodification. The scenario is a description and critique of these processes, an instance of strategic postmodern discourse. It is an attempt to recast modernist conceptions of deviance-labeling onto a textual terrain, to illuminate the contemporary conflict of self and cultural politics. Justice is an unfinished project in the postmodern turn, "the yet unrealized promise of the Enlightenment" (Lyman 1997d, 264).

Jean Baudrillard: The Problem of Meaning in Postmodern Culture

The work of Jean Baudrillard (1989) represents an influential critique of the American postmodern cultural terrain. Proceeding from a Marxist/structuralist stance, Baudrillard develops a thoroughgoing, if somewhat pessimistic, view of contemporary meaning-transformation (Kellner 1989, 2–6). He especially focuses on the centrality of meaning as found in popular cultural images.

Baudrillard's formulation, begun in his first book, *The System of Objects* (1968/96), rests on a critique of commodity in contemporary society.

His semiological analysis examines several types of objects, including functional (e.g., traditional consumer goods), nonfunctional or "marginal" (e.g., antiques, collections), and metafunctional (e.g., gadgets, robots). Furthermore, Baudrillard characterizes the interrelation of cultural objects as a "socio-ideological system" of consumption, in which credit and advertising play central roles. Utilizing the distinction in industrial society between "model" and "series," Baudrillard argues that cultural objects become personalized:

> *The psycho-sociological dynamic of model and series does not, therefore, operate at the level of the object's primary function, but merely at the level of a secondary function, at the level of the 'personalized' object.* That is to say: at the level of an object grounded simultaneously in individual requirements and in that system of differences which is, properly speaking, the cultural system itself. [*italics* in the original] (Baudrillard 1968/96, 140)

Our freedom to choose (e.g., one car instead of another), to make "our" objects personally relevant, is only apparently liberating or creative. At the same time it very definitely situates us within the integrative process of consumption (Baudrillard 1968/96, 141). Our specious choice is transmuted into conformity and acquiescence.

In *The Consumer Society* (1970/98) and "For a Critique of the Political Economy of the Sign" (1988b), Baudrillard further maps a postmodern theory of consumption to include signs as well as traditional objects. In consuming the former, contemporary culture links happiness with affluence. According to Baudrillard:

> We are here at the heart of consumption as total organization of everyday life, total homogenization, where everything is taken over and superseded in the ease and translucidity of an abstract 'happiness,' defined solely by the resolution of tensions. (Baudrillard 1970/98, 29–30)

Cultural meaning-creation is subject to the "social logic of consumption" whereby history is subverted to the satisfaction of increasingly symbolic needs: "Instead of prodigality, we have 'consumption,' consumption in perpetuity, twin sister to scarcity. It was social logic which brought primitive peoples the 'first' (and only) affluent society. It is our social logic which condemns us to luxurious and spectacular penury" (Baudrillard 1970/98, 68).

CHAPTER FIVE

The social logic of consumption is a practical ideology which constrains rather than liberates. The postmodern consumer replaces Marx's industrial worker-as-producer. Consumption is rationalized and elevated to unquestioned cultural status. As Baudrillard observes:

> Production and consumption are part of *one and the same process of expanded reproduction of the productive forces and their control*. This imperative, which is that of the system, passes into daily mentalities, ethics and ideology—and here is the great trick—in its *inverted* form: in the form of the liberation of needs, individual self-fulfillment, enjoyment and affluence, etc. The themes of Spending, Enjoyment and Non-Calculation ("Buy now, pay later") have taken over from the "puritan" themes of Saving, Work, and Heritage. [*italics* in the original] (Baudrillard 1970/98, 82)

This conflation of production into consumption and concomitant value reversal can be traced to Baudrillard's (1988b) critique of the "political economy of the sign." In short, postmodern consumer culture treats signs of consumption, of affluence, as possessing unique value (Storey 1999). While Thorstein Veblen (1899/1994) describes consumption among the wealthy "leisure class," Baudrillard contends that signs of consumption in postmodern culture are more dispersed. As Kellner writes:

> Baudrillard sees the entire society as organized around consumption and display of commodities through which individuals gain prestige, identity and standing. In this system, the more prestigious one's commodities—houses, cars, clothes and so on—the higher one's standing in the realm of sign value. Thus, just as words take on meaning according to their status in a differential system of language, so sign values take on meaning according to their place in a differential system of prestige and status. (Kellner 1989, 21)

Postmodern culture represents a kind of symbolic rupture with past ages, emerging from signification, meaning, and commoditization of experience. As Baudrillard (1988e, 135; 1981/94, 121) notes, there are three orders of *simulacra* (i.e., the relationship between images and the reality they supposedly represent). The first order is called counterfeit, in which signs were understood as more or less direct surrogates for the natural world. This scheme dominated from the Renaissance to the Industrial Revolution and was superseded by the order of production. Here, an underlying natural reality continues to be represented in the mass production and reproduction of commodities. Over time, the interrelationship of natural reality with its representational signs becomes increasingly less direct, problematic, even blurred. In the third order, that of simulation, the distinction between processes of signification and external signified reality has disappeared. Traditional modernist conceptions of commodities (effectively bounded in time and space) are replaced by signs-as-information. The latter come to represent "hyperreality" or systems of knowledge without meaningful empirical referents, so-called "copies without originals."

Baudrillard refers to this collapsing or conflation of the boundary which constitutes meaning as *implosion*. In his words:

> [the orders of simulacra] no longer constitute the imaginary in relation to the real, they are themselves an anticipation of the real, and thus leave no room for any sort of fictional anticipation—they are immanent, and thus leave no room for any kind of imaginary transcendence. The field opened is that of simulation in the cybernetic sense, that is, of the manipulation of these models at every level (scenarios, the setting up of simulated situations, etc.) but then *nothing distinguishes this operation from the operation itself and the gestation of the real: there is no more fiction.* [*italics* in the original] (Baudrillard 1981/94, 122)

In the order of hyperrealism and implosion, reality or truth does not disappear so much as it becomes hauntingly irrelevant. Thus, information is reproduced and consumed without regard to its truthfulness:

> Reality itself founders in hyperrealism, the meticulous reduplication of the real, preferably through another, reproductive medium, such as photography. From medium to medium, the real is volatilized, becoming an allegory of death. But it is also, in a sense, reinforced through its own destruction. It becomes *reality for its own sake*, the fetishism of the lost object: no longer the object of representation, but the ecstasy of denial and of its own extermination: the hyperreal. [*italics* in the original] (Baudrillard 1988d, 144–45)

For Baudrillard (1981/94, 79–86), postmodern hyperrealism is, above all, a mediated system of cultural meaning production. Like Foucault, he posits that the continuous subject/object dialectic of experience is intensified in the postmodern terrain. Reinserting (wo)man into the historical

CHAPTER FIVE

narrative accomplishes little; further, the increasing availability and circulation of commoditized cultural knowledge only exacerbates the problems of its truth value. The perfect crime is the "murder" of reality (Baudrillard 1996; 2000, 59–67). In the postmodern terrain, meaning is overproduced, mediated, and staged, at the expense of its relevance (Baudrillard 1981/94, 86). Compared to Lyotard, this view of the postmodern context is decidedly negative in outlook. Contemporary meaning processes stultify experience rather than liberate it. In the hyperreal, history is not at an end; instead, it is reversed and subject to erasure and effacement (Baudrillard 1994, 10–13).

Hyperrealism and implosion are particularly evident in the elevation of popular culture as a knowledge form. Baudrillard's (1981/94) analyses of Disneyland and Watergate, as well as the "holographic" process of television, explore the imploded boundary traditionally marking reality and cultural signification. With regard to television as a mass medium, Baudrillard writes the following:

> The TV studio transforms you into holographic characters: one has the impression of being materialized in space by the light of projectors, like translucid characters who pass through the masses (that of millions of TV viewers) exactly as your real hand passes through the unreal hologram without encountering any resistance—but without consequences: having passed through the hologram has rendered your hand unreal as well. (Baudrillard 1981/94, 105)

The subject sees a perfect double (i.e., the hologram), created for mass consumption. Implosion renders history as myth, created for the moment: "the hologram is now part of this 'subliminal comfort' that is our destiny, of this happiness now consecrated to the mental simulacrum and to the environmental fable of special effects" (Baudrillard 1981/94, 107).

Kellner refers to much of Baudrillard's cultural analysis as the "postmodern carnival." This term captures the simulated nature of much social exchange. Baudrillard examines fashion, life and death, art and architecture, utilizing the "carnivalesque 'logic of the turnabout and the inside out,' parodying modernity's rules of the game, codes, conventions and hierarchies and pointing to their conventionality, arbitrariness and frequent ludicrousness" (Kellner 1989, 93). Eventually the postmodern simulacrum transmutes into what Baudrillard calls the "end of the social" (Surber 1998, 224). The commodification of the subject precludes significant personal or political response:

> This is our destiny: subject to opinion polls, information, publicity, statistics; constantly confronted with the anticipated statistical verification of our behavior, and absorbed by this permanent refraction of our least movements, we are no longer confronted with our own will. We are no longer even alienated, because for that it is necessary for the subject to be divided in itself, confronted with the other, to be contradictory. Now, where there is no other, the scene of the other, like that of politics and of society, has disappeared. (Baudrillard 1988d, 210)

As does Derrida (and to a somewhat lesser extent, Foucault), Baudrillard views postmodern culture with much suspicion, even alarm. Human action, Lyotard's liberating postmodern condition, has been erased. The decentered subject, viewed through a modernist lens, has little voice. In his critique of Baudrillard, Kellner (1989, 188) exposes the "metaphysical imaginary" (the subject/object relativity of poststructuralism) and consequent instances of sexism and racism.

Interactionist Labeling and Cultural Studies: Scenarios of Meaning

Earlier in this chapter, I contrasted different senses of the postmodern context—as rupture or "turn" (Best and Kellner 1997). An historically informed cultural studies is best situated in the more gradual "turn." Such a conception allows a textual critique of reality and subject as ambiguous and contested without final erasure. It also links the emerging postmodern turn to the related linguistic one evident in cultural studies. Meaning is only glimpsed, never unequivocally stated. The scenario represents the combination of a mature interactionist perspective on deviance-labeling with postmodern cultural studies. From chapter 2 I restate the guiding questions animating this combination:

> What is the social context of rule (i.e., norm) creation or construction?

CHAPTER FIVE

> How is the deviant label articulated as stigmatization in various situations (i.e., rendered representative of individual persons, groups, and social categories)?
> How do the larger culture- and meaning-making institutions of society (e.g., mass and popular media, film, social science, art, religion, politics, science, and education) shape the experience of individuals in everyday interaction?
> What is the historical context of cultural production and consumption in postmodern America?
> How do ideological narratives (e.g., those based on gender, youth, race, and class) give structure and meaning to lived existence?

With these questions as my backdrop, I turn now to readings of specific scenarios in the following two chapters. Chapter 6 examines the stigma of deviance as generated in post–World War II youth subculture, and chapter 7 situates an historical murder-event even earlier in the postmodern turn, critiquing its meaning-creation as both news and entertainment.

Notes

1. There are numerous works addressing this topic, representing varying degrees of treatment depth and, sometimes, difficulty for the reader. Madan Sarup (1988/93) offers a succinct introduction to the area; similarly, John Storey (1993, 1996) outlines a cultural studies approach to the study of popular culture.

2. For more complete treatments, see Connor (1989); Harvey (1990); Best and Kellner (1991); Jones, Natter, and Schatzki (1993); and Natoli and Hutcheon (1993).

3. Richard Johnson (1986/87, 41–42) identifies four definitional strategies under the rubric of cultural studies: an intellectual and political tradition, in the relation of the field to academic disciplines, with regard to theoretical paradigms, and with respect to representative objects of study. Following his lead I focus on the last of these strategies. Norman K. Denzin (1991a) and Ben Agger (1992) offer other summaries of definitional concerns.

4. Agger (1992) suggests a number of senses in which culture studies has problematized its subject matter, "culture is us, culture as practice, culture is conflict (over meaning)." Each of these viewpoints is fundamentally a critique of culture

as a social creation, as is the general elevation of popular culture forms to a legitimate status of inquiry.

5. Barry Smart (1990, 1992) and Bryan S. Turner (1990a, 1990b) offer summaries of definitional controversies, especially the interface of modernism and postmodernism.

6. In their development of a critical anthropology, George E. Marcus and Michael M. J. Fisher (1986) speak of a "crisis of representation" within the postmodern moment, substantially similar to the present one. In their words, "The crisis arises from uncertainty about adequate means of describing social reality. In the United States it is the expression of the failure of post–World War II paradigms, or the unifying ideas of a remarkable number of fields, to account for conditions within American society, if not within Western societies globally, which seem to be in a state of profound transition" (Marcus and Fisher 1986, 8–9).

7. Poststructuralism is the unique American designation to distinguish the ideas of first-generation thinkers (e.g., Levi-Strauss) from those following (e.g., Foucault and Derrida). No such French distinction is made; the entire movement is labeled structuralism (Lilla 1998, 37; Dosse 1997b, 17).

8. John Storey (1993, 43–68) gives a brief summary of this period. Stanley Aronowitz (1993, 109–30) provides a general overview of the emergence and development of British cultural studies.

9. Because of their Marxist contribution to the development of British cultural studies, I include a discussion of Althusser and Gramsci at this point rather than in sections on Marxism or materialism (Storey 1993, 67; Surber 1998, 85–91).

10. For additional interpretations of postmodern images in film, see Ryan and Kellner (1988), Kellner (1995), Lyman (1997a, 1997b) and Thompson (1998). John Storey (1996, 54–74) discusses the relationship of film criticism to the emergence of cultural studies.

11. Paul Rabinow (1984, 7–9) offers a fuller discussion of the three modes of self-transformation or objectification.

12. For in-depth presentations of Derrida's phenomenological critique, see *Speech and Phenomenon* (1967/73), *Dissemination* (1972/81a), and *Margins of Philosophy* (1972/82). Derrida's early writing is aimed at developing grammatology, a science of writing. Derrida quickly concludes this to be an "impossible" task since the unity of scientific thought is one focus of his philosophical critique (Derrida 1967/76, 74).

13. For a variety of philosophical perspectives on deconstruction, see Sallis (1987).

CHAPTER SIX

ROCK IN A HARD PLACE: HISTORICAL STIGMATIZATION OF ADOLESCENT SUBCULTURES IN POPULAR MUSIC

In the 1960s the Centre for Contemporary Cultural Studies in Great Britain began to demystify the interrelationships among consumption, production, and reproduction in everyday life (Hall et al. 1980; Grossberg et al. 1992). This effort involved exposing the ideological basis of meaning. In the words of Dick Hebdige: "All human societies *reproduce* themselves in this way through a process of 'naturalization.' It is through this process—a kind of inevitable reflex of all social life—that *particular* sets of social relations, *particular* ways of organizing the world appear to us as if they were universal and timeless" (1979/2002, 14). Ideology, then, is discursive, socially realized through consumption in corporate capitalism (Featherstone 1991). Ideological demystification was linked to images of popular culture. Political expression became a matter of subcultural style (Hebdige 1979/2002) and resistance to dominant social forms (Hall and Jefferson 1975/2002b). In this context, rock music was seen as an important site of deviance-generation and consumption (Cohen 1972/93; Frith 1981). More recently, this focus on the importance of ideology (Althusser 1971; Gramsci 1971)—and its relationship to popular culture—has given way to a postmodern turn (McRobbie 1994). In this vein, my studies of rock music (Dotter 1987, 1994, forthcoming) situate meaning in the interplay between artist and audience, cultural hero and active interpreters of heroism—in a mediated process of consumption/reproduction of identities and individual lives.

Popular culture narratives are mythical in the sense that they emerge over time, represent both social fact as well as individual experience, and are constantly rewritten. Greil Marcus captures this mythical interactive quality of popular music: "If they are in touch with their audiences and with the images of community their songs hint at, rock 'n' rollers get to see their myths and parables in action, and ultimately they may even find out what they are worth" (Marcus 1975/97).

This chapter has three interrelated purposes. First I detail the historical interrelation between rock music and the emergence of youth subculture from the 1950s to the 1970s. Particular attention will be paid to the development of youth as a social category as well as its shifting relationships to those of race, gender, and class. Second, I critique two deviant events within this historical scenario of youth subculture emergence: the staging of the Woodstock Festival in 1969 (Makower 1989; Goodman 1997) and the December 1979 tragedy at the Cincinnati Riverfront Coliseum, in which eleven concertgoers lost their lives in a stampede to enter the facility for a concert by the Who (Fuller 1981; Barnes 1982/2000). The media reconstructions of each of these events were extensive and helped frame the process of deviance-labeling associated with youth and rock as the music evolved.

Third, I take up the topic of aging rock performer as deviant master status through an interpretive biography (Denzin 1989a) of Pete Townshend, guitarist and songwriter of the Who. Not only was Pete a participant in both of the above events, he has continued to perform solo and in various incarnations of the Who to the present day.

Rock Music and Youth Subculture

Rock music emerged from an amalgam of social and cultural forces appearing after World War II. Although this early history is by now much-chronicled in popular sources (Gillett 1983; Ward et al. 1986; Altschuler 2003), it is best understood as a postmodern narrative of cultural meaning-creation with three primary strands: the continuing emergence of mass forms of entertainment, the centrality of age for the development of the rock audience as youth subculture, and the ambiguities and conflicts of meaning that marked the music and its relation to that subculture. By 1970 rock was the dominant form of popular music culturally and commercially, as a social category "teenager" was replaced by youth, and social deviance associated with the music, its performers, and audiences had broadened (Dotter 1994).

Rock Music as Popular Culture

The early history of rock and roll—and later, rock—music has been told in many forms: as an emerging style of popular music (Belz 1972; Gillett 1983; Bayles 1994; Miller 1999); as a developing commercial enterprise (Denisoff 1975, 1986; Chapple and Garofalo 1977; Goodman 1997); and as the cultural backdrop for political change (Rodnitzky 1976; London 1984; Orman 1984; Pielke 1986; Altschuler 2003). In all of these the music represents a post–World War II mediated popular culture. According to Philip Ennis (1992, 2), the story of rock and roll "illuminates deeper social issues not generally addressed. These include the nature of social and artistic boundaries, their creation and maintenance, their violation and repair." Furthermore, Ennis (1992, 1–2) contends that by the 1950s rock and roll represented "a new kind of music, different from the others not just artistically but in the way it engaged politics and commerce." Still, its historical development has not been linear, but rather marked by numerous trajectories. In *Rock and Roll: An Unruly History*, the companion volume to the ten-part PBS television documentary, Robert Palmer (1995, 11) observes, "History is never tidy, but rock and roll history is particularly resistant to neatness and order. It's almost as unruly as the music itself, which is saying a lot."

As popular culture rock and roll has been called the "seventh stream." The preceding six—from which rock and roll emerged—are pop, black pop, country pop, jazz, folk, and gospel (Ennis 1992, 16). A musical stream has three characteristics: an artistic system, an economic structure, and a social movement. Of particular importance for a stream is its ethos, the cultural backdrop of style and expression that it engenders (Ennis 1992, 21–22). Streams have not been discrete products of history, nor have they been mutually exclusive. Rather, their interrelationships are complex, ambiguous, and often conflicting. According to Ennis, "That turbulence was exacerbated for rocknroll because it was born not only from six streams whose artistic heritages were different from one another, but also because its birth took place in the postwar untidiness" (Ennis 1992, 23).

This untidiness included the changing sociocultural categories of age, gender, race, and class. In this connection, Martha Bayles identifies a "blood knot"[1] of race and sex, the propensity "to reduce African American music to a crude caricature of dehumanized sex" (Bayles 1994, 11). The "blood knot" predates the appearance of 1950s rock and roll, but found

CHAPTER SIX

singular expression there as early white artists like Elvis Presley and Jerry Lee Lewis popularized black musical style for white youthful audiences. Bayles notes the historical context in the culture of the American South: "[T]he galvanizing music of the early rock 'n' rollers can be seen as striking a blow, not against sexual morality per se, but against the moral hypocrisies of a color-coded double standard" (Bayles 1994, 141). While the blood knot was loosened a bit, earlier artists only took its transformation to a point. Still, as Nelson George notes, "[T]he term 'rock & roll'—perhaps the perfect emblem of white Negroism—was in itself powerful enough to create a sensibility of its own" (George 1988, 67).

The musical stream, its artists, audience, and ethos, continued to evolve as a commercial enterprise. While Ennis (1992) recognizes that the music is new in how it engages politics and commerce, he likewise sees its beginnings in earlier streams. Similarly, Bayles presents a nuanced view of rock history, contrasting its early blood knot encounter with the myth of cultural revolution, which came later: "In the 1960s rock 'n' roll became 'rock,' and ceased to be an expression of the American South, with its agonizing wrestling over the uses of enthusiasm. Figures like Presley, Lewis, and Little Richard, who conceived of life and music as a battleground between God and the Devil, got shunted aside by a new generation with a new battle" (Bayles 1994, 141). This battle, between "Art and Society," emerged in the 1960s and continues to the present. Thus Bayles contrasts the early Southern-rooted struggles of rock to define itself with the later commercialization of the music and the myth of early rock as revolution. In her view early rock was revolutionary only in the eventual control of the market by major record labels, "not in any sweeping musical, sexual, or racial sense" (Bayles 1994, 115).

In the 1960s and 1970s the rock stream developed an increasingly centralized economic structure, which exploited artists as cultural heroes (Dotter 1987) and the countercultural ethos of rebellion. Sales and profits climbed steadily, the former reaching $4 billion in 1978, surpassing any other type of entertainment revenues, including sports and movies (Friedlander 1996, 233; Goodman 1997, xi). Most importantly, by the 1970s the audience for rock was changing. As Friedlander writes:

> The rock audience of the late 1960s was now encompassing much of the American under-thirty population. It was no longer the exclusive province of the very young or the disenchanted; rock was part of main-

stream culture. In the seventies the older and middle-class audience segments continued to purchase music by artists that wrote meaningful lyrics and accentuated melody and harmony—characteristics they enjoyed during the sixties. Their younger brothers and sisters and working-class cousins were usually more attracted to the evolving music, which contained a stronger beat, loud distorted guitars, and simple, sexually oriented, escapist sentiments. (Friedlander 1996, 233–34)

This confluence of popular culture, commerce, and audience expansion led, by 1970, to a "pause point" in rock as a musical stream. As Ennis describes the pause, "It was a shudder, youth's sense of the fragility of the world they were trying to remake, a recognition that forces darker and stronger than previously known had suddenly come down on them" (Ennis 1992, 344). I turn now to the changing meaning of age for the formation of youth subculture. It is the primary narrative of the music, even as it is bound to images of gender and race as well as class.

From Teenager to Youth: Rock and Subculture Formation

The rise of rock and roll as popular music in the 1950s and its dominance of the form in the 1960s is linked to the development of age as a social category. As James Miller frames the questions, "How did such a distinctly youthful form of music come to play a defining role in the global culture? Why should rock have become the music lingua franca of the last half of our century? And what can its evident power—and equally striking limits—tell us about the broader cultural character of our time?" (Miller 1999, 20).

To be sure, the importance of age as a social status predates the twentieth century, rooted especially in the biology of sexual development. Furthermore, the psychologist G. Stanley Hall (1904) is arguably the first to systematically develop a modern conception of adolescence. According to biographer Dorothy Ross, he "linked the turbulence of adolescence to a wide spectrum of physiological and psychological changes determined by evolution" (1972, 333). His ideas contained the seeds of adolescence as a social construction. Hall "worried over the degeneration of modern life and recalled an idealized version of a simpler and purer youth," As well, "he gloried in the passionate life of youth, which rose above the flat, workaday world of maturity and age" (Ross 1972, 335).

CHAPTER SIX

Adolescence assumed an even larger importance following World War II, as a summary description of sociocultural processes. In the 1940s popular press the usage of the term "adolescent" began to be interchanged with that of "teenager." Initially the latter was not laden with negative connotation. Rather it tended to be viewed as a more or less natural developmental stage on the way to adulthood. The high school experience gradually became central to this process. In fact, marketers of the day "usually portrayed teenagers as fun-loving, wholesome high school students eager to try out adult freedom, but willing to live by adult rules" (Palladino 1996, xv).

Ennis (1992, 6–7) traces the rise of rock and roll to two broader demographic and sociocultural process in postwar America, both of which amplify the importance of age for in the study of popular music. First, as the postwar generation began to reach teenage years, the optimistic flush of the victorious war had begun to wane. "By the time they got to high school in the late fifties . . . it was clear that the promise had been broken, or at least was not coming out the way the kids thought it would. Their response was to question, raise hell, do anything to avoid doing what the adults wanted" (Ennis 1992, 6). Second, the war's end witnessed a cultural explosion of the arts, popularizing them to a greater and greater number of Americans. As Ennis (1992, 7) notes, while the elite arts remained fairly insulated, other forms—due to democratization and mass marketing—proliferated. In the process artistic boundaries of both content and taste were expanded.

Ennis (1992, 19–20) refers to the first of these as "outside in" changes, and to the second as "inside out" ones. Their overlap linked culture and commerce, artist and audience, in an increasingly leisure-based economy. As one of the popularized arts of this process, music was slowly transformed. Amid the activity of the six streams, the seventh emerged. As Ennis writes, "There is simply no way to understand rocknroll without taking these two aspects into account: the young audience with all its adventures and misadventures on the one side and, on the other, the convoluted story of the music industry's internal plumbing" (Ennis 1992, 20).

Teenagers were not initially exploited as a distinct subcultural or economic group. Rock historian Charlie Gillett describes the relationship between music and audience:

> The growth of rock 'n' roll cannot be separated from the emergence, since the Second World War, of a new phenomenon: the adolescent or youth culture. Since the War, adolescents have made a greater show of enjoying themselves than they ever did before. Their impact has been particularly sharp because there were so few facilities that easily accommodated their new attitudes, interests, and increased wealth. Neither individual communities nor the mass communications industries anticipated the growth of adolescent culture, or responded quickly to it. (Gillett 1983, 15)

The emergence of rock and roll as a musical stream in the 1950s, then, was rife with ambiguity and conflict, on the fronts of both commerce and teen subculture. The economic viability of the music originally depended on independent labels and airplay by radio stations aimed at the black audience. Atlantic Records, under Ahmet Ertegun, became a purveyor of the expanding rhythm and blues style and eventually of crossovers to rock and roll (Chapple and Garofalo 1977, 28–32). The latter emerged in no small part from these "cover" versions of rhythm and blues songs which landed on the pop chart. The country charts largely resisted the new trend until Elvis appeared on Sam Phillips's Sun Records in 1955. That year "Rock Around the Clock" by Bill Haley and the Comets was also rehearsed (Ennis 1992, 210–28; Friedlander 1996, 11). Two radio stations in particular, WDIA in Memphis and WLAC in Nashville (with a fifty-thousand-watt transmitter), broadcast notable alternative programming (Ennis 1992, 174–76; Palmer 1995, 18–21).

The commercial development of rock and roll was inextricably tied to the emergence of teen subculture, "a category based on age, not race, a demographic shift that would change the very nature of pop music" (Palladino 1996, 124). This shift signaled that the teen audience was white, middle class, and, not insignificantly, female. The economic expansion of the music may have been predicated on age-based marketing images of wholesomeness and fun, but those of race and gender were also present from the beginning (Dotter 1994).

Bayles's (1994) blood knot (a crude racial and sexual stereotype), then, was enmeshed with simplistic images of age. Similarly, gender was linked to teenage subculture as well. Elvis, Bill Haley, and equally important, a black artist singing to a largely white audience, Chuck Berry, loosened the blood knot, thereby whitening the music for the teen audience (Marcus

CHAPTER SIX

1975/97, 154–57; Dotter 1994; Palladino 1996, 125–26; George 1988, 68). Crossing over to tap this audience continued at a number of record labels catering to the rhythm and blues and soul markets, including Atlantic, Vee-Jay, Chess, Stax, and Motown, among others. Still, to the black audience there was a distinction between rhythm and blues and rock and roll: "Rock & roll was young music; R&B managed to be young and old, filled both with references to the past and with fresh interpretations, all at the same time" (George 1988, 68–69).

The 1950s evidences a relative absence of women's voices in traditional histories of rock and roll, even as the teen subculture was identified as decidedly female (Dotter 1994; Palladino 1996). In fact, women had from the beginning been label owners, songwriters, and performers. Willie Mae "Big Mama" Thorton recorded "Hound Dog" in 1953, three years before Elvis (Gaar 1992, 1–2). The "girl groups" of the early 1960s homogenized popular music's gender content. Numerous artists created this adolescent female voice (the Crystals, Ronettes, Shirelles, and Shangri-Las, to name a few), which was stylistically expropriated by the Beatles:

> The demise of the girl-group era is often blamed on the Fab Four; it's ironic that in appropriating the girl-group a male band inadvertently destroyed it through their own success. In the same way that a white person (Elvis) made millions out of the previously segregated blues, so it took a male band to capitalize on the female group sound, and when they moved on to rock, their teen muses were left behind. (O'Brien 1995, 65–66)

The appearance of the Beatles specifically, and the British Invasion more generally, mark the beginning of the shift from teen to youth subculture, the gradual transformation of rock and roll to rock.[2] In America the cultural trauma of the Vietnam War expanded the political context of the music beyond harmless, if socially questionable, content to the formation of youth subculture and age-based identities. Simon Frith (1981, 181) describes this sociocultural transition as a movement from "teenager" to "youth." The former referred to consumption patterns and lifestyle, the latter to a self-conscious ideological category. With this expansion came more sophisticated forms of social protest and subcultural identification (in addition to the traditional focal points of sex and drugs) (Dotter 1994).

Media culture, situated in the historical context of an emerging American consumer capitalism, sowed the seeds of youthful rebellion in the name of corporate profits. Popular music, then, became a site of meaning-creation even as it was exploited for corporate gain. Youth audiences created gendered and race-based identities around consumption patterns. According to Ennis:

> An American youth culture was forming. Not only distinctive dress styles, including preeminently hair, but a wide variety of visual and ideological guides were being fabricated in high schools and colleges to mark the boundaries of the spreading alternative culture. (Ennis 1992, 288–89)

The problematic of meaning in rock and roll music was always situated in the relationships of teen subculture to images of race and gender; the appearance of youth subculture complicated the process. In both cases behavior of the young was subject to the process of deviance-labeling.

Popular Music and Social Deviance

From its inception postwar youth subculture was viewed as closely linked to deviant behavior by the wider society from which it spread. Historian James Gilbert (1986) uses the concept of "episodic notion" to describe this link. The term refers to widely professed ideas which recur through history. Specifically with regard to teen and youth, the criticism is the "seduction of youth by culture" (Gilbert 1986, 4).

This episodic notion exhibits identifiable characteristics (Gilbert 1986, 4–5). First, its meaning may not be readily apparent; it requires decoding across the range of culture to which it applies, including the categories of gender, race, and class. Thus the linkage of age to popular music and forms of social deviance is a complex tangle of layers to be deciphered. Second, the episodic notion possesses social functions which are broadly political and ideological. In Gilbert's words: "[D]uring the 1950s those who denounced mass culture for misleading American adolescents—even though they used the same words—often had very different purposes in mind when making this accusation" (Gilbert 1986, 4). Finally, the episodic notion as a broadly conceived idea has deep roots in both culture and social structure. Simple descriptions of causation are inadequate. Instead, the episodic notion likely reflects and contradicts these wider contexts. The

CHAPTER SIX

historical development of youth subculture as a scenario of social deviance is a multilayered moment of meaning-creation. Events overlap through time, and definitions of conformity and stigmatization emerge as a textual historical narrative. Changes in youth misbehavior after World War II "became increasingly difficult to isolate from the simultaneous development of a vast and increasingly commercialized youth culture" (Gilbert 1986, 5). Increased postwar birth rates impacted the structure of age-graded high school experience. At the same time that experience became enmeshed in the emerging consumer culture, in which youth for the first time became self-conscious participants. Film, as well as music, became a popular cultural site of meaning-creation, ambivalently portraying images of postwar delinquency in the number of productions, including *The Wild One*, *Blackboard Jungle*, *Rebel Without a Cause*, and *Blue Denim* (Gibert 1986, 178–79).

Still, the scenario of teen and youth subculture found widest expression in popular music, representing a stigma contest (Schur 1980) situated in the context of consumer culture:

> In its first decade and a half of existence, then, rock music and the youth subculture associated with it were part of two simultaneous processes of social construction: the deviance-generating efforts of claims-making interest groups and the positive social typing of mass media which tended to make cultural heroes of performers even as they and the subculture were exploited. (Dotter 1994, 101)

In the early years the stigma contest generated what I call "lifestyle deviance" with respect to teen subculture. "The music was 'different' in content, style, and presentation and therefore bad. Performers such as Elvis Presley, Jerry Lee Lewis, and Chuck Berry were labeled as relatively non-serious threats to authority" (Dotter 1994, 102). Youth subculture, by the 1960s, had developed a style of "political deviance"—based on resistance to middle-class lifestyle *and* values. The claims against this form were made in the context of its increasing opposition to the Vietnam War.

British cultural studies viewed the relationship of deviance claims-making as a matter of subcultural resistance and style. In his study of the social creation of the Mods and Rockers subcultures as moral panics, Stanley Cohen (1972/93) originally presented a fundamentally conventional view of the labeling process. In the preface to the 1980 edition of the book, Cohen articulates this process within a multilevel neo-Marxian framework (i.e., structure, culture, and biography). He describes his updated contextualization: "Much of the new work of British post-war youth cultures is a teasing out of the relationships between these three levels. And all of this work is more or less informed by the Marxist categorization of structure, culture and biography as the determinant conditions ('being born into a world not of your own choosing') to which the subculture is one of the possible working-class responses ('making your own history')" (Cohen 1972/93, v).

The edited volume *Resistance Through Rituals* (Hall and Jefferson 1975/2002b) examines the sociopolitical context of several British youth subcultures (e.g., Teds, Mods, Skinheads). Using Cohen as a springboard, the collection demonstrates an early series of attempts at "doing" cultural studies. The initial thrust of the project was interactionist labeling as articulated in Becker's (1963/73) *Outsiders*. But as the editors explain:

> Our reading of this text—and subsequent British work in this rapidly emerging tradition—and our engagement with the perspective in general was always, however, double-edged: both a sense of exhilaration about the importance of some of the ideas generated by this 'sceptical [sic] revolution' (the viewing of social action as *process* rather than as event, for example, and crucially, the idea that deviance was a social creation, a result of the power of some to label others) and a sense of unease; a feeling that these accounts, whilst containing many, important, new insights, were not comprehensive enough; a feeling, particularly, that deviant behaviour had other origins besides public labelling. [*italics* in the original] (Hall and Jefferson 1975/2002a, 5)

In his own related and later work, *Subculture*, Hebdige describes those "other origins" as crossing the "concepts of homology and *bricolage* to provide a systematic explanation of why a particular subcultural style should appeal to a particular group of people" [*italics* in the original] (Hebdige 1979/2002, 113–14). In short, the process (bricolage) by which subculture members give meaning to their experience (homology) becomes the focus. Homology (Willis 1978) or subcultural meaning-creation is a site of political resistance, describing expropriation of ideologized symbols by members for their own use.

CHAPTER SIX

British cultural studies distinguished between youth *culture* and *subculture*:

> The term 'Youth Culture' appropriates the situation of the young almost exclusively in terms of the commercial and publicity manipulation and exploitation of the young. As a concept, it has little or no explanatory power. We must try to get behind this market phenomenon, to its deeper social economic, and cultural roots. In short, our aim is to de-throne or *de-construct* the term, 'Youth Culture,' in favour of a more complex set of categories. [*italics* in the original] (Clarke et al. 1975/2002, 16)

The aim is to "reconstitute" the ideological basis of youth culture into subculture as a fruitful explanatory concept, "to show how youth subcultures are related to class relations, to the division of labour and to the productive relations of society, without destroying what is specific to their content and position" (Clarke et al. 1975/2002, 16). Subculture is thus embedded structurally in the wider sense of class-cultures, as well as intersubjectively in the capacity of style to signify active resistance on the part of subcultural actors.

Simon Frith, in his highly influential work *Sound Effects: Youth, Leisure and the Politics of Rock and Roll*, juxtaposes the Frankfurt mass cultural argument with British subcultural theory in an effort to "determine the relationship between rock's commercial function and its cultural use." (Frith 1981, 57) This determination is to be found in the ideological (i.e., seemingly objective) reality of the music's consumption and the intersubjective meanings generated by audiences. As Frith argues:

> It is difficult, then, to say how musical texts mean or represent something, and it is difficult to isolate structures of musical creation or control. (Who owns the means of music-making—the musicians? their record companies? broadcasters?) Radical music critics usually analyze rock not in terms of form and content but in terms of production and consumption: the argument is either that the ideological meaning of music lies in the way it is commercially produced, in its commodity form, or that consumers create their own meanings out of the commodities offered. (Frith 1981, 56)

Cultural and subcultural meaning-generation is a frequently untidy and contradictory process. Alongside overt resistance to mainstream values and material cultural expression, subculture embodies alternatives born in the relationship of artist to audience. This dialectic of production and consumption inevitably leads to ambiguity. The Mod experience in Britain is a case in point:

> The mods, many stuck in low-echelon white-collar and service jobs, emphasized the appearance of affluence, which they effectively subverted simply by the apparent incongruity of the caricature. Their opulence implicitly belied the dead-end clerical jobs that funded their finery, an irony explaining the seeming paradox that their well-groomed appearance caused so much offense. (Nehring 1993, 239)

This early literature critiquing youth culture and subculture as a site of meaning- (and style-) creation permits little space for gender interpretations, "contradictions that patterns of cultural resistance pose in relation to women" (McRobbie 1990, 69). Rather, subculture is situated in the ideology of either class or race categories. As McRobbie observes: "No commentary on the hippies dealt with the countercultural division of labor, let alone the hypocrisies of 'free love.'" (McRobbie 1990, 68). Treatments of subculture were synthesized initially from deviance-labeling (Cohen) and Marxist perspectives (Hall and Jefferson). Hebdige highlighted the importance of race as a signifier of youth style. Not excusing this silence on gender, it was a reflection of the ambiguous, emerging quality of women's voices in the cultural narrative of the late 1960s.

McRobbie summaries this gender problematic in early cultural studies: "Writing about subcultures isn't the same thing as being in one. Nonetheless, it's easy to see how it would be possible in sharing some of the same symbols—the liberating release of rock music; the thrill of speed, of alcohol, or even of football—to be blinded to some of their more oppressive features" (McRobbie 1990, 69). Similarly, in the 1970s punk had style elements of resistance to images of not only race and class, but gender as well; "the prevalence in punk of bohemians as much as working-class youths also helped diminish the sexism that had afflicted more purely working-class subcultures" (Nehring 1993, 322). While race was, as I have demonstrated, a central theme in the historical development of rock and roll, gender emerged on a less direct—but similarly conflicted—path. The latter more gradually appeared as subcultural narratives and expanded through the 1980s (Gaines 1991; McRobbie 1994; Weinstein 1991). Youth identity, then, is a subcultural negotiated process with layered outcomes. Fragmentation along dimensions of gender, race, and class leads to multiple "youths." In turn, these subcultural constructions of age ground these dimensions in historical time and place (Austin and Willard 1998, 6).

In the scenario of youth subculture formation, meaning is constantly created and modified in the nexus of production and consumption, the intersection of music as commercial product *and* as an intersubjective subcultural experience. In this public drama social typing—the interplay between artists, audiences, and other claims-makers—creates three types of images: those which reinforce cultural values, those which suggest seductive, deviant experience, and those offering a transcendence of cultural norms (Klapp 1962; 1969, 219–29). As cultural texts (Denzin 1989a, 1989b), these images are scripts for the search for identity in postmodern society. In particular, the scenario of youth subcultural formation led to an expansion of the seductive deviant search. Numerous events in the history of rock have become part of this public drama, to which I now turn.

The Scenario of Youth Subculture: The Public Drama of Rock and Roll

By the 1960s, with the cross-fertilization of American and British forms, rock had become commercially dominant popular music. Simultaneously, youth subculture was broadly institutionalized, especially its forms of deviant behavior (Dotter 1994). The problematic of this institutionalization received media coverage in countless events. As public dramas (Klapp 1964), these events highlight the social creation of deviance, its connection with consumer culture, the ambiguity of its meaning, and the increasing importance of rock musicians as postmodern cultural heroes (Dotter 1987).

The Woodstock Music and Art Fair

This complex connection of rock music to youth subcultural meaning and style is historically evident by the late 1960s. A key event of this emerging scenario was the Woodstock Music and Art Fair. To be sure, the contemporary significance of Woodstock is shrouded in myth and controversy. Over the years an idealistic purpose has come to be associated with the event: the creation of a society, even if only transitory, that celebrated peace and love (Pepper 1989). Joel Makower (1989, 1), in his oral history of Woodstock constructed from interviews with principals, acknowledges that there are multiple other "stories" to be told as well, "tales of art and politics, life and death, Utopian visions and broken dreams, enlightenment and disenchantment."

Woodstock emerged from the entrepreneurial efforts of four individuals. Michael Lang, one of the producers of the Miami Pop Festival in 1968, approached Artie Kornfeld, then vice president for Capitol Records and former producer/songwriter for the Cowsills. Together they developed the idea of a concert at Woodstock, tied in with the construction of a music studio (Makower 1989, 24–34; Spitz 1979, 3–4). Through attorney Miles Lourie, the two were introduced to John Roberts and Joel Rosenman as potential investors. Roberts recalls the partnership's beginning: "We were, in fact, the same age. Lang and I were both twenty-three and Joel and Artie were both twenty-five. So we were exact contemporaries" (Makower 1989, 28).

The four split stock ownership equally in Woodstock Ventures Incorporated. Similarly four other legal entities were formed at or near the same time. These five corporations controlled not only the planned concert but the music studio, band management company, and publishing company that were to follow from it (Makower 1989, 36). From the beginning, then, the Woodstock festival was conceived for its commercial possibilities.

The location of the concert was a persistent problem (Spitz 1979, 42–50). Two sites in Woodstock scouted by Lang were unsuitable, and negotiations for property in Saugerties proved fruitless. Roberts and Rosenman located property in Wallkill, Howard Mills Industrial Park, and secured its lease. Crews had begun construction and landscaping, but final permits were denied (Makower 1989, 55–56, 99–100).

After the breakdown of Wallkill negotiations the eventual site, Max Yasgur's 600-acre farm in Bethel, was identified and rented for $50,000 (Ward et al. 1986, 430). Miriam Yasgur, Max's widow, recalls a circumstance in their decision to lease property for the festival:

> down at the end of the field we saw a sign had been erected. Now we knew we didn't have any signs down there. Eventually, of course, we checked it. On the sign it said something like, Don't buy Yasgur's milk,

CHAPTER SIX

he loves the hippies. And I thought "You don't know Max, because we're going to have a festival." (Makower 1989, 120)

Promotion of the festival was not neglected and was tied to symbols of the emerging counterculture. Ads were placed in both the underground and mainstream press. Kornfeld sensed the cultural and generational significance of the event. "For him, the festival was always a state of mind, a happening that would exemplify the generation. . . . 'The cool PR image was intentional,' he said" (*Times Herald-Record* 1994, 3–4). The promoters could not interest major Hollywood studios in producing a feature film, and instead commissioned independent director Michael Wadleigh for the project (*Times Herald-Record* 1994, 5).

As a public drama, then, the meaning of Woodstock reflected commercial and political themes as well as the traditional sex and drugs lifestyle deviance associated with rock music. According to Abbie Hoffman:

> I wanted to see a good presentation of the Woodstock Nation, of an alternative lifestyle that showed all these people could come together and weren't going to stab each other, could enjoy the music. And I also wanted them to be able to know at the proper moment they were supposed to be raising fists and not "Vs," and it wasn't all love, love, love. It was about justice too. It was about ending a war. It was about changing our society. (Makower 1989, 112)

The festival took place August 15–17, 1969, with attendance estimated as high as 500,000 people (Dotter 1994, 100). Thirty-one performers provided the music; a partial list includes The Who, Joan Baez, Jimi Hendrix, Janis Joplin, Santana, The Grateful Dead, Creedence Clearwater Revival, Jefferson Airplane, and Sly and the Family Stone (Music Festival Home Page 2003). There were bad drug trips, three deaths, and three births (Ward et al. 1986, 431).

In the week after the festival the *New York Times* published two editorials, the first a negative interpretation and the second a contradictory positive one (Ward et al. 1986, 431). Jan Hodenfield and Greil Marcus covered the event for *Rolling Stone*: "Hodenfield had seen the *New York Times* editorial condemning the Woodstock wasteland as 'an outrageous episode.' How dead wrong they were, he thought, . . . believing as he never had before that it would be up to *Rolling Stone* to set matters straight"

(Draper 1990, 105). Similarly, Marcus sensed a significance to the concert, both commercially and subculturally: "'The limits have changed now,' he wrote, 'they've been pushed out, the priorities have been re-arranged, and new, 'impractical' ideas must be taken seriously. The mind boggles'" (Draper 1990, 106).

The connecting of white middle-class youth counterculture with rock music was an amorphous process. Media reconstructions of the Woodstock event were central to this process. Still, the music's audience was arguably attracted more to forms of lifestyle deviance like drug use and sexual freedom than to radical political activity. As Frith notes, "Nineteen-sixties rock politicized leisure—gave public, collective expression to usually private issues of risk and pleasure and sex" (1981, 185). Gender and race constructions, the voices of women and blacks, were subsumed in those of youth-as-politicized-leisure, as these performers assimilated the values of the white counterculture (Ward et al. 1986, 427).

As part of the stigma movie of youth subcultural formation, Woodstock is an indelible narrative of rock and roll's public drama. The focus of much mainstream media coverage of the event centered on the representation of lifestyle and political deviance. These mediated constructions were part of a process of moral enterprise. As Cohen observes, "the media might leave behind a diffuse feeling of anxiety about the situation: 'something should be done about it,' 'where will it end?' or 'this sort of thing can't go on forever'" (Cohen 1972/93, 17). In the view of these claims-makers Woodstock was seen as seductive deviance, stigmatizing youth culture for "its presumed advocacy of hedonism, nihilism, mysticism, and related 'countercultural' orientations" (Sanders 1990, 5).

Against this backdrop of moral entrepreneurship were counterdefinitions of youth subculture. Rock music suggested that popular culture was—for the moment at least—not a trivial artifact, meant only for consumption. Performers and audience were testing, even transcending, the boundaries of mass-produced art (Dotter 1987). Youth subculture, then provided a fertile ground for this stigma contest:

> A rock star's integrity (and that of his audience) was defined by his contempt for the old pop hype, a contempt that was matched by the sudden unfashionability of early sixties pop acts, matching suits, publicity stunts,

CHAPTER SIX

fan mags, and all. It was quickly obvious that rock artists would still have to cooperate with the music industry (as one by one the "countercultural" acts signed their record deals). But from now on the argument was that they were using that industry for their own ends. (Harron 1988, 181)

Race and gender constructions were part of this contest as well. In his discussions of Jimi Hendrix and Sly Stone, Nelson George writes:

> [A]ll the great black musicians working in a pop idiom—be it rock & roll, R&B, or funk—become cultural curators or cultural critics. By taking established black forms, preserving their essence but filtering these textures through an ambitious creative consciousness, they make astounding music that is in the tradition yet singular from it. For example, Jimi Hendrix used blues and R&B as his building blocks, and Sly Stone worked from gospel and soul. Yet black America's reaction to each was different: Hendrix was rejected, while Sly was viewed, before drug days, as a hero. (George 1988, 108)

Similarly, gender stigmatization overlapped with that of youth in the 1960s. According to McRobbie, "the shock of subcultures can be partially diffused because they can be seen as, among other things, boys having fun," an opportunity less willingly afforded to young women (McRobbie 1990, 75).

As part of the "pause point" in the maturation of rock, Woodstock and other festivals such as Monterey and the notorious Altamont highlight the importance of music in subcultural meaning-expression. By the late 1960s the connection was becoming increasingly tenuous:

> The question as to whether it was a "youth thing" or "generational" was still open. There is no doubt, on the other hand, about whether the Woodstock nation fought for love and unleashed "all fucking hell." They didn't; what broke instead was the once solid youth ranks. The branching of young people into a cultural and political wing was a step toward the general unraveling of the coalition. (Ennis 1992, 350–51)

Woodstock is an important event in the historically constructed stigma movie of youth subculture formation, decidedly ambivalent in its narrative. Forms of lifestyle and political deviance played on a commercial stage:

Woodstock represents the degeneration of rock's political deviance rather than its summit. As many performers suggested, they participated for the musical experience itself and not for any political ramifications. Indeed, Abbie Hoffman was forced from the stage by Pete Townshend when Hoffman attempted to make a political announcement during the Who's set. (Dotter 1994, 106)

By the late 1960s, then, deviant youth subculture had become institutionalized as a commercial commodity, continuing to offer deviant and transcendental narratives (Klapp 1969). As public mediated drama these narratives often changed quickly, as much about personal destruction as "flower power" (London 1984, 119–20). The rock audience broadened in the 1970s and the economics of the music promoted groups both in and out of the studio.

Violence in Rock: The Who Cincinnati Concert Tragedy

On May 23, 1969, the Who released the rock opera *Tommy* (Marsh 1983, 339–40). Prior to their Woodstock performance in August, the band had toured America in support of the album. The convergence of *Tommy* and Woodstock solidified the band's international reputation, and resulting commercial success placed the group alongside the Rolling Stones among British acts. The original Who was comprised of lead singer Roger Daltrey, guitarist Pete Townshend, bassist John Entwistle, and drummer Keith Moon. From the beginning Pete was the primary composer of the band's material.

While *Tommy* represents the group's breakthrough album, the Who had performed for a number of years as a club band in native Great Britain (Dotter forthcoming). The band grew out of that country's mod/rocker subculture mix of the early 1960s as an expression of the former style. Mod was in some ways "a more female than a male phenomenon" (Cohen 1972/93, 186). The movement found voice in fashion and style, music and clothes. Still, the oblivious coolness of mods was coupled with a current of violence. Pete Meaden, the first manager of the Who, offers this description of mod: "It's a continuous party, sustain it for as long as you can without doing too much damage to your body. You mustn't damage yourself too much, but take it right out on the rim" (Marsh 1983, 92–93). In his analysis of mod and rocker subcultures as moral panics, Cohen (1972/93, 189) sees the Who as "pure and complete Mod." Similarly, Gary Herman (1971, 37) links the group's

CHAPTER SIX

identity to being a survivor of the short-lived movement: "Their music has extended the limits of the mod outlook, and it is to that extension that we can attribute their continued development."

In his first *Rolling Stone* interview (published in September 1968) Pete connects preliminary ideas for the rock opera *Tommy* to the importance of modism for youthful identity: "It was an incredible youthful drive. It was the closest thing to patriotism that I have ever felt" (Wenner 1968, 40). In the same interview Pete offers this further characterization (Wenner 1968, 40): "It could be anyone. Any kid, you know, however ugly or however fucked up, if he had the right haircut and the right clothes and the right motorbike, he was a mod. He was mod! There was no big Fred Mod or something."

On stage the Who defined the mod performance style honed from the early club days, "an orgy of smashed instruments and deafening feedback" (Cohen 1972/93, 189). Pete's energetic playing, acrobatics, and guitar destructions were a central component of that style: "In addition to trademark displays of 'power chords' and incessant 'windmilling,' he frequently ended concerts by smashing his guitar and abandoning it to the audience" (Dotter 1994, 97). Regarding the relative violence symbolized in the group's performances Marsh observes, "It was the fans who gave the event meaning, by choosing to interpret Townshend's original broken instrument not just as part of the show but as a part that could and *should* be repeated" [*italics* in the original] (Marsh 1983, 126).

In 1973 Pete and the Who released a second rock opera, *Quadrophenia*, which even more explicitly than *Tommy* drew on the narrative of the mod subculture and the group's roots in it. As well, "the songs were carefully integrated into characterizations and plotline" (Giuliano 1996, 98). The opera's narrative relates the saga of Jimmy, a conflicted, ambivalent adolescent mod, through four interwoven voices. Pete offers the following observation linking the opera to the band's own story: "Its about the Who and what happens to us. It starts out in 1965 and ends now, and I left it open-ended on a note of spiritual desperation because we're in the middle of nowhere, not sure where we're going." He frequently told live audiences, "It's about growing up. At the end of the album the hero is in grave danger of maturing" (Giuliano 1996, 98).

The film version of *Quadrophenia*, directed by Franc Rodham and released in August 1979, coincided with a revival of modism in Britain. This new generation of mod adolescents took cues from the film and gave a nod to the Who's history in the subculture (Marsh 1983, 510). This mod revival overlapped with the ascendence of punk in significant ways for the group and for Pete: They were freed relatively from their mod past, but as both wealthy and aging rockers the band now was at best an uneasy bridge for generations of listeners. In his biography of Pete, Geoffrey Giuliano frames the dilemma: "Rock was now, like it or not, in the hands of the punksters, a generation not part of the Who history. The Who were growing further away from their once awesome and unchallenged power base" (Giuliano 1996, 175). This conflict of commerce and aging is the general theme of "Who Are You," written by Pete in 1978 after a chance drunken encounter with Paul Cook of the Sex Pistols. As Pete raved at the time: "Rock & roll's going down the fucking pan!. . . You've got to take over where the Who left off—and this time, you've got to finish the fucking job!" (Marsh 1983, 485).

On September 8, 1978 Keith Moon died from an overdose of tranquillizers prescribed to combat his alcoholism (Dotter forthcoming). Despite its profound emotional impact on the remaining three members, the event completed the break of the band with its earlier history. Kenney Jones was recruited to replace Keith, and as Marsh (1983, 509) observes, "What remained was still an exceptional rock band but not anybody's standard bearer." Following the release of *Quadrophenia*, the reconstituted Who played five consecutive nights at New York's Madison Square Garden in September 1979 and planned a wider American tour to begin in December (Marsh 1983, 510).

On December 3 at Cincinnati Riverfront Coliseum, eleven people were killed in a crowd crush before and during the opening of the venue's doors (*Cincinnati Enquirer* 1979l). Marsh describes the scene:

> A good share of the 18,000 patrons had arrived early, and still they were herded into the small plaza in front of that single rank of doors. Although there were warnings from the police outside, the Coliseum staff and the concert promoters, Electric Factory Concerts of Philadelphia, refused to open the doors before 7:00 P.M., even when the crowd started shoving furiously as the Who went through its sound check just after six o'clock. When the doors were opened, the crowd rushed in, ignoring the pleas of those caught in the middle and thrust forward rapidly against their will. Some of the glass in the doorways shattered. In the wake of the stampede

CHAPTER SIX

for the seats, many were injured. Eleven died: Walter Adams, Jr., age seventeen; Peter Bowes, eighteen; Connie Burns, twenty-one; Jacqueline Eckerle, fifteen; David J. Heck, nineteen; Teva Ladd, twenty-seven; Karen Morrison, fifteen; Stephan Preston, nineteen; Philip K. Snyder, twenty; Bryan Wagner, seventeen; and James Warmouth, twenty-one. Most were trampled; some suffocated. The dead included seven teens, four adults; seven men, four women—a representative ratio of Who fans. It could have been anybody. (Marsh 1983, 512)

Immediately the issue of responsibility and blame was paramount in press reconstructions of the event. En route to Buffalo, New York, the next tour stop, Roger spoke for the band, saying "the Who has a 'clear conscience as far as the band is concerned' as well as 'a total feeling of total helplessness'" (*Cincinnati Enquirer* 1979q). Similarly, local city officials as well as the promoter either declined comment or failed to admit responsibility. Two upcoming concerts at the privately owned venue were cancelled (*Cincinnati Enquirer* 1979a, 1979f).

Coverage by the national press delved even deeper into the responsibility issue. The *Rolling Stone* cover story (Flippo 1980) focused on the unreserved "festival" seating for most of the show's tickets (14,770 of the total 18,348). Electric Factory, headed by Larry Magid, had been the defendant in five antitrust suits in the previous three years—filed by competing promoters. Furthermore, "[p]romoters across the country blamed festival seating. Larry Magid said that he felt terrible and that her personally didn't like festival seating, but that's what the kids wanted. A kid in Cincinnati printed up a few T-shirts that read I SURVIVED THE WHO CONCERT" (Flippo 1980, 24). The December 17 *Time* cover story proclaimed the Who as "rock's outer limits" (Cocks 1979). The piece interwove the Cincinnati tragedy with the band's history, affording considerably more coverage to the latter.

Following the event, efforts of moral entrepreneurship understandably focused on explanation of and proposing changes in seating policies at rock concerts (*Cincinnati Enquirer* 1979c, 1979d, 1979h, 1979i, 1979n, 1979o), as well as the introduction of legislation addressing crowd control at indoor events (*Cincinnati Enquirer* 1979b). Previous debates and recommendations were brought to light: A 1976 city committee study of festival seating at Riverfront Coliseum had suggested the gradual voluntary reduction of the practice (*Cincinnati Enquirer* 1979k), and Cincinnati fire officials had previously called for reduced capacity at festival seating events (*Cincinnati Enquirer* 1979e). Finally, within seventy-two hours a broad-based investigative panel was formed, charged with reviewing current reports, policies, and laws on crowd control for effectiveness (*Cincinnati Enquirer* 1979j, 1979m). No criminal prosecution was ever brought, and by 1994 all civil suits brought by victims' survivors had been settled out of court (Purdy 1994).

Moral entrepreneurship also intensely examined the connection between hard rock/heavy metal and violence. These contemporary forms were seen as more volatile when compared to those of a generation before (*Cincinnati Enquirer* 1979p). Lifestyle and political deviance of the 1960s were transmuted into psychological and psychiatric summaries of "crowd behavior." Dr. Vytautus Bieliauskas, Xavier University psychology professor, explained the event and the Who's impact on its audience: "This was not only barbaric but animal-like. I don't know this group (the Who), but they must be magnetizing these young people" (*Cincinnati Enquirer* 1979g).

In a book-length account, *Are the Kids All Right?*, John G. Fuller (1981) somewhat sensationally links the event to "the rock generation and its hidden death wish!" He offers a popular history of hard rock and heavy metal as well as a narrative of the tragedy told in the voices of those who experienced it: concertgoers, family and friends, police, promoters. Fuller summarizes his thesis: "Any wide sample of spectators at a hard or heavy-metal rock concert would show fundamentally that 'the kids are all right.' Yet collected en masse for this specific kind of concert, something happens, something that even the concert-goers are not aware of. As for the promoters, the arena managers and the superstars, the phenomenon goes to the heart of their exploitation of a whole generation" (Fuller 1981, 255).

For Fuller—dubbed the "king of popular epidemiology" on the book's jacket—the Who's genesis in the mod subculture is one of countless examples of rock's historical connection with violence. While the violence grows out of lifestyle deviance of drugs and sexual promiscuity, it is all the more perverse as psychologized crowd behavior, the vicarious identification of its audience with the Who:

> The idolatry tendered Frank Sinatra and Elvis Presley in America was far less riotous than the adoration beginning to be showered on The

CHAPTER SIX

> Who. The crowd response moved beyond the thrill of the music, into a lifestyle that swallowed that music whole, so that those who heard it carried the tribal beat before, during, and after the gig. The scene created an emotional release for the Mods, and other kids who joined them in increasing numbers. It also created monumental problems for the police, the street cleaners, the dance hall managers, and any innocent bystanders who got in the way. (Fuller 1981, 51)

Reconstruction of the Cincinnati tragedy, then, led to a reexamination of the group's reputation for violence on stage (*Cincinnati Enquirer* 1979r); the well-known propensity for private physical confrontation between Pete and Roger; and the untimely death of Keith the year before (Cocks 1979). The film version of *Quadrophenia* dramatized earlier British subcultural violence and suggested a connection with contemporary forms. The coincidence of its release in the same year as the concert deaths furthered the identification of the Who with themes of violence. Despite the gender and age diversity of the Cincinnati victims, from the event the rock audience was characterized as not only white, but young—"kids"—and male. As an episode in the stigma movie of youth subculture, the Cincinnati tragedy suggested fundamental shifts in rock culture: Its performers were sometimes near middle age, and its audiences were a mix of generations.

The deaths at the Cincinnati concert and the media reconstructions of the event highlighted the relationship of the Who to its audience, especially in the context of live performance. The demonstrated potential for violence in the public drama of rock and roll heightened mediated stigmatization. It also intensely personalized the drama in the biographies of the victims, survivors, and the Who.

Through the years Pete has expressed an evolving conflicted view of the event and the deaths associated with it. During their first post-Cincinnati American tour he told Greil Marcus:

> It was, fuck it! We're not gonna let a *little thing* like this stop us. That was the way we *had* to think. We had to reduce it. We had to reduce it, because if we'd actually *admitted* to ourselves the *true* significance of the event, the *true* tragedy of the event—not just in terms of "rock," but the fact that it happened at one of our concerts—the tragedy to us, in par-

ticular if we'd admitted to that, we could not have gone on and worked. And we had a tour to do. We're a rock & roll band. You know, *we don't fuck around*, worrying about eleven people dying. We *care* about it, but there is a particular attitude I call the "tour armor": when you go on the road, you throw up an armor around yourself, you almost go into a trance. [*italics* in the original] (Marcus 1980, 38)

In a 1994 *Playboy* interview Pete reflects further on the band's decision not to halt the tour after the tragedy:

> The kids were gone. We then should have attended to the families. We should have stayed in Cincinnati. It looked as if we had gone in like commando's created this havoc, then fucked off to do the same things somewhere else. (Sheff 1994, 54)

By 1979 the Who were fast becoming aging rockers. The Cincinnati tragedy as well as the death of Keith were historical markers for the band as well as significant events in the biography of Pete Townshend.

Who's Life: Pete Townshend as Postmodern Aging Rocker

As players in the public drama of rock and roll—the stigma movie of youth subculture—Pete and the Who, albeit imperfectly, mirror the collective identity search by audiences and society-at-large (Dotter 1987; Klapp 1969). In the interpretive context of the deviance-generating scenario, these symbolic representations make contradictory claims regarding the nature of meaning in contemporary society.

The textual biography of Pete Townshend is at both unique and forever tied to his membership in the Who. His creative role was from the beginning ambiguous: While Pete wrote the overwhelming bulk of the group's material, Roger lay claim to the roles of its founder and leader as vocalist. In his solo career Pete has sought to free himself from the group's history even as he is immersed in it. Popular culture as postmodern knowledge situates the self in media-generated stories, a self at once historical and present, personal and political, mythical and stigmatized, ideological and creative. I turn now to the story of Pete Townshend as postmodern aging rocker.

CHAPTER SIX

Self-As-Text: Ideological and Creative Narratives

Pete Townshend is a relatively unique aging rocker—a highly visible, controversial member of the Who in his early years and later a successful solo artist, considered an "elder statesman" by rock press and audiences alike (Dotter forthcoming). Many other rock superstars have attempted to follow this path, finding it choked with creative difficulties and nostalgic memories. Pete himself has hardly found the popular culture landscape familiar in middle age.

As applied to rock performers, the term elder statesman is more than slightly ironic, an oxymoron in a youthful subcultural discourse stressing rebellion, defiance, even generational warfare. In fact, the two chief biographical trajectories for the aging rocker have been pop stardom and death. Pete has, so far, avoided both.

In so doing, his public career (and therefore his textual biography) in middle age reflects two ongoing concerns. First is his continuing relationship to the life of the Who as a classic rock band. In 1989—seven years after its breakup—the group mounted the first of many reunion tours, with an accompanying double-disc live album. On June 27, 2002, the eve of yet another American tour, John Entwhistle died in his sleep at the Hard Rock Hotel in Las Vegas. With the first two shows rescheduled, the tour continued (Dansby 2002). Most of the band's earlier catalogue has been remastered and expanded. A compilation released by BMG/RCA Victor is entitled *Who's Serious: Symphonic Music of the Who*; eight of the album's ten tracks are performed by the London Philharmonic Orchestra.

The second important aspect of Pete's career at middle age is related to the first: his creative focus continues to cast art as a form of therapeutic storytelling. The voice of the "aging rocker," first apparent in later Who material, has continued to emerge in solo works. Pete's interpretive biography, then, has transmuted from the redeemed Tommy Walker to the alienated Jimmy of *Quadrophenia* to Pete in *White City* to Ray High in *PsychoDerelict*.

White City and *PsychoDerelict* are musical renditions of Pete's aging rocker status. As both lyrical and video works of art, they represent a postmodern literary style. That is, postmodern texts are not confined to a written narrative (Attridge 1992, 7; Derrida 1992), but include other forms of communication as well (Barthes 1977). In short, the postmodern literary text—musical, video, or even virtual—tells stories (Roemer

1995). As postmodern texts, *White City* and *PsychoDerelict* are sources of biographical and autobiographical storylines in the life of Pete Townshend (Dotter forthcoming). The postmodern self represents textual processes of meaning-creation and discovery. It is realized as a dialogue of ideological and creative self-narratives.

The ideological self-narrative refers to the process by which individuals are rendered as coherent textual subjects (Dotter forthcoming). This activity occurs in conventional everyday interactions; in the case of celebrity, the ideological self-narrative is a mythical creation embodied in mass-media forms of communication (Dotter 1987, forthcoming). Conversely, the creative self-narrative is "the subject's attempt to transform and recapture the ideological myth" (Dotter forthcoming). The concept of "myth as stolen language" (Barthes 1957/72) describes the dialogue between the two. Furthermore, "[t]he creative expression of the subject is transmuted into an ideological narrative biography (story or myth) by the mass media. Commoditized in this way, the ideological narrative is further embedded in the subject's creative autobiographical storyline" (Dotter forthcoming). This discursive emergence of ideology through consumption, displacement, and recapture constitutes mediated storytelling as postmodern literary creation. Works of art interweave with the interpretation of life events in the multilayered narratives.

The musical career of Pete Townshend has endured for some forty years, as rhythm guitarist and singer-songwriter of the Who, as well as solo artist (and occasional producer of other acts). The dominant self-dialogue of this life has been "rock storyteller as postmodern punk" (Dotter forthcoming). Through writing and performing Pete has been fervently searching for and creating the rock and roll dream. On the one hand this dream emphasizes the power of rock to change individual lives and social conditions (i.e., rock storyteller). On the other, it is shaped by the materialistic context of consumption and the quest for celebrity in rock media culture (i.e., postmodern punk).

In later years this dialogue has evolved into a more complex storyline incorporating the "aging rocker." This latter subtext is layered within the creative storyteller narrative and further challenges the ideologized discourse of the postmodern punk. The rock dream does not disappear, but is reinterpreted and presented to his audience in biographical form through various creative works. Chief among these are *White City* and

CHAPTER SIX

PsychoDerelict. Like the earlier efforts *Tommy* and *Quadrophenia*, these later compositions are presented as loosely constructed stories, told in song as well as in interviews with Pete. Unlike the two operas, these aging rocker storylines elaborate Pete's solo, post-Who search for the rock and roll dream.

White City: Aging and Communication of the Rock and Roll Dream

Released in 1985 (when Pete was forty years old), *White City* takes both album and video form (originally shot on 35mm film). The former is subtitled *A Novel* and the latter *The Music Movie*. Each contains music not found in the other, and the video format includes an interview with Pete on the story's evolution. Taken alone, the album does not convey the narrative thrust of the story (certainly not as well as those for the previous operas).

It is quickly apparent that the story is to some extent autobiographical. White City is a deteriorating estate, dating from World War II, a Shepherd's Bush community not unfamiliar to Pete. He none too subtly layers perspectives from his life into the work. The following provides a context for the story:

> The idea was sparked by a visit to the World War II–era White City council estate. Townshend admits that he was shocked at the marked disrepair of the area, shops boarded up, and street corners bearing stately names like Commonwealth and Crown now teeming with pimps and pushers. In this immigrant community of Jamaicans, Africans, Irish, and gypsies all living within an estate bordered by walls, making it, in effect, a fortress, Townshend found a seamy microcosm of postwar Britain, a tidy metaphor for the decline of the empire. (Giuliano 1996, 209)

Thus, the White City estate symbolizes postmodern British society, or at least Pete's perception of his own place in it. The neighborhood's deterioration dramatizes the decay of the old empire; at the same time, youth presents hope to the aging observer.

Giuliano summarizes the video's plot:

> Townshend focused on a married couple: Jim, an unemployed update of *Quadrophenia*'s Jimmy, and Alice, the estate's swim team coach. Jim's old mate, Pete (played with surprising ease by Townshend), is the local boy

turned rock star who's come home to shoot a video. Jim and Alice's emotional and economic struggles are set against Townshend's theme: that evil is always lurking, but through hope one can endure. (Giuliano 1996, 210)

The basic dramatic tension of the story, as realized through the action and words of the above three characters, is based on age and the resulting differences in perspectives it engenders. By his own generation's verdict, Pete, the rock entrepreneur, is a success story. In the same judgment, Jimmy and Alice (some ten years younger) fail to measure up. Neither has left White City for any length of time, and both seem resigned, if not content, with their lives.

In spite of these biographical differences, Pete obviously cares for and communicates with them. In the process his postwar middle-aged perspective is attenuated, though not necessarily transformed: Jimmy and Alice represent the future, however uncertainly. As they struggle to find their spiritual path, the importance of economic success is rendered secondary to self-knowledge. Since Pete's own awareness is bound up in the former, and the freedom it provides, the dialogue between generations is an uneasy one.

In returning to White City, Pete can only reflect on his life. Simultaneously, he is powerless to change his past or to significantly affect the lives of Jimmy and Alice, beyond his role of friend and confidant. Indeed, the younger couple is equally important to his own search for self. From their everyday struggles, the older Pete is learning to turn the rock and roll dream inward. In this sense generational communication is essential to the viability of the dream. The music may be altered stylistically, but its core of hope remains. The rock and roll dream of social and biographical change now speaks haltingly across generations.

Two songs from the album, "Give Blood" and "Face the Face," encapsulate this transformation of the rock and roll dream in generational dialogue. One is expected to "give blood" in many ways: literally, in wartime combat; in the conflict and betrayal between lovers; in the gradual growing apart experienced by parents and children, siblings, and friends. It may never "be enough," but recognize we shed it collectively.

"Face the Face" further addresses the need for honesty in generational dialogue and the difficulty in achieving it. In facing ourselves, with our imperfections and confusion, we may know others as well. The song was

CHAPTER SIX

inspired by the T. S. Eliot poem "The Love Song of J. Alfred Prufrock" (Giuliano 1996, 211). Eliot's (1934/62, 4) verse summarizes the multiple perspectives brought by aging and our response to growing old.

A number of other songs contain images of age or imply a middle-aged point of view. "Crashing By Design" paints a haunting word portrait of being alone, without family; it also alludes to the raging child found inside every man. "Hiding Out" and "I Am Secure" describe literal imprisonment within his home and emotional bondage within his heart, as he longingly observes the women and children in the streets below. "Secondhand Love" is an angry plea for intimate communication, and "Brilliant Blues" deals with depression and its aftermath, particularly feelings of personal freedom. "White City Fighting" examines the estate from aging eyes. "Come To Mama" is a complex, compact examination of pride, as seen by men and women in relationships. Finally, in "Night School," found only on the video and presented as a recording session montage, Pete sings of life as "nocturnal education."

For Pete Townshend, aging rocker, the ultimate expression of the rock and roll dream is found in its applicability to the above observations. Rock must transform specifics of its narrative content to link generations. In the process, the music offers hope in the face of inevitable mortality.

PsychoDerelict: Aging Rocker as Mediated Cultural Hero

Released in 1993, *PsychoDerelict* continues the storyline of Pete Townshend as aging rocker begun in *White City*. While there is no direct narrative link between the two, *PsychoDerelict* amplifies the theme of aging as a mediated process, involving artist and audience, and between them, the rock press. Giuliano outlines the plot:

> Townshend tackles a new format: songs threaded within a radio play. The plot revolves around Ray Highstreet [Highsmith, *sic*] (professionally known as Ray High), a sixties rock star turned nineties recluse whose return to the limelight is manipulated by his irascible manager, Rastus Knight, and muckraking broadcaster Ruth "Life's a Bitch and so am I" Streeting. The scam involves Ruth inventing a persona as Roz Nathan, High's precocious fourteen-year-old pen pal and aspiring singer. A flattered Ray takes the bait and writes a song for this ingenue, initially unaware of a conspiracy to engineer a rejuvenation of his career.

Interspersed throughout is a techno, sci-fi subplot lifted from Townshend's aborted *Lifehouse* project in which Ray is writing a concept called *Grid Life*, a virtual reality concept that espouses the lost dream of the sixties anchored by the familiar search for universal harmony through music. (Giuliano 1996, 249)

The cynical aging rocker is the victim of a greedy plot by Rastus and Ruth to fleece him of millions. Thus, his long-distance relationship with Roz (Ruth in disguise), is at once unreal, founded on his rock celebrity, and redemptive, as he rediscovers the ideals of the rock dream through connection with an audience of new, younger listeners. The dramatic thrust of the work rests in the mediated nature of rock stardom. Without the attention of the press, Ray's career is waning; with it, he must constantly strive, through his work, to refute the image of star and communicate the power of the rock dream for radical change to his audience.

As in *White City*, age is a complicating and liberating factor. In the psuedorelationship of Ray and Roz, it is discursively located in the reciprocal dialogue linking artist and audience. Ruth Streeting, the journalist masquerading as Roz, represents the ambivalence of the media for the story. Media generate consumption-based materialistic cultural heroes. In turn, these heroes articulate a powerful dream for listeners, drawn from the creative interpretation of their own life experiences. Finally, the audience is an active participating element in the drama, consuming the images and reproducing them as elements of postmodern biography.

Though not without digressions, *PsychoDerelict* remains an intriguing statement of aging in rock media culture. Unlike the structure of *White City*, individual songs are woven into the narrative, propelling the story along in a kind of "virtual unreality." Eventually, the listener learns that Ray himself has discovered the plot and attempted to undermine its success.

Several pivotal songs go to the heart of the deviant, stigmatized image of the aging rocker. "Outlive the Dinosaur" is not a lamentation of this image, but observations on the difficulty of living up to earlier stardom. Furthermore, "English Boy" deals at once with the historical emergence of punk and the disappearance, since World War II, of nonmediated heroes in postmodern society. The relationship between the rock artist and audience is elaborated in "Don't Make Me Real" and "Fake It." Similarly, "Let's Get Pretentious" is a knowing take on the celebrity-self, and "Early

CHAPTER SIX

Morning Dreams" introduces Ray's first letter to Roz. Three songs, "Now and Then," "I Am Afraid," and "Predictable" are mature, searching descriptions of intimate relationships through their uncertain courses. Finally, "Flame" is a pop tune written by Ray especially for Roz to record.

Though *PsychoDerelict* has sold fewer copies than any other solo effort by Pete (Giuliano 1996, 253), the album dramatically portrays the importance of aging in a medium that for all of its history has denied the process. Pete knows better than anyone the negative consequences of his serious examination of aging and rock celebrity. In his own words:

> You know what happens to the likes of Bowie, Jagger, and me? Our teenage kids turn around and say, "You look like mutton dressed as lamb. How can I possibly have my friends round? You look fucking ridiculous. Why are you suddenly wearing an earring?" (Giuliano 1996, 248)

In both *White City* and *PsychoDerelict*, Pete dramatically articulates the subtext of aging within the rock and roll dream. The importance of aging is its narrative reversal of the emphasis on youth. Still, for Pete, the dream maintains a hopeful significance.

Self-Narratives, Stigmatization, and the Postmodern Context

The aging rocker narrative is an open-ended interpretive process realized in popular culture media—in which meaning-creation is never completely accomplished. At any given moment meaning is negotiated within media culture (Kellner 1995). Furthermore, contextualized in the scenario as an episode of the stigma movie, the postmodern self is found only in textual expression; its meaning is de-centered, singularly located within the text itself (Derrida 1967/76, 1972, 1972/81b). As a dialogue of ideological and creative self-narratives, meaning is continually changing. The interrelated narratives "are expressed as a struggle to define the subject" (Dotter forthcoming). In this sense, the biographical and autobiographical narrative-subject is only temporarily present in the moment of realization. Creative self-expression gives way to ideological consumption.

For fifty-something-year-old Pete Townshend, the aging rocker storyline represents a nascent creative self-narrative. It simultaneously emerges from and recasts the ideological, commodified, media-generated postmodern punk, focusing on his life and achievements as a member of the Who. That is, the *White City* and *PsychoDerelict* texts contain frames of both. Pete, the returning rock entrepreneur, has achieved celebrity and stardom. Still, he must place these in the context of his White City roots. As a media-generated hero (Dotter 1987), his fame links him vicariously with his audience. Yet, his present story (an extension of the search for the rock and roll dream) of aging in rock divides him from rock culture generally, and his audience particularly.

Similarly, at the beginning of *PsychoDerelict* Ray High has been reduced to a parody of his former stardom, an ideological symbol of an earlier, more rebellious persona. He must combat the manipulations of his crafty manager and relentless stigmatization at the hands of the press. *Grid Life*, a reworked take on his 1960s dream for change through music, may be dismissed as irrelevant by contemporary audiences. Indeed, Ray cannot initially bring himself to entrust this revised vision to his fans.

The ambiguous, incomplete salvation of both textual characters lies in reaching out, somewhat painfully, to younger participants in media culture. Pete must face his own still-substantial pop heroism and reputation among White City residents. Ray faces a more daunting task; he must come to terms with his waning commodified celebrity even as the "Roz Nathan affair" introduces him to a young audience, reviving his career. Jim and Alice firmly root Pete in his White City origins, and Roz Nathan is mentored temporarily by Ray concerning the pitfalls of fame for the creative artist.

Neither story suggests a resolution of the conflict generated by the ideological and creative narratives. In each the creative aging rocker is confronting an ideologized postmodern punk. The latter, manufactured within rock media culture (and embellished by Pete over the years) is based on youthful, not middle-aged, rebellion. As Pete fashions a contemporary identity, he is outside the mainstream of rock culture, separated from nearly all audiences. The young find it impossible to relate to his age, and his contemporaries care only for the nostalgia of past glory. His discursive, textual subjectification is thus a product of "dividing practices" and self-transformation (Foucault 1983): the performer who is no longer worshipped as a star and who, simply through fortune and the passing of time, did not die before he got old.

Within rock media culture the story of the aging rocker is ambiguous at best. Rather than providing a coherent structure, its plots are often muddled,

CHAPTER SIX

and our knowledge of the main character, his actions, and thoughts is hardly reassuring. The celebrity-as-hero (Dotter 1987) presents a profoundly contradictory narrative image. As Michael Roemer observes:

> Despite the guarantees that a story, both fictive and factual, appears to offer, what happens is at once uncertain *and* fated—uncertain before it occurs and precluded in hindsight. It is hardly a reassuring prospect and suggests that even escapist fictions are not simply escapist. They may confirm a "reality" we continue to encounter even if we no longer have a way of accommodating it. (Roemer 1995, 179)

In short, Pete Townshend's aging rocker, created as textual biography, challenges the dominant narrative of the music as youthful rebellion. This episode of the stigma movie is anchored in images of disvaluement even as it suggests new meaning-potential for the rock and roll dream.

White City and *PsychoDerelict* represent Pete Townshend's continuing search for the rock and roll dream. The deconstruction of this search hinges on two related "reversals" or ruptures (Lynn 1994). First is the juxtaposition of the pre- and post-Who Pete Townshend, the intertextual ideological and creative self-narratives. Indeed, traces of both "selves" are found in each story and within one another. They are layered and shifting, neither one a pure text existing independently. *White City* portrays a confident if vaguely uneasy Pete communicating with his friend Jim (an extension of the alienated Jimmy from *Quadrophenia*). *PsychoDerelict* revisits the failure of Pete's *Lifehouse* project and his conflicts with bandmate Roger Daltrey. In fact, Pete himself has suggested that Ray High is a dual image of Roger and himself (Giuliano 1996, 252).

The second rupture centers on images of aging in rock media culture. The aging rocker narrative generates images of stigmatization and possibilities for transformation of the rock dream of hopeful change. The former are anchored in Pete's ideological self-narrative as a youthful member of the bygone Who, a "postmodern punk" celebrity created for, relevant to the experience of, and consumed by 1960s audiences (Dotter 1987, forthcoming). The stigmatization, or disvaluement, represents a complex process of deviance-generation (Dotter and Roebuck 1988; Dotter and Fisher-Giorlando 1997). Middle age as a social category is defined as "naturally" outside the ideological discourse of the rock dream (Barthes 1957/72), subject to the "reality of commodification" (Best 1994).

Pete's creative self-narrative suggests the transformative potential of the scenario for a postmodern turn on the rock dream. In this sense he is developing a reconstituted vocabulary of motives (Gerth and Mills 1953) anchored in contemporary constructions of age. As Richard Harvey Brown notes, this "political semiotics of selfhood" has important implications for the creation of meaning and the range of identities within the postmodern scenario:

> The self would be seen as revealed in statements that are guaranteed by a cultural grammar of intentions, a vocabulary of motives, and so on. In such a political semiotics it would be possible to conceive the self as neither an atomized monad nor a mere medium for larger social forces. Instead, the self would become an author, at once creating and "authoring" her own experience, while at the same time emerging from and merging into a pregiven structure of text, context, and audience interpretation. (Brown 1987, 57–58)

The novelty of Pete's self-dialogue, then, is "deviantized" in the nostalgic interpretation of his audience. Simultaneously, the aging rocker can symbolize a negotiated language of relationships for his listeners (Goffman 1963b, 3). That is, the stigma of age is never absolutely conferred, even in rock culture: It is mediated and open to biographical, textual interpretation.

The appearance of Pete Townshend's aging rocker creative self-narrative is historically situated in the postmodern context. This context interrelates knowledge, self, and the nature of meaning-creation. In the interpretive strategy of the scenario, each of these elements connects and reconnects to the others, constituting an interactional script for the given historical moment. The narrative-self-as-meaningful-experience is imbedded in the moment, dissolving the boundary between public and private discourse.

Similarly, knowledge in the postmodern context is largely without boundaries. Popular culture forms are simultaneously produced and reproduced alongside others (i.e., scientific, spiritual). Furthermore, the critique of knowledge forms has altered the relationship between cultural spheres of consumption, especially between high and popular culture. As Stanley Aronowitz comments:

> [T]he *generalized* challenge to the very idea of Great Art opposed to mass culture can be located in the turbulent 1960s, in the wake of the

CHAPTER SIX

> coming of age of rock 'n' roll as the characteristic cultural expression of the generation born around 1940. (Aronowitz 1994, 2)

In this moment the seeds of the rock dream were nurtured and spread by Pete and his generation, even as the dream was ideologized by corporate capitalism. Thus, rock was and is a product for consumption as well as a discourse of rebellion (Dotter 1987, 1994). This contradiction leads to an uncertain connection between performers and audiences. As the "seventh stream" (Ennis 1992) of American popular music, early rock was unique stylistically and in relation to its listeners. In the latter instance, the music was rooted in the present, in the performance. With commodification came reproduction and a backward eye to the past (Aronowitz 1993, 197).[3]

While the dream of biographical and social change through music has remained, the relationship of performer to audience has changed. The creation and maintenance of this boundary is mediated and multilayered (Ennis 1992, 2; Kellner 1995). As the aging rocker, Pete is telling stories, relating experiences for which hitherto there has been no audience. The postmodern self, a product of creative and ideological narratives, becomes fragmented. The plot shifts from rock storyteller to postmodern punk to aging rocker in layers of experience. The aging rocker is stigmatized as a superfluous narrative of contemporary existence; furthermore, young audiences experience him only through technological reproduction. According to Aronowitz:

> Social interaction is unthinkable without technological mediation. In these processes, the individual withers in proportion as she is unable to distance herself from the givens of the social world. Every act of independence from approved norms is labelled pathology. At the same time as the pace of life quickens, memory is obliterated, so that the past is recalled only in the form of nostalgia. [*italics* in the original] (Aronowitz 1994, 16)

As textual expressions of Pete Townshend, Pete and Ray live in a postmodern sociocultural milieu characterized by doubt and risk-taking. For these mediated cultural heroes, age and the aging process become their primary, but tenuous, creative links to audiences. In *White City* and *PsychoDerelict*, then, the textual post-Who Pete Townshend *risks* telling the story of the aging rocker to his listeners. Such activity leads to both psychological benefits and burdens. In the words of Anthony Giddens, "A self identity has to be created and more or less continually reordered against the backdrop of shifting experiences of day-to-day life and the fragmenting tendencies of modern institutions" (Giddens 1991, 186).

Pete's aging rocker is both creatively expressed and eventually ideologically consumed. As a deviant master status (Dotter and Roebuck 1988), it speaks to both youth and middle age. The former is challenged to consider perspectives of aging within the music, the latter to expand the interpretation of the rock dream beyond nostalgia. The aging rocker is a vital storyline within rock media culture. If its appearance seems inconvenient, it will remain no less important for future performers and audiences.

Rock music as a cultural form has endured for nearly half a century. A polyvocal medium of communication, it is simultaneously an object of consumption and site for meaning-creation and interpretation. As represented in the interpretive biography (Denzin 1989a) of Pete Townshend, the aging rocker is a potentially fertile text for creative self-discovery. If only the young can be truly postmodern (Best and Kellner 1997, 12), perhaps their elders can point the way. The Who's manager, Bill Curbishley, makes this point on Pete's interpretation of the rock and roll dream:

> Rock music is really a quest for Pete. He's always used rock to answer his own problems and questions. "I Can't Explain," "Substitute," all those songs were really him coming to terms with his own problems and by extension the problems of millions of others. I think that principle still holds true today. He really does believe that rock 'n' roll has the capacity to change the world: that if enough people were to actually listen to what he and a few others have to say, then things might be a bit better. (Giuliano 1996, 218)

Coda for the Aging Rocker

I have characterized Pete's textual biography in the phrase "rock storyteller as postmodern punk"—the interplay of ideological and creative self narratives (Dotter forthcoming). Within this dialogue Pete as aging rocker seeks expression, a stigmatized but no less heroic voice seeking to connect with the audience. To this end, Pete launched his website, petetownshend.com, to showcase news, diaries, and upcoming projects. The related site,

CHAPTER SIX

eelpie.com, offers Pete solo material for sale, including a number of exclusive double-disc live solo performances as well as a reworked radio play version of *Lifehouse* (Townshend 1999).

In January 2003 Pete was questioned in Britain for allegedly downloading illegal images of children from an Internet pornography site. He claimed he had himself been abused as child and was doing research for his autobiography. He also stated that he was shocked at the wide Internet availability of such images and had since 1995 been preparing a brief on the proliferation of child pornography. He was eventually not charged, but issued a formal caution and placed on a register of sex offenders. The police investigation determined that he had used a credit card to access the site, but did not download any images (*New York Times* 2003; *London Times* 2003; Kent 2003a, 2003b).

Phoenix Survivors, a group representing victims of pedophiles, initially issued "various robust" statements on the allegations against Pete, but after the investigation the organization was critical of his placement on the sex offender list: "Mr. Townshend should have been 'less publically cautioned' and given a second chance. It seems that Roger Daltry's [sic] assertions of a 'witch hunt' may indeed have real substance" (Kent 2003c).

Following the investigation Pete offered these thoughts in an e-mail to *Rolling Stone*:

> I intend to work my way back to normality. As a result of all this shit, I've decided to greatly formalize the structure of my charity (Double-O) and the way I work with "survivors"—so that in future my work is more well known to everyone. I've kept my profile low in this area out of modesty I suppose, and it has worked against me. I am going to complete my autobiography, Pete Townshend (who he?) [sic]. I put it down and did not plan to finish it until much later. But now I am going to push ahead until it is done. People need to read about my entire life to get a real picture of who I am. I hope to finish it by the end of the year. So it may come out next year sometime. I am also going to get up and play just as soon as I can. (Kent 2003c)

Sharing an ironically similar fate with his protagonist Ray in *PsychoDerelict*, Pete will continue to negotiate the status of aging rocker, only now with the added stigma conferred by these recent events. Ultimately, the stigma movie is viewed through the voyeur's gaze into the narrative self. In Denzin's words, "Thus the mystery of experience. There is no secret key that will unlock its meanings" (Denzin 1995, 218).

Notes

1. Bayles (1994, 68) traces the term to a stage play of the same title by the South African writer Athol Fugard.

2. Ennis describes the increasing importance of the guitar for the music during this period. The rise of the virtuoso guitarist had an echo of the blues: "the adulation given virtuoso guitar players whose repertoire was blues based was part of the reason black musicians held that rock of this style was old hat and not worthy of their attention" (Ennis 1992, 279).

3. For an analysis of the contemporary commodification of big band music and its relationship to audience identification with the genre, see Leslie and Dotter (1999).

CHAPTER SEVEN
MURDER IN THE MEDIA: CULTURAL CRIMINOLOGY, CONSTRUCTIONS OF VIOLENCE, AND A CRIME OF THE EARLY CENTURY

For most of the twentieth century, development of criminological theory was animated by classical/neoclassical and positivist approaches. The former focuses on the degree of choice by perpetrators of crime and the latter on establishing the causes of crime through the use of the scientific method. These schools grew from the eighteenth-century Enlightenment and its modernist pillars of reason and science. More broadly, classical and positivist philosophies have dominated discourse in practically all fields of social science (Bohm 1997; Vold, Bernard, and Snipes 1998). While there is an ebb and flow characterizing their relative influences, arguably from the 1950s to today criminology has been heavily positivistic in orientation; in textbooks the field is summarily defined as the scientific study of crime, criminals, and victims.

Criminology is commonly acknowledged as inter- or "multi-"disciplinary, and its primary roots are in sociology (Hunter and Dantzker 2002, 23–24). Its theories and methods distinguish the area quite clearly from related ones such as abnormal psychology or jurisprudence. Labeling or interactionist perspectives have presented the most durable contrast to the narrow classical/positivist debate, particularly with the demise of Marxist criminology (Dotter and Roebuck 1988). As I demonstrated in chapter 4, this perspective has accommodated many proponents from the broadest spectrum of sociology—including a share of positivists.

Criminal labeling is part of the larger interactional process of stigmatization common to all types of deviance-generation (Schur 1971). A thoroughly interpretive interactionist labeling, informed with a cultural

CHAPTER SEVEN

studies critique, presents an alternative to mainstream approaches and is in no small part responsible for the emerging subfield of cultural criminology (Ferrell and Sanders 1995a; Dotter 1997). Its focus is "the common ground between cultural and criminal practices in contemporary social life—that is, collective behavior organized around imagery, style, and symbolic meaning, and that characterized by legal and political authorities as criminal" (Ferrell and Sanders 1995b, 3). A primary emphasis of cultural criminology is the expanding presence and complex qualitative linkages of crime coverage in the mass media. This emphasis includes all types of media, but most especially print, film, and video, as well as electronic sources. It conceives of crime as both news and entertainment (Fishman and Cavender 1998; Ferrell and Websdale 1999a).

Following this lead, then, the focus of this chapter is the cultural construction of murder or homicide as news and entertainment. It is organized along three lines. First, I present a summary of the development of cultural criminology, linking it with the scenario as an interpretive strategy. Second, I examine the social construction of violence in both interactionist and cultural studies texts, giving particular emphasis to conceptions of literary theory and film criticism in the latter. Third, I present a reading of an historical scenario of murder. In 1906 Chester Gillette was convicted of murdering Grace Brown at Big Moose Lake in New York's Adirondack Mountains and eventually executed for the crime (Brandon 1986; Brownell and Wawrzaszek 1986). The event was fictionalized in Theodore Dreiser's (1925/2003) massive novel, *An American Tragedy*, which itself was produced as a motion picture entitled *A Place in the Sun*. My interpretation of this scenario—"The Story of Grace and Chester"—moves between various texts, fictional and nonfictional: historical accounts of the events; Dreiser's 1925 novel as well as literary criticism of it; elements of Dreiser's biography; and the 1951 film, directed by George Stevens and featuring Elizabeth Taylor, Montgomery Clift, and Shelley Winters in major roles.

I argue that both actual events and novelistic ones are intertwined in this interpretive scenario of violence. The stigma associated with the crime emerges from the social status of characters and is part of the wider backdrop of the story. The murder-event is narratively linked to the textual biographies of Grace and Chester—and thereby his trial and execution as additional story elements. The reconstruction of these elements in the novel give a dramatic glimpse of actors' textual selves—perpetrator, victim, and others linked through the crime. The stigma movie—Dreiser's own biography, literary criticism of the novel, and the film version of the story—adds further literary and visual layers to the textual narrative. Images of conventional and stigmatized status are mediated in the larger early-twentieth-century ideology of the Social Gospel and emerging consumer culture (Curtis 1991). This historical confluence contextualizes class (Kaplan 1988; Eby 1998), age (Ziff 1966, 146–65; Fass 1977; Shi 1995, 294–99; Austin and Willard 1998), and gender (Edwards and Gifford 2003) in the labeling process. Additionally, a minority racialized voice (White 1990; Baker 1998, 81–98; Goldberg 1993; Lemert 2002, 43–44) is notably absent from the white-middle-class-emerging-American-Dream-turned-to-nightmare storyline.

In the postmodern moment of the scenario, philosophical and historical discourses are joined through literature. Derrida summaries the fluidity of narratives and their textual connectedness: "The 'economy' of literature *sometimes* seems to me more powerful than that of other types of discourse: such as, for example, historical or philosophical discourse. *Sometimes*: it depends on singularities and contexts. Literature would be potentially more potent" [*italics* in the original] (Derrida 1992, 43). Literary narratives may both obscure and illuminate the creation of stigma, and as such be a fruitful space to glimpse the turn from modern to postmodern. Derrida speaks further to this ambiguous but inescapable quality of literature: "If it is not almost everything, it is anything but nothing—or, if it is nothing, it's a nothing which *counts*, which in my view counts a lot" [*italics* in the original] (Derrida 1992, 73).

Cultural Criminology, the Scenario, and the Social Creation of Violence

Emergence of Cultural Criminology

As introduced in chapter 2, the scenario represents a multidimensional sensitizing concept, combining interactionist labeling with the cultural studies emphasis on the social creation of meaning. I view it as central to the developing subfield of cultural criminology, a fluid intersection of disciplines and points of view including "criminology, cultural and media studies, critical theory" and "postmodern, feminist, and other

CHAPTER SEVEN

perspectives"—"less a closed analytic system than an open road into the study of culture, crime, and their interconnections" (Ferrell and Sanders 1995c, 297). Both cultural criminology and the scenario bring into bold relief the importance of mass media—as agents and process—for the study of contemporary crime. The cultural context of crime is described and critiqued as part of meaning-generation.

Cultural criminology is a reflexive project simultaneously examining "crime as culture" and "culture as crime" (Ferrell and Sanders 1995b, 4–11). In the first instance crime is taken as primarily subcultural in origin, reflecting patterns of style and expression based on age, gender, race, and social class. The long history of the Chicago School and its theoretical influence is reflected here, from social disorganization through differential association to interactionist labeling. In the second case popular culture is seen as a particularly fruitful site for the study of crime. Traditional concepts like white-collar or corporate crime, terrorism, and so on are now part of broader cultural discourse, not merely confined to closed debates among experts. Similarly, the shifting boundaries of criminality and broader characterizations of social deviance (Sagarin 1975) are daily on display in media coverage and rooted in the social categories of gender, race, and class (Barak, Flavin, and Leighton 2001). As Ferrell and Sanders (1995c, 299) observe, "'culture' and 'crime' exist less as discrete phenomena to be perceived and experienced than as processes interwoven along continua of political power, social stigma and marginality, and style."

With its emphasis on meaning-generation, the scenario is an important concept for cultural criminology. The dynamics of crime construction are taken beyond descriptions of the actual event to layers of representations (media reconstruction) and implosion (stigma movie). Mediated images of crime are overlaid with those of celebrity (Boorstin 1962/87) even as they blur the distinction between reality and "unreality" (Mitroff and Bennis 1989/93). The scenario is a roadmap for "a journey into the spectacle and carnival of crime, a walk down an infinite hall of mirrors where images created and consumed by criminals, criminal subcultures, control agents, media institutions, and audiences bounce endlessly one off the other" (Ferrell and Websdale 1999b, 4).

As a script for untangling mediated crime images, the scenario presents at least two possibilities. A single criminal event—historical or contemporary—can be the focus, or several events can be grouped under a general crime category for comparison. In either case meaning-generation, from the occurrence of an event to media reconstructions and the production of the stigma movie, is paramount. The narrative can be followed through its handling in different types of media (e.g., newspapers, books, and film) as well. While any specific type of crime may constitute the scenario, murder (i.e., homicide) and, more generally, violent crime are the most frequently found storylines. The scenario views the meaning of violence through mediated storytelling. Murder is the most serious and fearful of such narratives and takes countless forms: acts between intimates, traditional predatory homicide, and today, instances of mass murder and terrorism.

Images of Crime: News and Entertainment

There are two broad categories of mass media–generated crime meaning: news or information and entertainment. For analytical purposes the two can be treated separately, but within the dynamics of the scenario, they are often intertwined. Media presentations of events are fundamentally summaries of description and analysis, characterizing what I term the documentary scenario. When such reconstructions assume an independent existence as "stigma movies" their original functions tend to blur.

The cultural context of crime as news and information is dynamic. As Barak observes, that context reflects "the socially constructed perspectives of both the privileged elites and the popular masses." He states further, that the focus "concerns the various contradictions and tensions involved in the subjective and organizational production of crime news, and in the implicit and explicit crime control policies advocated by the mass media" (Barak 1994b, 8). In short, crime news emerges from a complex process of negotiated meaning at multiple levels and is treated as commodity. This process is characterized as "contextual constructionism" (Surette, 1998, 8–9), in which the negotiation has an impact on the meaning being created.

As a broad social product, crime news is experienced intersubjectively, "an expanded personal reality constructed from knowledge from both experienced and symbolic realities. It is perceived as the 'real' world by each individual—what we individually believe the world to be like" (Surette 1998, 11). In short, while individual experience can play a significant role in perceptions of crime, they are most fully realized in a mediated context.

CHAPTER SEVEN

The interweaving of race and violent crime in newsmaking demonstrates this complexity. Minority, especially black, images dominate television crime coverage—as perpetrators if not victims of violence. In the process, context is largely sacrificed to drama. The result is a racialized treatment of violence as news:

> Even if the proportion of Black victims and criminals were to reflect defensibly "accurate" readings of actual crime patterns, *in the absence of contextual explanations*, the heavy prominence of a racial minority in these stories may worsen negative stereotyping. Additionally, relying upon crime statistics accepts constructions of social reality that we should regard skeptically. Comparing news to official crime data neglects subtleties in defining violence and in categorizing it as criminal—or as newsworthy. [*italics* in the original] (Entman and Rojecki 2000, 81)

More than biased or even selective, coverage of violence is thus decontextualized and a racial stereotype emerges.

In addition to its news or information content, crime meaning is also generated as entertainment. The twentieth-century development of mass media moved from print sources (newspapers, books) to electronic ones (film, radio, television, and Internet) (Whetmore 1985). Crime has been a central topic of concern throughout this history, evolving particularly as a subject of entertainment. With the appearance of television, feature films were replaced as the dominant media source of crime images. As Surette summarizes:

> by the second half of the nineteenth century the dominant image of the criminal in the popular media had shifted from earlier romantic, heroic portraits to more conservative and negative images. The media of this period were already presenting the stereotypical portraits and themes of crime and justice that would later dominate movies and television—portraits and themes still to be found in modern entertainment media. (Surette 1998, 26)

Information/entertainment overlap is found throughout the history of mediated crime portrayals—from nineteenth-century tabloid journalism to contemporary reality-based television as well as twenty-four-hour cable news coverage. Reality-based television is a development of the last generation, including "happy talk" and "action news" styles, syndicated talk shows, tabloid news magazine productions, and reality crime series (Cavender and Fishman 1998, 12). Examples of reality crime programming include "America's Most Wanted" and "Unsolved Mysteries." The growth of cable networks through the new millennium has seen a proliferation of "infotainment" programming, most especially focusing on crime as well as war (Leslie 1997).

In distinguishing between meaning as entertainment and information, scenarios have different analytical properties. The documentary scenario functions primarily to convey information about a particular criminal event. The crime scenario whose primary aim is entertainment may be called dramatic, based on a fictional event. In purely fictional storylines, reconstruction of the event lies more firmly in the interpretations of audiences (i.e., viewers or readers) (Kellner 1995). The blending of an historical event into an otherwise novel storyline—the layering of documentary and dramatic—leads to a more complex reconstruction in which the narrative is creatively embellished beyond the historical record.

Prelude to Scenario: Interactionist and Cultural Studies Concerns

Social Construction of Violence: Interactionist Perspectives

Violence, including murder, is a multidimensional social phenomenon, "the threat, attempt, or use of physical force" to gain "dominance over another or others" (Brownstein 2000, 6). Social science for the most part compartmentalizes violence in the search for its causes, in criminal-legal definitions, in the identification of historical trends, and in various typologies (Holmes and Holmes 2001; Miethe and McCorkle 2001; Fox and Levin 2001; Clinard et al. 1994; Gurr 1989a, 1989b). Two specific types of homicide that have particularly been the focus of such mainstream analyses are serial murder (Holmes and Holmes 1998) and hate crime (Levin 2002).

Contrasting with these objective points of view—legal, historical, psychological, and so on—are interactionist constructions of violence and its meaning in different contexts, with various labels. The thrust of this work is on the situational relativity of violence and the emergence of its meaning from the interplay of numerous sociocultural factors. No specific act is universally defined as violent in human societies, and certain definitions of

CHAPTER SEVEN

violence are viewed as normal (i.e., as demonstrations of bravery or altruism) (Curra 2000, 61).

Lonnie H. Athens (1989/92, 1997) utilizes an interactionist conception of self to describe the interpretive process by which acts of criminal violence are rendered meaningful by perpetrators. In so doing, he identifies a number of different violent criminal types, levels of violent criminal action, and careers of the violent criminal. Similarly, Jack Katz argues that actors find a moral and even sensual dimension in the violent criminal experience. In his words:

> The challenge for explanation is to specify the steps of the dialectic process through which the person empowers the world to seduce him. On the one hand, we must explain how the individual himself *conjures up* the spirit. On the other hand we must accept the attraction or compulsion as *authentic*. [italics in the original] (Katz 1988, 7)

Katz examines a range of violent crimes, most notably forms of homicide he calls "righteous slaughter" and "senseless" murder. He chillingly concludes the monograph with this observation: "the reason we so insistently refuse to look closely at how street criminals destroy others and bungle their way into confinement to save their sense of purposive control over their lives—is the piercing reflection we catch when we steady our glance at those evil men" (Katz 1988, 324).

Philip Jenkins critiques the social construction of violence in several historical contexts: serial murder (1994), child sexual abuse by Roman Catholic priests (1996, 2003b, 133–56), and post–9/11 terrorism (2003a). Mediated images are drawn from popular culture and criminal justice. In so doing his work expands the traditional labeling perspective to include elements of a cultural studies feminist interpretation. Describing the appearance in the media of serial murder as a social problem, he writes, "[T]he gap between objective social reality and subjective definition is enormous. This type of crime involves minuscule numbers of people, either victims or perpetrators, and the likelihood of becoming a victim of this activity is extremely low" (Jenkins 1994, 19).

The dramatization of crime news, lacking any context, goes well beyond the case of serial murder. In fact, "the less common a crime is, the more coverage it will generate. Sensational and rare crimes which can be fitted into news themes with moralistic messages are particularly popular" (Potter and

Kappeler 1998, 5). Exotic drug abuse (Jenkins 1998) or rape (Benedict 1992)—which inevitably revolves around constructed images of the woman making the charge—are cases in point. Furthermore, sensationalized crimes are very much part of "moral panics" (Goode and Ben-Yehuda 1994). Increasingly crime, especially as covered on twenty-four-hour cable, becomes not only an important news category, but a primary one. Glassner's (1999) term "culture of fear" goes beyond the interactional dynamics of moral panic to locate the production of crime news as a commodity.

Cultural Studies: Tragedy and the Mediated Textuality of Violent Events

Interactionism and cultural studies share the emphasis on the importance of the meaning-generation process. For example, the creation of race and gender stigmatization may often be linked to crime, resulting in complex historical cases of deviance-labeling. The newspaper coverage of the 1855 murder of New Orleans businessman Levi Smelser reveals textually what we call "the story of Kitty, Theresa, and Adam." The three are charged with the crime; thus they are linked in the media narrative. Kitty was Smelser's slave; Theresa Smelser, his wife; and Adam Scott, his laborer, who apparently was romantically involved with Theresa (Dotter and Fisher-Giorlando 1997; Fisher-Giorlando and Dotter 2003). The antebellum patriarchal slave culture produced intertwining stigma contests in the media coverage of the events. The textual narrative suggests not an additive model of oppression, but a reflexive one, better characterized by "both/and scripts in which all groups and actors possess relative amounts of privilege and stigma" (Dotter and Fisher-Giorlando 1997, 265).

Furthermore, the gender/race "imaginary" (Ingraham 1994) historically prevented a criticism of the ascriptive categories as sites of labeling and social control. In the antebellum South patriarchy and racism suffused both the legal system and the wider culture, finding normative expression in conceptions of honor and shame (Wyatt-Brown 1982, 400). As we conclude, "Simultaneously, stigmatization based on race and gender is a layered, interactive, nonlinear process. Thus Kitty the slave and Adam Scott, a white male, were imprisoned for the murder of Levi Smelser, while the widow Theresa Smelser was eventually released" (Dotter and Fisher-Giorlando 1997, 266).

Contemporary criminal events have likewise led to analyses of the mediated construction of violence. The trial of O. J. Simpson and his

CHAPTER SEVEN

eventual acquittal on the 1994 charges of double murder has been critiqued as a site of cultural heroism (Moore and Moore 1997) and of postmodern spectacle (Barak 1999). In both instances the focus is the contradiction between Simpson's previous conventional celebrity and the heinous crime of dual homicide. The September 11, 2001, mass murder and terrorist attack on New York City is the subject of an interpretive volume of essays, focusing on a multilayered dialogue including the personal and biographical, the media and ideological, and a national conversation on 9/11 and its aftermath (Denzin and Lincoln 2003, xv–xvi). The work represents an attempt to establish the importance of voices from social sciences and humanities in the ongoing debate regarding terrorism. Similarly, autoethnography frames emotional response to the event by those not directly involved (Ellis 2002), and a performance-based cultural studies situates narratives of the event's experience in a community moral dialogue (Denzin 2003a). Finally, Baudrillard (2003) offers a "requiem for the Twin Towers." Habermas and Derrida are engaged in interview dialogues in the wake of the event as well (Borradori 2003).

From literary theory, violence can be seen as tragedy (Williams 1966; Eagleton 2002), differing from pathos (i.e., "acts of God") or accident. As tragedy, violence involves social relationships, emotional ties, and expectations, and the fundamental severing of these in the story of victim and victimizer (Gilligan 1997, 6–7). Finally, the definition of tragedy is multilayered in at least three senses: as works of art, lived experience, or worldviews and structures of feeling (Eagleton 2002, 9). In *The Birth of Tragedy* Nietzsche argues that modernist philosophical rationalism and the dominance of scientific method have stripped culture of its mythic quality—and thereby "its healthy creative natural power" (Nietzsche 1927/95, 84–85). As art, tragedy offers an ironic counterpoint to this loss of meaning:

> [T]ragedy must embody value; but it is odd, even so, that an art form which portrays human anguish and affliction should have been so brandished as a weapon to combat a typically "modern" pessimism and passivity. Tragedy for a great many commentators is all about cheering us up. (Eagleton 2002, 9)

To culturally and artistically embody value, tragedy must examine the conflicts of human existence, particularly those pitting individual desire against the social organization of experience. In short, the character of knowledge is unavoidably tragic. Thus, the textual self—the postmodern audience for tragedy—"risks gazing into the abyss of the Real and dancing on its edge without being turned to stone, reading what the scholars decorously call history as a squalid genealogy of blood, toil and terror" (Eagleton 2002, 53).

These layers of definition frame the difficulty in analytically separating the tragic from the violent, and equally as problematic, the event from its reconstruction. Each suggests a dynamic process of meaning-creation. According to Williams, "We are not looking for a new universal meaning of tragedy. We are looking for the structure of tragedy in our own culture. Once we begin to doubt, in experience and then in analysis, the ordinary twentieth-century idea, other directions seem open" (Williams 1966, 62). One such direction is West's (1989, 211–39) vision of prophetic pragmatism (first introduced in chapter 3). Pragmatic instrumentalism, marked by its "evasion" of traditional philosophical epistemology, is transformed into a tool for human agency and social change. As cultural criticism, then, prophetic pragmatism is not without a sense of the tragic, exposing "the irreducible predicament of unique individuals who undergo dread, despair, disillusionment, disease, and death *and* the institutional forms of oppression that dehumanize people" [*italics* in the original] (West 1989, 228). The sense of loss is experienced by the individual, but there is hope in the struggle that social transformation is possible.

Furthermore, Sidney Hook (1974) argues that pragmatism is linked to "the tragic sense of life" through the experience of moral choice. Moral experiential choice, involving value conflict, is most critical not in the alternative between "good and evil," but in that between "good and good." Thus the moral dilemma has a dialectical tragic quality, gleaned from the voice not heard or ultimately silenced, imagined in "the possible selves we have sacrificed to become what we are" (Hook 1974, 13).

The connection of violence to tragedy, then, is above all a textual one (Barker 1993, 230). Eagleton writes, "For most people today, tragedy means an actual occurrence, not a work of art. Indeed, some of those who nowadays use the word of actual events are probably unaware that it has an artistic sense at all" (Eagleton 2002, 14). Tragedy as lived experience is constantly, if unevenly, juxtaposed to its literary reconstruction: Violence and/or death are the inevitable outcome of both the event and its reconstruction.

CHAPTER SEVEN

New historical criticism holds that the meaning of texts is uncertain and ambiguous—best grasped, however temporarily, as a relational expression in space and time. Derrida observes, "There is nothing outside of the text" (Derrida 1967/76, 158). As a deconstructive project, Lynn likens new historical criticism to cinematic imagery and "history as a movie." In his words:

> [B]iographical and historical critics watch the movie in the usual fashion, trying to figure out the plot, keeping track of the characters. A new historical critic may select one frame of the film, carefully analyzing minute details, and then compare that frame to another one ten minutes later, showing the radical differences between the two. Whereas, traditional historians see connections, new historians see ruptures and revolutions. (Lynn 1994, 13)

Postmodern literary constructions of violence include visual images as well as written narrative, situated, as I have shown, in texts of information and entertainment. The impact of such visualization is more than the mere technological innovation and historical development of television and film. In documentation of historical events after the passage of time and especially in visual coverage as it unfolds, the textual expression of violence has been recast in the relationship of the event to its reconstruction. As Derrida observes:

> [a textual description] is already a weave of pure traces, differences in which meaning and force are united—a text nowhere present, consisting of archives which are *always already* transcriptions. Originary prints. Everything begins with reproduction. Always already: repositories of a meaning which was never present, whose signified presence is always reconstituted by deferral. [*italics* in the original] (Derrida 1967/78, 211)

Regarding the role of television, Williams observes, "Much of the real content of news has been altered by the facts of visual presentation. In certain kinds of report there seems to be an absolute difference between the written or spoken account and the visual record with commentary. It is true that much can be altered by selection and editing, but of course this is true of any observer's account. It can be reasonably argued that the televised impression of 'seeing the events for oneself' is at times and perhaps always deceptive" (Williams 1975, 48).

The ability of contemporary cable television to present immediate real-time satellite transmission of events heightens the textual quality of event and its reconstruction. Williams calls this the "drama-documentary"—television's "capacity to enter a situation and show what is actually happening in it" (Williams 1975, 72). Violence is the frequent subject of such visual texts, the vicarious, often real-time experience of events whose mediated nature is often not readily apparent.

Hall (1986a) introduces the concept of articulation in critiquing the mediated process of meaning-generation. The concept describes the process in a double sense of expression (i.e., communicating through language) and connection (i.e., the context of mass communication). In Hall's words, "So the so-called 'unity' of a discourse is really the articulation of different, distinct elements which can be rearticulated in different ways because they have no necessary 'belongingness'" (1986a, 53). Hall is particularly interested in the mediated expression of ideological images (racism, sexism, inequality, the desirability of consumption, and so on) and the articulation/rearticulation of their meaning in the context of audience interpretation: "the theory of articulation asks how an ideology discovers its subject rather than how the subject thinks the necessary and inevitable thoughts which belong to it." Thus meaning-construction is a dynamic process in which articulation "enables us to think how an ideology empowers people, enabling them to begin to make some sense or intelligibility of their historical situation" (Hall 1986a, 53).

Hall (1980b, 1980c) characterizes the emergence of meaning from a mediated process of "encoding" and "decoding." The process is a multilayered articulation of "moments," including production, circulation, distribution/consumption, and reproduction. Hall applies it specifically to television communication, but it can be extended to other mass media. Images of an event are encoded by media (production), circulated to and decoded by audiences (consumption-as-interpretation), and eventually recirculated as the meaning changes.

For Hall (1980b, 136–38), decoding is the interrelationship of three hypothetical meaning "positions" between and among audiences. In the dominant-hegemonic position, the viewer operates "inside the dominant code" put forth in the production of the event by media, accepting the meaning relatively "full and straight." In the second position, the negotiated code or version, "decoding contains a mixture of adaptive and oppositional elements," and the dominant ideology is "shot through with contradictions, though these are only on certain occasions brought to full visibility." The third decoding position is a completely oppositional one, in which audience members, most likely fully aware of other meaning levels, choose to reinterpret images in radical ways. Hall notes that the boundary between negotiation and opposition marks the struggle of the "politics of signification" (Hall 1980b, 138).

As articulated discourse, the scenario's deviant event immediately passes from "actuality" to reconstruction and interpretation. For example, the particulars of a death labeled a murder may or may not be established in a short period of time. Even from its initial reporting, the event is constructed as such by potentially numerous groups such as police; countless news agencies (most offering "live" coverage as the event unfolds over minutes, days, weeks, and sometimes months—long after the homicide itself); friends and family of the victim and other established actors in the event; as well as community groups. As the discursive acts (Perinbanayagam 1985, 20–21) unfold, the story inevitably encompasses more than merely the facts of the case—even when these are not in question. Thus, constructions of race or gender of the actors as known enter the discourse initially as event-facts and gradually become part of the "politics of signification." Hegemonic and oppositional positions may evolve from reporting the occurrence of the event to a widening discussion of how the event characterizes community or even national values. Celebrity may at first be one of several attributes associated with victim or accused, but through articulation become the overriding context of the scenario (even generated where none existed prior to the event).

Hall's model of the articulation of meaning and the politics of signification can be extended to literary theory and to film theory and criticism as well. Both literature and the cinema evidence important historical traditions of realism which may be critiqued with Hall's notion of coding. In American literature realism appeared in the 1880s and 1890s and developed throughout the twentieth century (Ziff 1966; Kaplan 1988). The movement focused on novelistic portrayals of everyday life, particularly the moral trials and dilemmas of choice faced by those living in complex industrial, urban society. As such, the form was inherently critical of modern society and its alienation of individuals (Berthoff 1965). Naturalism is either synonymous with realism or seen as emerging from it, in that characters are once again plotted in everyday situations, but find their individual agency either severely circumscribed or negated by sociocultural forces beyond their control (Cowley 1950; Pizer 1966/76, 1982).

Naturalism sought to even more objectively portray experience than did realism, exemplified by the distinction between naturalist "characters" and realist "selves" (Mitchell 1989, 14–15). As well, in historical terms realism refers roughly to post–Civil War fiction (1870s and 1880s), and naturalism to that appearing from the turn of the century (Pizer 1966/76, 11–12; 1995, 4–5). This historical movement from realism to naturalism, occurring as literature became more widely available to mass audiences in emerging consumer society and culture, is illuminated by Hall's (1980b, 1980c) conceptualizations of coded meaning. The subjects and plots of literary texts were mediated (i.e., articulated through moments of production, circulation, distribution/consumption, and reproduction). It can be argued that neither realism nor naturalism fully emerged beyond negotiation of dominant normative narratives, attempting descriptions of modern society at the century's turn and beyond. In various forms these narratives focused on the everyday struggle to forge self-identity in a changing world—one marked by impersonal industrial forces and the importance of wealth accumulation (Budd 1995; Pizer 1995).

By the 1920s American naturalism is juxtaposed with an evolving literary modernism (Ruland and Bradbury 1991, 247–49). Retrospectively, a vague outline of postmodern sociocultural terrain is evident in the opening decades of twentieth-century America, marked by emergence of a "modern temper" (Dumenil 1995). Peter Conrad offers a dramatic description of its literary effects:

> Bodies now did things which, at least according to literature, they had never done before. A man ponders his own bowel movement, relishing its sweet smell. Later in the day he surreptitiously masturbates in a public place and takes part in a pissing contest, proud of the arc his urine describes. A woman has a noisily affirmative orgasm or perhaps more than one. The same people did not think in paragraphs or logical completed sentences, like characters in nineteenth-century novels. Their mental life proceeded in associative jerks and spasms; they mixed up shopping lists with sexual fantasies, often forgot verbs and (in the woman's case) scandalously abandoned all punctuation. The modern mind was not a quiet, tidy cubicle for cogitation. (Conrad 1999, 15)

CHAPTER SEVEN

The flourish of modernity presages the extended meaning crisis of the postmodern. Moreover, "this first full-blown generation of American moderns experienced the imperatives of the age as plainer, if no less complex," including "the pressures of democracy and the claims of women" (Stansell 2001, 7) as well as the emergence of a class-based consumer society (Leach 1993; Douglas 1995; Eby 1998). If, as I contend, postmodern culture and society can be glimpsed in the modern, then turn-of-century portrayals of literary naturalism are a rich textual site of meaning-generation, ambiguity, stigma, and turn (Blair 1999; Trotter 1999, 74–76).[1]

From its birth with the new century (Cook 1981), cinema began to develop its own tradition of realism alongside that of literature's naturalistic realism. Moreover, the visual "language" of film, despite the initial absence of sound, led classical film theorist Siegfried Kracauer to argue that only film "is uniquely equipped to record and reveal physical reality and, hence, gravitates toward it." (Kracauer 1960, 28).

Andre Bazin, a second-generation realist, goes beyond Kracauer in conceptualizing "the myth of total cinema" (Bazin 1967, 17–22), in which reality can never be fully recaptured, only approached. His was a perceptual realism in which "the daily life habit of apperception, recognition, and mental elaboration is structurally reproduced in the cinema" (Andrew 1984, 50). Furthermore, cinematic reality is rendered through montage (the ordering of shots to convey meaning of "events") as well as depth-of-field technique (which permits action to develop over time and on multiple spatial planes). In montage meaning emerges from relationships between frames, while depth-of-field (i.e., *mise-en-scène*) creates meaning through interrelationships, particularly spatial ones, within the frame. Bazin considered depth-of-field the more realistic style (Andrew 1976, 155–58). Regarding the addition of sound to visual image, Bazin observes, "Every new development added to the cinema must, paradoxically, take it nearer and nearer to its origins. In short, cinema has not yet been invented!" (Bazin 1967, 21) Still, the addition of sound and color to motion pictures (Cook 1981, 245) further enhanced film's realism and cemented the century's status as that of the "cinematic society" (Denzin 1995).

The new visual medium began to develop theory, especially regarding its artistic functions and its relations to growing audiences (Andrew 1976, 1984). Cinematic realism overlapped not only with that in literature, but also with similar perspectives in newspaper reporting (Shi 1995, 93). Denzin summarizes the contribution of the emerging cinematic form of communication in that mix of cultural mass media: "This was the system of ideas and representation the movies implemented as they moved into the sound and colour phase. These discursive systems, and their reproduction in Hollywood films, aligned the industry with dominant American values" (Denzin 1995, 22).

From the beginning of media culture to the present, crime—especially violence and murder—has been a central site of meaning-generation (Surette 1998). It is consistently found as a genre of literature, film, and news reporting—both print and television. In scenarios violent events are reconstructed and continuously articulated as cultural knowledge. The remainder of this chapter will present a critical reading of an historical scenario of homicide.

Murder in the Media: The Story of Grace and Chester

In mass-mediated society the overlap of crime news with its potential value as entertainment has long been evident (Surette 1998). With the development of motion pictures and television in the twentieth century their interrelationship became increasingly complex, often interweaving print texts with visual images. Crime scenarios that intermix documentary and dramatic construction are now a common form of media-generated knowledge. Violent crime, especially murder and its aftermath, is with little doubt the most frequent narrative of these scenarios.

Before the advent of electronic media, newspapers offered the reading public journalistic narratives of crime. By the beginning of the twentieth century, such coverage had split into informational and entertainment styles as newspapers courted expanding urban markets (Surette 1998, 57–58). Various "crimes of the century" took the media stage in national print and radio coverage as well as in fictionalized literary accounts.[2] In 1925 Theodore Dreiser published his massive, controversial novel *An American Tragedy*. The criminal event at the heart of the work is the 1906 murder of Grace Brown at Big Moose Lake in the Adirondack Mountains in New York, for which her lover Chester Gillette was convicted and executed.

My reading of the scenario—"The Story of Grace and Chester"—emerges from a variety of texts. There are two book-length accounts,

CHAPTER SEVEN

Adirondack Tragedy (Brownell and Wawrzaszek 1986) and *Murder in the Adirondacks* (Brandon 1986). These monographs go well beyond description of Grace's murder (i.e., the deviant event) to include accounts of Chester's trial and execution from original newspaper coverage and trial records. Dreiser's novel represents both a mediated reconstruction of the event and a bridge to the stigma movie production. The layer of stigma movie links the novel to literary criticism related to it, to various Dreiser biographical texts, and to the feature film based on the novel, *A Place in the Sun*. The reading is an articulation of these sources and represents my own textual discovery (Dotter and Fisher-Giorlando 1997, 254) of the scenario.

The Context of the Deviant Event: More than Murder

The murder of Grace Brown on July 11, 1906, has been called "the first 'crime of the century'" (Fitzpatrick 1999). A description of this historical event is immediately a reproduction, "always already" (Derrida, 1967/78, 211). Problems surrounding the event's meaning arise in the interpretation of the historical record: there were no direct witnesses to Grace's death and Chester Gillette gave various accounts:

> At first, he said it was an accident. Later, at the trial, he said Grace committed suicide. Still later, he is said to have confessed that he was responsible for her death, but a full account of how it happened wasn't included. (Brandon 1986, 134)

The textual event may be described as the layering of social acts in space and especially time. Perinbanayagam (2000, 8) captures the importance of this signification process:

> The present of the act is richly textured and to the extent that the actor is neither amnesiac nor autistic, the act will incorporate a constructed past and a construed future. The human typically confronts a situation and produces an act, all the while remembering his or her own past and that of the others. To the extent that he or she remembers the past, however incompletely and selectively, and anticipates a future, a self is involved in the act.

In the scenario's linguistic turn the event is grasped retrospectively in a variety of texts, especially newspaper accounts and monographs published by smaller area publishers (Brandon 1986; Brownell and Wawrzaszek 1986). Also, the murder-event can only be understood by placing it in the wider context of past situations (i.e., the relationship of Grace and Chester to themselves and others) and future developments (in particular, the trial of Chester, his conviction and execution for the crime) (Perinbanayagam 1985, 21). The narrative links the textual biographies of Grace and Chester in a dramatic storyline, generating meaning from the murder-event to others before and afterward.

On July 11, 1906, during the busy tourist season at Big Moose Lake in upstate New York, Robert Morrison rented a rowboat to a young couple:

> The man had looked like a college student, about 22, well-dressed in a neat gray suit and a white tie, with a tan complexion and an athletic build. The girl was slightly younger, but looked pale and unhappy and, Morrison thought, her plain green skirt, white shirtwaist and the black silk jacket she carried in her hand suggested she was not quite the man's social equal. (Brandon 1986, 2)

The pair did not return with the boat that evening. The next day, as Morrison began searching for the craft and its passengers, he recalled the suitcase carried by the young man with a tennis racket attached to its side. Shortly, Morrison spotted the boat in a cove, floating upside down some forty feet from the shore. On the upturned keel he noted a black jacket, and there were various objects floating in the water. Morrison righted the rowboat and it was then that he noticed two locks of dark brown hair attached to screws securing the seats (Brandon 1986, 1–4).

A search was organized and the woman's bruised body was recovered from the water, still clad in the green skirt and white shirtwaist. The remains were transported to the local Glenmore Hotel, and a check of the register tentatively identified the couple as Carl Grahm of Albany and Grace Brown of S. Otselic (Brandon 1986, 7). The search for the man's body continued the next day, July 13:

> [B]ut by afternoon word had reached them from the Albany police that there was no one in the area with a name like Carl Grahm. More of the searchers gave up, joining others in thinking the worst. When the afternoon paper, the Utica *Observer*, arrived, they were informed that the man in the boat was probably not Carl Grahm at all, but Chester

CHAPTER SEVEN

> Gillette, the nephew of the owner of the factory in Cortland, N.Y. where Grace Brown had worked. The article also noted that Grace Brown had often been seen "keeping company" with Gillette. That was enough to convince everyone and the search was not resumed. (Brandon 1986, 8)

Grace Brown was a farmer's daughter, born in 1886 near the town of South Otselic and known to her family as "Billy." The life of farm families in upstate New York, never easy, was circumscribed even further by the widespread mechanization of agriculture. The farm became increasingly uncompetitive, especially as markets expanded, and Grace's father lost his mortgage, reduced to a tenant on the land he had once owned. The future prospects for Grace and her sisters were clear but limited: marriage and establishment of their own families, often in the same county as their parents. In 1905, unmarried and seeking a fresh start, nineteen-year-old Grace followed her sister Ada's family to Cortland. She "quickly found work in the newly completed Gillette Skirt Company where she was soon seen as a pleasant, hard working employee. The pay was but a few dollars a week, but it was more money than she had ever seen back on the farm." Soon Ada and her husband left Cortland; Grace, determined to make a life of her own, remained in Cortland as a boarder in a house within sight of the skirt factory. She made infrequent trips home and, despite friendships with several girls met at the factory, was necessarily isolated from family. Grace's life took what must initially have seemed a positive turn when she met Chester Gillette (Brownell and Wawrzaszek 1986, 40–41).

Chester's arrival in Cortland in 1905 was the latest stop on a convoluted journey—including a summer there three years before as well as a stint at prep school in Oberlin, Ohio. He had struck out on his own, tired of an austere family life. His parents, Frank and Louisa, had for years served as street missionaries in various cities—first with the Salvation Army and later, Zion City. During this time Chester and his younger siblings lived in poverty, largely without roots (Brandon 1986, 30–38). Reaching Cortland, Chester contacted his uncle Horace Gillette, his father's younger brother. Horace offered Chester employment in his factory's stockroom, which the latter accepted. By all accounts Chester was quite a charismatic personality, an ambitious youth seeking his way in the world. As Brandon continues:

But the Chester Gillette who stepped off the train at the Cortland railroad station in late March of 1905 was quite a different person from the college student who had last been there in the summer of 1902. He was a mass of contradictions. The student who had studied Wordsworth and Shelley had been tempered with the hard life and rough habits of the railroad brakeman. The young gentleman scholar had been thrust into the worst kind of influences. When he wanted to, he could still project the image of the prep school student. His uncle, aunt and cousins saw a well-dressed, immaculately-groomed, intelligent and well-spoken young gentleman, who could discuss literature and poetry at an evening soiree, always knew the proper courtesies and never stepped out of line. He was an intelligent gentleman who, through the unfortunate circumstance of his family's conversion to a bizarre religious cult, had not become all he was capable of being. All this person needed, his uncle thought, was a chance and his abilities and talents would make him a valuable asset to society. (Brandon 1986, 57)

Despite the fact that two of his cousins had been taken in as full-fledged members of Horace's household, Chester was not offered accommodation there and instead rented a room in the city. Most likely during the summer of 1905, the paths of Chester and Grace crossed at the factory—he based in the stockroom, she in the adjacent cutting room. Their relationship grew throughout the fall of 1905 and Chester wrote several intimate letters to Grace during her visit home (Brownell and Wawrzaszek 1986, 53–58). The relationship continued into the next year. Despite the written declarations of his feelings for her, gifts, and time spent together, Chester was by no means completely committed:

Chester did not call on Grace every night, nor did he see her every weekend. There were other girls in the factory whom he saw occasionally, much to Billy's distress, and he soon discovered girls among the students at the Normal School. Chester's loyalty was far from total. (Brownell and Wawrzaszek 1986, 58)

In the spring of 1906 Grace again journeyed to South Otselic for a vacation. During this time her regular and increasingly anxious letters were largely ignored by Chester. Her moods became more desperate as she realized she might be losing him to another (Brownell and Wawrzaszek 1986, 58–60). They continued to see each other upon Grace's return to

CHAPTER SEVEN

Cortland, albeit amid strain and an important dilemma: "Somewhere in the months after her return, a new and ominous factor emerged. It had begun in the spring, probably just before her April trip to South Otselic. Now, in the aftermath of her vacation and the bickering with Chester came the first clues, the first slow fears, and then the frightening realization. Billy Brown was pregnant" (Brownell and Wawrzaszek 1986, 61).

Apparently Chester's attachment to Grace was from their first meeting never solitary, or had been so for only a short time. By the fall of 1905 he had begun to receive invitations to private parties among youth of Cortland's upper class, owing no doubt to his kinship with Horace Gillette. At one of these affairs he met Harriet Benedict, an eighteen-year-old socialite who had just graduated from high school. The relationship is a mystery in the historical record, spawning legends of deep romance or even a marriage proposal. In any case, as Chester's social circle expanded he had similar contacts with Harriet and other women as well, even until Grace's death (Brandon 1986, 70–72).

In June 1906 Grace planned her third visit home since meeting Chester. The trip hardly represented a solution to either her pregnancy or to the increasing uncertainty of Chester's intentions regarding their future. She would return home and Chester was to call for her after a time:

> While there are clues that the two planned to leave on a trip at the conclusion of her stay, there is no indication that Grace knew exactly what Chester had in mind. Every day at home would be one during which she would be completely reliant on Chester's ultimate arrival with a solution. The "vacation" in South Otselic promised to be an anxious rather than a happy one. Her only link with Chester would be by mail. (Brownell and Wawrzaszek 1986, 65)

On the morning of July 14 Chester was arrested at the Arrowhead Hotel, in the town of Old Forge on Fourth Lake, tracked there by District Attorney George Ward:

> From the moment he was arrested, Chester did not hesitate to talk freely about the case, but kept changing his mind about the story, getting himself deeper and deeper into trouble. First he said he was on vacation but could not explain why he had so little money, not even enough, he admitted, to pay his bill at the Arrowhead. He said he had been intimate

with Grace for over a year and that he had been aware since April that she was pregnant. He then said the trip to the woods was a wedding trip, but couldn't answer when Ward asked him where he planned to marry Grace. When Ward asked him about the letters in Grace's trunk [Clyde's own letters to Grace, written since June], Chester foolishly volunteered the information that the return letters, that Grace had written to him from South Otselic, were in his room in Cortland. So, casually, he gave away one of the most important pieces of evidence later used against him. (Brandon 1986, 146)

An autopsy was performed apparently only after embalming, due to a communication mix-up between Ward and the attending physician. Anonymous newspaper accounts report that air had been found in Grace's lungs, an indication that her death resulted from drowning. The source further suggested that she had been struck by Chester before entering the water, and it was also known that Grace could not swim (Fitzpatrick 1999; Brandon 1986, 147–48).

Ward, the district attorney, had begun assembling a chain of evidence linking Chester to the murder:

> The owner of the Arrowhead and many of his guests had already identified Chester. Now it was the turn of those who worked at Big Moose [the site of the murder]. By train, boat and road they came to Old Forge and pointed to the man they had known as Carl Grahm. During the day Grace's trunk was located and opened. In it were letters Chester had written. Chester did not deny this when questioned. He did not deny taking Grace to Big Moose Lake, but his story of the row on that lake was one of accident and panic and a girl who could not swim. (Brownell and Wawrzaszek 1986, 101)

Finally, Frank Brown, Grace's father, offered this assessment at the time he identified her body and shortly after he had been told of her "delicate condition" (as her pregnancy became described in the press):

> It was Gillette all right who was with Grace up there. They had been keeping company for some time. Lately, however, I had noticed that she had acted rather cool towards Gillette, but I did not think anything of it because from what I could learn he was as attentive to her as ever. Why they should go up there I do not know. I cannot explain it. (Brandon 1986, 148)

CHAPTER SEVEN

Ward's investigation established as Chester's motive that "'the birth of an illegitimate child would put a dark blot on his life'" (Brandon 1986, 161), and that he had repeatedly struck Grace with either an oar or his tennis racket before she entered the water. The racket had not been found when Chester, with no admission of guilt, informed the sheriff of its location (Brandon 1986, 153–64).

The section of Big Moose Lake where Grace had died is in Herkimer County. Consequently, Chester was to stand trial before the County Court in the town of Herkimer. As the investigation unfolded in the fall of 1906, Ward was elected to a judgeship but stood ready to prosecute the case. In fact, he requested and received from the governor the creation of a special Supreme Court term for handling the grand jury indictment of Chester and selection of the trial jury. With no real legal representation to this point, Chester was granted his request to the grand jury that he be defended by attorneys Albert Mills and Charles Thomas. Mills, a former state senator, was thoroughly reluctant to serve and thereby suggested Thomas's participation as co-counsel. Not unexpectedly, Chester was also indicted on a charge of first-degree murder, to which he pleaded not guilty (Brandon 1986, 169–72; Brownell and Wawrzaszek 1986, 107–11).

The trial commenced on November 12, 1906, seated with an all-male jury; its high point was Chester's appearance on the stand. A summary of his account as testimony in his own defense:

> After picnicking on the shore he and Grace had gone out in the boat for the final time. At long last they began to talk out their common problem. Grace wanted to continue on to Fourth Lake. Chester thought it was time to return to South Otselic and confess all to Grace's parents. Grace protested. She could not face her parents. Chester insisted and then, without warning, Grace jumped over the side of the boat. There was confusion. Chester attempted to help. (It was no secret to anyone in the courtroom that Grace could not swim.) But as Chester attempted to effect a rescue the boat overturned. When he surfaced there was no sign of Grace. He never saw her again. (Brownell and Wawrzaszek 1986, 136)

Ward's cross-examination of Chester was aimed at attacking his credibility and truthfulness, to introduce doubt concerning his uncorroborated description of the death scene, the spontaneity of his testimony, and the nature of his character. Jury deliberation began the evening of December

4, and midnight a verdict was reached. Chester Gillette was found guilty of first-degree murder (Brownell and Wawrzaszek 1986, 137–39).

The sentencing hearing was set for December 10. Louisa Gillette, Chester's mother, was in attendance. To pay her expenses for the trip from Denver to Herkimer, she had agreed to serve as a correspondent for the *Denver Times* and the *New York Journal* and to report on her son's sentencing hearing. Judge Irving R. Devendorf ordered the Herkimer County sheriff to deliver Chester to the state prison at Albany where the sentence of death by electrocution would be carried out. Louisa relinquished her press post and set about working for an appeal; her activities included investigations in Cortland and elsewhere, a fruitless attempt to meet with Grace's mother, and finally a series of unsuccessful lectures ("Chester Gillette—Guilty or Not Guilty—A Mother's Plea for her Son") to finance an appeal. Following the lectures, Louisa returned to family in Denver (Brandon 1986, 258–68).

Mills filed an appeal over a year later in January 1908. Louisa journeyed to Albany in March 1908 for a meeting with New York Governor Charles Evans Hughes, in which she sought clemency for Chester. Both were denied and Chester Gillette was executed March 30, 1908 (Brownell and Wawrzaszek 1986, 137–39). To the end Chester maintained his innocence. He resisted his mother's direct pleas to repent and similarly rebuffed the appeals of other evangelists. Sometime during his last year, Chester consented to meet with Henry MacIlravy, who had made the acquaintance of Louisa—on the condition that MacIlravy refrain from any mention of religion:

> Chester, who called him "Mac," seems to have liked him right away and MacIlravy came to visit him every two weeks. Eventually, of course, the topic did turn to religion and MacIlravy did what Chester's own parents and their friends could not do—converted him into a full-fledged, born-again Christian. This seems not to have happened overnight in a flash of revelation, but came gradually during the year Chester saw no one but his sister and MacIlravy. Perhaps it was the closeness of their ages, plus the fact that MacIlravy had no competition from Chester's other interests: the outdoors and women. Chester added the Bible to his small library of books and even a self-help book MacIlravy had given him called *A Young Man's Questions*. Gradually Biblical language began to enter his letters. His parents, of course, could not have been more pleased. (Brandon 1986, 271–72)

CHAPTER SEVEN

As an historical event the murder of Grace Brown is meaningful only in its relation to events that both precede and follow it in time. This narrative context is central to the labeling process and links events to actors, normative constructions, and audiences (Becker 1963/73; Dotter and Roebuck 1988). The deviant/criminal event is, as I have argued, known only as a reproduced reality of definition (stigma) and process (social reaction) (Schur 1979, 160). Thus, Grace's death was ultimately constructed as a criminal homicide; in Ward's prosecution narrative her relationship with Chester—one of intimacy leading to pregnancy—provided the motive through which the latter was tried and executed for first-degree murder. As actor/subjects Grace and Chester are juxtaposed in two disvalued acts, pregnancy and murder. In the first instance Grace may be labeled a co-conspirator with Chester, but the second situation transforms her into a tragic victim. The generation of meaning, then, is both contextual and historical:

> The concept of meaning implies that humans and the social and physical world they inhabit have particular significance. It implies that this significance might coincide with that held by others in the past, present and future, and that, by changing how one acts individually or collectively, what is meaningful can be changed as it is being generated. (Henry and Milovanovic 1996, 23)

The meaning of deviant events emerges in the stigma contest, the struggle to define disvalued behavior and the assignment of deviantized master status to actors. Schur summarizes the generation of meaning in the stigma contest:

> Definitional struggles, furthermore, will often involve competing versions of "what it is about" the kinds of persons fitting into the stigmatized categories that put them there in the first place. Different versions of the "causes" of individual deviation may carry varying moral and political implications. To that extent, kinds-of-people depictions and prescriptions regarding what should be done will be interrelated. (Schur 1980, 147)

In this manner the labeling process is expanded and the generation of meaning becomes multilayered.

Almost from the moment that Grace Brown's body was pulled from Big Moose Lake, moral entrepreneurs and audiences began constructing the story of her death. First, she (along with an apparent companion) might have accidentally drowned. Then, Chester's identity (as Carl Grahm), confirmed in the hotel register, as well as the failure to recover his body in the lake, led to suspicions of homicide. Criminal justice personnel as well as journalists began construction and reconstruction of this mediated narrative. The murder/event of July 11, 1906, was but the beginning of the story of Grace and Chester and was therefore "more than murder." The textual scenario is marked by what Derrida calls supplements, "substantive significations which could only come forth in a chain of differential references, the 'real' supervening, and being added only while taking on meaning from a trace and from an invocation of the supplement" to infinity. (Derrida 1967/76, 159) Furthermore, the story of Grace and Chester is defined only in the process of supplemental meaning-creation: "the possibility of repetition and trace do not simply inhabit the present, they constitute it in the movement of difference which they introduce into it" (Howells 1999, 22). Once the labeling process is even preliminarily presented as a mediated site, it is marked by dissemination (Derrida 1972/81a; Howells 1999, 78)—multiple and changing readings of the text. In successive media reconstructions the story of Grace and Chester frames a wider construction of their biographies as both information and entertainment.

Murder as Interpretive Biography: Yellow Journalism and Literary Greatness

Media reconstructions in the story of Grace and Chester situate the event—Grace's murder—in the relationship between the two immediately prior to Grace's death, especially as framed in the "love letters" Grace had written and in Chester's less frequent and emotional replies. Chester testified in his own defense at trial as well. These narrative details of the relationship embellished the murder's description and site interpretive biographies (Denzin 1989a) of Grace and Chester in the stigma of her pregnancy and murder. At the same time the details converge on Chester as the convicted murderer of Grace. These reconstructions are presented in journalistic accounts as the story unfolded, in the trial transcript, and in Dreiser's novel.

CHAPTER SEVEN

Grace's letters, written during her last visit home, serve as her voice-testimony during the trial. They portray Grace as hiding her pregnancy as it progresses, desperately hoping that Chester will acknowledge and willingly offer his support, if not his heartfelt love. Shortly after arrival at her parents' farm in mid-June Grace wrote:

> Chester, if I could only die. I know how you feel about the affair and I wish for your sake you need not be troubled. If I die I hope that you can be happy. I hope I can die. . . . Oh dear, please come and take me away. You won't ever know how much I wish you would come. Chester I do want you to have a good time now and I won't be cross. I think when I see you, dear, I will be so glad I can't live. I hope you will be glad to see me. Go where you want to dear and don't be angry with me. I want you tonight and I am so blue.
> Lovingly,
> The Kid
> P.S. Write often please. (Brownell and Wawrzaszek 1986, 67)

On June 22, Grace offered:

> I don't suppose you will ever know how I regret being all this trouble to you. I know you hate me, and I can't blame you one bit. My whole life is ruined and, in a measure, yours is too. Of course it is worse for me than for you, but the world and you too may think I am the only one to blame, but somehow I can't, just simply can't, think I am, Chester. I said no so many times dear [to Chester's advances for sexual intercourse]. Of course the world will not know that, but it's true all the same. (Brandon 1986, 95)

Chester's responses were both infrequent and without apparent passion. In one exchange he instructed Grace about his own plans as well as their coming reunion:

> Please excuse paper and pencil as I am not writing this at home and have nothing else here. I received your letter last night and was just a little surprised although I thought you would be discouraged. Don't worry so much and think less about how you feel and have a good time. Your trip with your father and mother ought not to make any difference as you can go from wherever they are at any time. . . . I cannot get

away before the 7th or 8th [of July]. . . . I also think you should go with your parents and write while with them and we can make arrangements then.
Yours lovingly,
C. (Brownell and Wawrzaszek 1986, 68)

As the date for their reunion neared, Grace wrote:

> Oh! dear, dear, dear! I can't see anything but just trouble. What if I should not be able to travel. There are so many things to think about. If I had the strength, dear, I do believe I should walk to the river and throw myself in. . . . You would smile if you knew how I am trying to get strong, for I don't care how rough my life is after next Saturday. I think I could carry packs like women peddlers. (Brownell and Wawrzaszek 1986, 68)

And she expressed concern about Chester's social rounds, informed by letters from her own girlfriends—who had seen Chester out and about:

> I do wish you could read some of the letters from the girls. It is no wonder I write blue letters. I don't believe what they say now, dear. I wish you could have read one letter, giving an account of your trip to the lake. Of course I had received your letter telling me about it so I did not believe the other one, but it was so different. Of course you boys all had girls and all that stuff and nonsense. I was awfully glad I had your letter first though. (Brownell and Wawrzaszek 1986, 71)

Chester responded with references to his unfolding social plans, the conflicting accounts Grace has suggested, and, more vaguely, their reunion:

> I really have no plans beyond that as I do not know how much money I can get or anything about the country. If you have any suggestions to make I wish you would and also just when and where you can meet me. I have said nothing more about going away but shall simply leave Sunday the 8th. . . . As for my plans for the Fourth . . . I have made none as the only two girls I could get to go with me have made other arrangements because I did not ask them until Saturday and today, so that someone is mistaken. (Brownell and Wawrzaszek 1986, 72)

CHAPTER SEVEN

The letter exchanges between Grace and Chester carry the story up to Grace's death. In trial testimony Chester relates their conversation in the boat:

> "I finally said I thought the best thing we could do would be, well, to get her home and tell her father and mother just everything that had occurred, and then explain to her. I thought we might better do that than have them find it out, as they would find it out anyway. She said she couldn't tell her mother. Then she started to cry." (Brandon 1986, 203)

He describes the event:

> "Then she said, 'Well, I will end it here,' and she, well, jumped into the lake; stepped up onto the boat, kind of throwed herself in." (Brandon 1986, 203)

And further:

> "I tried to reach her and, well, I was not quick enough. I went in the lake, too. The boat tipped over as I started to get up. The boat went right over then. Of course, I went into the lake. . . . Then I came up. I hallooed, grabbed hold of the boat. Then as soon as I could get the water out of my eyes and see, I got hold of the boat or got to the boat. . . . I stayed there at the boat but a minute or two. It seemed like a long time, anyway, and I didn't see her. Then I swam to shore." (Brandon 1986, 203)

Brandon (1986, 303–5) refers to much of the coverage of the story of Grace and Chester as "purple prose and yellow journalism." While he acknowledges the textual nature of the story as it emerged—confirming and correcting facts through supplementation and dissemination—there were also "deliberate attempts by some of the journalists covering the arrest and especially the trial to play the case for all it was worth." Indeed, by the second day, newspaper headlines were referring to unfolding events as "The Big Moose Tragedy." Coverage even pitted local reporters against those from out of town, the former charging that the latter "didn't even go to the trial at all, but wrote their articles from the bar of the Palmer House." In fact, by the time of the trial the national press had largely departed the scene.

The scenario I have entitled "The Story of Grace and Chester" is both dramatic and documentary. From the time of Grace Brown's murder, it was reconstructed as information and entertainment. The national press, even more than the local, focused on the sensational aspects of the case, "weaving fictional tales of passionate love triangles, suicide attempts, escape attempts, assassination plots, lynch mobs and plots to conceal evidence" (Brandon 1986, 304). Especially after his arrest Chester's guilt was largely taken for granted and speculation was rampant in an effort to complete the tale. Particularly important was coverage given to the role of Harriet Benedict, with whom Chester publicly celebrated the July Fourth holiday, and the intentions of Chester's Cortland kin after his arrest. The upper-class-based glamor of these subplots were mirror images of those portraying Chester's humble, largely unknown, background and the sordid nature of his scandalous affair with a naive farm-girl-turned-factory-worker (Brownell and Wawrzaszek 1986, 103–7).

Theodore Dreiser began his writing career as a journalist and reporter. *An American Tragedy*, published in two volumes in 1925,[3] represented his sixth novel, following, most notably, *Sister Carrie* (1900), *Jennie Gerhardt* (1911), and *The Financier* (1912). He had also published books of short stories, autobiography, and travel. The story of Grace and Chester, despite the passage of more than a decade since its events, fascinated Dreiser:

> The young people in Dreiser's work in progress faced a dilemma that urban sophisticates would regard as quaintly antique, something more typical of 1906 than 1923. (In his first draft he set the novel in Chester Gillette's day—remarking on the rarity of automobiles, for example. But in subsequent versions, the story is vaguely located in the late teens and early twenties, as evident by scattered references to clothes, songs, and movies of the time.) (Lingeman 1990, 231)

Dreiser (1920, 126–28) offhandedly mentions the case of "Billy Brown" as one of several that have created "convulsive interest" in the public. As a former reporter, he was convinced that sexually motivated crimes and other crimes of passion, especially those carried out in the general pattern of urban upward mobility, were unique to the society of the day. He began the novel in 1920 but eventually set it aside for two years, during which time the story of Roberta Alden (Grace) and Clyde Griffiths

CHAPTER SEVEN

(Chester) became his preferred narrative (Dreiser 1935/77; Riggio 2003, 966). After settling on Grace Brown's death as the murder-event he intended to novelize, Dreiser set about conducting research into the case:

> He inspected the scene of the murder, examined the courtroom in which the Gillette trial was held, and even succeeded in getting permission to visit death row at Sing Sing. He consulted with an attorney and he discussed the psychology of murder with Dr. A. A. Brill, the psychologist who was Freud's official translator. (Lundquist 1974, 88)

An American Tragedy is 934 pages in length and is divided into three sections. It is related by an unknown narrator and follows Clyde's biographical path. Book One relates Clyde's life up to his arrival in Lycurgus, New York (Cortland transformed). Book Two covers his life in Lycurgus: his establishment of family ties and employment; the gradual expansion of Clyde's circle into Lycurgus upper-class youth culture and his acquaintance with socialite Sondra Finchley (Harriet Benedict); the meeting and courtship of Clyde and Roberta; Roberta's pregnancy and her eventual demise. Book Three narrates Clyde's flight, and his arrest, trial, and execution.

With the opening of Book Two (Dreiser 1925/2003, 167–566) Clyde arrives in Lycurgus, freed not only from a dreary youth in his missionary family but also from potentially criminal consequences of events in Kansas City (where he had worked in a hotel amid a comparatively busy, if unsatisfying, youthful social life). Having established contact with his uncle and secured employment at the factory, Clyde on separate occasions makes the acquaintances of first Sondra and then Roberta. The two women represent for Clyde his search as framed from the novel's beginning: Must he be satisfied with a respectable but (to his thinking) dull working-class existence? Or might he aspire (especially now, if his uncle's sponsorship continues) to enter polite society with all its gaiety and action? As Clyde reflects:

> In loneliness, resentment and disappointment his mind now wandered from the Griffiths and their world, and particularly that beautiful Sondra Finchley, whom he recalled with a keen and biting thrill, to Roberta and the world which she as well as he was occupying here. For although a poor factory girl, she was still so much more attractive than any of these other girls with whom he was every day in contact. (Dreiser 1925/2003, 295)

At the same time:

> For poor or not—a working girl by misfortune only—he could see how he could be very happy with her if only he did not need to marry her. For now his ambitions toward marriage had been firmly magnetized by the world to which the Griffiths belonged. (Dreiser 1925/2003, 296)

From this point forward, Clyde is pulled in both directions, never fully a part of Sondra's world and not able to completely escape Roberta's and his own. Instead, he moves back and forth between the two—women as well as worlds—even as time with Roberta leads to eventual sexual intimacy:

> She was not of his station, really—at least not of that of the Griffiths to which still he most eagerly aspired. . . . he would still return to Roberta, picturing her, since the other mood which had drawn him to her and by no means palled as yet, as delightful, precious, exceedingly worthwhile from the point of view of beauty, pleasure, sweetness—the attributes and charms which best identify any object of delight. (Dreiser 1925/2003, 347)

Roberta's pregnancy does nothing to alleviate the conflict either of them is experiencing. From the beginning of their relationship she has been aware—even wary—of Clyde's family connections and eventually learns of his interest in Sondra Finchley; likewise Roberta has come to realize that Clyde harbors dreams of wealth and success which mean little to her—and in fact may not include her in the end. With Roberta's pregnancy Clyde continues to move between worlds and, particularly in his fantasies, his relationship with Sondra deepens. Seeking to free himself from Roberta, he obtains pills to induce abortion, which are unsuccessful. Finally, he accompanies Roberta to an out-of-town doctor, where her efforts to secure help for terminating the pregnancy are fruitless. Afterward, Roberta departs for her parents' farm to await a reunion with Clyde, while he continues to court Sondra.

One day, amid his increasing desperation, Clyde reads a newspaper account of accidental drowning at a nearby lake, a "double tragedy" involving a young couple:

> He must not even think of such a thing. It was wrong—wrong—terribly wrong. And yet, supposing—by accident, of course—such a thing as this

CHAPTER SEVEN

did occur? That would be the end, then, wouldn't it, of all his troubles in connection with Roberta? No more terror as to her—no more fear and heartache even as to Sondra. A noiseless, pathless, quarrelless solution of all his present difficulties, and only joy before him forever. Just an accidental, unpremeditated drowning—and then the glorious future which would be his! (Dreiser 1925/2003, 506–7)

Thus is the seed of the possibility of Roberta's accidental death planted in Clyde's mind, though it does not grow easily. Roberta and Clyde meet at Gun Lodge and take the journey to Big Bittern where they are to picnic and canoe the lake—all the while Clyde, almost dreamily, contemplates the coming event:

And all this time Roberta at his side was imagining that she was not going to anything but marriage to-morrow morning sure; and now only to the passing pleasure of seeing this beautiful lake of which he had been talking—talking, as though it were something more important and delectable than any that had as yet been in her or his life for that matter. (Dreiser 1925/2003, 553)

Later, in the water, Roberta screams while Clyde continues to struggle with his motivation:

For she was stunned, horror-struck, unintelligible with pain and fear—her lifelong fear of water and drowning and the blow he had so accidentally and all but unconsciously administered.
"Help! Help!
"Oh my God, I'm drowning, I'm drowning. Help! Oh my God!
"Clyde, Clyde!"
And then the voice at his ear!
"But this—this—is not this that which you have been thinking and wishing for this while—you in your great need! And behold! For despite your fear, your cowardice, this—this—has been done for you. An accident—an accident—an unintentional blow on your part is now saving you the labor of what you sought, and yet did not have the courage to do!" (Dreiser 1925/2003, 564–65)

Convicted and sentenced to death, Clyde befriends Reverend McMillan while he awaits the appeal. A letter arrives from "Miss X"—as Sondra was designated at trial. It is typewritten and unsigned, postmarked New York. Its contents:

> "Clyde—This is so that you will not think that some one once dear to you has utterly forgotten you. She has suffered much, too. And though she can never understand how you could have done as you did, still, even now, although she is never to see you again, she is not without sorrow and sympathy and wishes you freedom and happiness." (Dreiser 1925/2003, 906)

With Reverend McMillan as his confidant and spiritual guide, Clyde struggles in retrospect to give order to his motivations and actions in the death of Roberta (Dreiser 1925/2003, 916): "Oh, these evasive and tangled and torturesome thoughts!! Would he never be able—quite—to get the whole thing straightened out in his own mind?" Finally, his appeal denied, Clyde faces his execution with these words: "'So they've decided against me. Now I will have to go through that door after all, like all those others.'" (Dreiser 1925/2003, 918).

In its movement from historical event to media reconstruction, "the Story of Grace and Chester" frames interwoven textual biographies of the two, an expanded illustration of "contextual constructionism" (Surette 1998, 8), discussed earlier. As applied to interpretive biography, the process represents "writers making biographical claims about their ability to make biographical and autobiographical statements about themselves and others" (Denzin 1989a, 21). In Dreiser's novelization the story is transformed into the narrative of Roberta and Clyde. It is overlaid on the historical construction of events, especially as the latter were reported in newspaper and trial coverage.

My own reading of the story of Grace and Chester as presented above is thus a project in interpretive biography, yet another retelling of the tragic tale. The method seeks to critically interpret "supplemented" de-centered textual representations of life (Derrida 1967/76; 1972). Following Denzin (1989b, 38–39), the method of interpretive biography encompasses "variations on narratives and stories. The emphasis on self, biography, history and experience must always work back and forth between a concern for process and the analysis of the specific lives of individuals who live the process that is being studied."

CHAPTER SEVEN

The selves of Grace and Chester—as well as of Roberta and Clyde—are textually constructed in relation to one another, particularly as linked through the murder-event. Grace's pregnancy and her death are overlapping epiphanies in the biography she shares with Chester. They are transformative events in the story (Denzin 1989a, 71; 1989b, 128–30). Pregnancy represents a minor epiphany, a problematic moment in their relationship, which propels the narrative toward her tragic death. In a fundamental way, Grace's death is a relived epiphany for Chester: After his conviction for murder Chester, in turning to religion, seeks meaning by constantly reexamining his role in her death as well as his ambiguous motivations therein. With death, Grace and Chester's shared biography is relocated in Dreiser's novel. In this added layer of reconstruction the pregnancy and murder become instances of shared deviant status for Roberta and Clyde. As related by Dreiser in *An American Tragedy*, their stigma is interwoven from the trajectories of their individual lives. Roberta is reconstructed as a naive farm girl "in trouble" through pregnancy; Clyde is the ambitious charmer—a "young man in a hurry," the details of whose life are never quite as apparent as they seem. The novel portrays Clyde as "the fortune hunter de luxe" and stakes the literary claim that "America had bred fortune hunting as a disease" (Dreiser 1935/77, 292).

The play of meaning between events and their reconstruction in journalism and Dreiser's novel emerges uncertainly from gender and class differences between Grace and Chester, Roberta and Clyde. The narratives "are gendered, class productions, reflecting the biases and values of patriarchy and the middle class" (Denzin 1989a, 18). These differences produce deviance as master status, within and between the two lives. Grace, with precious few prospects even before her pregnancy, clings to Chester in the hopes of a better, happier married life. Chester, aspiring to the middle and upper class—with a wealthy uncle in the bargain—sees marriage only as a step toward his mobility. Turning as they do on gender and class myths, the textual lives of Grace and Chester are part of the politics of signification (Hall 1980b, 1980c). Their shared biographies are reconstituted first journalistically as murder victim and perpetrator. Even after death, both lives continue in the novel—an "act of literature" (Derrida 1992)—historical actors submerged in a changing story.

As primary sites of deviance-labeling, class and gender contradictorily overlap for Grace and Chester (Di Stephano 1990; Walby 1990). Her experience is completely encoded within patriarchy as subservient to the wishes of her male-dominated family and to those of Chester. Chester's self-narrative is similarly circumscribed, but by class images. Still, Grace is from the beginning more constrained as an actor than Chester (Schur 1984, 1988). While she struggles with the inevitable discredit of pregnancy, his deviant status is assured only with conviction as her killer. Grace is twice-marginalized as poor and female. She represents what Butler calls the "culturally enmired subject," negotiating "its constructions, even when those constructions are the very predicates of its own identity" (Butler 1990/99, 182). Conversely, Chester, his poverty neutralized by family connections and an otherwise relatively unknown past, is criminally labeled only after his ambitions for success turn murderous. Finally, moving from event to reconstruction, from information to entertainment, their voices are decentered in the media process (Benhabib 1990). As their story unfolded in 1906, celebrity (naive victim for Grace; notorious degenerate for Chester) was its wellspring. Dreiser shaded his novel more toward Chester's experience, especially in the plot device of a developing love affair between Clyde and Sondra. The latter was more a new character than a simple transposition of Harriet Benedict (Brandon 1986, 345–46; Brownell and Wawrzaszek 1986, 176).

Stigma Movie: Literary Criticism and Hollywood Transformation

Dreiser's retelling of the story of Grace and Chester became notable American literature, situated by way of criticism as an example of literary naturalism. As he achieved his own measure of notoriety for the novel, the voices of Grace and Chester continued to fade. In effect, Dreiser's entrance into the scenario shifted its focus from historical event to popular culture staple, a process furthered by the story's production on the stage and in the cinema.

Dreiser (1871–1947) was born to poor parents of German ancestry, a second-generation child of Gilded Age America. His father was a man of "iron conventionalism and moral intolerance" and his mother a woman "beyond or behind so-called good and evil," "neither moral nor immoral," "a poet who suffers much, yet unfailingly and irresistibly continues to contemplate beauty—her one enduring earthly reward, as I came to know" (Dreiser 1931, 10). Critics and biographers have commonly noted that the

CHAPTER SEVEN

economic disadvantage of Dreiser's early life had a notable impact on the themes of his writing (Lundquist 1974, 1–14; Lingeman 1986, 13–15). Dreiser himself observes:

> Brought up in a conventional and successful world, I might have assumed that the rich had all those virtues which the poor are too often assumed not to have—wisdom, refinement, ambition, sensitivity—whereas as it was, and per circumstances, the shoe was on the other foot. Being poor, I thought the poor were very much underestimated and underpaid and misunderstood—myself a shining illustration, as it were. At the same time, there was growing in me a fairly clear perception of the value of personality as distinct from either poverty or riches. (Dreiser 1931, 542)

Thus, Dreiser evidenced a profound ambivalence to the pursuit of success that he understood to be the norm in turn-of-the-century America. In particular, he noted the widening gap between rich and poor and the increasing influence of corporations on the economy and in daily life: "The great quarrel in America to-day is between wealth and poverty—whether an individual, however small or poor, shall retain his self respect and his life, or whether a commercial oligarchy shall at last and finally take charge" (Dreiser 1932, 9). Furthermore, while his naturalism allowed that social, psychological, economic, and other forces constrained historical actors, he also held hope that progressive cultural change could liberate them, at least to a degree (Lehan 1969, 35–36). This tension is reflected in Dreiser's own biography:

> Looked at in retrospect, his life towers like a lonely mesa, striated with layers of American time, beginning in nineteenth-century Indiana and encompassing those epical social temblors that altered the landscape—the mass migration to the cities, the widening fissure between rich and poor, the rise of industry, the centralization of economic (and political) power in the corporations and trusts. It offers many glimpses of journalism in the pre-Yellow and Yellow eras, of New York City in the Mauve Decade, of America in the age of enterprise and the age of progressivism; of the optimism and budding imperialism of the early 1900s, as reflected in the popular magazines of the day; and of the literary tides and crosscurrents that boiled up in the twentieth century. (Lingeman 1986, 15)

Dreiser was a crucial transitional writer in the American literary scene of his time: "He was one of those—in America, the most important one of those—who put their shoulder to the wheel turning past into present; one of the great international company of *survivors*, men formed before the turn of the century but dominant after the first World War" [*italics* in the original] (Moers 1969, viii). From his career as a journalist, Dreiser acquired an appreciation for the complexity of everyday life and the realist style for its textual presentation. He began as a reporter in 1892, serving papers in numerous cities and finally arriving in New York.[4] In 1894 he became editor of *Ev'ry Month*, an arts magazine in that city. In 1900 his first novel, *Sister Carrie*, was published (under the enthusiastic sponsorship of Frank Norris) (Kaplan 1988, 110–31; Shi 1995, 240–42). For Dreiser, then, literary naturalism represented a from with which he was quite familiar: storytelling stripped of at least a measure of the veneer of traditional romanticized depictions. He summarizes the naturalist critique of such fiction at the new century:

> Immoral! Immoral! Under this cloak hide the vices of wealth as well as the vast unspoken blackness of poverty and ignorance; and between them must walk the little novelist, choosing neither truth nor beauty, but some half-conceived phase of life that bears no honest relationship to either the whole of nature or to man. (Dreiser 1903/98, 180)

I take Dreiser's novel as a fluid historical representation of literary naturalism. As such, the novel offers glimpses of four naturalist boundaries: determinism, survival, violence, and taboo (Walcutt 1956/98, 288–90). These boundaries marked experience in emerging modern society. As well, they are substantially similar to naturalism as found in the early Chicago school (covered in chapter 4). In their studies of urbanism and social disorganization, Park and Burgess, Shaw and McKay, as well as others, grappled with the extent to which life experience was socially constrained or a matter of individual choice (determinism versus survival). As well, in their case studies these Chicagoans described normative conflict as social disorganization (real and potential urban violence and failure of the systemic normative process meant to control it), even as diversity was evident in the variety of "social worlds" and emerging subcultures of the modern. Matza (1969, 99) goes further still, describing the naturalistic affinity of disorganization and poverty, linking deviance to the anonymity

CHAPTER SEVEN

of metropolitan life. In *An American Tragedy*, Dreiser offers a literary take on this disorganization narrative, demonstrating "how, given certain hereditary and environmental conditions, what did happen had to happen; and he communicates this conviction because he is able to present so detailed an account of events that Clyde Griffiths is shown as powerless to choose at the very climax of the action and is never held morally responsible for his 'crime'" (Walcutt 1956/98, 292).

As I pointed out above, Book One of the novel is a biographical narrative of Clyde's life up to his arrival in Cortland/Lycurgus. As such, this section is more purely inventive fiction, not based so much on firm historical record, journalistic accounts, or the trial transcript. In particular it portrays Clyde's family life as well as his abandonment of that life for employment at a Kansas City hotel. Clyde's family, painfully poor, is involved in street missionary work—all of its members participate in the "act." Thus, Dreiser frames the contradiction between class structure and the emerging ideology of mass cultural consumption. As well, from the novel's beginning Clyde is caught in the raging cultural war of the day between religion and the secular (Shi 1995, 244; Rhodes 1998, 130–31). On his own, he gradually is enmeshed in 1920s youth culture, defined by sexual awakening, conspicuous consumption, and the pursuit of a wide variety of pleasures. Even early in the century, this subculture was something more than a microcosm of modern America's broader terrain:

> It was a social product made possible, even necessary, by those changes which historians variously called the industrialization, modernization, or rationalization of American life. What the society experienced in large terms as a maturing economy, an urbanized geography, and a nationalized culture—all bewildering and threatening to those who remembered when things were otherwise—individuals born in the new century experienced on a more intimate (but no less significant) level in the changing experience of growing up. (Fass 1977, 120)

Clyde's development, then, in Book One is crucial to the event-death of Roberta as well as his heightened desires to move among the upper class of his relatives and Sondra (Pizer 1976, 232–44; 1977/98, 353). In this sense the novel's textual tragedy is dual: that linking the shared biographies of Roberta and Clyde through her death and that emerging from following cultural values extolling financial success and social advancement. In the end, the former is encapsulated within the latter, and "personal identity is reduced by society's values to a matter of *having* (and appearing), at a cost of true (intrinsic) *being*. From the start of his story, Clyde gains from observations of his acquisitive American world a distorted sense of how to achieve meaningful selfhood" [*italics* in the original] (Orlov 1998, 103). The rise of a mass culture of consumption in the 1920s included the proliferation of literature and the authors that created it (Allen 1931/2000, 195–211; Bowlby 1985, 83–97). *An American Tragedy* is foremost a textual statement of the American Dream as found in consumption and the ambiguities and perils of living within this narrative. It is "a protest novel which points backward to earlier naturalism and forward to the social protest fiction of the Depression 1930s" (Ruland and Bradbury 1991, 248).

In the historical context of consumption, the novel's naturalism rendered both a relentless description and critique regarding the construction of the modern self. The crucial point of this construction (in literary and other cultural spheres) "is that through goods and services, Americans found a way to understand themselves, others, the past, and the future" (Cross 2000, 24). What I have identified as the dual tragedy in Dreiser's novel marks nothing less than the gradual transformation of experience categories in modern society. As Thorstein Veblen (1899/1994, 20) has noted, "So soon as the possession of property becomes the basis of popular esteem, therefore it becomes also a requisite to that complacency which we call self-respect."

The intersection of youth and class in Dreiser's tragedy is coupled with gender and race constructions. The latter are likewise situated in the context of mass consumption. Dreiser's characterization of Roberta Alden, though based on real-life Grace Brown, did not evidence the nuances of personality and motivation found in those of Sister Carrie and Jennie Gerhardt. Dreiser created Roberta almost exclusively from press reports focusing on Grace's life at the time of Chester's trial. These accounts were of two types: sensational physical descriptions of her death and medical reports concerning it, and sentimentally drawn portraits of a naive young girl met with terrible misfortune. The latter relied heavily on Grace's letters to Chester, which when read at trial brought some jurors to tears; these letters were reproduced, bound as a pamphlet, and sold on the courthouse steps during the trial (Fishkin 1995, 3–5).

CHAPTER SEVEN

Dreiser wrote Roberta largely as Grace had been portrayed by the press many years before: as a stereotypical unworldly young woman who clung to Chester and was otherwise quite alone in her distress.[5] This stereotype was not unknown to readers at the turn of the century, but surely had begun to seem outdated by the time *An American Tragedy* was published:

> Work outside the home for a woman was viewed throughout most of the culture as a sometimes necessary and always unfortunate way station along the road to marriage. For this reason, whether a woman was good at her work simply did not matter. Marriage was really the only plot women could enact in literature as well as life. (Fishkin 1995, 8)

By contrast, Clyde's own sexual development was marked by a measure of gender anxiety. In Book One he doggedly, if unsuccessfully, pursues women and routinely is denied any sexual contact. Later, his dilemma of eventual intimacy with Roberta and her resulting pregnancy is heightened by the unexpected warmth shown him by Sondra Finchley. Still, the novel turns on the gender differences between Clyde and Roberta: "Clyde, a momma's boy, has to overcome his initial fear of women, only to discover through Roberta's pregnancy the awful hold women seem to have over men" (Eby 1998, 174).

The textuality of their converging biographies plays off these sexual and larger personality inadequacies. Gender, for both Roberta and Clyde, is a key site of problematic meaning-creation. Their relationship is characterized as a kind of psychological doubling: "Clyde's inability to acknowledge how fully he displaces himself upon Roberta—much like her own inability to admit having projected similar desires onto Clyde—later causes his resentment to become overpowering" (Mitchell 1989, 61).

Roberta's death leaves countless ambiguities relating to Clyde's motivation and the causes of his behavior:

> Thus the sympathetic reader is left uncertain about where to place blame for the central act of the novel: Who killed Roberta? Did Clyde? Or did the "America" of the novel's title, and if so, what does that mean? Clyde goes to his death unsure if he has committed murder; readers can debate for hours "what happened" on the rowboat (as classroom discussions

readily confirm); only for the community that has constructed him does Clyde Griffiths become a fixed entity: exactly what they want him to be. (Eby 1998, 145)

The duality (i.e., doubling) of the tragedy is gendered, placed by Dreiser in the modern sociocultural context of mass consumption. Roberta and Clyde are linked through her death and, just as surely, through his internalization of social values celebrating wealth and consumption as success. At the same time both are circumscribed by the "feminization" of consumer culture (Douglas 1977/88; Bowlby 1985, 18–34). In the emergence of consumer society, feminine images were a basis for interpreting style, beauty, desirability, and so on across the spectrum of goods and services:

The boundaries of subject and object, active and passive, owner and owned, unique and general, break down in this endless reflexive interplay of consumer and consumed. One consequence is that the clear separation of masculine and feminine roles as applied to the consumer/commodity relation cannot be maintained. (Bowlby 1985, 29)

In moving from Dreiser's novel to literary criticism of it, his reconstruction of events is gradually transformed into the stigma movie of the scenario. Key elements of that movie, as I have shown, are the constructions of youth, class, and gender in emerging modern society. As a frame for the emerging consumer society, youth and class are sites of stigma-generation, textually grounding the murder-event. Gender, its differences, and meaning-construction is the key site for viewing Grace's death as well as looking backward and forward from it in the narrative. I turn now to race as a final element.

Race is not merely a muted voice in the story of Grace and Chester—it is completely silent. The question of racial identity is never raised in either the novel or earlier accounts of events. Certainly, the actors in the story are white, a fact which only serves to question the construction of race—not only in the story itself but in wider society as well. In America of the early twentieth century, dialogue about race was rarely openly evident, even less so than those surrounding age, class. and gender. Ideologies were "invariably inflected with the codes, strategies and embedded assumptions concerning racial difference that had always been part of the

CHAPTER SEVEN

maintenance of social control and nationalist identity on the Anglo-American continent" (Rhodes 1998, 170).

Legal and social segregation was institutionalized in everyday Southern life through the early twentieth century (Woodward 1955/74), supported by an ideology that linked "invisible" whiteness with power:

> By the early twentieth century, whites were constructing modern racial identity: a mass cultural rather than a localized, socially embodied, particularized self, an absolute division that dissolved any range of racially mixed subjectivities, a natural and embodied but not strictly biological or legal category, a way to mediate the fragmentation of modernity and still enjoy its freedom. (Hale 1998, 8)

Carried by consumer culture this invisibility of whiteness was found not only in the South, but gradually across the nation. The presence of the absence of a racial voice (Ashley 1997, 4) in the story of Grace and Chester—from the event, through Dreiser's novel, to its criticism—is hardly surprising then. The notorious historical celebrity-deviance-labeling of the two has largely faded, but their textual, changing biographies remain within the linguistic turn.

Literature was an increasingly important source of cultural meaning-creation in the 1920s. In a naturalist/realist style the problems of modern consumer-based society were dramatized for all to read if not to enjoy (Kaplan 1988). At the same time the political context of youth, class, gender, and race were ambiguously framed in the national movement of Progressivism (Diner 1998; Goldberg 1999; McGerr 2003). The differences among these status categories and voices gave seed to pragmatic philosophy as well as to early Chicago School deviance studies (Rock 1979). Each of these constructed categories were central to the American modernist narrative of emerging consumer society. Leading up to the war, Progressivism embodies the social and cultural tensions of modern America, secular and sacred, urban and rural:

> Progressivism had influenced many aspects of American life. Painters associated with the ashcan school shocked the art word by portraying and often celebrating urban life. Charles Beard and other progressive historians challenged those who idealized American history. Academics connected to the new discipline of sociology called attention to the in-

equalities in American society. Progressives and socialists, whites and blacks joined to form the National Association for the Advancement of Colored People. (Goldberg 1999, 4–5)

Crime, especially urban crime, was seen as a consequence of the developing modern society and its naturalistic Darwinian "survival of the fittest" (Hofstadter 1944/55). In particular, class, race, and gender inequalities were framed in the religious-political ideology of the Social Gospel. Arising after the Civil War, this ideology represented an attempt to graft the principles of Christianity onto emerging social institutions and to preach the desirability of individual salvation. The movement was part and parcel of consumer society (Curtis 1991) and the emerging conflicts over class (Altschuler 1982), gender (Edwards and Gifford 2003), and race (White 1990). After World War I, the movement became increasingly secularized:

> The cultural affirmation of youth and the emphasis on immediate psychic and material rewards resulted from Americans' impatience with deferred, ethereal promises and found expression in such widely divergent impulses as modernism and antimodernism, literary realism, and spectator sports. Cultural spokesmen—literati, artists, and increasingly, advertisers—were responding to their own yearnings when they proposed new cultural forms that undercut deferred gratification, faith in the unseen, and self-control. What they may not have realized, however, was that the very act of consuming—that is, participating in and being part of a consumer culture—became an act of faith, faith in the messages of corporate and scientific experts and in the ability of commodities and therapeutic professionals to advance a general process of social identification and self realization. (Curtis 1991, 229)

The story of Grace and Chester, retold by Dreiser in *An American Tragedy*, is a biographical construction located in this historical space. As a naturalist Dreiser novelized the event, information transformed into entertainment. All that remains for the scenario is its cinematic presentation.

Dreiser's novel was released as a feature film, *A Place in the Sun*, in 1951, produced and directed by George Stevens (Weiler 1951/2003). The book had been filmed once before in 1931, but the remake is considered the more faithful—if itself now dated—adaptation.[6] It won Academy

CHAPTER SEVEN

Awards for Best Director (Stevens), Editing (William W. Hornbeck), Score (Franz Waxman), and Screenplay (Harry Brown and Michael Wilson); as well, the effort secured four other nominations, including Best Picture. Clyde Griffiths becomes George Eastman, played by Montgomery Clift; Grace Brown is now Alice Tripp, portrayed by Shelley Winters; and most notably, Harriet Benedict-as-Sondra Finchley-as-Angela Vickers is played by nineteen-year-old Elizabeth Taylor. In adapting the major events of the novel's narrative, the film is largely faithful, but the character emphases have changed:

> The forces pushing young Eastman to the final, horrible retribution are obvious and a tribute to Dreiser as the youth is suddenly exposed to the overwhelming opulence of his family and Angela Vickers, to whose love and beauty he succumbs. (Weiler 1951/2003)

Dreiser kept his primary focus on Grace/Roberta and Chester/Clyde, textually bound by her pregnancy and death; Harriet/Sondra, while not a minor character, is obviously secondary to the "tragedy" in the book's title. Conversely, Stevens focuses more on the relationship between Chester/George and Harriet/Angela. The Hollywood treatment, then, becomes "The Story of George and Angela" or, more realistically, that of Monty and Liz. In this narrative, Grace/Alice becomes the secondary character in the love triangle. In fact, the inescapable tragedy of the film is that George's execution precludes the fulfillment of Angela's love for him and their never-to-be marriage. Grace/Alice is portrayed, similar to Dreiser's Roberta, as first naive to Clyde's sexual manipulations, then worried over the moral stigma of their affair, and finally desperate to the point of exposing Clyde to his family. By the time of her death, the viewer has been thoroughly saturated with numerous close-up images of George and Angela at parties, on solitary outings, falling in love. Similarly, in the film's most obvious narrative deviation from the novel, Angela visits George in the prison prior to his execution (Hussman 1995, 193).

Another change in focus for the film is its time and place settings: The script was substantially updated and moved the story from New York State to the California Sierras. Most of the exterior scenes were shot in the area around Lake Tahoe. The new script, like the novel and movie which preceded it, made the story a contemporary one, with all of the automobiles and technology of midcentury America (Brownell and Wawrzaszek 1986, 181). In his own temporal relocation, Dreiser went to great length portraying his characters in the historical period of the 1920s, giving his book a realistic, almost documentary, sense of style and place (if not pacing). The film has no such sense of time, and despite its two-hour length treats the social context of the story superficially. Abandoning the historical context of the novel might have rendered the film contemporary upon release, but ultimately forces it to play as a dated melodrama. One telling example: Raymond Burr plays the minor part of the prosecutor at trial. His over-the-top, histrionic cross-examination of George includes relentless probing of answers and in particular, the smashing of an oar to dramatize George's alleged murder of Alice.

A Place in the Sun was released over forty years after the Grace Brown murder as well as the conviction and execution of Chester Gillette—and some twenty-six years following the publication of Dreiser's novel. The original deviant events and facsimiles of personalities are constituted as subjects in a drama of entertainment (Foucault 1983; Dotter forthcoming). Dreiser's novel, a rich naturalistic narrative of stigmatization and ambiguity of meaning, is itself transformed into another layer of text in the stigma movie. This scenario, as I have argued, is about more than the murder of Grace Brown by Chester Gillette: In it we can glimpse the historical emergence of the "perfect crime." As Baudrillard writes:

> And indeed, the main objection to reality is its propensity to submit unconditionally to every hypothesis you can make about it. With this its most abject conformism, it discourages the liveliest minds. You can subject it—and its principle (what do they get up to together, by the way, apart from dully copulating and begetting reams of obviousness?)—to the most cruel torments, the most obscene provocations, the most paradoxical insinuations. It submits to everything with unrelenting servility. Reality is a bitch. And that is hardly surprising, since it is the product of stupidity's fornication with the spirit of calculation—the dregs of the sacred illusion offered up to the jackals of science. (Baudrillard 1996, 3)

For quite some time Grace Brown and Chester Gillette have been caught up in Hall's (1980b, 1980c) politics of signification. Their biographies were originally created as notorious master status/celebrity in the 1906

CHAPTER SEVEN

press accounts. Much later, Dreiser reconstituted them as classic literature and Hollywood made them stars.

Notes

1. An exhaustive reading of literary naturalism as well as the many "modernisms" that followed, their periodization and overlap, is beyond my scope. These fuller treatments are instructive: on the development of American literary naturalism (Pizer 1982), realism (Berthoff 1965), and comparison of the two (Pizer 1966/76; Pizer 1998); panoramic views of modern culture (Conrad 1999; Watson 2001); on the roots of modernism in European literature (Bradbury and McFarlane 1976/91a, 1976/91c); regarding the relationship between European literary modernism and naturalism as well as their development in America (Bradbury and McFarlane 1976/91b; Ruland and Bradbury 1991; Lehan 1995); the overlay of the modern with American realism (Shi 1995, 275–302) and that between modernism and the Harlem Renaissance (Baker 1987; Lewis 1994; Douglas 1995); general critiques of the modern novel (Bradbury 1983/94; Trotter 1999). Darwinian biological determinism served as a bridge between naturalism and modernism not only in literature, but in the social sciences as well (McFarlane 1976/91, 72–77). Lehan summarizes the relationship of naturalist concerns to those of modernism and postmodernism in twentieth-century American literature:

> As an ideology and a mode of narration, naturalism rose and then fell. It was replaced by literary modernism and then by postmodernism. But even in this context its meaning was not entirely lost: new narrative modes transformed (or what can be called *re-presented*) naturalism, rather than totally superseded it. [*italics* in the original] (Lehan 1995, 70)

2. Examples from this general time period include these cases: Leopold and Loeb (1924), the Scottsboro "boys" (1931), and Bruno Richard Hauptmann (1932) (Geis and Bienen 1998).

3. The novel's original chapters were written in Hollywood, where Dreiser lived from 1919 to 1923 with his eventual second wife, Helen Richardson (Dreiser 1982, 275–413).

4. In *The Color of a Great City* Dreiser (1923) offers impressionistic studies of New York life in his first years there, including among others, "the bread-line" and "the push-cart man." For a selection of his turn-of-the-century magazine articles, see Dreiser (1985).

5. Fishkin (1995, 13–18) imagines a provocative reading of the "other" Billy Brown we will never see in Dreiser's novel. She contends that Dreiser "knew" her

in his personal and especially professional relationships with women. Furthermore, "exploitation and abandonment were not the only risks a women undertook by working for Dreiser; there was always the chance that he would plagiarize from her as well" (Fiskin 1995, 18).

6. Hussman (1995) offers a comprehensive survey of film adaptations of Dreiser's novels, including a never-filmed screenplay by famed Russian director Sergei Eisenstein.

CHAPTER EIGHT
THEORIZING DEVIANCE IN THE POSTMODERN: THE TURN CONTINUES

The study of deviance and crime has been a focal point in the development of American sociology through the twentieth century to the present. The Chicago School theories, especially interactionist labeling, have been central to this enterprise (Becker 1963/73; Matza 1969; Schur 1971; Dotter and Roebuck 1988). My purpose has been to articulate interactionist perspectives with those from cultural studies (Denzin 1992; Lemert 1997; Best and Kellner 1997, 2001), offering the scenario as a context for the contemporary understanding of disvalued behavior. Chapters 6 and 7 demonstrate the versatility of the scenario as a qualitative method in the postmodern turn (Dotter 1997; Denzin and Lincoln 2000). The scenario is, if I must pin a label on it, interdisciplinary. It draws from sociology, history, philosophy, film and literary theories, and feminist, race, and cultural studies.

In the more familiar terms of symbolic interactionism it is, broadly speaking, a sensitizing concept (Blumer 1969). But the scenario goes beyond the construction of meaning as argued by the original pragmatists (West 1989; Menand 2001) and Chicago ecologists (Ericksen 1980), as well as in differential association and labeling (Matza 1969): It is a narrative about narratives. I have attempted to situate deviance-labeling in the context of the postmodern moment. Thus previous chapters cover much familiar ground in my reviews of pragmatism, interactionism in the thought of both Blumer and Mead, and the various strands of labeling. The cultural studies part of my story relies heavily on Denzin's (1989a, 1989b) and Mills's (1959) critiques of modernism as implied in the sociological imagination. The narrative quality of deviance is increasingly clustered around the status sites of class, age, gender, and race. It is embedded in the larger process of commodification (Baudrillard 1970/98) and spectacle (Debord 1967/94). The construction of self is a narrative process of meaning creation and change (Denzin 1989a; Holstein and Gubrium 2000; Perinbanayagam 2000; Dotter forthcoming).

In this final chapter I will broadly and briefly assess the current state of deviance theorizing, particularly the charge of the "death" of the sociological study of deviance (Sumner 1994), framing my answer in the context of the scenario. Neither the study of deviance—nor of sociology from which the field emerged—is dead. The charge is not without grave intellectual drama, but processes of stigmatization remain with us all the same—and await study. Also, I suggest other contemporary scenarios, for clues to the future of deviance theorizing—what might be called contemporary symbolic studies of stigma.[1]

Interactionist Labeling and Cultural Studies: The Scenario and Meaning Construction in the Postmodern Turn

The Scenario as Interpretive Cultural Studies

The impact of the postmodern turn has been felt throughout the humanities and social sciences. This turn is a gradual shift characterizing "the transition from modern to postmodern society, from modern to postmodern theory" (Best and Kellner 1997, x). The scenario is a qualitative method to describe and probe these changes in meaning-construction, summarized by Denzin (1994) as "the art and politics of interpretation." As critical theory, the scenario combines cultural studies perspectives with deviance-labeling ones in the style of interpretive interactionism:

> The slices, sequences, and instances of social interactionism that are studied by the interpretivist carry layers of meaning, nuance, substance and fabric, and these layers come in multiples and are often contradictory. Some flow from other peoples's histories, and some are of the person's own making. (Denzin 1989b, 26)

As storyteller, the slices and sequences I chose to critique were two historically based scenarios of deviance-creation: early youth subculture formation and the story of Grace and Chester and its transformation in literature and film. These choices were both personal and illustrative, for my own textual autobiography interweaves, among other strands, rock music and the persistent intellectual affinity for labeling theory (Manning and Cullum-Swan 1994). The inclusion of a literary scenario as found in *An American Tragedy* can be neatly summarized as my desire to "do" an interdisciplinary project in cultural studies interpretation. The scenarios were chosen as intriguing stories in the postmodern turn: early- and mid-to-later-twentieth-century sites where textual selves, my own and others', can be glimpsed. Neither story is a final version, and indeed both have been told before. They represent tales in the unfolding "postmodern adventure" of mediated society (Best and Kellner 2001). On this terrain, deviance—its events and behaviors as well as constructed categories—remain fiercely contested issues.

The Death of the Sociology of Deviance: Obituary Absent a Demise

With drama, if not pretension, Colin Sumner (1994) has announced the death of the sociology of deviance. This claim seemed utterly surprising to me as I had been completely unaware the field was even ill, much less fatally so. Before my guilt could set in, I attempted to give Sumner the benefit of a doubt: that he employed a theoretical bias, a deliberate overstatement, to make his point; that he surely does not mean all that his obituary notice suggests:

> The fact is that, in the social sciences, the world we study changes, partly because of the knowledge we provide about it and because of our 'scientific' interventions within its politics; and that, in turn, transforms the way we look at the world. In our case, this is certainly what has happened. We have changed the world that gave rise to the sociology of deviance and those changes have altered the way we look at that old world. The sociology of deviance no longer expresses our vision in the very new world of the 1990s. In that sense, it is dead. Its voice cannot speak. (Sumner 1994, x)

Sumner offers what I consider to be an excellent history of the field. My main objection is in his announcement of its death. Perhaps I am quibbling, but although intellectual projects wax and wane, they need not die. Critiques of the field, my own in chapter 4, Sumner's, or others, are necessary to tell us where we have been; they also point toward the future:

to articulations, and rearticulations, that make publication of obituaries risky intellectual business. His observation that a "sociology of censure" had arisen by the late 1970s, especially in Britain, may be accurate to a point. Not content with well-reasoned accuracy, Sumner presses for the drama of demise: "Both the definition and practice of deviance were now to be seen as ideological practices. Politicization had exacted its toll: Transformation of the field was now in the offing. The category 'ideological' certified the intellectual death of the field" (Sumner 1994, 308).

In America by 1980, the study of deviance was indeed joined by a renewed interest in criminology (Best 2004, 71–86), with the latter's alignment in the developing discipline of criminal justice. This development was fraught with the politics of professionalization and boundary maintenance. Those of us trained in the sociology of deviance—especially in the labeling tradition—could not fail to note the shift toward a "correctional criminology" (Hester and Eglin 1992, 3–7). By this time I myself was teaching in a criminal justice department, responsible for courses in both deviance and criminology. While I can identify with the spirit of Sumner's critique, at the very least I lack his flair for drama. Deviance as a concept—and a field of study—continues to stand on its own. As Goode notes: "Cut out deviance, and, in effect, crime does not exist. It seemed blatantly obvious that the theoretical death of deviance implies the death of criminology. Indeed, I believe, the death of deviance, implies the death of sociology itself" (Goode 2003, 519). The foregoing chapters are my articulation of deviance theorizing in the postmodern turn, and in retrospect serve to refute his death charge. As well, I might offer Best's (2004, 87) observation as a caveat to those prone to such announcements: "We tend to recall confused events in straightforward tales of intellectual progress and to treat research findings as if they are timeless, but of course this simplifies and distorts the messy ways ideas emerge. Ideas are always products of their times."

The Scenario: A Framework for Contemporary Symbolic Studies

A Recapitulation

My articulation of interactionist labeling and cultural studies in the concept of scenario is not without contradictions. Classical pragmatism as well as labeling constantly were marked by the "messy" engagement of meaning-creation and its relationship to the scientific method. Entering cultural studies, one must confront, as Sumner suggests, the very process by which deviance is transformed to ideology. The poststructuralist linguistic turn of Derrida (1972, 1972/81b) and Foucault's (1972b, 1983) wide-ranging historical critiques are bound to frustrate even most symbolic interactionists. I contend that Derrida's deconstruction of meaning is not synonymous with its destruction. Rather, the textuality of meaning is its multiple decentered contexts: ambiguity, layers, referrals, restatement. As I observed earlier, Foucault in particular cannot be labeled uncritically as a "postmodernist." Instead, his historical critiques represent an articulation of modern and postmodern elements: "Foucault produces a new kind of critical theory that is somewhere between the modern and the postmodern, that reworks certain modern elements in a postmodern framework. Within this new context, Foucault emphasizes principles of difference and discontinuity" (Best 1995, 89).

I view the postmodern meaning crisis (Dotter 1997) not as a rupture (Lyotard 1979/84), but a gradual emergence characterized by both continuity and discontinuity (Jervis 1998, 333–38). The use of film imagery in the scenario (i.e., screenplay) and its transmutation into the stigma movie historically grounds the concept in early cinematic realism (Denzin 1995, 16–24). Thus, the scenario is most fruitfully situated as a practice in strategic postmodernism, a reworking of the ideas of modernity (Lemert 1997). I argue that the seeds of postmodernism are found in early-twentieth-century consumer culture. Social science and its physical counterpart, as well as philosophy, literature, and other mass entertainments of this time, were viewed through realist and naturalist lenses—all bearing the mark of Darwinian evolutionary biology (Hofstadter 1944/55; Persons 1950).

For social science, especially the early Chicago School of social ecology and disorganization, naturalism was contradictorily constructed. It represented the foundation for scientifically studying social processes in their own right. In the emergence of the interactionist study of deviance, the school promoted a bifurcated focus on relatively personalized "social worlds" against the wider backdrop of "disorganization." Later, Sutherland's differential association combined subculture proliferation with interactional normative conflict, and labeling developed its critique of signification (Matza 1969). In retrospect, 1960s labeling represented the "flowering" (Sumner 1994) of social deviance in its "unorthodox moral

CHAPTER EIGHT

vision" (Best 2004, 31). As I have shown, throughout the 1970s—by default if not design—the perspective also became the site of emerging feminist critiques of gender stigmatization (Schur 1980).

These feminist alternatives serve as a bridge to a critical cultural studies based on Denzin's (1989b) interpretive interactionism and Rorty's (1967) reworking of pragmatism in the linguistic turn. In the scenario, then, constructions of gender are framed with those of class, age, and race (Heller 1993). The textual scenario moves the deviance-creation process from individually labeled actors and events to the dramatic negotiation of cultural politics. The stigma contest (Schur 1980) involves culture (i.e., norms, values, and their practice) as a politicized terrain. Furthermore, cultural politics "fundamentally determine the meanings of social practices and, moreover, which groups and individuals have the power to define these meanings" (Jordan and Weedon 1995, 5). Emotional expression, self, and identity are inevitably part of this struggle of resistance and domination. Finally, in cultural politics "the subject, rather than be identified strictly with the individual, ought to be designated as a linguistic category, a placeholder, a structure in formation. Individuals come to occupy the site of the subject" (Butler 1997b, 10).

The labeled deviant is transmuted into a textual subject, and the language of stigmatization describes a fluid terrain of transgression (Foucault 1977). Transgression implies that normative boundaries are marked by increasing ambiguity and is characteristic of the turn from modern to postmodern. As Jervis (1999, 4) contends, modernity is "a consciousness and way of life that are implicitly (and at times explicitly) set against an unacceptable 'other,' thereby unwittingly providing the resources for transgression." As a stigma contest, labeling frames both individual and collective definitions. In the postmodern scenario traditional processes such as retrospective interpretation and role engulfment (Schur 1971)—the construction of a deviant identity after-the-fact and its management by the actor—become aspects of the politics of signification (Hall 1980b). Constructions of age, class, race, and gender become commodities in this discourse.

My readings of specific scenarios highlight the importance of these constructions within the deviance-generating process. In both Dreiser's time and after World War II, youth subculture emerged as a consumer audience and cultural voice, especially within the developing middle class.

Race and gender constructions contextualize the stories of stigma. Rock music from the 1950s onward has been a site of both deviance as subcultural resistance and commercial exploitation (Cohen 1972/93; Hall and Jefferson 1975/2002b; Hebdige 1979/2002). Dreiser's *An American Tragedy* situates a very personal story of intimacy-turned-to-murder against a tapestry of emerging American modernism. My choice of scenarios reflects the attitude of strategic postmodernism. The story of Grace and Chester emerged in the early twentieth century, a time when media coverage was dominated by print journalism and film was just appearing as a popular culture form. The saturation of daily life by television's images was nearly fifty years distant. Dreiser's (1920, 126–41) fascination with murderous crimes of passion was always reportorial, and *An American Tragedy* is written in a documentary style full of rich description. In its naturalism, the novel is a narrative of emerging modern America, early in the postmodern turn:

> I was witnessing the upbuilding of the great American fortunes. And once these fortunes and the families which controlled them were established, there began to develop our "leisure class," the Four Hundred of New York and the slave aristocracy in the South, plus their imitators in the remainder of the states. (Dreiser 1935/77, 292)

The emerging class distinctions in early American consumer society both isolated the wealthy and symbolically bound them with those below in the narrative of the American Dream of financial success. Dreiser frames this context of class, youth, and consumption:

> I saw also that the maintaining of those privileges was likewise the principal business of those who were not heirs to anything—the young and ambitious in nearly all walks of life. In fact, between 1875 and 1900 it became an outstanding American madness which led first to the Great War of 1914–18 and culminated finally in the financial debacle of 1929. (1935/77, 292)

Grace's murder situates gender construction in the tragic narrative. Speaking retrospectively of the event, Dreiser asks and answers, "But why so widely heralded at the time? Why the sorrow, sympathy, pain really, to the hearts of millions not only for Billy Brown but for him? Why? I will tell

CHAPTER EIGHT

you. Because the emotions, so much more quickly than the far more commonplace scales of the brain, register the essential truth. That is why" (1935/77, 299). The truth for Dreiser was naturalistic: Clyde and Grace were actors in a drama of which they had little control, staged against the backdrop of Dreiser's (1932) "tragic America."

The 1951 movie portrays the tragedy very narrowly through the eyes of its stars, Montgomery Clift and Elizabeth Taylor. Constructed with no historical sense of time and place—so unlike Dreiser's novel—the deviant event points only to dated images of class, gender, and youth. In the process the characters, especially Shelly Winters's portrayal of fictionalized Grace, translate only pathos to the screen and no sense of Dreiser's broader tragedy.

The scenario of youth subcultural creation is situated later in the postmodern turn. In the narrative of rock music, youth becomes a singular category, typed as deviant in both its lifestyle and political voice (Dotter 1994). By the time of Woodstock, its commodification was largely accomplished. Still, cultural expression is not a one-way street: Resistance, though made ideological as subcultural style, may be reconstituted, glimpsed as authentic and even as a radical creative voice (Hebdige 1979/2002; Kellner 1995, 336–41; Storey 1999, 54–60).

Pete Townshend is the principal player in this draft of the scenario, an historical actor and a textual voice (Dotter forthcoming). Other versions, especially those yet to be written, will doubtlessly feature other performers.[2] Pete is important as a voice of the aging rocker. This subtext has emerged alongside developing race and gender voices in the narrative of rock music (Rose 1994). A middle-age white male narrative, Pete's story no longer dominates the terrain either commercially or artistically. Yet the stigma narrative of the aging rocker remains an important one in the postmodern turn.

Contemporary Scenarios

The postmodern turn continues, and within it there are countless examples of scenarios awaiting discovery. Film remains a central medium for the presentation of crime as entertainment (Ferrell and Sanders 1995a). Throughout the 1990s until the present many controversial films have taken crime, especially violence, as their subject: among others, *JFK* and

THEORIZING DEVIANCE IN THE POSTMODERN

Natural Born Killers (Oliver Stone); *Miller's Crossing* and *Fargo* (Joel and Ethan Coen); *Reservoir Dogs* and *Pulp Fiction* (Quentin Tarantino); *Lone Star* (John Sayles); *Things to Do in Denver When You're Dead* (Gary Fleder); and *Traffic* (Steven Soderbergh). For the most part these efforts are marketed to adult audiences. Violence may be jarringly portrayed, in some instances juxtaposed with humor, and placed in the narrative to highlight its effects on everyday life. The shifting overlap of events, characters, time, and place are important narrative elements as well. A reconstruction of the assassination of President Kennedy, Stone's *JFK* combines history, conspiracy theory, memoir, and latter-day speculation in a multisourced screenplay. The project sparked much debate over its historical portrayal of the event and charges that Stone had "rewritten" history (Stone and Sklar 1992).

The emergence of satellite cable television has led to the endless proliferation of true deviance/crime stories for consumption (Ferrell and Websdale 1999a, 1999b; Fishman and Cavender 1998). Arguably the most sensationalized of these is the investigation and impeachment of President Clinton during his second term in office for sexual and other actions (U.S. Congress 1998). An even longer-running scenario is the connection of the Presidency of George H. W. Bush with that of his son, George W. Bush. The linking includes Gulf Wars I and II—emerging narratives of "postmodern war" (Gray 1997)—punctuated by the Clinton scenario itself, the contested election of 2000 (Bugliosi 2001; Kellner 2001), and the 9/11/01 terrorist attack on the New York World Trade Center (Kellner 2003a).

These intertwined "stories-within-stories" (Dotter forthcoming) combine political biography, constitutional interpretation, foreign and domestic policy, and long-term global politics and stability. Each scenario overlays deviant and criminal acts-as-plots,[3] conveyed daily in the full range of postmodern media. Indeed Kellner (2003b, 160–78) aptly describes presidential politics as an ever-present "megaspectacle" of contemporary media culture and analyzes each administration from Kennedy to the present in a narrative he calls "Presidential Politics, the Movie." According to Kellner,

> The centrality of media spectacle and political narrative to contemporary politics means that making sense of the current era requires the

CHAPTER EIGHT

tools of a critical social theory and cultural studies in order to analyze the images, discourses, events, and narratives of presidential politics. Of course, politics is more than merely narrative, there are real events with material interests and consequences, and often behind the scenes maneuvering that is not part of the public record. Yet the public sees presidencies and administrations in terms of narrative and spectacle, so that theorizing the cinematic and narrative nature of contemporary politics can help us to understand, analyze, and transform our political system. (2003b, 176–77)

As Kellner points out, narrative spectacle, in presidential politics or in other scenarios, is a multimedia concern but is most effectively realized in video and cinematic form. Postmodern narrative is visual mass communication. Such spectacle, even when reported as news, is simultaneously a popular culture storyline for consumption, the primary product of media culture (Debord 1967/94, 14–16). The production of the stigma movie, then, blurs, erases, and "dramatizes" events in the practice of cultural politics—with the immediacy of visual presentation and (re)presentation. The scenario from which the stigma movie emerges is a textual process of popular culture mythmaking:

[Popular culture] is an arena that is *profoundly* mythic. It is a theater of popular desires, a theater of popular fantasies. It is where we discover and play with the identifications of ourselves, where we are imagined, where we are represented, not only to the audiences out there who do not get the message, but to ourselves for the first time. [*italics* in the original] (Hall 1993, 113)

Contemporary Symbolic Studies of Stigma: The Turn Continues

This mediated mythic quality of spectacle has important implications for self and identity in the continuing postmodern turn. As I argued in the last chapter, at the turn of the twentieth century self-experience transmuted from the basis of *being* to *having* in the emerging consumer society. Currently, that basis is further changing from *having* to *appearing*. The narrative of appearance is the hallmark of the spectacle (Debord 1967/94, 16). Similarly, cultural politics (stigma contests in the construction of master status) is inextricably communicated in its "appearing." The decentered self is realized in this same meaning-as-appearance. Lemert describes the problematic of the contemporary self-as-narrative in several imagined questions asked by those confronting the new millennium:

> Why should anyone be put in a cell without due process? Why should we think of ourselves as individuals? What is this thing "society" that once was so local and common? Why should our passports be assigned by our societies and their national administrators when we also belong to groups that are the more important intimate associations? And, most telling of all, they asked and still ask, What's wrong with figuring out who we are without the bother of that dreadful choice between individual and society? Why can't we, as individuals, also be members of the intimate associations we are accustomed to, and not the one's imposed by law? And so on. (Lemert 2002, 37–38)

My conceptualization of scenario in a general way frames Lemert's questions in the context of deviance creation—in the postmodern crisis of meaning (Dotter 1997). In the stigma movie, the politics of signification—constructions of age, class, race, and gender—are textualized as linguistic narratives of which transgressions are an important part (Perinbanayagam 2000, 39–46). I use the term transgression (Foucault 1977) freely, as a description of the textual quality of deviance in the postmodern turn. A part of that textuality is the silence of marginalized voices. As Denzin remarks, "One out of ten (greater depending on race and gender) postmodern subjects will be one or more of the following: gay, lesbian, alcoholic or drug-addicted, ill, elderly, battered, homeless, and unemployed. Yet each type will be electronically connected to the American dream; even if they have to watch themselves on TV sets in shelters for the homeless, while their age, sex, and race are being recorded by 1990 census takers" (Denzin 1991c, 14).

The scenario, a commodity of information and entertainment, frames the creation of deviance in the space between self-as-subject and mediated cultural politics. As a "narrative about narratives" the scenario is interpretive and interactional, and locates "self construction at the doorstep of the particular, in the varied self stories that populate the identity landscape" (Holstein and Gubrium 2000, 231). The self—particularly the stigmatized, labeled self—is glimpsed in Derrida's (1972/81b) textualized *différance* and Foucault's (1983) dividing practices. Ideological and creative self-narratives are in constant juxtaposition in the contemporary subject (Dotter forthcoming). As an interpretive project the scenario views popular culture as a

CHAPTER EIGHT

primary site for the negotiation of stigmatized identities (Denzin 2003b). Finally, the scenario displays self stories as contemporary symbolic studies of stigma. With the latter term I mean to call attention to the linguistic, mediated character of deviant identity. Symbolic studies seek to highlight the transformation of normative meaning in cinematic and, increasingly, virtual contexts.

In the postmodern moment social deviance is neither dead nor meaningless. It is embedded in the contesting of cultural meaning, in the media spectacle. The media spectacle represents the third stage of the sign (Baudrillard 1981/94, 121; 1983, 83), hyperreality, simulation, a narrative of appearances. A century ago, early in the postmodern turn, realist constructions of deviance were natural as well (Matza 1969), portrayed so by reporters, novelists, social scientists, and others. Later, the traditional labeling perspectives of the 1950s and 1960s recognized that stigma was interactional and its meaning ambiguous, if not entirely arbitrary in its placement. Textual sociocultural reality in the third order is characterized as a continuous circuit of simulation. For Baudrillard, the postmodern context of self, media, and meaning-creation represents a double challenge, difficult but not insurmountable:

> It is essential today to evaluate this double challenge: the challenge to meaning by the masses and their silence (which is not at all a passive resistance), and the challenge to meaning which comes from the media and their fascination. (Baudrillard 1988d, 217)

The strands of traditional interactionist approaches to deviance-theorizing—Chicago School labeling, interactional conflict, and sociological phenomenology—were unmediated descriptions of stigma-creation and the relationship of that process to the acting self. Feminist critiques of these strands bridge to a critical cultural studies, an interpretive interactionism (Denzin 1989b, 2003b). Biographical voices are glimpsed in the multitude of mediated texts (Manning 2003), especially popular culture ones. These scenarios are descriptive and critical stories, with deviance transformed from normative violation to fluid transgression. Such symbolic studies of stigmatization occur on the shifting boundaries of subject and society, voices and their absence, in the postmodern turn.

Notes

1. I would like to thank Peter Manning for his suggestion of this term.

2. In his history of classic rock Altschuler (2003, 189–91) offers a brief Bruce Springsteen narrative.

3. Three examples: Kellner (2003a, 1–45) summarizes the actions of the Bush Administration following the 9/11/01 terrorist attacks. For a critical account of secret U.S.–Taliban "oil diplomacy" dating from the elder Bush Administration, see Brisard and Dasquié (2002). Finally, French philosopher Bernard-Henri Lévy (2003) reconstructs the 2002 murder of *Wall Street Journal* reporter Daniel Pearl in Karachi, Pakistan.

REFERENCES

Agger, Ben. 1992. *Cultural Studies as Critical Theory.* London: Falmer Press.
Akers, Ronald L. 1968. "Problems In the Sociology of Deviance: Social Definition and Behavior." *Social Forces* 46: 455–65.
———. 1985. *Deviant Behavior: A Social Learning Approach.* Third Edition. Belmont, CA: Wadsworth.
Allen, Frederick Lewis. 1931/2000. *Only Yesterday: An Informal History of the 1920's.* New York: HarperCollins.
Althusser, Louis. 1969/96. *For Marx.* Ben Brewster (tr.). London: Verso.
———. 1971. *Lenin and Philosophy and Other Essays.* New York: Monthly Review Press.
Altschuler, Glenn C. 1982. *Race, Ethnicity, and Class in American Thought: 1865–1919.* Arlington Heights, IL: Harlan Davidson.
———. 2003. *All Shook Up: How Rock 'n' Roll Changed America.* New York: Oxford University Press.
Alway, Joan. 1995. "The Trouble With Gender: Tales of the Still-Missing Feminist Revolution In Sociological Theory." *Sociological Theory* 13: 209–28.
Andersen, Margaret L., and Patricia Hill Collins. 2004a. "Introduction." Pp. 1–14 in *Race, Class, and Gender: An Anthology*, Margaret L. Andersen and Patricia Hill Collins (eds.). Fifth Edition. Belmont, CA: Wadsworth.
——— (eds). 2004b. *Race, Class, and Gender: An Anthology.* Fifth Edition. Belmont, CA: Wadsworth.
Anderson, Nels. 1923/65. *The Hobo: The Sociology of the Homeless Man.* Chicago: University of Chicago Press.
Andrew, Dudley. 1976. *The Major Film Theories: An Introduction.* London: Oxford University Press.

REFERENCES

———. 1984. *Concepts in Film Theory.* Oxford: Oxford University Press.

Appleby, Joyce, Lynn Hunt, and Margaret Jacob. 1994. *Telling the Truth About History.* New York: W. W. Norton.

Arato, Andrew, and Eike Gebhardt. 1982/97. *The Essential Frankfurt School Reader.* New York: Continuum.

Aronowitz, Stanley. 1992. *The Politics of Identity: Class, Culture, Social Movements.* New York: Routledge.

———. 1993. *Roll over Beethoven: The Return of Cultural Strife.* Hanover, NH: University Press of New England.

———. 1994. *Dead Artists, Live Theories and Other Cultural Problems.* New York: Routledge.

———. 2003. *How Class Works: Power and Social Movement.* New Haven, CT: Yale University Press.

Ashley, David. 1997. *History Without a Subject: The Postmodern Condition.* Boulder, CO: Westview Press.

Athens, Lonnie H. 1989/92. *The Creation of Dangerous Violent Criminals.* Urbana: University of Illinois Press.

———. 1997. *Violent Criminal Acts and Actors Revisited.* Urbana: University of Illinois Press.

Attridge, Derek. 1992. "Introduction: Derrida and the Questioning of Literature." Pp. 1–29 in *Jacques Derrida: Acts of Literature* by Jacques Derrida, Derek Attridge (ed.). New York: Routledge.

Austin, Joe, and Michael Nevin Willard. 1998. "Introduction: Angels of History, Demons of Culture." Pp. 1–20 in *Generations of Youth: Youth Cultures and History in Twentieth-Century America,* Joe Austin and Michael Nevin Willard (eds.). New York: New York University Press.

Baca Zinn, Maxine, and Bonnie Thornton Dill. 1996. "Theorizing Difference from Multiracial Feminism." *Feminist Studies* 22: 321–31.

Bailey, Frankie Y. 1996. "The 'Tangle of Pathology' and the Lower Class African-American Family: Historical and Social Science Perspectives." Pp. 49–71 in *Justice With Prejudice: Race and Criminal Justice In America,* Michael J. Lynch and E. Britt Patterson (eds.). Albany, NY: Harrow and Heston.

Baker, Houston A. 1987. *Modernism and the Harlem Renaissance.* Chicago: University of Chicago Press.

Baker, Lee D. 1998. *From Savage to Negro: Anthropology and the Construction of Race, 1896-1954.* Berkeley: University of California Press.

Bannet, Eve Trevor. 1989. *Structuralism and the Logic of Dissent: Barthes, Derrida, Foucault, and Lacan.* Urbana: University of Illinois Press.

Barak, Gregg (ed.). 1994a. *Media, Process, and the Social Construction of Crime: Studies in Newsmaking Criminology.* New York: Garland.

REFERENCES

———. 1994b. "Media, Society, and Criminology." Pp. 3–45 in *Media, Process, and the Social Construction of Crime: Studies in Newsmaking Criminology*, Gregg Barak (ed.). New York: Garland.

——— (ed.). 1999. *Media, Criminal Justice and Mass Culture*. Revised Edition. Monsey, NY: Criminal Justice Press.

Barak, Gregg, Jeanne M. Flavin, and Paul S. Leighton. 2001. *Class, Race, Gender, and Crime: Social Realities of Justice in America*. Los Angeles: Roxbury.

Barker, Francis. 1993. *The Culture of Violence: Essays on Tragedy and History*. Chicago: University of Chicago Press.

Barnes, Richard. 1982/2000. *The Who: Maximum R&B*. London: Plexus.

Barthes, Roland. 1957/72. *Mythologies*. Annette Lavers (tr.). New York: Hill and Wang.

———. 1977. *Image-Music-Text*. Steven Heath (tr.). New York: Hill and Wang.

Baudrillard, Jean. 1968/96. *The System of Objects*. James Benedict (tr.). London: Verso.

———. 1970/98. *The Consumer Society: Myths and Structures*. London: Sage.

———. 1981/94. *Simulacra and Simulation*. Sheila Faria Graham (tr.). Ann Arbor: University of Michigan.

———. 1983. *Simulations*. Paul Foss, Paul Patton, and Philip Beitchman (trs.). New York: Semiotext[e].

———. 1988a. "Consumer Society." Pp. 29–56 in *Jean Baudrillard: Selected Writings*, Mark Poster (ed.). Stanford, CA: Stanford University Press.

———. 1988b. "For a Critique of the Political Economy of the Sign." Pp. 57–97 in *Jean Baudrillard: Selected Writings*, Mark Poster (ed.). Stanford, CA: Stanford University Press.

———. 1988c. *Jean Baudrillard: Selected Writings*. Mark Poster (ed.). Stanford, CA: Stanford University Press.

———. 1988d. "The Masses: The Implosion of the Social in the Media." Pp. 207–19 in *Jean Baudrillard: Selected Writings*, Mark Poster (ed.). Stanford, CA: Stanford University Press.

———. 1988e. "Symbolic Exchange and Death." Pp. 119–48 in *Jean Baudrillard: Selected Writings*, Mark Poster (ed.). Stanford, CA: Stanford University Press.

———. 1989. *America*. Chris Turner (tr.). London: Verso.

———. 1994. *The Illusion of the End*. Chris Turner (tr.). Stanford, CA: Stanford University Press.

———. 1996. *The Perfect Crime*. Chris Turner (tr.). London: Verso.

———. 2000. *The Vital Illusion*. Julia Witwer (ed.). New York: Columbia University Press.

———. 2003. *The Spirit of Terrorism and Requiem for the Twin Towers*. New Edition. Chris Turner (tr.). London: Verso.

REFERENCES

Bauman, Zygmunt. 1988. "Is There a Postmodern Sociology?" *Theory, Culture and Society* 5: 217–37.

———. 1995. "Sociology and Postmodernity." Pp. 74–83 in *Class*, Patrick Joyce (ed.). Oxford: Oxford University Press.

Bayles, Martha. 1994. *Hole In Our Soul: The Loss of Beauty and Meaning in American Popular Music*. New York: Free Press.

Bazin, Andre. 1967. *What is Cinema?* Volume 1. Hugh Gray (tr.). Berkeley: University of California Press.

Becker, Howard S. 1951. "The Professional Dance Musician and His Audience." *American Journal of Sociology* 57: 136–44.

———. 1953. "Becoming a Marihuana User." *American Journal of Sociology* 59: 235–42.

———. 1963/73. *Outsiders: Studies in the Sociology of Deviance*. Enlarged Edition. New York: Free Press.

———. 1964. *The Other Side: Perspectives on Deviance*. New York: Free Press.

———. 1967. "Whose Side Are We On?" *Social Problems* 14: 239–47.

Becker, Howard S., and Michal M. McCall (eds.). 1990. *Symbolic Interaction and Cultural Studies*. Chicago: University of Chicago Press.

Belz, Carl. 1972. *The Story of Rock*. Second Edition. New York: Oxford University Press.

Benedict, Helen. 1992. *Virgin or Vamp: How the Press Covers Sex Crimes*. New York: Oxford University Press.

Benhabib, Seyla. 1990. "Epistemologies of Postmodernism: A Rejoinder to Jean-Francois Lyotard." Pp. 107–30 in *Feminism/Postmodernism*, Linda J. Nicholson (ed.). New York: Routledge.

Benjamin, Walter. 1968. *Illuminations: Essays and Reflections*. Hannah Arendt (ed.). Harry Zohn (tr.). New York: Schocken.

Bennington, Geoffrey. 2000. *Interrupting Derrida*. London: Routledge.

Ben-Yehuda, Nachman. 1988. "The Politicization of Deviance: Reversing Degradation and Stigmatization." *Deviant Behavior* 8: 259–82.

———. 1990. *The Politics and Morality of Deviance: Moral Panics, Drug Abuse, Deviant Science and Reversed Stigmatization*. Albany: State University of New York Press.

Bercovitch, Sacvan. 1993. *The Rites of Assent: Transformations in the Symbolic Construction of America*. New York: Routledge.

Berthoff, Warner. 1965. *The Ferment of Realism: American Literature 1884-1919*. New York: Free Press.

Best, Joel (ed.). 1989. *Images of Issues: Typifying Contemporary Social Problems*. New York: Aldine de Gruyter.

———. 2004. *Deviance: Career of a Concept*. Belmont, CA: Wadsworth.

REFERENCES

Best, Steven. 1994. "The Commodification of Reality and the Reality of Commodification." Pp. 41–67 in *Baudrillard: A Critical Reader*, Douglas Kellner (ed.). Cambridge, MA: Blackwell.

———. 1995. *The Politics of Historical Vision: Marx, Foucault, Habermas.* New York: Guilford Press.

Best, Steven, and Douglas Kellner. 1991. *Postmodern Theory: Critical Interrogations.* New York: Guilford Press.

———. *The Postmodern Turn.* Oxford: Blackwell.

———. 2001. *The Postmodern Adventure: Science, Technology, and Cultural Studies at the Third Millennium.* New York: Guilford Press.

Bittner, Egon. 1967. "The Police on Skid-Row: A Study of Peace Keeping." *American Sociological Review* 32: 699–715.

Blair, Sara. 1999. "Modernism and the Politics of Culture." Pp. 157–73 in *The Cambridge Companion to Modernism*, Michael Levenson (ed.). Cambridge: Cambridge University Press.

Blumer, Herbert. 1939/69. "An Appraisal of Thomas and Znaniecki's The Polish Peasant in Europe and America." Pp. 117–26 in *Symbolic Interactionism: Perspective and Method*, by Herbert Blumer. Englewood Cliffs, NJ: Prentice-Hall.

———. 1966. "Sociological Implications of the Thought of George Herbert Mead." *American Journal of Sociology* 71: 535–48.

———. 1969. *Symbolic Interactionism: Perspective and Method.* Englewood Cliffs, NJ: Prentice-Hall.

———. 1972. "Action vs. Interaction." Review of *Relations in Public: Microstudies of the Public Order*, by Erving Goffman. *Society* 9 (April): 50–53.

———. 1973. "Comment on Symbolic Interaction as a Pragmatic Perspective: The Bias of Emergent Theory." *American Sociological Review* 38: 797–98.

Bohm, Robert M. 1997. *A Primer on Crime and Delinquency.* Belmont, CA: Wadsworth.

Boorstin, Daniel J. 1962/87. *The Image: A Guide to Pseudo-Events in America.* New York: Vintage.

Bordua, David J. 1967. "Recent Trends: Deviant Behavior and Social Control." *The Annals of the American Academy of Political and Social Science* 369: 149–63.

Borradori, Giovanna. 2003. *Philosophy in a Time of Terror: Dialogues with Jurgen Habermas and Jacques Derrida.* Chicago: University of Chicago Press.

Bourdieu, Pierre. 1995. "The Reality of Representation and the Representation of Reality." Pp. 99–101 in *Class*, Patrick Joyce (ed.). Oxford: Oxford University Press.

Bowlby, Rachel. 1985. *Just Looking: Consumer Culture in Dreiser, Gissing and Zola.* New York: Methuen.

REFERENCES

Bradbury, Malcolm. 1983/94. *The Modern American Novel.* London: Penguin.

Bradbury, Malcolm, and James McFarlane (eds.). 1976/91a. *Modernism: A Guide to European Literature 1890-1930.* London: Penguin.

———. 1976/91b. "Movements, Magazines, and Manifestos: The Succession from Naturalism." Pp. 192–205 in *Modernism: A Guide to European Literature 1890–1930.* London: Penguin.

———. 1976/91c. "The Name and Nature of Modernism." Pp. 19–55 in *Modernism: A Guide to European Literature 1890-1930.* London: Penguin.

Braithwaite, John. 1989. *Crime, Shame and Reintegration.* Cambridge: Cambridge University Press.

———. 1995. "Shaming Theory." Pp. 35–40 in *Readings in Deviant Behavior*, Alex Thio and Thomas Calhoun (eds.). New York: HarperCollins.

Brandon, Craig. 1986. *Murder in the Adirondacks: An American Tragedy Revisited.* Utica, NY: North Country Books.

Brent, Joseph. 1993/98. *Charles Sanders Peirce: A Life.* Revised and Enlarged Edition. Bloomington: Indiana University Press.

Brisard, Jean-Charles, and Guillaume Dasquié. 2002. *Forbidden Truth: U.S.-Taliban Secret Oil Diplomacy and the Failed Hunt for Bin Laden.* Lucy Rounds (tr.), with Peter Fifield and Nicholas Greenslade. New York: Thunder's Mouth Press/Nation Books.

Bromwich, David. 1998. "The Novelist of Everyday Life." Pp. 370–76 in *The Revival of Pragmatism: New Essays on Social Thought, Law, and Culture*, Morris Dickstein (ed.). Durham, NC: Duke University Press.

Brown, Richard Harvey. 1987. *Society as Text: Essays on Rhetoric, Reason, and Reality.* Chicago: University of Chicago Press.

Brownell, Joseph W., and Patricia A. Wawrzaszek. 1986. *Adirondack Tragedy: The Gillette Murder Case of 1906.* Interlaken, NY: Heart of the Lakes Publishing.

Brownmiller, Susan. 1975. *Against Our Will: Men, Women and Rape.* New York: Fawcett Columbine.

Brownstein, Henry H. 2000. *The Social Reality of Violence and Violent Crime.* Boston: Allyn and Bacon.

Budd, Louis J. 1995. "The American Background." Pp. 21–46 in *The Cambridge Companion to American Realism and Naturalism: Howells to London*, Donald Pizer (ed.). Cambridge: Cambridge University Press.

Bugliosi, Vincent. 2001. *The Betrayal of America: How the Supreme Court Undermined the Constitution and Chose Our President.* New York: Thunder's Mouth Press/Nation Books.

Bulmer, Martin. 1984. *The Chicago School of Sociology.* Chicago: University of Chicago Press.

REFERENCES

Butler, Judith. 1990/99. *Gender Trouble: Feminism and the Subversion of Identity.* New York: Routledge.

———. 1993. *Bodies That Matter: On the Discursive Limits of "Sex."* New York: Routledge.

———. 1997a. *Excitable Speech: A Politics of the Performative.* New York: Routledge.

———. 1997b. *The Psychic Life of Power: Theories in Subjection.* Stanford, CA: Stanford University Press.

Cagle, Van M. 1995. *Reconstructing Pop/Subculture: Art, Rock, and Andy Warhol.* Thousand Oaks, CA: Sage.

Carey, James T. 1975. *Sociology As Public Affairs: The Chicago School.* Beverly Hills, CA: Sage.

Carey, James W. 1989. *Communication as Culture.* Boston: Unwin Hyman.

Carlen, Pat. 1994. "Gender, Class, Racism, and Criminal Justice: Against Global and Gender-Centric Theories, For Poststructuralist Perspectives." Pp. 134–44 in *Inequality, Crime, and Social Control*, George S. Bridges and Martha A. Myers (eds.). Boulder, CO: Westview.

Carrington, Kerry. 1998. "Postmodernism and Feminist Criminologies: Disconnecting Discourses?" Pp. 69–84 in *Criminology at the Crossroads: Feminist Readings in Crime and Justice*, Kathleen Daly and Lisa Maher (eds.). New York: Oxford University Press.

Cavender, Gray, and Mark Fishman. 1998. "Television Reality Crime Programs: Context and History." Pp. 1–14 in *Entertaining Crime: Television Reality Programs*, Mark Fishman and Gray Cavender (eds.). New York: Aldine de Gruyter.

Chambliss, William J. 1985. "Toward a Political Economy of Crime." Pp. 423–41 in *Theories of Deviance*, Stuart H. Traub and Craig B. Little (eds.). Third Edition. Itasca, IL: Peacock.

Chapple, Steve, and Reebee Garofalo. 1977. *Rock 'n' Roll Is Here to Pay: The History and Politics of the Music Industry.* Chicago: Nelson-Hall.

Cincinnati Enquirer. 1979a. "All Deny Blame For Tragedy." (December 5): A1–2.

———. 1979b. "Aronoff to Offer Crowd Bill." (December 6): B1.

———. 1979c. "Changes Could Be on the Way for Seating Policies." (December 5): B4.

———. 1979d. "City Seeks Festival Seating Ban, More Police Power." (December 6): B1.

———. 1979e. "Coliseum Capacity Figure Too High, Officials Say." (December 5): B1.

———. 1979f. "Concert Promoters Cancel Two Events Set for December." (December 5): B1.

REFERENCES

———. 1979g. "Crowds Capable of Developing Own Personalities, Expert Says." (December 5): B1.
———. 1979h. "General Admission 'A Way of Life.'" (December 5): B3.
———. 1979i. "Hoosiers Say They Have Crowd Control Answers." (December 5): B1.
———. 1979j. "Panel Named to Probe Tragedy at Rock Concert." (December 7): A1.
———. 1979k. "'76 Study Recommended Coliseum Reduce 'Festival Seating.'" (December 5): A1–2.
———. 1979l. "Stampede Kills 11 Persons at Coliseum Rock Concert." (December 5): A1–2.
———. 1979m. "Tough, Objective Probe Urged in Coliseum Deaths." (December 6): A1–2.
———. 1979n. "The Tragedy." (December 5): A14.
———. 1979o. "Two Cities Move to Ban Festival Seating." (December 6): B1.
———. 1979p. "Violence A Companion of Festivals." (December 5): B5.
———. 1979q. "Who's Daltrey Feels Helpless, Guiltless." (December 5): A1.
———. 1979r. "The Who's Violence Always Kept to Stage." (December 4): D1.
Clark, Gary. 1990. "Defending Ski-Jumpers: A Critique of Theories of Youth Subculture." Pp. 81–96 in *On Record: Rock, Pop, and the Written Word*, Simon Frith and Andrew Goodman (eds.). New York: Pantheon.
Clarke, John, Stuart Hall, Tony Jefferson, and Brian Roberts. 1975/2002. "Subcultures, Cultures and Class: A Theoretical Overview." Pp. 9–74 in *Resistance Through Rituals: Youth Subcultures in Post-War Britain*, Stuart Hall and Tony Jefferson (eds.). London: Routledge.
Clinard, Marshall B., and Robert F. Meier. 2004. *Sociology of Deviant Behavior.* Twelfth Edition. Belmont, CA: Wadsworth.
Clinard, Marshall, Richard Quinney, and John Wildeman. 1994. *Criminal Behavior Systems: A Typology.* Third Edition. Cincinnati, OH: Anderson.
Cocks, Jay. 1979. "Rock's Outer Limits." *Time* (December 17): 86–94.
Cohen, Lizabeth. 2003. *A Consumer's Republic: The Politics of Mass Consumption in Postwar America.* New York: Knopf.
Cohen, Stanley. 1972/93. *Folk Devils and Moral Panics: The Creation of the Mods and Rockers.* Oxford: Blackwell.
Collins, Patricia Hill. 1988. "The Social Construction of Black Feminist Thought." Pp. 297–325 in *Black Women In America: Social Science Perspectives*, Michele R. Malso, Elizabeth Mudimbe-Boyi, Jean F. O'Barr, and Mary Wyer (eds.). Chicago: University of Chicago Press.
———. 1991. *Black Feminist Thought: Knowledge, Consciousness, and the Politics of Empowerment.* New York: Routledge, Chapman and Hall.

REFERENCES

Collins, Randall. 1975. *Conflict Sociology.* New York: Academic Press.

Colomy, Paul, and J. David Brown. 1995. "Elaboration, Revision, Polemic, and Progress in the Second Chicago School." Pp. 17–81 in *A Second Chicago School?: The Development of a Postwar American Sociology,* Gary Alan Fine (ed.). Chicago: University of Chicago Press.

Commager, Henry Steele. 1950. *The American Mind: An Interpretation of American Thought and Character Since the 1880's.* New Haven, CT: Yale University Press.

Connell, R. W. 1987. *Gender and Power: Society, the Person and Sexual Politics.* Stanford, CA: Stanford University Press.

Connor, Steven. 1989. *Postmodernist Culture: An Introduction to Theories of the Contemporary.* Oxford: Blackwell.

Conrad, Peter. 1999. *Modern Times, Modern Places.* New York: Aldred A. Knopf.

Cook, David A. 1981. *A History of Narrative Film.* New York: W.W. Norton.

Cooley, Charles Horton. 1902/83. *Human Nature and the Social Order.* Philip Rieff (in.). New Brunswick, NJ: Transaction.

———. 1909/62. *Social Organization: A Study of the Larger Mind.* Philip Rieff (in.). New York: Schocken.

Coreno, Thaddeus. 1994. "Guerrilla Music: Avant-Garde Voice as Oppositional Discourse." Pp. 189–224 in *Adolescents and Their Music: If It's Too Loud, You're Too Old,* Jonathon S. Epstein (ed.). New York: Garland.

Cowley, Malcolm. 1950. "Naturalism in American Literature." Pp. 300–33 in *Evolutionary Thought in America,* Stow Persons (ed.). New Haven, CT: Yale University Press.

Cressey, Paul G. 1932/69. *The Taxi-Dance Hall: A Sociological Study of Commercialized Recreation and City Life.* Montclair, NJ: Patterson Smith.

Cross, Gary. 2000. *An All-Consuming Century: Why Commercialism Won in Modern America.* New York: Columbia University Press.

Culler, Jonathan D. 1975. *Structuralist Poetics: Structuralism, Linguistics, and the Study of Literature.* Ithaca, NY: Cornell.

———. 1982. *On Deconstruction: Theory and Criticism After Structuralism.* Ithaca, NY: Cornell.

———. 1988. *Framing the Sign: Criticism and Its Institutions.* Norman: University of Oklahoma Press.

———. 1997. *Literary Theory: A Very Short Introduction.* New York: Oxford University Press.

———. 2000. "The Literary in Theory." Pp. 273–92 in *What's Left of Theory?: New Work on the Politics of Literary Theory,* Judith Butler, John Guillory, and Kendall Thomas (eds.). New York: Routledge.

Curra, John. 2000. *The Relativity of Deviance.* Thousand Oaks, CA: Sage.

REFERENCES

Curti, Lidia. 1992. "What is Real and What is Not: Female Fabulations in Cultural Analysis." Pp. 134–53 in *Cultural Studies,* Lawrence Grossberg, Cary Nelson, and Paula Treichler (eds.). New York: Routledge.

Curtis, Susan. 1991. *A Consuming Faith: The Social Gospel and Modern American Culture.* Baltimore: Johns Hopkins University Press.

Daly, Kathleen, and Meda Chesney-Lind. 1988. "Feminism and Criminology." *Justice Quarterly* 5 (December): 497–538.

Daly, Kathleen, and Lisa Maher (eds.). 1998a. *Criminology at the Crossroads: Feminist Readings in Crime and Justice.* New York: Oxford University Press.

———. 1998b. "Crossroads and Intersections: Building from Feminist Critique." Pp. 1–17 in *Criminology at the Crossroads: Feminist Readings in Crime and Justice,* Kathleen Daly and Lisa Maher (eds.). New York: Oxford University Press.

Daly, Kathleen, and Deborah J. Stephens. 1995. "The 'Dark Figure' of Criminology: Towards a Black and Multi-ethnic Feminist Agenda for Theory and Research." Pp. 189–215 in *International Feminist Perspectives in Criminology: Engendering a Discipline,* Nicole Hahn Rafter and Frances Heidensohn (eds.). Philadelphia: Open University Press.

Dansby, Andrew. 2002. (June 28, 2002). "The Who Tour Goes On." *Rolling Stone.* Retrieved June 30, 2003 from http://www.rollingstone.com/news/newsarticle.asp?nid=16197.

Darden, Donna K., Steven K. Worden, and Lori Holyfield. 1997. "Cockfighting and Backsliding: Deviance and Postmodernism." *Sociological Spectrum* 17: 363–73.

Davis, Nanette J. 1975. *Sociological Constructions of Deviance: Perspectives and Issues in the Field.* Dubuque, IA: William C. Brown.

Davis, Nanette J., and Clarice Stasz. 1990. *Social Control of Deviance: A Critical Perspective.* New York: McGraw-Hill.

Debord, Guy. 1967/94. *The Society of the Spectacle.* New York: Zone Books.

Degler, Carl N. 1991. *In Search of Human Nature: The Decline and Revival of Darwinism in American Thought.* New York: Oxford University Press.

Denisoff, R. Serge. 1975. *Solid Gold: The Popular Record Industry.* New Brunswick, NJ: Transaction.

———. 1986. *Tarnished Gold: The Record Industry Revisited.* New Brunswick, NJ: Transaction.

Denzin, Norman K. 1978. "Crime and the American Liquor Industry." Pp. 87–118 in *Studies in Symbolic Interaction* (Volume 1), Norman K. Denzin (ed.). Greenwich, CT: JAI.

———. 1984. "On Interpreting an Interpretation." *American Journal of Sociology* 89: 1426–33.

———. 1986a. "On a Semiotic Approach to Mass Culture: Comment on Gottdiener." *American Journal of Sociology* 92: 678–83.

———. 1986b. "Postmodern Social Theory." *Sociological Theory* 4: 194–204.

———. 1987/93. *The Alcoholic Society: Addiction and Recovery of the Self.* New Brunswick, NJ: Transaction.

———. 1987. "The Death of Sociology in the 1980s." *American Journal of Sociology* 93: 175–80.

———. 1988a. "Act, Language, and Self in Symbolic Interactionist Thought." Pp. 51–80 in *Studies in Symbolic Interaction* (Volume 9), Norman K. Denzin (ed.). Greenwich, CT: JAI.

———. 1988b. "*Blue Velvet*: Postmodern Contradictions." *Theory, Culture and Society* 5: 461–73.

———. 1989a. *Interpretive Biography.* Newbury Park, CA: Sage.

———. 1989b. *Interpretive Interactionism.* Newbury Park, CA: Sage.

———. 1990a "The Sociological Imagination Reconsidered." *Sociological Quarterly* 31: 1–23.

———. 1990b "Reading Cultural Texts: Comment of Griswold." *American Journal of Sociology* 95: 1577–80.

———. 1991a. "Empiricist Cultural Studies in America: A Deconstructive Reading." Pp. 17–39 in *Current Perspectives in Social Theory* (Volume 11), Ben Agger (ed.). Greenwich, CT: JAI Press.

———. 1991b. *Hollywood Shot by Shot: Alcoholism in American Cinema.* New York: Aldine de Gruyter.

———. 1991c. *Images of Postmodern Society: Social Theory and Contemporary Cinema.* London: Sage.

———. 1992. *Symbolic Interactionism and Cultural Studies: The Politics of Interpretation.* Cambridge, MA: Blackwell.

———. 1994a. "The Art and Politics of Interpretation." Pp. 500–15 in *Handbook of Qualitative Research*, Norman K. Denzin and Yvonna S. Lincoln (eds.). Thousand Oaks, CA: Sage.

———. 1994b. "Chan Is Missing: The Asian Eye Confronts Cultural Studies." *Symbolic Interactionism* 17: 63–89.

———. 1994c. "Postmodernism and Deconstructionism." Pp. 182–202 in *Postmodernism and Social Inquiry*, David R. Dickens and Andrea Fontana (eds.). New York: Guilford Press.

———. 1995. *The Cinematic Society: The Voyeur's Gaze.* London: Sage.

———. 1996. "Prophetic Pragmatism and the Postmodern: A Comment on Maines." *Symbolic Interaction* 19: 341–55.

———. 2002a. "Confronting Ethnography's Crisis of Representation." *Journal of Contemporary Ethnography* 31 (August): 482–90.

REFERENCES

———. 2002b. *Reading Race: Hollywood and the Cinema of Racial Violence.* London: Sage.

———. 2003a. "The Call to Performance." *Symbolic Interaction* 26 (winter): 187–207.

———. 2003b. "Cultural Studies." Pp. 997–1019 in *Handbook of Symbolic Interactionism*, Larry T. Reynolds and Nancy J. Herman-Kinney (eds.). Walnut Creek, CA: AltaMira Press.

Denzin, Norman K., and Yvonna S. Lincoln. 1994. "Introduction: Entering the Field of Qualitative Research." Pp. 1–17 in *Handbook of Qualitative Research*, Norman K. Denzin and Yvonna S. Lincoln (eds.). Thousand Oaks, CA: Sage.

———. 2000. "The Discipline and Practice of Qualitative Research." Pp. 1–29 in *Handbook of Qualitative Research*, Norman K. Denzin and Yvonna S. Lincoln (eds.). Second Edition. Thousand Oaks, CA: Sage.

———. 2003. "Introduction: 9/11 in American Culture." Pp. xiii–xxi in *9/11 in American Culture*, Norman K. Denzin and Yvonna S. Lincoln (eds.). Walnut Creek, CA: AltaMira Press.

Derrida, Jacques. 1967/73. *Speech and Phenomena: And Other Essays on Husserl's Theory of Signs.* David B. Allison (tr.). Evanston, IL: Northwestern University Press.

———. 1967/76. *Of Grammatology.* Gayatri Chakravorty Spivak (tr.). Baltimore: Johns Hopkins University Press.

———. 1967/78. *Writing and Difference.* Alan Bass (tr.). Chicago: University of Chicago Press.

———. 1972. "Structure, Sign, and Play in the Discourse of the Human Sciences." Pp. 247–72 in *The Structuralist Controversy*, Richard Macksey and Eugenio Donato (eds.). Baltimore: Johns Hopkins University Press.

———. 1972/81a. *Dissemination.* Barbara Johnson (tr.). Chicago: University of Chicago Press.

———. 1972/81b. *Positions.* Alan Bass (tr.). Chicago: University of Chicago Press.

———. 1972/82. *Margins of Philosophy.* Alan Bass (tr.). Chicago: University of Chicago Press.

———. 1977. "Signature, Event, Context." *Glyph* 1: 172–97.

———. 1989. *Of Spirit: Heidegger and the Question.* Geoffrey Bennington and Rachel Bowlby (trs.). Chicago: University of Chicago Press.

———. 1991. "Letter to a Japanese Friend." Pp. 269–76 in *A Derrida Reader: Between the Blinds.* Peggy Kamuf (ed.). New York: Columbia University Press.

———. 1992. *Acts of Literature.* Derek Attridge (ed.). New York: Routledge.

———. 1994. *Specters of Marx: The State of the Debt, the Work of Mourning, and the New International.* Peggy Kamuf (tr.). New York: Routledge.

REFERENCES

———. 1997. *Politics of Friendship.* George Collins (tr.). London: Verso.

Dewey, John. 1896/1981. "The Reflex Arc Concept in Psychology." *Psychological Review* III (July): 357–70. Reprinted in *The Philosophy of John Dewey: Two Volumes in One,* pp. 136–48, John J. McDermott (ed.). Chicago: University of Chicago Press.

———. 1910/81. "The Experimental Theory of Knowledge." Pp. 77–111 in *The Influence of Darwin on Philosophy: And Other Essays in Contemporary Thought.* New York: Henry Holt. Reprinted in *The Philosophy of John Dewey: Two Volumes in One,* pp. 175–93, John J. McDermott (ed.). Chicago: University of Chicago Press.

———. 1929/81. "Experience and Philosophic Method." *In Experience and Nature.* Second Edition. Chapter One. New York: W. W. Norton and Company. Reprinted in *The Philosophy of John Dewey: Two Volumes in One,* pp. 249–77, John J. McDermott (ed.). Chicago: University of Chicago Press.

———. 1930/81. "Toward a New Individualism." Pp. 74–100 in *Individualism Old and New.* New York: Minton, Balch and Company. Reprinted in *The Philosophy of John Dewey: Two Volumes in One,* pp. 608–20, John J. McDermott (ed.). Chicago: University of Chicago Press.

———. 1981. *The Philosophy of John Dewey: Two Volumes In One,* John J. McDermott (ed.). Chicago: University of Chicago Press.

Di Stephano, Christine. 1990. "Dilemmas of Difference: Feminism, Modernity, and Postmodernism." Pp. 63–82 in *Feminism/Postmodernism,* Linda J. Nicholson (ed.). New York: Routledge.

Dickens, David R. 1990. "Deconstruction and Marxist Inquiry." *Sociological Perspectives* 33 (spring): 147–58.

Dickstein, Morris. 1998a. "Introduction: Pragmatism Then and Now." Pp. 1–18 in *The Revival of Pragmatism: New Essays on Social Thought, Law, and Culture,* Morris Dickstein (ed.). Durham, NC: Duke University Press.

——— (ed.). 1998b. *The Revival of Pragmatism: New Essays on Social Thought, Law, and Culture.* Durham, NC: Duke University Press.

Diggins, John Patrick. 1994. *The Promise of Pragmatism: Modernism and the Crisis of Knowledge and Authority.* Chicago: University of Chicago Press.

Diner, Steven J. 1998. *A Very Different Age: Americans of the Progressive Era.* New York: Hill and Wang.

Dodge, David L. 1985. "The Over-Negativized Conception of Deviance: A Programmatic Exploration." *Deviant Behavior* 6: 1–37.

Donovan, Josephine. 1985/96. *Feminist Theory: The Intellectual Traditions of American Feminism.* Expanded Edition. New York: Continuum.

Donziger, Steven R. (ed.). 1996. *The Real War on Crime: The Report of the National Criminal Justice Commission.* New York: HarperCollins.

REFERENCES

Doob, Christopher Bates. 1999. *Racism: An American Cauldron.* Third Edition. New York: Addison Wesley Longman.

Dosse, Francois. 1997a. *History of Structuralism.* Volume 1 *(The Rising Sign, 1945–1966).* Deborah Glassman (tr.). Minneapolis: University of Minnesota Press.

——. 1997b. *History of Structuralism.* Volume 2 *(The Sign Sets, 1967–Present).* Deborah Glassman (tr.). Minneapolis: University of Minnesota Press.

Dotter, Daniel. 1978. "Beyond the Chicago School: Deviance and Social Conflict." Paper presented at the annual meeting of the Mid-South Sociological Association, Jackson, MS.

——. 1980a. "Pragmatism in the Thought of George H. Mead." Paper presented at the annual meeting of the Southern Sociological Society, Knoxville, TN.

——. 1980b. "The Social Construction of Territory: Metaphor, Self, and the Meaning of Space." *Sociological Forum* 3: 19–30.

——. 1987. "Growing Up is Hard to Do: Rock and Roll Performers as Cultural Heroes." *Sociological Spectrum* 7: 25–44.

——. 1994. "Rock and Roll is Here to Stray: Youth Subculture, Deviance and Social Typing in Rock's Early Years." Pp. 87–114 in *Adolescents and Their Music: If It's Too Loud, You're Too Old,* Jonathon S. Epstein (ed.). New York: Garland.

——. 1997. "Introduction: The Scenario As Postmodern Interpretive Strategy." *Sociological Spectrum* 17: 249–57.

——. forthcoming. "Who Are You: Pete Townshend, 'Going Solo,' and the Postmodern Search for Self in Rock Music." *Studies in Symbolic Interaction* (Volume 27), Norman K. Denzin (ed.). Greenwich, CT: JAI.

Dotter, Daniel, and Marianne Fisher-Giorlando. 1997. "The Social Creation of Deviant Status: Gender, Race, and Criminality in Antebellum Louisiana." Pp. 241–73 in *Studies in Symbolic Interaction* (Volume 21), Norman K. Denzin (ed.). Greenwich, CT: JAI.

Dotter, Daniel, and Julian B. Roebuck. 1988. "The Labeling Approach Re-Examined: Interactionism and the Components of Deviance." *Deviant Behavior* 9: 19–32.

Douglas, Ann. 1977/88. *The Feminization of American Culture.* New York: Anchor.

——. 1995. *Terrible Honesty: Mongrel Manhattan in the 1920s.* New York: Farrar, Straus and Giroux.

Douglas, Jack D. 1967. *The Social Meanings of Suicide.* Princeton, NJ: Princeton University Press.

——. 1970. "Understanding Everyday Life." Pp. 3–44 in *Understanding Everyday Life: Toward the Reconstruction of Sociological Knowledge,* Jack D. Douglas (ed.). Chicago: Aldine.

——. 1971. *American Social Order: Social Rules in a Pluralistic Society.* New York: Free Press.

REFERENCES

———. (ed.). 1984. *The Sociology of Deviance.* Boston: Allyn and Bacon.

Douglas, Jack D., and John M. Johnson (eds.). 1977. *Existential Sociology.* New York: Cambridge University Press.

———. 1978. *Business and Professional Deviance.* Philadelphia: Lippincott.

Douglas, Jack D., and Paul Rasmussen (With Carol Ann Flanigan). 1977. *The Nude Beach.* Beverly Hills, CA: Sage.

Douglas, Jack D., and Frances C. Waksler. 1982. *The Sociology of Deviance: An Introduction.* Boston: Little Brown.

Downes, David, and Paul Rock. 1982/98. *Understanding Deviance: A Guide to the Sociology of Crime and Rule-Breaking.* Third Edition. New York: Oxford University Press.

Draper, Robert. 1990. *Rolling Stone Magazine: The Uncensored History.* New York: Doubleday.

Dreyfus, Hubert L., and Paul Rabinow. 1983. *Michel Foucault: Beyond Structuralism and Hermeneutics.* Second Edition. Chicago: University of Chicago Press.

Dreiser, Theodore. 1903/98. "True Art Speaks Plainly." Pp. 179–80 in *Documents of American Realism and Naturalism,* Donald Pizer (ed.). Carbondale: Southern Illinois University Press.

———. 1920. *Hey Rub A Dub Dub Or A Book of the Mystery and Wonder and Terror of Life.* New York: Boni and Livewright.

———. 1923. *The Color of a Great City.* C.B. Falls (il.). New York: Boni and Liveright.

———. 1925/2003. *An American Tragedy.* Thomas P. Riggio (nt). New York: Library of America.

———. 1931. *Dawn.* New York: Horace Liveright.

———. 1932. *Tragic America.* New York: Horace Liveright.

———. 1935/77. "I Find the Real American Tragedy." Pp. 291–99 in *Theodore Dreiser: A Selection of Uncollected Prose,* Donald Pizer (ed.). Detroit, MI: Wayne State University Press.

———. 1982. *American Diaries: 1902–1926.* Thomas P. Riggio (ed.). Philadelphia: University of Pennsylvania Press.

———. 1985. *Selected Magazine Articles of Theodore Dreiser.* Yoshinobu Hakutani (ed., in., nt). Cranbury, NJ: Associated University Presses.

Dumenil, Lynn. 1995. *The Modern Temper: American Culture and Society in the 1920s.* New York: Hill and Wang.

Eagleton, Terry. 1991. *Ideology: An Introduction.* London: Verso.

———. 1996. *Literary Theory: An Introduction.* Second Edition. Minneapolis: University of Minnesota.

———. 2000. *The Idea of Culture.* Oxford: Blackwell.

REFERENCES

———. 2002. *Sweet Violence: The Idea of the Tragic.* Oxford: Blackwell.

Eby, Clare Virginia. 1998. *Dreiser and Veblen: Saboteurs of the Status Quo.* Columbia, MO: University of Missouri Press.

Edwards, Wendy J. Deichmann, and Carolyn De Swarte Gifford (eds.). 2003. *Gender and the Social Gospel.* Urbana: University of Illinois Press.

Eliot, T. S. 1934/62. *The Waste Land and Other Poems.* San Diego, CA: Harcourt Brace and Company.

Ellis, Carolyn. 2002. "Shattered Lives: Making Sense of September 11th and Its Aftermath." *Journal of Contemporary Ethnography* 31 (August): 375–410.

Ennis, Philip H. 1992. *The Seventh Stream: The Emergence of Rocknroll in American Popular Music.* Hanover, NH: Wesleyan.

Entman, Robert M., and Andrew Rojecki. 2000. *The Black Image in the White Mind: Media and Race in America.* Chicago: University of Chicago.

Erenberg, Lewis A. 1981. *Steppin' Out: New York Nightlife and the Transformation of American Culture, 1890-1930.* Westport, CT: Greenwood Press.

Ericksen, E. Gordon. 1980. *The Territorial Experience: Human Ecology as Symbolic Interaction.* Austin: University of Texas Press.

Erikson, Kai T. 1964. "Notes On the Sociology of Deviance." Pp. 9–21 in *The Other Side: Perspectives On Deviance,* Howard S. Becker (ed.). New York: Free Press.

———. 1966. *Wayward Puritans: A Study in the Sociology of Deviance.* New York: Wiley.

———. 1976. *Everything In Its Path: Destruction of Community in the Buffalo Creek Flood.* New York: Simon and Schuster.

Farganis, Sondra. 1994a. "Postmodernism and Feminism." Pp. 101–26 in *Postmodernism and Social Inquiry,* David R. Dickens and Andrea Fontana (eds.). New York: Guilford Press.

———. 1994b *Situating Feminism: From Thought to Action.* Thousand Oaks, CA: Sage.

Faris, Robert E. L. 1970. *Chicago Sociology: 1920–1932.* Chicago: University of Chicago Press.

Fass, Paula S. 1977. *The Damned and the Beautiful: American Youth in the 1920s.* New York: Oxford University Press.

Featherstone, Mike. 1988. "In Pursuit of the Postmodern: An Introduction." *Theory, Culture and Society* 5: 195–215.

———. 1991. *Consumer Culture and Postmodernism.* London: Sage.

Ferrell, Jeff, and Clinton R. Sanders (eds.). 1995a. *Cultural Criminology.* Boston: Northeastern University Press.

———. 1995b. "Culture, Crime, and Criminology." Pp. 3–21 in *Cultural Criminology,* Jeff Farrell and Clinton R. Sanders (eds.). Boston: Northeastern University Press.

REFERENCES

———. 1995c. "Toward a Cultural Criminology." Pp. 297–326 in *Cultural Criminology,* Jeff Farrell and Clinton R. Sanders (eds.). Boston: Northeastern University Press.

Ferrell, Jeff, and Neil Websdale (eds.). 1999a. *Making Trouble: Cultural Constructions of Crime, Deviance, and Control.* New York: Aldine de Gruyter.

———. 1999b. "Materials for Making Trouble." Pp. 3–21 in *Making Trouble: Cultural Constructions of Crime, Deviance, and Control.* New York: Aldine de Gruyter.

Fine, Gary Alan. 1993. "The Sad Demise, Mysterious Disappearance, and Glorious Triumph of Symbolic Interactionism." Pp. 61–87 in *Annual Review of Sociology* (Volume 19), Judith Blake (ed.). Palo Alto, CA: Annual Reviews.

———. 1995a. "Introduction." Pp. 1–16 in *A Second Chicago School?: The Development of a Postwar American Sociology,* Gary Alan Fine (ed.). Chicago: University of Chicago Press.

——— (ed.). 1995b. *A Second Chicago School?: The Development of a Postwar American Sociology.* Chicago: University of Chicago Press.

Fisher-Giorlando, Marianne, and Daniel Dotter. 2003. "Murder in Black and White: A Crime and Media Story in Antebellum Louisiana." *Women & Criminal Justice* 14: 59–87.

Fishkin, Shelley Fisher. 1995. "Dreiser and the Discourse of Gender." Pp. 1–30 in *Theodore Dreiser: Beyond Naturalism,* Miriam Gogol (ed.). New York: New York University Press.

Fishman, Mark. 1996. "Crime Waves as Ideology." Pp. 53–72 in *Constructing Crime: Perspectives on Making News and Social Problems,* Gary W. Potter and Victor E. Kappeler (eds.). Prospect Heights, IL: Waveland.

Fishman, Mark, and Gray Cavender. 1998. *Entertaining Crime: Television Reality Programs.* New York: Aldine de Gruyter.

Fitzpatrick, Edward. 1999. "The First 'Crime of the Century' as Grace Joined Chester on the Lake, She had No Idea Fate Was Rowing Their Boat." *Times Union* (Albany, NY) (January 24): A3.

Flax, Jane. 1990. "Postmodernism and Gender Relations in Feminist Theory." Pp. 39–62 in *Feminism/Postmodernism,* Linda J. Nicholson (ed.). New York: Routledge.

Flippo, Chet. 1980. "Rock & Roll Tragedy." *Rolling Stone* (January 24): 1; 10–12; 22–24.

Foucault, Michel. 1965/88. *Madness and Civilization: A History of Insanity in the Age of Reason,* Richard Howard (tr.). New York: Vintage Books.

———. 1970/94. *The Order of Things: An Archaeology of the Human Sciences.* New York: Vintage Books.

REFERENCES

———. 1972a. *The Archaeology of Knowledge*, A. M. Sheridan Smith (tr.). New York: Pantheon.

———. 1972b. "The Discourse on Language." Pp. 215–37 in *The Archaeology of Knowledge*, A. M. Sheridan Smith (tr.). New York: Pantheon.

———. 1973/94. *The Birth of the Clinic: An Archaeology of Medical Perception*, Alan Sheridan (tr.). New York: Vintage Books.

———. 1975/79. *Discipline and Punish: The Birth of the Prison*, Alan Sheridan (tr.). New York: Vintage Books.

———. 1976/90. *The History of Sexuality*. Volume 1: *An Introduction*, Robert Hurley (tr.). New York: Vintage Books.

———. 1977. *Language, Counter-Memory, and Practice: Selected Essays and Interviews*. Donald F. Bouchard (ed.), Donald F. Bouchard and Sherry Simon (trs.). Ithaca, NY: Cornell University Press.

———. 1983. "Afterword: The Subject and Power." Pp. 208–26 in *Michel Foucault: Beyond Structuralism and Hermeneutics*, by Hubert L. Dreyfus and Paul Rabinow. Second Edition. Chicago: University of Chicago Press.

———. 1984/88. *The Care of the Self:* Volume 3 of *The History of Sexuality*, Robert Hurley (tr.). New York: Vintage Books.

———. 1984. *The Foucault Reader*, Paul Rabinow (ed). New York: Pantheon.

———. 1984/90. *The Use of Pleasure:* Volume 2 of *The History of Sexuality*, Robert Hurley (tr.). New York: Vintage Books.

———. 1997. "What is Enlightenment?" Pp. 303–14 in *Michel Foucault: Ethics, Subjectivity and Truth* (*The Essential Works of Foucault 1954–1984*, Volume 1), Paul Rabinow (ed.). New York: New Press.

Fox, James Alan, and Jack Levin. 2001. *The Will to Kill: Making Sense of Senseless Murder*. Boston: Allyn and Bacon.

Fraser, Nancy, and Linda Nicholson. 1988. "Social Criticism Without Philosophy: An Encounter between Feminism and Postmodernism." *Theory, Culture and Society* 5: 373–94.

Friedlander, Paul. 1996. *Rock and Roll: A Social History*. Boulder, CO: Westview.

Frith, Simon. 1981. *Sound Effects: Youth, Leisure, and the Politics of Rock and Roll*. New York: Pantheon.

Fuller, John G. 1981. *Are the Kids All Right?: The Rock Generation and Its Hidden Death Wish*. New York: Times Books.

Gaar, Gillian G. 1992. *She's a Rebel: The History of Women in Rock & Roll*. Seattle, WA: Seal.

Gabler, Neal. 1998. *Life the Movie: How Entertainment Conquered Reality*. New York: Knopf.

Gaines, Donna. 1991. *Teenage Wasteland: Suburbia's Dead End Kids*. New York: HarperCollins.

REFERENCES

Garfinkel, Harold. 1967. *Studies in Ethnomethodology.* Englewood Cliffs, NJ: Prentice-Hall.

Gates, Henry Louis, Jr. 1988. *The Signifying Monkey: A Theory of African-American Literary Criticism.* New York: Oxford University Press.

Gay, Peter. 1966. *The Enlightenment: An Interpretation.* Volume 1 *(The Rise of Modern Paganism).* New York: Norton.

———. 1969. *The Enlightenment: An Interpretation.* Volume 2 *(The Science of Freedom).* New York: Norton.

Geis, Gilbert, and Leigh B. Bienen. 1998. *Crimes of the Century: From Leopold and Loeb to O.J. Simpson.* Boston: Northeastern University Press.

Gelsthorpe, Loraine, and Allison Morris. 1988. "Feminism and Criminology in Britain." *British Journal of Criminology* 28 (spring): 223–40.

———. 1990. "Introduction: Transforming and Transgressing Criminology." Pp. 1–6 in *Feminist Perspectives In Criminology,* Loraine Gelsthorpe and Allison Morris (eds.). Philadelphia: Open University Press.

George, Nelson. 1988. *The Death of Rhythm & Blues.* New York: Pantheon.

Gerth, Hans, and C. Wright Mills. 1953. *Character and Social Structure: The Psychology of Social Institutions.* New York: Harcourt, Brace and Company.

Gibbs, Jack P. 1966. "Conceptions of Deviant Behavior: The Old and the New." *Pacific Sociological Review* 9: 9–14.

———. 1995. "Major Notions and Theories in the Sociology of Deviance." Pp. 64–83 in *Readings In Deviant Behavior,* Alex Thio and Thomas Calhoun (eds.). New York: HarperCollins.

Giddens, Anthony. 1990. *The Consequences of Modernity.* Stanford, CA: Stanford University Press.

———. 1991. *Modernity and Self Identity: Self and Society in the Late Modern Age.* Stanford, CA: Stanford University Press.

Gilbert, James. 1986. *A Cycle of Outrage: America's Reaction to the Juvenile Delinquent in the 1950s.* New York: Oxford University Press.

Gillett, Charlie. 1983. *The Sound of the City: The Rise of Rock and Roll.* Second Edition. New York: Pantheon.

Gilligan, James. 1997. *Violence: Reflections on a National Epidemic.* New York: Vintage.

Giuliano, Geoffrey. 1996. *Behind Blue Eyes: The Life of Pete Townshend.* New York: Dutton.

Glassner, Barry. 1999. *The Culture of Fear: Why Americans Are Afraid of the Wrong Things.* New York: Basic Books.

Goffman, Erving. 1959. *The Presentation of Self in Everyday Life.* New York: Doubleday Anchor.

———. 1961. *Asylums: Essays on the Social Situation of Mental Patients and Other Inmates.* New York: Doubleday Anchor.

REFERENCES

———. 1963a. *Behavior in Public Places: Notes on the Social Organization of Gatherings.* New York: Free Press.

———. 1963b. *Stigma: Notes on the Management of Spoiled Identity.* Englewood Cliffs, NJ: Prentice-Hall.

———. 1967. *Interaction Ritual.* Chicago: Aldine.

———. 1971. *Relations in Public: Microstudies of the Public Order.* New York: Basic Books.

———. 1974. *Frame Analysis.* New York: Harper.

———. 1979. *Gender Advertisements.* New York: Harper and Row.

———. 1981. *Forms of Talk.* Philadelphia: University of Pennsylvania Press.

Goldberg, David J. 1999. *Discontented America: The United States in the 1920s.* Baltimore: Johns Hopkins University Press.

Goldberg, David Theo. 1993. *Racist Culture: Philosophy and the Politics of Meaning.* Oxford: Blackwell.

———. 1997. *Racial Subjects: Writing on Race in America.* New York Routledge.

Goode, Erich. 1975. "On Behalf of Labeling Theory." *Social Problems* 22: 570–83.

———. 1981. "Deviance, Norms, and Social Reaction." *Deviant Behavior* 3: 47–53.

———. 1996a. "Preface." Pp. vii–ix in *Social Deviance,* Erich Goode (ed.). Boston: Allyn and Bacon.

———. 1996b. "The Stigma of Obesity." Pp. 332–40 in *Social Deviance,* Erich Goode (ed.). Boston: Allyn and Bacon.

———. 2001. *Deviant Behavior.* Sixth Edition. Upper Saddle River, NJ: Prentice-Hall.

———. 2003. "The MacGuffin That Refuses to Die: An Investigation into the Condition of the Sociology of Deviance." *Deviant Behavior* 24: 507–33.

Goode, Erich, and Joanne Preissler. 1983. "The Fat Admirer." *Deviant Behavior* 4: 175–202.

Goode, Erich, and Nachman Ben-Yehuda. 1994. *Moral Panics: The Social Construction of Deviance.* Cambridge, MA: Blackwell.

Goodman, Fred. 1997. *The Mansion on the Hill: Dylan, Young, Geffen, Springsteen, and the Head-on Collision of Rock and Commerce.* New York: Times Books.

Gottdiener, Mark. 1994. "The System of Objects and the Commodification of Everyday Life." Pp. 25–40 in *Baudrillard: A Critical Reader,* Douglas Kellner (ed.). Cambridge, MA: Blackwell.

Gouldner, Alvin W. 1968. "The Sociologist as Partisan: Sociology and the Welfare State." *American Sociologist* 3: 103–16.

———. 1970. *The Coming Crisis of Western Sociology.* New York: Basic Books.

Gove, Walter R. (ed.). 1980. *The Labelling of Deviance: Evaluating a Perspective.* Second Edition. Beverly Hills, CA: Sage.

REFERENCES

Gramsci, Antonio. 1971. *Selections From the Prison Notebooks of Antonio Gramsci.* Quintin Hoare and Geoffrey Nowell Smith (eds. and tr.). New York: International Publishers.

Gray, Chris Hables. 1997. *Postmodern War: The New Politics of Conflict.* New York: Guilford Press.

Greenberg, David F. 1988. *The Construction of Homosexuality.* Chicago: University of Chicago Press.

Gross, Edward. 1978. "Organizational Crime: A Theoretical Perspective." Pp. 55-86 in *Studies in Symbolic Interaction* (Volume 1), Norman K. Denzin (ed.). Greenwich, CT: JAI.

Grossberg, Lawrence, Cary Nelson, and Paula Treichler (eds.). 1992. *Cultural Studies.* New York: Routledge.

Gumpert, Gary, and Robert Cathcart. 1986. "Mediated Interpersonal Communication: Toward a New Typology." Pp. 9–16 in *Inter/Media: Interpersonal Communication in a Media World,* Gary Gumpert and Robert Cathcart (eds.). New York: Oxford University Press.

Gurr, Ted Robert (ed). 1989a. *Violence in America.* Volume 1 *(The History of Crime).* Thousand Oaks, CA: Sage.

——— (ed.). 1989b. *Violence in America.* Volume 2 *(Protest, Rebellion, Reform).* Thousand Oaks, CA: Sage.

Gusfield, Joseph R. 1963/86. *The Symbolic Crusade: Status Politics and the American Temperance Movement.* Urbana: University of Illinois Press.

Habermas, Jurgen. 1993. "Modernity Versus Postmodernity." Pp. 91–104 in *A Postmodern Reader,* Joseph Natoli and Linda Hutcheon (eds.). Albany: State University of New York Press.

Hale, Grace Elizabeth. 1998. *Making Whiteness: The Culture of Segregation in the South, 1890–1940.* New York: Pantheon Books.

Hall, G. Stanley. 1904. *Adolescence.* Two Volumes. New York: D. Appleton.

Hall, John A. 1990. "Social Interaction, Culture, and Historical Studies." Pp. 16–45 in *Symbolic Interaction and Cultural Studies,* Howard S. Becker and Michal M. McCall (eds.). Chicago: University of Chicago Press.

Hall, Peter. 1972. "A Symbolic Interactionist Analysis of Politics." *Sociological Inquiry* 42: 35–75.

———. 2003. "Interactionism, Social Organization, and Social Processes: Looking Back and Moving Ahead." *Symbolic Interaction* 26 (winter): 33–55.

Hall, Stuart. 1980a. "Cultural Studies and the Centre: Some Problematics and Problems." Pp. 17–47 in *Culture, Media, Language: Working Papers in Cultural Studies, 1972–1979,* S. Hall, D. Hobson, A. Lowe, and P. Willis (eds.). London: Hutchinson.

REFERENCES

———. 1980b. "Encoding/decoding." Pp. 128–38 in *Culture, Media, Language: Working Papers in Cultural Studies, 1972–1979,* S. Hall, D. Hobson, A. Lowe, and P. Willis (eds.). London: Hutchinson.

———. 1980c. "Introduction to Media Studies at the Centre." Pp. 117–21 in *Culture, Media, Language: Working Papers in Cultural Studies, 1972–1979,* S. Hall, D. Hobson, A. Lowe, and P. Willis (eds.). London: Hutchinson.

———. 1986a. "On Postmodernism and Articulation: An Interview." *Journal of Communication Inquiry* 10: 45–60.

———. 1986b. "The Problem of Ideology—Marxism Without Guarantees." *Journal of Communication Inquiry* 10: 28–44.

———. 1992. "Cultural Studies and its Theoretical Legacies." Pp. 277–94 in *Cultural Studies,* Lawrence Grossberg, Cary Nelson, and Paula Treichler (eds.). New York: Routledge.

———. 1993. "What Is This 'Black' in Black Popular Culture?" *Social Justice* 20: 104–14.

Hall, Stuart, and Tony Jefferson. 1975/2002a. "Introduction." Pp. 5–7 in *Resistance through Rituals: Youth Subcultures in Post-War Britain,* Stuart Hall and Tony Jefferson (eds.). London: Routledge.

Hall, Stuart, and Tony Jefferson (eds.). 1975/2002b. *Resistance through Rituals: Youth Subcultures in Post-War Britain.* London: Routledge.

Hall, Stuart, Dorothy Hobson, Andrew Lowe, and Paul Willis (eds.). 1980. *Culture, Media, Language: Working Papers in Cultural Studies.* London: Hutchinson.

Halley, Janet E. 2000. "'Like Race' Arguments." Pp. 40–74 in *What's Left of Theory?: New Work on the Politics of Literary Theory,* Judith Butler, John Guillory, and Kendall Thomas (eds.). New York: Routledge.

Haraway, Donna. 1995. "Fractured Identities." Pp. 95–99 in *Class,* Patrick Joyce (ed.). Oxford: Oxford University Press.

Harding, Sandra. 1990. "Feminism, Science, and the Anti-Enlightenment Critiques." Pp. 83–106 in *Feminism/Postmodernism,* Linda J. Nicholson (ed.). New York: Routledge.

Harman, Lesley D. 1985. "Acceptable Deviance as Social Control: The Cases of Fashion and Slang." *Deviant Behavior* 6: 1–15.

Harron, Mary. 1988. "McRock: Pop as a Commodity." Pp. 173–220 in *Facing the Music,* Simon Frith (ed.). New York: Pantheon.

Hartsock, Nancy. 1987. "The Feminist Standpoint: Developing the Ground for a Specifically Feminist Historical Materialism." Pp. 157–80 in *Feminism and Methodology,* Sandra Harding (ed.). Milton Keynes: Open University Press.

Harvey, David. 1990. *The Condition of Postmodernity: An Enquiry into the Origins of Cultural Change.* Cambridge, MA: Blackwell.

Hebdige, Dick. 1979/2002. *Subculture: The Meaning of Style.* London: Routledge.

REFERENCES

Heller, Agnes. 1993. "Existentialism, Alienation, Postmodernism: Cultural Movements As Vehicles of Change In Everyday Life." Pp. 497–509 in *A Postmodern Reader,* Joseph Natoli and Linda Hutcheon (eds.). Albany: State University of New York Press.

Henry, Stuart, and Dragan Milovanovic. 1996. *Constitutive Criminology: Beyond Postmodernism.* Thousand Oaks, CA: Sage.

Herman, Gary. *The Who.* 1971. New York: Macmillan.

Herman, Nancy J. 2002. "'Mixed Nutters,' 'Looney Tuners,' and 'Daffy Ducks.'" Pp. 244–56 in *Deviance: The Interactionist Perspective,* Earl Rubington and Martin S. Weinberg (eds.). Eighth Edition. Boston: Allyn and Bacon.

Hester, Stephen, and Peter Eglin. 1992. *A Sociology of Crime.* London: Routledge.

Hildebrand, David L. 2003. *Beyond Realism and Antirealism: John Dewey and the Neopragmatists.* Nashville, TN: Vanderbilt University Press.

Hofstadter, Richard. 1944/55. *Social Darwinism in American Thought.* Revised Edition. Boston: Beacon Press.

Hoggart, Richard. 1957/98. *The Uses of Literacy.* New Brunswick, NJ: Transaction.

Hollinger, Robert. 1994. *Postmodernism and the Social Sciences: A Thematic Approach.* Thousand Oaks, CA: Sage.

Holmes, Ronald M., and Stephen T. Holmes (eds.). 1998. *Contemporary Perspectives on Serial Murder.* Thousand Oaks, CA: Sage.

Holmes, Ronald M., and Stephen T. Holmes. 2001. *Murder in America.* Second Edition. Thousand Oaks, CA: Sage.

Holstein, James A., and Jaber F. Gubrium. 2000. *The Self We Live By: Narrative Identity in a Postmodern World.* New York: Oxford University Press.

Hook, Sidney. 1974. *Pragmatism and the Tragic Sense of Life.* New York: Basic Books.

hooks, bell. 1982. *Ain't I a Woman?* London: Pluto Press.

———. 1990. *Yearning: Race, Gender, and Cultural Politics.* Boston: South End Press.

———. 1992. *Black Looks: Race and Representation.* Boston: South End Press.

Hoopes, James. 1991. "Introduction." Pp. 1–13 in *Peirce on Signs: Writings on Semiotic by Charles Sanders Peirce,* James Hoopes (ed.). Chapel Hill: University of North Carolina Press.

Horkheimer, Max, and Theodor Adorno. 1972. *Dialectic of Enlightenment.* New York: Herder and Herder.

Horowitz, Irving Louis. 1983. *C. Wright Mills: An American Utopian.* New York: Free Press.

Howe, Adrian. 1990. "Prologue to a History of Women's Imprisonment: In Search of a Feminist Perspective." *Social Justice* 17 (summer): 5–22.

REFERENCES

Howells, Christina. 1992. "Conclusion: Sartre and the Deconstruction of the Subject." Pp. 318–52 in *The Cambridge Companion to Sartre*, Christina Howells (ed.). Cambridge: Cambridge University Press.

———.1999. *Derrida: Deconstruction from Phenomenology to Ethics.* Cambridge: Polity Press.

Huey, Jacklyn, and Michael J. Lynch. 1996. "The Image of Black Women In Criminology: Historical Stereotypes As Theoretical Foundation." Pp. 72–88 in *Justice with Prejudice: Race and Criminal Justice In America*, Michael J. Lynch and E. Britt Patterson (eds.). Albany, NY: Harrow and Heston.

Hughes, Everett C. 1958. *Men and Their Work.* New York: Free Press.

Humphreys, Laud. 1970/75. *Tearoom Trade: Impersonal Sex in Public Places.* Enlarged Edition. New York: Aldine de Gruyter.

Hunter, Ronald D., and Mark L. Dantzker. 2002. *Crime and Criminality: Causes and Consequences.* Upper Saddle River, NJ: Prentice-Hall.

Hussman, Lawrence E. 1995. "Squandered Possibilities: The Film Versions of Dreiser's Novels." Pp. 176–200 in *Theodore Dreiser: Beyond Naturalism*, Miriam Gogol (ed.). New York: New York University Press.

Huyssen, Andreas. 1990. "Mapping the Postmodern." Pp. 234–77 in *Feminism/Postmodernism*, Linda J. Nicholson (ed.). New York: Routledge.

Ibarra, Peter R., and John I. Kitsuse. 1993. "Vernacular Constituents of Moral Discourse: An Interactionist Proposal for the Study of Social Problems." Pp. 21–54 in *Constructionist Controversies: Issues in Social Problems Theory*, Gale Miller and James Holstein (eds.). New York: Aldine de Gruyter.

Ingraham, Chrys. 1994. "The Heterosexual Imaginary: Feminist Sociology and Theories of Gender." *Sociological Theory* 12 (July): 203–19.

Jacobs, Jerry. 1967. "A Phenomenological Study of Suicide Notes." *Social Problems* 15: 60–72.

James, William. 1890/1950. *The Principles of Psychology.* Two Volumes. New York: Dover.

———. 1907/91. *Pragmatism.* Buffalo, NY: Prometheus.

———. 1909/87. *The Meaning of Truth.* Pp. 821–978 in *William James: Writings 1902-1910*, Bruce Kuklick (ed.). New York: Library of America.

Jameson, Fredric. 1991. *Postmodernism or, The Cultural Logic of Late Capitalism.* Durham, NC: Duke University Press.

———. 2002. *A Singular Modernity: Essay on the Oncology of the Present.* London: Verso.

Jenkins, Philip. 1994. *Using Murder: The Social Construction of Serial Homicide.* New York: Aldine de Gruyter.

———. 1996. *Pedophiles and Priests: Anatomy of a Contemporary Crisis.* New York: Oxford University Press.

REFERENCES

———. 1998. "'The Ice Age': The Social Construction of a Drug Panic." Pp. 137–60 in *Constructing Crime: Perspectives on Making News and Social Problems,* Gary W. Potter and Victor E. Kappeler (eds.). Prospect Heights, IL: Waveland.

———. 2003a. *Images of Terror: What We Can and Can't Know About Terrorism.* New York: Aldine de Gruyter.

———. 2003b. *The New Anti-Catholicism: The Last Acceptable Prejudice.* New York: Oxford University Press.

Jervis, John. 1998. *Exploring the Modern: Patterns of Western Culture and Civilization.* Oxford: Blackwell.

———. 1999. *Transgressing the Modern: Explorations in the Western Experience of Otherness.* Oxford: Blackwell.

Joas, Hans. 1985. *G. H. Mead: A Contemporary Re-examination of His Thought.* Cambridge, MA: MIT Press.

———. 1993. *Pragmatism and Social Theory.* Chicago: University of Chicago Press.

Johnson, Barbara. 1981. "Translator's Introduction." Pp. vii–xxxii in *Dissemination* by Jacques Derrida. Chicago: University of Chicago Press.

Johnson, John M. 1985. "Symbolic Salvation." Pp. 289–305 in *Studies in Symbolic Interaction,* Volume 6, Norman K. Denzin (ed.). Greenwich, CT: JAI Press.

———. 1988. "Media Manslaughter." Pp. 201–8 in *Studies in Symbolic Interaction,* Volume 9, Norman K. Denzin (ed.). Greenwich, CT: JAI Press.

———. 1989. "Horror Stories and the Construction of Child Abuse." Pp. 5–19 in *Images of Issues: Typifying Contemporary Social Problems,* Joel Best (ed.). New York: Aldine de Gruyter.

Johnson, Richard. 1986/87. "What is Cultural Studies Anyway?" *Social Text* 16: 38–80.

Jones, John Paul, III, Wolfgang Natter, and Theodore R. Schatzki (eds.). 1993. *Postmodern Contentions: Epochs, Politics, Space.* New York: Guilford Press.

Jordan, Glenn, and Chris Weedon. 1995. *Cultural Politics: Class, Gender, Race and the Postmodern World.* Oxford: Blackwell.

Joyce, Patrick (ed.). 1995. *Class.* Oxford: Oxford University Press.

Kaplan, Amy. 1988. *The Social Construction of American Realism.* Chicago: University of Chicago Press.

Katovich, Michael A. 2003. "Hall's Hope and the Focus Next Time: Let Us Now Study Social Structure." *Symbolic Interaction* 26 (winter): 57–66.

Katz, Ephraim. 1994. *The Film Encyclopedia.* Second Edition. New York: HarperCollins.

Katz, Jack. 1988. *Seductions of Crime: Moral and Sensual Attractions in Doing Evil.* New York: Basic Books.

REFERENCES

Kellner, Douglas. 1988. "Postmodernism as Social Theory: Some Challenges and Problems." *Theory, Culture and Society* 5: 239-69.

———. 1989. *Jean Baudrillard: From Marxism to Postmodernism and Beyond.* Stanford, CA: Stanford University Press.

———. (ed.). 1994. *Baudrillard: A Critical Reader.* Cambridge, MA: Blackwell.

———. 1995. *Media Culture: Cultural Studies, Identity and Politics Between the Modern and Postmodern.* London: Routledge.

———. 2001. *Grand Theft 2000: Media Spectacle and a Stolen Election.* Lanham, MD: Rowman and Littlefield.

———. 2003a. *From 9/11 to Terror War: The Dangers of the Bush Legacy.* Lanham, MD: Rowman and Littlefield.

———. 2003b. *Media Spectacle.* London: Routledge.

Kent, Matt. (May 7, 2003a). "Pete Not To Be Charged." Retrieved June 30, 2003 from http://petetownshend.co/uk/diary/display.cmf?id=37&zone=pr

———. (May 20, 2003b). "Pete Emails Rolling Stone." Retrieved June 30, 2003 from http://petetownshend.co.uk/diary/display.cmf?id=40&zone=pr

———. (June 2, 2003c). "Phoenix Survivors Issue New Statement Regarding Pete." Retrieved June 30, 2003 from http://petetownshend.co.uk/diary/display.cmf?id=42&zone=pr

Kitsuse, John I. 1962. "Societal Reaction to Deviant Behavior: Problems of Theory and Method." *Social Problems* 9: 247–56.

Klapp, Orrin E. 1962. *Heroes, Villains, and Fools: The Changing American Character.* Englewood Cliffs, NJ: Prentice-Hall.

———. 1964. *Symbolic Leaders: Public Dramas and Public Men.* Chicago: Aldine.

———. 1969. *Collective Search for Identity.* New York: Holt, Rinehart, and Winston.

———. 1991. *Inflation of Symbols: Loss of Values in American Culture.* New Brunswick, NJ: Transaction.

Klein, Dorie. 1995a. "Crime Through Gender's Prism: Feminist Criminology in the United States." Pp. 216–40 in *International Feminist Perspectives in Criminology: Engendering a Discipline,* Nicole Hahn Rafter and Frances Heidensohn (eds.). Philadelphia: Open University Press.

———. 1995b. "The Etiology of Female Crime: A Review of the Literature." Pp. 30–47 in *The Criminal Justice System and Women: Offenders, Victims, and Workers,* Barbara Raffel Price and Natalie J. Sokoloff (eds.). New York: McGraw-Hill.

———. 1995c. "Twenty Years Ago . . . Today: Afterword to 'The Etiology of Female Crime.'" Pp. 47–53 in *The Criminal Justice System and Women: Offenders, Victims, and Workers,* Barbara Raffel Price and Natalie J. Sokoloff (eds.). New York: McGraw-Hill.

REFERENCES

Kotarba, Joseph A. 1994. "The Postmodernization of Rock and Roll Music: The Case of Metallica." Pp. 141–63 in *Adolescents and Their Music: If It's Too Loud, You're Too Old,* Jonathon S. Epstein (ed.). New York: Garland.

Kracauer, Siegfried. 1960. *Theory of Film: The Redemption of Physical Reality.* New York: Oxford University Press.

Krzycki, Lenny. 1996. "Race, Popular Culture and the News." Pp. 89–103 in *Justice With Prejudice: Race and Criminal Justice In America,* Michael J. Lynch and E. Britt Patterson (eds.). Albany, NY: Harrow and Heston.

Kuhn, Manford H. 1964a. "Major Trends in Symbolic Interaction Theory in the Past Twenty-Five Years." *Sociological Quarterly* 5: 61–84.

———. 1964b. "The Reference Group Reconsidered." *Sociological Quarterly* 5: 5–21.

Kuklick, H. 1973. "A 'Scientific Revolution': Sociological Theory in the United States 1930–45." *Sociological Inquiry* 43: 3–22.

Kurtz, Lester R. 1984. *Evaluating Chicago Sociology: A Guide to the Literature with an Annotated Bibliography.* Chicago: University of Chicago Press.

Layder, Derek. 1994. *Understanding Social Theory.* London: Sage.

Leach, William. 1993. *Land of Desire: Merchants, Power, and the Rise of a New American Culture.* New York: Pantheon.

Lehan, Richard. 1969. *Theodore Dreiser: His World and His Novels.* Carbondale: Southern Illinois University Press.

———. 1995. "The European Background." Pp. 47–73 in *The Cambridge Companion to American Realism and Naturalism: Howells to London,* Donald Pizer (ed.). Cambridge: Cambridge University Press.

Lemert, Charles. 1979. *Sociology and the Twilight of Man: Homocentrism and Discourse in Sociological Theory.* Carbondale: Southern Illinois University Press.

———. 1992. "Series Editor's Preface." Pp. xii–xi in *Symbolic Interactionism and Cultural Studies: The Politics of Interpretation,* by Norman K. Denzin. Cambridge, MA: Blackwell.

———. 1994. "Dark Thoughts About the Self." Pp. 100–29 in *Social Theory and the Politics of Identity,* Craig Calhoun (ed.). Cambridge, MA: Blackwell.

———. 1995. *Sociology After the Crisis.* Boulder, CO: Westview.

———. 1997. *Postmodernism Is Not What You Think.* Malden, MA: Blackwell.

———. 2002. *Dark Thoughts: Race and the Eclipse of Society.* New York: Routledge.

Lemert, Edwin M. 1951. *Social Pathology.* New York: McGraw-Hill.

———. 1972. *Human Deviance, Social Problems, and Social Control.* Second Edition. Englewood Cliffs, NJ: Prentice-Hall.

———. 1974. "Beyond Mead: The Societal Reaction to Deviance." *Social Problems* 21: 457–68.

REFERENCES

Leonard, Eileen. 1995. "Theoretical Criminology and Gender." Pp. 54–70 in *The Criminal Justice System and Women: Offenders, Victims, and Workers*, Barbara Raffel Price and Natalie J. Sokoloff (eds.). New York: McGraw-Hill.

Lerner, Gerda (ed.). 1972/92. *Black Women In White America.* New York: Vintage.

———. 1976. "New Approaches to the Study of Women in American History." Pp. 349–56 in *Liberating Women's History: Theoretical and Critical Essays*, Berenice A. Carroll (ed.). Urbana: University of Illinois Press.

———. 1986. *The Creation of Patriarchy.* New York: Oxford University Press.

———. 1990. "Reconceptualizing Differences Among Women." *Journal of Women's History* 1 (winter): 106–22.

———. 1993. *The Creation of Feminist Consciousness: From the Middle Ages to Eighteen-seventy.* New York: Oxford University Press.

Leslie, Paul (ed.). 1997. *The Gulf War as Popular Entertainment: An Analysis of the Military-Industrial Media Complex.* Lewiston, NY: Edwin Mellen.

Leslie, Paul, and Daniel Dotter. 1999. "Postmodern Paradox of the Real and the Night Train To Nowhere: Big Bands As Embedded Popular Culture." *Quarterly Journal of Ideology* 22 (December): 1–16.

Levin, Jack. 2002. *The Violence of Hate: Confronting Racism, Anti-Semitism, and Other Forms of Bigotry.* Boston: Allyn and Bacon.

Levi-Strauss, Claude. 1963. *Structural Anthropology.* New York: Basic Books.

Lévy, Bernard-Henri. 2003. *Who Killed Daniel Pearl?* James X. Mitchell (tr.). Hoboken, NJ: Melville House Publishing.

Lewis, J. David, and Richard L. Smith. 1980. *American Sociology and Pragmatism.* Chicago: University of Chicago Press.

Lewis, David Levering. 1994. "Introduction." Pp. xiii–xli in *The Portable Harlem Renaissance Reader,* David Levering Lewis (ed.). New York: Penquin.

Liazos, Alexander. 1972. "The Poverty of the Sociology of Deviance: Nuts, Sluts, and 'Preverts.'" *Social Problems* 20: 103–20.

Lichtman, Richard T. 1970. "Symbolic Interactionism and Social Reality: Some Marxist Queries." *Berkeley Journal of Sociology* 15: 75–94.

Lilla, Mark. 1998. "The Politics of Jacques Derrida." *New York Review of Books* XLV (June 25): 36–41.

Lincoln, Yvonna S., and Norman K. Denzin. 1994. "The Fifth Moment." Pp. 575–86 in *Handbook of Qualitative Research,* Norman K. Denzin and Yvonna S. Lincoln (eds.). Thousand Oaks, CA: Sage.

Lingeman, Richard. 1986. *Theodore Dreiser.* Volume 1 *(At the Gate of The City, 1871–1907).* New York. G. P. Putnam's Sons.

———. 1990. *Theodore Dreiser.* Volume 2 *(An American Journey, 1908–1945).* G. P. Putnam's Sons.

Lofland, John. 1969. *Deviance and Identity.* Englewood Cliffs, NJ: Prentice-Hall.

Lofquist, William S. 1996. "Constructing 'Crime': Media Coverage of Individual and Organizational Wrongdoing." Pp. 241–61 in *Constructing Crime: Perspectives on Making News and Social Problems,* Gary W. Potter and Victor E. Kappeler (eds.). Prospect Heights, IL: Waveland.

London, Herbert I. 1984. *Closing the Circle: A Cultural History of the Rock Revolution.* Chicago: Nelson-Hall.

London Times. (May 8, 2003). "Pete Townshend on Sex Register over Child Porn" Retrieved June 30, 2003 from http://www.timesonline.co.uk/printFriendly/0,,1-2-673078,00.html

Lorber, Judith (ed.). 1998. *Gender Inequality: Feminist Theories and Politics.* Los Angeles: Roxbury.

Loseke, Donileen R. 1993. "Constructing Conditions, People, Morality, and Emotion: Expanding the Agenda of Constructionism." Pp. 207–14 in *Constructionist Controversies: Issues in Social Problems Theory,* Gale Miller and James Holstein (eds.). New York: Aldine de Gruyter.

Lucy, Niall. 1997. *Postmodern Literary Theory: An Introduction.* Oxford: Blackwell.

Lundquist, James. 1974. *Theodore Dreiser.* New York: Frederick Ungar Publishing.

Lyman, Stanford M. 1995. "1994 MSSA Presidential Address: The Bequests of 20th Century Sociology To the 21st Century." *Sociological Spectrum* 15: 209–25.

———. 1997a. "Anhedonia: Gender and the Decline of Emotions in American Film, 1930–1988." Pp. 210–33 in *Postmodernism and a Sociology of the Absurd and Other Essays on the "Nouvelle Vague" in American Social Science,* by Stanford M. Lyman. Fayetteville: University of Arkansas Press.

———. 1997b. "Postmodernism and the Construction of Ethnocultural Identity: The Jewish-Indian Theory and the Lost Tribes of Israel." *Sociological Spectrum* 17: 259–82.

———. 1997c. "Postmodernism and a Sociology of the Absurd." Pp. 11–43 in *Postmodernism and a Sociology of the Absurd and Other Essays on the "Nouvelle Vague" in American Social Science,* by Stanford M. Lyman. Fayetteville: University of Arkansas Press.

———. 1997d. "Without Morals or Mores: Deviance in Postmodern Social Theory." Pp. 234–64 in *Postmodernism and a Sociology of the Absurd and Other Essays on the "Nouvelle Vague" in American Social Science,* by Stanford M. Lyman. Fayetteville: University of Arkansas Press.

Lyman, Stanford M., and Marvin B. Scott. 1970. *A Sociology of the Absurd.* Pacific Palisades, CA: Goodyear.

Lyman, Stanford M., and Arthur J. Vidich. 1988. *Social Order and the Public Philosophy: The Analysis and Interpretation of the Work of Herbert Blumer.* Fayetteville: University of Arkansas Press.

REFERENCES

Lynn, Steven. 1994. *Texts and Contexts: Writing About Literature With Critical Theory.* New York: HarperCollins.

Lyotard, Jean-Francois. 1979/84. *The Postmodern Condition: A Report on Knowledge.* Geoff Bennington and Brian Massumi (trs.). Minneapolis: University of Minnesota Press.

———. 1988. *Pereginations: Law, Form, Event.* New York: Columbia University Press.

———. 1991. *The Inhuman,* Geoffrey Bennington and Rachel Bowlby (trs.). Stanford, CA: Stanford University Press.

———. 1997. *Postmodern Fables,* Georges Van Den Abbeele (tr.). Minneapolis: University of Minnesota Press.

MacIntyre, Alasdair. 1970. *Herbert Marcuse: An Exposition and Polemic.* New York: Viking.

Maines, David R. 1996a. "On Choices and Criticism: A Reply to Denzin." *Symbolic Interaction* 19: 357–62.

———. 1996b. "On Postmodernism, Pragmatism, and Plasterers: Some Interactionist Thoughts and Queries." *Symbolic Interaction* 19: 323–40.

———. 2001. *The Faultline of Consciousness: A View of Interactionism in Sociology.* New York: Aldine de Gruyter.

———. 2003. "Interactionism's Place." *Symbolic Interaction* 26 (winter): 5–18.

Makaryk, Irena R. (ed.). 1993. *Encyclopedia of Contemporary Literary Theory: Approaches, Scholars, Terms.* Toronto: University of Toronto Press.

Makower, Joel. 1989. *Woodstock: The Oral History.* New York: Doubleday.

Mankoff, Milton. 1985. "Societal Reaction and Career Deviance: A Critical Analysis." Pp. 314–31 in *Theories of Deviance,* Stuart H. Traub and Craig B. Little (eds.). Third Edition. Itasca, IL: Peacock.

Mann, Coramae Richey, and Marjorie S. Zatz. 1998. *Images of Color; Images of Crime: Readings.* Los Angeles: Roxbury.

Manning, Peter K. 2002. "The Sky Is Not Falling." *Journal of Contemporary Ethnography* 31 (August): 490–98.

———. 2003. "Semiotics, Pragmatism, and Narratives." Pp. 1021–39 in *Handbook of Symbolic Interactionism,* Larry T. Reynolds and Nancy J. Herman-Kinney (eds.). Walnut Creek, CA: AltaMira Press.

Manning, Peter K., and Betsy Cullum-Swan. 1994. "Narrative, Content, and Semiotic Analysis." Pp. 463–77 in *Handbook of Qualitative Research,* Norman K. Denzin and Yvonna S. Lincoln (eds.). Thousand Oaks, CA: Sage.

Manning, Philip. 1992. *Erving Goffman and Modern Sociology.* Stanford, CA: Stanford University Press.

Marcus, George E. 1994. "What Comes (Just) After 'Post'?: The Case of Ethnography." Pp. 563–74 in *Handbook of Qualitative Research,* Norman K. Denzin and Yvonna S. Lincoln (eds.). Thousand Oaks, CA: Sage.

REFERENCES

Marcus, George E., and Michael M. J. Fisher. 1986. *Anthropology as Cultural Critique: An Experimental Moment in the Human Sciences.* Chicago: University of Chicago Press.

Marcus, Greil. 1975/97. *Mystery Train: Images of America in Rock 'n' Roll Music.* New York: Plume.

———. 1980. "Pete Townshend: The Rolling Stone Interview." *Rolling Stone* (June 26): 34–39.

Marcuse, Herbert. 1964/91. *One-Dimensional Man: Studies in the Ideology of Advanced Industrial Society.* Second Edition. Boston: Beacon Press.

Marsh, Dave. 1983. *Before I Get Old: The Story of the Who.* New York: St. Martin's Press.

Martindale, Don. 1960. *The Nature and Types of Sociological Theory.* Boston: Houghton Mifflin.

Matthews, Fred H. 1977. *Robert E. Park and the Chicago School: Quest for an American Sociology.* Montreal: McGill-Queen's University Press.

Matza, David. 1964. *Delinquency and Drift.* New York: John Wiley.

———. 1969. *Becoming Deviant.* Englewood Cliffs, NJ: Prentice-Hall.

McCall, Michal M., and Howard S. Becker. 1990. "Introduction." Pp. 1–15 in *Symbolic Interaction and Cultural Studies,* Howard S. Becker and Michal M. McCall (eds.). Chicago: University of Chicago Press.

McDermott, John J. 1981. "Introduction." Pp. xv–xl in *The Philosophy of John Dewey: Two Volumes in One.* John J. McDermott (ed.). Chicago: University of Chicago Press.

McFarlane, James. 1976/91. "The Mind of Modernism." Pp. 71–93 in *Modernism: A Guide to European Literature 1890–1930.* London: Penguin.

McGerr, Michael. 2003. *A Fierce Discontent: The Rise and Fall of the Progressive Movement in America, 1870-1920.* New York: Free Press.

McRobbie, Angela. 1990. "Settling Accounts with Subcultures: A Feminist Critique." Pp. 66–80 in *On Record: Rock, Pop, and the Written Word,* Simon Frith and Andrew Goodman (eds.). New York: Pantheon.

———. 1992. "Post-Marxism and Cultural Studies." Pp. 718–30 in *Cultural Studies,* Lawrence Grossberg, Cary Nelson, and Paula Treichler (eds.). New York: Routledge.

———. 1994. *Postmodernism and Popular Culture.* London: Routledge.

Mead, George Herbert. 1903/64. "The Definition of the Psychical." Pp. 25–59 in *George Herbert Mead: Selected Writings,* Andrew J. Reck (ed.). Chicago: University of Chicago Press.

———. 1910/64. "What Social Objects Must Psychology Presuppose?" Pp. 105–13 in *George Herbert Mead: Selected Writings,* Andrew J. Reck (ed.). Chicago: University of Chicago Press.

REFERENCES

———. 1932/80. *The Philosophy of the Present.* Arthur E. Murphy (ed.). Chicago: University of Chicago Press.

———. 1934. *Mind, Self, and Society from the Standpoint of a Social Behaviorist.* Charles W. Morris (ed.). Chicago: University of Chicago Press.

———. 1936. *Movements of Thought in the Nineteenth Century.* Merrit H. Moore (ed.). Chicago: University of Chicago Press.

———. 1938. *The Philosophy of the Act.* Charles W. Morris (ed.). Chicago: University of Chicago Press.

———. 1964a. *George Herbert Mead: On Social Psychology.* Anselm Strauss (ed.). Chicago: University of Chicago Press.

———. 1964b. *Selected Writings: George Herbert Mead.* Andrew Reck (ed.). Chicago: University of Chicago Press.

———. 1982. *The Individual and the Social Self: Unpublished Work of George Herbert Mead.* David L. Miller (ed.). Chicago: University of Chicago Press.

Menand, Louis. 1997. "An Introduction to Pragmatism." Pp. xi–xxxiv in *Pragmatism: A Reader,* Louis Menand (ed.). New York: Vintage.

———. 2001. *The Metaphysical Club: A Story of Ideas in America.* New York: Farrar, Straus and Giroux.

Messerschmidt, James W. 1993. *Masculinities and Crime: Critique and Reconceptualization of Theory.* Lanham, MD: Rowman and Littlefield.

Meyrowitz, Joshua. 1985. *No Sense of Place: The Impact of Electronic Media on Social Behavior.* New York: Oxford University Press.

Miethe, Terance, D., and Richard C. McCorkle. 2001. *Crime Profiles: The Anatomy of Dangerous Persons, Places, and Situations.* Second Edition. Los Angeles: Roxbury.

Miller, David L. 1973/80. *George Herbert Mead: Self, Language, and the World.* Chicago: University of Chicago Press.

Miller, Gale, and James A. Holstein (eds.). 1993. *Constructionist Controversies: Issues in Social Problems Theory.* New York: Aldine de Gruyter.

Miller, James. 1999. *Flowers in the Dustbin: The Rise of Rock and Roll, 1947–1977.* New York: Simon & Schuster.

Miller, Leslie J. 1993. "Claims-Making from the Underside: Marginalization and Social Problems Analysis." Pp. 21–54 in *Constructionist Controversies: Issues in Social Problems Theory,* Gale Miller and James Holstein (eds.). New York: Aldine de Gruyter.

Millman, Marcia. 1975. "She Did It All for Love: A Feminist View of the Sociology of Deviance." Pp. 251–79 in *Another Voice: Feminist Perspectives on Social Life and Social Science,* Marcia Millman and Rosabeth Moss Kantor (eds.). Garden City, NY: Doubleday-Anchor.

Mills, C. Wright. 1948. *The New Men of Power: America's Labor Leaders.* New York: Harcourt.

———. 1951. *White Collar.* New York: Oxford University Press.

———. 1956. *The Power Elite.* New York: Oxford University Press.

———. 1959. *The Sociological Imagination.* New York: Oxford University Press.

———. 1963. *Power, Politics and People: The Collected Essays of C. Wright Mills.* Irving Louis Horowitz (ed.). New York: Ballantine.

———. 1964. *Sociology and Pragmatism.* New York: Oxford University Press.

Mitchell, Lee Clark. 1989. *Determining Fictions: American Literary Naturalism.* New York: Columbia University Press.

Mitroff, Ian I., and Warren Bennis. 1989/93. *The Unreality Industry: The Deliberate Manufacturing of Falsehood and What It is Doing to Our Lives.* New York: Oxford University Press.

Moers, Ellen. 1969. *Two Dreisers.* New York: Viking.

Monaco, James. 2000. *How to Read a Film: The World of Movies, Media, and Multimedia: Art, Technology, Language History Theory.* Third Edition. New York: Oxford University Press.

Moore, Michael C., and Lynda J. Moore. 1997. "Fall from Grace: Implications of the O. J. Simpson Trial for Postmodern Criminal Justice." *Sociological Spectrum* 17: 305–22.

Morris, Charles. 1970. *The Pragmatic Movement.* New York: George Braziller.

Mouffe, Chantal (ed.). 1996. *Deconstruction and Pragmatism: Simon Critchley, Jacques Derrida, Ernesto Laclau and Richard Rorty.* London: Routledge.

Mullins, Nicholas (with the assistance of Carolyn Mullins). 1973. *Theory and Theory Groups in Contemporary American Sociology.* New York: Harper and Row.

Murphy, John W. 1989. *Postmodern Social Analysis and Criticism.* New York: Greenwood Press.

Music Festival Home Page. 2003. "1969 Woodstock Performers Song List." Retrieved March 23, 2003, from http//www.geocities.com/~music-festival/wsonglist.htm.

Naffine, Ngaire. 1996. *Feminism and Criminology.* Philadelphia: Temple University Press.

Nasaw, David. 1993. *Going Out: The Rise and Fall of Public Amusements.* New York: Basic Books.

Natoli, Joseph, and Linda Hutcheon (eds.). 1993. *A Postmodern Reader.* Albany: State University of New York Press.

Nealon, Jeffrey T. 1993. *Double Reading: Postmodernism after Deconstruction.* Ithaca, NY: Cornell University Press.

Neff, Ronald. 1980. "Labeling vs. Conflict Perspectives on Crime and Deviance: A Proposed Synthesis." *Sociological Forum* 3: 31–46.

Nehring, Neil. 1993. *Flowers in the Dustbin: Culture, Anarchy, and Postwar England.* Ann Arbor: University of Michigan Press.

REFERENCES

Nelson, Cary, Paula A. Treichler, and Lawrence Grossberg. 1992. "Cultural Studies: An Introduction." Pp. 1–22 in *Cultural Studies,* Lawrence Grossberg, Cary Nelson, and Paula Treichler (eds.). New York: Routledge.

New York Times (May 7, 2003). "The Who's Pete Townshend Cautioned over Child Porn." Retrieved May 7, 2003 from http://www.nytimes.com/reuters/arts/entertainment-crime-britain-townshend.html.

Nicholson, Linda J. (ed.). 1990a. *Feminism/Postmodernism.* New York: Routledge.

———. 1990b. "Introduction." Pp. 1–16 in *Feminism/Postmodernism,* Linda J. Nicholson (ed.). New York: Routledge.

Nietzsche, Friedrich. 1927/95. *The Birth of Tragedy,* Clifton P. Fadiman (tr.). New York: Dover.

O'Brien, Lucy. 1995. *She Bop: The Definitive History of Women in Rock, Pop and Soul.* New York: Penguin.

Oleson, Virginia. 1994. "Feminisms and Models of Qualitative Research." Pp. 158–74 in *Handbook of Qualitative Research,* Norman K. Denzin and Yvonna S. Lincoln (eds.). Thousand Oaks, CA: Sage.

Orlov, Paul A. 1998. *An American Tragedy: Perils of the Self Seeking "Success."* Lewisburg, PA: Bucknell University Press.

Orman, John. 1984. *The Politics of Rock Music.* Chicago: Nelson-Hall.

Palladino, Grace. 1996. *Teenagers: An American History.* New York: Basic Books.

Palmer, Robert. 1995. *Rock & Roll: An Unruly History.* New York: Harmony.

Park, Robert E. 1922/70. *The Immigrant Press and Its Control.* Westport, CT: Greenwood Press.

———. 1950. *Race and Culture.* Glencoe, IL: Free Press.

———. 1952. *Human Communities: The City and Human Ecology.* New York: Free Press.

Park, Robert E., Ernest W. Burgess, and Roderick D. McKenzie. 1967. *The City.* Chicago: University of Chicago Press.

Peirce, Charles S. 1940/55. *Philosophical Writings of Peirce.* Justus Buchler (ed.). New York: Dover.

———. 1958/66. Charles S. Peirce: *Selected Writings (Values in a Universe of Chance).* Philip P. Wiener (ed.). New York: Dover.

———. 1991. *Peirce on Signs: Writings on Semiotic by Charles Sanders Peirce.* James Hoopes (ed.). Chapel Hill: University of North Carolina Press.

Pepper, Jon. 1989 "1960s Flower Children Now Grown Up." *Monroe (Louisiana) News-Star* (August 13): 1D.

Perinbanayagam, R. S. 1985. *Signifying Acts: Structure and Meaning in Everyday Life.* Carbondale: Southern Illinois University Press.

———. 2000. *The Presence of Self.* Lanham, MD: Rowman and Littlefield.

REFERENCES

Persons, Stow (ed.). 1950. *Evolutionary Thought in America.* New Haven, Conn.: Yale University Press.

Pfohl, Steven. 1977. "The 'Discovery' of Child Abuse." *Social Problems* 24: 310–23.

———. 1985/94. *Images of Deviance and Social Control: A Sociological History.* New York: McGraw-Hill.

Pielke, Robert G. 1986. *You Say You Want a Revolution: Rock Music in American Culture.* Chicago: Nelson-Hall.

Pizer, Donald. 1966/76. *Realism and Naturalism in Nineteenth-Century American Literature.* New York: Russell and Russell.

———. 1976. *The Novels of Theodore Dreiser: A Critical Study.* Minneapolis: University of Minnesota Press.

———. 1977/98. "American Literary Naturalism: The Example of Dreiser." Pp. 344–54 in *Documents of American Realism and Naturalism,* Donald Pizer (ed.). Carbondale: Southern Illinois University Press.

———. 1982. *Twentieth-Century American Literary Naturalism: An Interpretation.* Carbondale: Southern Illinois University Press.

———. 1995. "Introduction." Pp. 1–18 in *The Cambridge Companion to American Realism and Naturalism: Howells to London,* Donald Pizer (ed.). Cambridge: Cambridge University Press.

——— (ed.). 1998. *Documents of American Realism and Naturalism.* Carbondale: Southern Illinois University Press.

Plummer, Kenneth. 1979. "Misunderstanding Labelling Perspectives." Pp. 85–121 in *Deviant Interpretations,* David Downes and Paul Rock (eds.). London: Martin Robertson.

Potter, Gary W., and Victor E. Kappeler. 1998. "Introduction." Pp. 1–24 in *Constructing Crime: Perspectives on Making News and Social Problems,* Gary W. Potter and Victor E. Kappeler (eds.). Prospect Heights, IL: Waveland.

Probyn, Elspeth. 1990. "Travels in the Postmodern: Making Sense of the Local." Pp. 176–89 in *Feminism/Postmodernism,* Linda J. Nicholson (ed.). New York: Routledge.

Punday, Daniel. 2003. *Narrative after Deconstruction.* Albany, NY: State University of New York Press.

Purdy, Mark. 1994. "15 Years Later, We Still Ask, Who? Why?" *Cincinnnati Enquirer* (December 4): B1.

Quinney, Richard. 1970. *The Social Reality of Crime.* Boston: Little Brown.

———. 1977. *Class, State and Crime: On the Theory and Practice of Criminal Justice.* New York: David McKay.

Rabinow, Paul. 1984. "Introduction." Pp. 3–29 in *The Foucault Reader,* by Michel Foucault, Paul Rabinow (ed.). New York: Pantheon.

REFERENCES

Rafter, Nicole Hahn. 1990. "The Social Construction of Crime and Crime Control." *Journal of Research in Crime and Delinquency* 27 (November): 376–89.

Rafter, Nicole Hahn, and Frances Heidensohn (eds.). 1995. *International Feminist Perspectives in Criminology: Engendering a Discipline.* Philadelphia: Open University Press.

Rafter, Nicole Hahn, and Elizabeth A. Stanko (eds.). 1982. *Judge, Lawyer, Victim, Thief: Women, Gender Roles, and Criminal Justice.* Boston: Northeastern University Press.

Rains, Prudence. 1975. "Imputations of Deviance: A Retrospective Essay on the Labeling Perspective." *Social Problems* 23: 1–11.

Rajan, Tilottana. 2002. *Deconstruction and the Remainders of Phenomenology: Sartre, Derrida, Foucault, Baudeillard.* Stanford, CA: Stanford University Press.

Reck, Andrew J. 1964. "Introduction." Pp. xiii–lxix in *Selected Writings: George Herbert Mead,* Andrew J. Reck (ed.). Chicago: University of Chicago Press.

Reinarman, Craig, and Ceres Duskin. 1996. "Dominant Ideology and Drugs in the Media." Pp. 317–31 in *Constructing Crime: Perspectives on Making News and Social Problems,* Gary W. Potter and Victor E. Kappeler (eds.). Prospect Heights, IL: Waveland.

Reynolds, Larry T. 1987. *Interactionism: Exposition and Critique.* Dix Hills, NY: General Hall.

Rhodes, Chip. 1998. *Structures of the Jazz Age: Mass Culture, Progressive Education, and Racial Disclosures in American Modernism.* London: Verso.

Rice, Marcia. 1990. "Challenging Orthodoxies in Feminist Theory: A Black Feminist Critique." Pp. 57–69 in *Feminist Perspectives In Criminology,* Loraine Gelsthorpe and Allison Morris (eds.). Philadelphia: Open University Press.

Riggio, Thomas P. 2003. "Note on the Text." Pp. 966–68 in *An American Tragedy* by Theodore Dreiser. New York: Library of America.

Rock, Paul. 1979. *The Making of Symbolic Interaction.* Totowa, NJ: Rowman and Littlefield.

Rodnitsky, Jerome L. 1976. *Minstrels of the Dawn: The Folk-Protest Singer as a Cultural Hero.* Chicago: Nelson-Hall.

Roemer, Michael. 1995. *Telling Stories: Postmodernism and the Invalidation of Traditional Narrative.* Lanham, MD: Rowman and Littlefield.

Rorty, Richard (ed.). 1967. *The Linguistic Turn: Recent Essays in Philosophical Method.* Chicago: University of Chicago Press.

———. 1979. *Philosophy and the Mirror of Nature.* Princeton, NJ: Princeton University Press.

———. 1982. *Consequences of Pragmatism.* Minneapolis: University of Minnesota Press.

———. 1989. *Contingency, Irony, and Solidarity.* New York: Cambridge University Press.

———. 1996. "Remarks on Deconstruction and Pragmatism." Pp. 13–18 in *Deconstruction and Pragmatism: Simon Critchley, Jacques Derrida, Ernesto Laclau, and Richard Rorty,* Chantal Mouffe (ed.). London: Routledge.

———. 1999. *Philosophy and Social Hope.* London: Penguin.

Rose, Tricia. 1994. *Black Noise: Rap Music and Black Culture in Contemporary America.* Hanover, NH: Wesleyan University Press/University Press of New England.

Rosecrance, John. 1986. "You Can't Tell the Players Without a Scorecard: A Typology of Horse Players." *Deviant Behavior* 7: 77–97.

Ross, Dorothy. 1972. *G. Stanley Hall: The Psychologist as Prophet.* Chicago: University of Chicago Press.

Royle, Nicholas. 2000. "What Is Deconstruction?" Pp. 1–13 in *Deconstructions: A User's Guide.* Nicholas Royle (ed.). Basingstoke, U.K.: Palgrave.

Rubington, Earl, and Martin S. Weinberg. 1995. *The Study of Social Problems: Seven Perspectives.* Fifth Edition. New York: Oxford University Press.

———. 2002. *Deviance: The Interactionist Perspective.* Eighth Edition. Boston: Allyn and Bacon.

Rucker, Darnell. 1969. *The Chicago Pragmatists.* Minneapolis: University of Minnesota Press.

Ruland, Richard, and Malcolm Bradbury. 1991. *From Puritanism to Postmodernism: A History of American Literature.* London: Penguin.

Russell, Katheryn K. 1992. "Development of a Black Criminology and the Role of the Black Criminologist." *Justice Quarterly* 9: 667–83.

Ruth, David E. 1996. *Inventing the Public Enemy: The Gangster in American Culture, 1918–1934.* Chicago: University of Chicago Press.

Ryan, Alan. 1995. *John Dewey and the High Tide of American Liberalism.* New York: W. W. Norton.

Ryan, Michael. 1982. *Marxism and Deconstruction: A Critical Articulation.* Baltimore: Johns Hopkins University Press.

Ryan, Michael, and Douglas Kellner. 1988. *Camera Politica: The Politics and Ideology of Contemporary Hollywood Film.* Bloomington: Indiana University Press.

Sacco, Vincent F., and Leslie W. Kennedy. 2002. *The Criminal Event: Perspectives in Space and Time.* Second Edition. Belmont, CA: Wadsworth.

Sagarin, Edward. 1969. *Odd Man In: Societies of Deviants in America.* Chicago: Quadrangle Books.

———. 1975. *Deviants and Deviance: An Introduction to the Study of Disvalued People and Behavior.* New York: Praeger.

———. 1985. "Positive Deviance: An Oxymoron." *Deviant Behavior* 6: 169–81.

REFERENCES

Sallis, John (ed.). 1987. *Deconstruction and Philosophy: The Texts of Jacques Derrida.* Chicago: University of Chicago Press.

Sanders, Clinton R. 1990. "'A Lot of People Like It': The Relationship Between Deviance and Popular Culture." Pp. 3–13 in *Marginal Conventions: Popular Culture, Mass Media, and Social Deviance.* Clinton R. Sanders (ed.). Bowling Green, OH: Bowling Green State University Popular Press.

Sartre, Jean-Paul. 1988. *"What Is Literature?" and Other Essays.* Steven Ungar (in.). Cambridge, MA: Harvard University Press.

Sarup, Madan. 1988/93. *An Introductory Guide to Post-Structuralism and Postmodernism.* Second Edition. Athens: University of Georgia Press.

———. 1996. *Identity, Culture and the Postmodern World.* Athens: University of Georgia Press.

Saussure, Ferdinand de. 1986. *Course in General Linguistics.* Chales Bally and Albert Sechehaye (eds.) and Roy Harris (tr.). Chicago: Open Court.

Scheff, Thomas. 1964. "The Societal Reaction to Deviance: Ascriptive Elements in the Psychiatric Screening of Mental Patients In a Midwestern State." *Social Problems* 11: 401–13.

———. 1966. *Being Mentally Ill: A Sociological Theory.* Chicago: Aldine.

———. 2003. "Shame in Self and Society." *Symbolic Interaction* 26 (spring): 239–62.

Schur, Edwin M. 1969a. *Our Criminal Society: The Social and Legal Sources of Crime In America.* Englewood Cliffs, NJ: Prentice-Hall.

———. 1969b. "Reactions To Deviance: A Critical Assessment." *American Journal of Sociology* 75: 309–22.

———. 1971. *Labeling Deviant Behavior: Its Sociological Implications.* New York: Harper and Row.

———. 1973. *Radical Nonintervention: Rethinking the Delinquency Problem.* Englewood Cliffs, NJ: Prentice-Hall.

———. 1979. *Interpreting Deviance: A Sociological Introduction.* New York: Harper and Row.

———. 1980. *The Politics of Deviance: Stigma Contests and the Uses of Power.* Englewood Cliffs, NJ: Prentice-Hall.

———. 1984. *Labeling Women Deviant: Gender, Stigma, and Social Control.* New York: Harper and Row.

———. 1988. *The Americanization of Sex.* Philadelphia: Temple University Press.

Schwandt, Thomas A. 1994. "Constructivist, Interpretivist Approaches to Human Inquiry." Pp. 118–37 in *Handbook of Qualitative Research,* Norman K. Denzin and Yvonna S. Lincoln (eds.). Thousand Oaks, CA: Sage.

Scraton, Phil. 1990. "Scientific Knowledge or Masculine Discourses?: Challenging Patriarchy In Criminology." Pp. 10–25 in *Feminist Perspectives In Crimi-*

REFERENCES

nology, Loraine Gelsthorpe and Allison Morris (eds.). Philadelphia: Open University Press.

Scull, Andrew. 1984. "Competing Perspectives on Deviance." *Deviant Behavior* 5: 275–89.

Seigfried, Charlene Haddock. 1996. *Pragmatism and Feminism: Reweaving the Social Fabric.* Chicago: University of Chicago Press.

Shalin, Dmitri. N. 1993. "Modernity, Postmodernism, and Pragmatist Inquiry: An Introduction." *Symbolic Interaction* 16(4): 303–32.

Shaskolsky, Leon. 1970. "The Development of Sociological Theory in America: A Sociology of Knowledge Interpretation." Pp. 6–30 in *The Sociology of Sociology*, Larry T. Reynolds and Janice M. Reynolds (eds.). New York: McKay.

Shaw, Clifford R. 1930/66. *The Jack-Roller: A Delinquent Boy's Own Story.* Chicago: University of Chicago Press.

——— (with the collaboration of Maurice E. Moore). 1931/68. *The Natural History of a Delinquent Career.* New York: Greenwood Press.

Shaw, Clifford R., and Henry D. McKay. 1942/69. *Juvenile Delinquency and Urban Areas.* Revised Edition. Chicago: University of Chicago Press.

Sheff, David. 1994. "Pete Townshend: The Playboy Interview." *Playboy* (February): 51–59; 148–51.

Shi, David E. 1995. *Facing Facts: Realism in American Thought and Culture 1850–1920.* New York: Oxford University Press.

Short, James F., Jr. (ed.). 1971. *The Social Fabric of the Metropolis: Contributions of The Chicago School of Urban Sociology.* Chicago: University of Chicago Press.

Showalter, Elaine. 1997. *Hystories: Hysterical Epidemics and Modern Media.* New York: Columbia.

Simmel, Georg. 1964. *Conflict and the Web of Group-Affiliations,* Kurt H. Wolff and Reinhard Bendix (trs.). New York: Free Press.

———. 1971. *On Individuality and Social Forms,* Donald N. Levine (ed. and tr.). Chicago: University of Chicago Press.

Simons, Herbert W., and Michael Billig (eds). 1994. *After Postmodernism: Reconstructing Ideology Critique.* London: Sage.

Smart, Barry. 1990. "Modernity, Postmodernity and the Present." Pp. 14–29 in *Theories of Modernity and Postmodernity,* Bryan S. Turner (ed.). London: Sage.

———. 1992. *Modern Conditions, Postmodern Controversies.* London: Routledge.

Smart, Carol. 1995. *Law, Crime and Sexuality: Essays in Feminism.* Thousand Oaks, CA: Sage.

Smith, Dorothy E. 1989. "Sociological Theory: Methods of Writing Patriarchy." Pp. 34–64 in *Feminism and Sociological Theory,* Ruth A. Wallace (ed.). Newbury Park, CA: Sage.

REFERENCES

Spector, Malcolm, and John I. Kitsuse. 1987. *Constructing Social Problems.* New York: Aldine de Gruyter.

Spitz, Robert Stephen. 1979. *Barefoot in Babylon: The Creation of the Woodstock Music Festival, 1969.* New York: Viking.

Spitzer, Steven. 1975. "Toward a Marxian Theory of Deviance." *Social Problems* 22: 638–51.

Stanfield, John H., II. 1994. "Ethnic Modeling Qualitative Research." Pp. 175–88 in *Handbook of Qualitative Research,* Norman K. Denzin and Yvonna S. Lincoln (eds.). Thousand Oaks, CA: Sage.

Stansell, Christine. 2001. *American Moderns: Bohemian New York and the Creation of a New Century.* New York: Henry Holt.

Steedman, Carolyn. 1992. "Culture, Cultural Studies, and the Historians." Pp. 613–22 in *Cultural Studies,* Lawrence Grossberg, Cary Nelson, and Paula Treichler (eds.). New York: Routledge.

Stevenson, Nick. 2002. *Understanding Media Cultures: Social Theory and Mass Communication.* Second Edition. London: Sage.

Stone, Oliver, and Zachary Sklar. 1992. *JFK: The Book of the Film.* New York: Applause Books.

Storey, John. 1993. *An Introductory Guide to Cultural Theory and Popular Culture.* Athens: University of Georgia Press.

———. 1996. *Cultural Studies and the Study of Popular Culture: Theories and Methods.* Athens: University of Georgia Press.

———. 1999. *Cultural Consumption and Everyday Life.* New York: Oxford University Press.

Stuhr, John J. 2003. *Pragmatism, Postmodernism, and the Future of Philosophy.* New York: Routledge.

Sumner, Colin. 1994. *Deviance: An Obituary.* New York: Continuum.

Surber, Jere Paul. 1998. *Culture and Critique: An Introduction to the Critical Discourses of Cultural Studies.* Boulder, CO: Westview.

Surette, Ray. 1994. "Predator Criminals as Media Icons." Pp. 131–58 in *Media, Process, and the Social Construction of Crime: Studies in Newsmaking Criminology,* Gregg Barak (ed.). New York: Garland.

———. 1998. *Media, Crime, and Criminal Justice: Images and Realities.* Belmont, CA: Wadsworth.

Sutherland, Edwin H. 1949/83. *White Collar Crime: The Uncut Version.* New Haven, CT: Yale University Press.

Sutherland, Edwin H., Donald R. Cressey, and David F. Luckenbill. 1992. *Principles of Criminology.* Eleventh Edition. Dix Hills, NY: General Hall.

Tannenbaum, Frank. 1938. *Crime and the Community.* New York: Ginn.

REFERENCES

Taylor, Ian, Paul Walton, and Jock Young. 1973. *The New Criminology: For a Sociology of Deviance.* London: Routledge and Kegan Paul.

Thio, Alex. 1995. "A Posthumanist Perspective." Pp. 91–98 in *Readings in Deviant Behavior,* Alex Thio and Thomas Calhoun (eds.). New York: HarperCollins.

———. 2004. *Deviant Behavior.* Seventh Edition. Boston: Allyn and Bacon.

Thomas, W. I. 1923/71. "On the Definition of the Situation." Pp. 274–77 in Marcello Truzzi (ed.), *Sociology: The Classic Statements.* New York: Random House.

Thomas, W. I., and Dorothy Swaine Thomas. 1928. *The Child in America: Behavior Problems and Programs.* New York: Alfred A. Knopf.

Thomas, W. I., and Florian Znaniecki. 1984. *The Polish Peasant in Europe and America.* Eli Zaretsky (ed. and ab.). Urbana: University of Illinois Press.

Thompson, Carol Y. 1998. "The Psycho-femme: Identity Norm Violations and the Interactional Dynamics of Assignment." *Deviant Behavior* 19: 207–26.

Thompson, E. P. 1963. *The Making of the English Working Class.* New York: Vintage.

Thompson, John B. 1990. *Ideology and Modern Culture: Critical Social Theory in the Era of Mass Communication.* Stanford, CA: Stanford University Press.

Thrasher, Frederic. 1927/68. *The Gang: A Study of 1,313 Gangs in Chicago.* Chicago: University of Chicago Press.

Times Herald-Record (Middletown, NY). 1994. "How Woodstock Happened...." Woodstock Commemorative Edition. Retrieved March 23. 2003, from http://www.geocities.com/~music-festival/how-w.htm.

Townshend, Pete (with Jeff Young). 1999. *Lifehouse.* London: Simon and Schuster.

Trotter, David. 1999. "The Modernist Novel." Pp. 70–99 in *The Cambridge Companion to Modernism,* Michael Levenson (ed.). Cambridge: Cambridge University Press.

Turk, Austin T. 1982. *Political Criminality: The Defiance and Defense of Authority.* Newbury Park, CA: Sage.

Turner, Bryan S. 1990a. "Periodization and Politics in the Postmodern." Pp. 1–13 in *Theories of Modernity and Postmodernity,* Bryan S. Turner (ed.). London: Sage.

———. 1990b. *Theories of Modernity and Postmodernity.* London: Sage.

Turner, Graeme. 1990/2003. *British Cultural Studies: An Introduction.* London: Routledge.

Twitchell, James B. 1999. *Lead Us Into Temptation: The Triumph of American Materialism.* New York: Columbia.

Ulmer, Jeffery. 2003. "Demarginalizing Symbolic Interaction: A Comment on 'Interactionism's Place.'" *Symbolic Interactionism* 26 (winter): 19–31.

U.S. Congress. 1998. *The Starr Report: The Findings of Independent Counsel Kenneth W. Starr on President Clinton and the Lewinsky Affair.* New York: Public Affairs.

REFERENCES

Veblen, Thorstein. 1899/1994. *The Theory of the Leisure Class*. New York: Dover.
Vold, George B., Thomas J. Bernard, and Jeffrey B. Snipes. 1998. *Theoretical Criminology*. Fourth Edition. New York: Oxford University Press.
Wagner, David. 1997. *The New Temperance: The American Obsession with Sin and Vice*. Boulder, CO: Westview.
Walby, Sylvia. 1990. *Theorizing Patriarchy*. Oxford: Blackwell.
Walcutt, Charles C. 1956/98. "New Ideas in the Novel." Pp. 277–95 in *Documents of American Realism and Naturalism,* Donald Pizer (ed.). Carbondale: Southern Illinois University Press.
Wallace, Michele. 1992. "Negative Images: Towards a Black Feminist Cultural Criticism." Pp. 654–64 in *Cultural Studies,* Lawrence Grossberg, Cary Nelson, and Paula Treichler (eds.). New York: Routledge.
Ward, Ed, Geoffrey Stokes, and Ken Tucker. 1986. *Rock of Ages: The Rolling Stone History of Rock and Roll*. New York: Summit.
Waters, Malcolm. 1994. *Modern Sociological Theory*. London: Sage.
Watson, Peter. 2001. *The Modern Mind: An Intellectual History of the 20th Century*. New York: HarperCollins.
Weiler. A. H. 1951/2003. "A Place in the Sun." *New York Times*. Retrieved October 30, 2003, from http://movies2.nytimes.com/mem/movies/review.html
Weinstein, Deena. 1991. *Heavy Metal: A Cultural Sociology*. New York: Lexington.
Wenner, Jann S. 1968. "Pete Townshend: The Rolling Stone Interview." *Rolling Stone* (October 15): 39–40.
West, Candace, and Don H. Zimmerman. 1998. "Doing Gender." Pp. 161–66 in *Gender Inequality: Feminist Theories and Politics,* Judith Lorber (ed.). Los Angeles: Roxbury.
West, Cornel. 1989. *The American Evasion of Philosophy: A Genealogy of Pragmatism*. Madison: University of Wisconsin Press.
———. 1992. "The Postmodern Crisis of the Black Intellectuals." Pp. 689–96 in Cultural Studies, Lawrence Grossberg, Cary Nelson, and Paula Treichler (eds.). New York: Routledge.
Whetmore, Edward Jay. 1985. *Mediamerica: Form, Content, and Consequence of Mass Communication*. Third Edition. Belmont, CA: Wadsworth.
White, Roland C., Jr. 1990. *Liberty and Justice for All: Racial Reform and the Social Gospel (1877–1925)*. New York: Harper and Row.
Whyte, William Foote. 1943/55. *Street Corner Society*. Enlarged Edition. Chicago: University of Chicago Press.
Williams, Raymond. 1958/66. *Culture and Society: 1780–1950*. New York: Harper and Row.
———. 1961/2001. *The Long Revolution*. Ontario: Broadview.
———. 1966. *Modern Tragedy*. Stanford, CA: Stanford University Press.

———. 1975. *Television: Technology and Cultural Form.* New York: Schocken.

———. 1982. *The Sociology of Culture.* New York: Schocken.

———. 2001. *The Raymond Williams Reader,* John Higgins (ed.). Oxford: Blackwell.

Willis, Paul. 1978. *Profane Culture.* London: Routledge and Kegan Paul.

Winant, Howard. 2001. *The World Is a Ghetto: Race and Democracy since World War II.* New York: Basic Books.

Windschuttle, Keith. 1997. *The Killing of History: How Literary Critics and Social Theorists Are Murdering Our Past.* New York: Free Press.

Wirth, Louis. 1928/62. *The Ghetto.* Chicago: University of Chicago Press.

Woodward, C. Vann. 1955/74. *The Strange Career of Jim Crow.* Third Edition. New York: Oxford University Press.

Wyatt-Brown, Bertram. 1982. *Southern Honor: Ethics and Behavior in the Old South.* New York: Oxford University Press.

Young, Alison. 1996. *Imagining Crime: Textual Outlaws and Criminal Conversations.* London: Sage.

Zatz, Marjorie S., and Coramae Richey Mann. 1998. "The Power of Images." Pp. 1–12 in *Images of Color; Images of Crime: Readings,* Coramae Richey Mann and Marjorie S. Zatz (eds.). Los Angeles: Roxbury.

Ziff, Larzer. 1966. *The American 1890s: Life and Times of a Lost Generation.* New York: Viking.

Zorbaugh, Harvey W. 1929/48. *The Gold Coast and the Slum: A Sociological Study of Chicago's Near North Side.* Chicago: University of Chicago Press.

AUTHOR INDEX

Adorno, Theodor, 144–45
Althusser, Louis, 11, 19, 26, 140, 149–50, 185
Alway, Joan, 9, 137, 159–60
Andersen, Margaret L., 99, 152, 155, 162
Anderson, Nels, 105
Aronowitz, Stanley, 6–7, 42, 145–47, 152–53, 183n8, 155, 220

Barak, Gregg, 12, 35, 36, 43, 99, 120, 228–29, 234
Barthes, Roland, 11, 27, 137, 141–42, 150–51, 154, 164, 210–11, 218
Baudrillard, Jean, 6, 8, 16, 20, 26, 34, 40, 136, 176–79, 180–81, 234, 271, 276, 286
Bayles, Martha, 187–88, 191, 223n1
Bazin, Andre, 240
Becker, Howard S., 1, 3–5, 7, 11, 13, 16–17, 38, 54, 83–84, 87, 89, 93–98, 100–102, 108–10, 116, 121, 127–28, 132n6, 133n9, 135, 195, 250, 275
Benjamin, Walter, 146–47

Ben-Yehuda, Nachman, 39, 84, 128–30, 233
Best, Joel, 4, 14, 132n5, 278, 280
Best, Steven, 6, 8, 10, 15, 49, 135, 140–41, 165, 181, 182n2
Blumer, Herbert, 1, 7, 17, 25, 26, 49, 54, 68–73, 79n2, 80n3, 100, 102, 124, 133n6, 275
Bowlby, Rachel, 265, 267
Bradbury, Malcolm, 77, 239, 265, 272n1
Brandon, Craig, 226, 242–49, 252, 254, 255, 261
Brownell, Joseph W., 13, 226, 242–49, 252–53, 255, 261, 271
Bulmer, Martin, 53, 79n1, 133n11
Butler, Judith, 12, 75, 78, 159, 241, 280

Carrington, Kerry, 12, 100, 117–18, 120, 123
Clinard, Marshall B., 27, 108, 231
Cohen, Stanley, 6, 84, 185, 194–95, 201, 203–4
Collins, Patricia Hill, 6, 9, 12, 99, 116, 137, 152, 155, 160, 162

AUTHOR INDEX

Connor, Steven, 8, 49, 182n2
Conrad, Peter, 239, 272n1
Cooley, Charles Horton, 2–3, 80n7
Cowley, Malcolm, 239
Cressey, Paul G., 105
Culler, Jonathan D., 8, 20, 29, 30, 44
Curtis, Susan, 227, 269

Daly, Kathleen, 12, 99–100, 116–18, 120, 123, 159
Davis, Nanette J., 96, 105, 108, 132n5
Debord, Guy, 34, 136, 157, 276, 284
Denzin, Norman K., 2–3, 5–9, 11–13, 15–16, 19–29, 32, 39, 42, 44–45, 48, 49n1, 50n8–9, 53–54, 72, 74, 79n1, 79n2, 80n7, 81n11, 111, 131n1, 135–36, 138–41, 154, 156, 157, 182n3, 186, 198, 220, 223, 234, 240–41, 251, 259, 260, 275–76, 280, 285–86
Derrida, Jacques, 8, 9, 20, 25, 28, 30, 38, 43–47, 76–77, 136, 141–42, 154, 171–76, 183n12, 210, 216, 227, 234, 236, 242, 251, 259–60, 279, 285
Dewey, John, 5, 10, 58–61, 80n6, 80n7
Dickens, David R., 8, 25, 174–75
Diggins, John Patrick, 13, 54, 60–61, 75–76, 80n4, 80n6
Dosse, Francois, 141, 168, 173, 183n7
Dotter, Daniel, 5, 7–11, 13, 16–19, 24–25, 27, 29, 37, 40, 44, 46, 54, 56, 69, 71, 79n3, 84–85, 87, 90, 93, 99, 100, 104–5, 114, 121, 134, 141, 156, 158, 185–86, 188, 191–92, 194, 198, 200–201, 203–4, 209, 211, 217–18, 221, 225–26, 233, 242, 250, 275–76, 279, 282–83, 285

Douglas, Ann, 74, 240, 267, 272n1
Douglas, Jack D., 1–2, 7, 13, 83–84, 98–99, 101, 111–15, 121, 130, 133
Downes, David, 103, 106, 113
Dreiser, Theodore, 13, 226, 242, 255–63, 272n3, 272n4, 272–73n5, 273n6, 281–82
Dreyfus, Hubert L., 167–70
Dumenil, Lynn, 236, 239

Eagleton, Terry, 8, 11, 19, 29, 136, 140–41, 150, 234–35
Eby, Clare Virginia, 13, 227, 266–67
Eglin, Peter, 84, 111, 132n5, 278
Ennis, Philip H., 187–91, 193, 202, 220, 223n2
Ericksen, E. Gordon, 11, 69, 79n3, 132n3, 275
Erikson, Kai T., 1, 17, 101, 126

Farganis, Sondra, 133n14, 140, 159, 161
Fass, Paula S., 227, 264
Featherstone, Mike, 15, 135, 185
Ferrell, Jeff, 13, 33, 40, 226, 228, 282–83
Fisher-Giorlando, Marianne, 24, 37, 44, 218, 233, 242
Fishkin, Shelley Fisher, 265–66, 272–73n5
Fishman, Mark, 35, 39, 226, 231, 283
Foucault, Michel, 8, 20, 27, 40, 46, 78, 136, 141–42, 167–70, 217, 271, 279, 280, 285
Frith, Simon, 151, 185, 192, 196

Gabler, Neal, 29, 32
Garfinkel, Harold, 7, 99, 115
George, Nelson, 188, 202

AUTHOR INDEX

Gerth, Hans, 5, 219
Gibbs, Jack P., 4, 93–94
Giddens, Anthony, 47, 165, 220
Gilbert, James, 84, 121, 138, 193–94
Gillett, Charlie, 186–87, 190–91
Giuliano, Geoffrey, 204–5, 212–16, 218, 220
Goffman, Erving, 1, 7, 10, 13, 17–18, 50n3, 79–80n3, 83–84, 88–89, 99, 121, 130, 131n2, 132–33n8, 219
Goode, Erich, 39, 83–86, 93, 95, 99, 102–3, 126, 128–30, 131n1, 133n9, 233, 278
Gramsci, Antonio, 11, 19, 140, 149–51, 185
Grossberg, Lawrence, 6, 9, 19, 135, 185
Gubrium, Jaber F., 14, 26–27, 276, 285

Habermas, Jurgen, 147–48, 234
Hall, Stuart, 6, 10–11, 19, 43, 137–38, 140, 149–53, 185, 195, 237–39, 260, 271
Hebdige, Dick, 6, 12, 19–20, 26, 75, 137, 140, 149, 150–51, 185, 195, 281–82
Hester, Stephen, 84, 11, 132n5, 278
Hildebrand, David L., 54, 75–76
Hofstadter, Richard, 59, 279
Hoggart, Richard, 148
Holstein, James A., 14, 26–27, 132n5, 276, 285
Hook, Sidney, 54, 235
Horkheimer, Max, 144–45
Huey, Jacklyn, 7
Hughes, Everett C., 54, 133n12
Humphreys, Laud, 83, 132n6
Hussman, Lawrence E., 270, 273n6

Ingraham, Chrys, 137, 233

James, William, 10, 56–57, 80n4, 80n6, 80n7
Jameson, Fredric, 6, 19, 33–34, 48, 138, 153–54
Jefferson, Tony, 6, 19, 137, 185, 195, 281
Jenkins, Philip, 10, 36, 39, 84, 232–33
Jervis, John, 14, 27, 29, 32, 75, 279–80
Joas, Hans, 53–56, 59, 63, 66–67, 79–80n3
Johnson, Richard, 6, 136–37, 156, 182n3
Jordan, Glenn, 14, 75, 280

Kaplan, Amy, 13, 227, 238, 263, 268
Katz, Ephraim, 9, 29
Katz, Jack, 232
Kellner, Douglas, 6, 8, 10, 15, 32, 34, 36, 49, 135–36, 140–41, 143, 145, 153–55, 157, 165, 176, 178, 180–81, 182n2, 183n10, 216, 220, 231, 275–77, 282–84, 287n3
Kitsuse, John I., 93, 132n5
Klapp, Orrin E., 38, 40, 198, 203, 209
Kotarba, Joseph A., 158
Kracauer, Siegfried, 240
Kuhn, Manford H., 7
Kurtz, Lester R., 54, 79n1, 133n11, 133n13

Lehan, Richard, 262, 272n1
Leighton, Paul S., 12, 228
Lemert, Charles, 12, 30–31, 46, 51n10, 75–76, 147–48, 159–60, 227, 275, 279, 284–85
Lemert, Edwin M., 1, 13, 89, 94, 98
Leslie, Paul, 223n3, 231
Levi-Strauss, Claude, 141, 183n7
Liazos, Alexander, 4, 83, 96
Lilla, Mark, 47, 175–76, 183n7

AUTHOR INDEX

Lincoln, Yvonna S., 44–45, 50n8, 234, 275
Lingeman, Richard, 13, 255, 262
Lofland, John, 17, 114
Lorber, Judith, 12, 116, 118–19, 160
Lucy, Niall, 8, 13, 27, 29
Lundquist, James, 256, 262
Lyman, Stanford M., 47, 79n2, 81n12, 99, 115, 138, 140, 176, 183n10
Lynch, Michael J., 7
Lyotard, Jean-Francois, 8, 20, 28, 136, 139, 141, 164–66, 279

Maher, Lisa, 12, 99–100, 117, 120, 123, 159
Maines, David R., 4, 50n1, 79n1, 104
Makower, Joel, 186, 199–200
Manning, Peter K., 11, 45, 47, 74, 141, 277, 286, 287n1
Marcus, Greil, 186, 192, 209
Marcuse, Herbert, 146
Marsh, Dave, 203–6
Matza, David, 2, 11, 17, 84, 91–92, 97, 102, 104–7, 125, 263, 275, 279, 286
McCall, Michal M., 5, 16, 135
McKay, Henry D., 106
McKenzie, Roderick D., 104
McRobbie, Angela, 138, 140, 149, 152, 161, 185, 197, 202
Mead, George Herbert, 1, 5, 7, 25, 62–66, 80
Meier, Robert F., 37
Menand, Louis, 55, 57, 76, 275
Miller, David L., 65–66, 80n8, 80n9, 80n10
Mills, C. Wright, 4–6, 8, 11, 12, 16, 21, 54, 138–39, 155, 219, 275
Mitchell, Lee Clark, 13, 239, 266

Moore, Lynda J., 234
Moore, Michael C., 234

Naffine, Ngaire, 12, 99, 116–18, 159
Nelson, Cary, 6, 9, 19, 135, 149, 151
Nicholson, Linda J., 12, 137, 159–61, 164
Nietzsche, Friedrich, 234

Orlov, Paul A., 265

Palladino, Grace, 190–92
Palmer, Robert, 187, 191
Park, Robert E., 17, 72, 104–5
Peirce, Charles S., 53, 55, 57–58
Perinbanayagam, R. S., 14, 18, 25, 48, 65, 67, 79–80n3, 125, 238, 242–44, 276, 285
Persons, Stow, 279
Pizer, Donald, 13, 239, 264, 272n1
Plummer, Kenneth, 93, 97, 130

Quinney, Richard, 108, 132n7

Rabinow, Paul, 167–70, 183n11
Rafter, Nicole Hahn, 99, 116–17, 120
Reck, Andrew J., 62, 66, 80n8
Reynolds, Larry T., 4, 63, 67, 79n1
Rhodes, Chip, 264, 268
Rock, Paul, 53, 67, 72, 80n3, 103, 105–6, 113, 268
Roebuck, Julian B., 8, 13, 16, 18, 37, 46, 85, 87, 90, 93, 100, 114, 218, 220, 225, 250, 275
Roemer, Michael, 50n7, 210, 218
Rorty, Richard, 13, 20–21, 54, 76–77, 280
Rose, Tricia, 12, 121, 158, 282
Rubington, Earl, 83, 132n5
Ruland, Richard, 239, 265, 272n1

AUTHOR INDEX

Russell, Katheryn K., 12, 116, 118
Ryan, Alan, 59, 61
Ryan, Michael, 175, 183n10

Sagarin, Edward, 7, 18, 88, 90, 132n4, 133n10, 228
Sanders, Clinton R., 13, 40, 201, 226, 228, 282
Sartre, Jean-Paul, 28
Sarup, Madan, 5, 6, 16, 42, 48, 140–42, 182n1
Saussure, Ferdinand de, 171–73
Schur, Edwin M., 1, 6–7, 9–11, 17–18, 39, 83–85, 87, 89, 93–94, 99, 120, 122–23, 126, 129–30, 194, 225, 250, 261, 275, 280
Scott, Marvin B., 99, 115
Shaw, Clifford R., 105–6
Shi, David E., 227, 241, 264, 272n1
Short, James F., Jr., 104
Simmel, Georg, 104
Smith, Dorothy E., 137, 152, 161
Stansell, Christine, 240
Stasz, Clarice, 96, 108, 132n5
Stone, Oliver, 283
Storey, John, 6, 8, 14, 20, 29, 33–34, 141–42, 147, 150, 158, 166, 182n1, 183n9, 183n10, 282
Sumner, Colin, 14, 277–79
Surber, Jere Paul, 167–69, 172, 174, 176, 181, 183n9
Surette, Ray, 35, 229–30, 241, 259
Sutherland, Edwin H., 99, 106–7

Tannenbaum, Frank, 87, 98
Taylor, Ian, 98

Thio, Alex, 96, 131n1
Thomas, W. I., 2–3, 54, 73
Thompson, Carol Y., 183n10
Thompson, E. P., 149
Thrasher, Frederic, 105
Townshend, Pete, 186, 203–5, 208–22
Treichler, Paula, 6, 9, 19, 135
Trotter, David, 240, 272n1
Turk, Austin T., 111

Veblen, Thorstein, 178, 265
Vidich, Arthur J., 79n2, 81n12

Waksler, Frances C., 17, 53, 98, 115
Walcutt, Charles C., 263–64
Walton, Paul, 96
Ward, Ed, 186, 199–201
Watson, Peter, 272n1
Wawrzaszek, Patricia A., 13, 226, 242–49, 252–53, 255, 261, 271
Websdale, Neil, 33, 226, 228, 283
Weedon, Chris, 14, 75, 280
Weinberg, Martin S., 83, 132n5
West, Cornel, 5, 21, 47, 54, 56, 61, 74–75, 137, 235, 275
Whyte, William Foote, 105
Williams, Raymond, 149, 234–37
Willis, Paul, 6, 137, 195
Wirth, Louis, 105

Young, Alison, 40, 88, 159
Young, Jock, 96

Ziff, Larzer, 227, 238
Znaniecki, Florian, 73
Zorbaugh, Harvey W., 17, 105–6

SUBJECT INDEX

age. *See* status as social construction
aging rocker: as cultural hero, 214–20; as deviant master status, 186, 221; Pete Townshend as, 185–86, 210–12; and the postmodern self, 210–12, 216–21; and the rock and roll dream, 212–14, 218–21
American Dream, 265, 281
An American Tragedy (Dreiser), 13, 226, 256–69, 277, 281–82; and interpretive biography, 259–61; as literary naturalism, 263–67; race, class, gender in, 260–61, 264–65, 266–69; youth and consumer culture in, 264–65, 268–69

Chicago School. *See* deviance; symbolic interactionism
class. *See* status as social construction
cultural consumption, 6, 8–9, 19–21, 30, 40, 50n5, 151, 158, 162, 166, 177–78, 180, 196–98, 201, 211, 215–16, 219–21; and the Frankfurt School, 143–44, 146–47, 153; and media culture, 8–10, 152–57, 162–63, 193, 211, 215–18, 221, 241
cultural criminology, 13; constructions of violence, 231–32, 235–36; and crime images, 229; defined, 228; "infotainment," 230–31; and interactionist labeling, 225–26; and mainstream criminology, 226; racial stereotypes, 230; relationship to scenario, 228–29; role of television, 236–37; and tragedy, 233–35
cultural hero, 40, 185, 188, 194, 198, 234
cultural politics, 14, 75, 78, 176, 280, 284, 285
cultural studies, 5, 135–38; American history of, 152–58; and articulation, 237–39; British and American perspectives, 6, 19–20; British history of, 148–52; Derrida's formulation of poststructuralism, 171–81; feminist history of, 159–64; and history of Frankfurt School, 143–48; and interactionism, 6–7, 11–12, 15–16,

SUBJECT INDEX

135, 140, 276; interdisciplinary nature of, 6, 11, 19, 136–37, 182n1; key questions of, 18–19; and labeling, 151, 162, 176, 181–82; and media culture, 31–32, 77, 135–36, 140–43, 148, 152, 283–84; and politics of signification, 238, 260, 271, 280, 285; and popular culture, 8–10, 142–43, 145–48, 151–56, 162–63, 166, 180, 182n1, 183n4; and postmodernism, 5–12, 138–41, 164; and poststructuralism, 135–36, 141–42, 151–52, 158, 159–61, 163–64, 166–67, 169, 171, 183n7; and the study of deviance, 16–21, 45–49, 131, 151, 158–59, 176, 181. *See also* postmodernism

deconstruct(ion), 8–9, 20, 25, 27, 30–33, 44–47, 171, 278–79; Derrida and Saussure, 172–73; and *différance*, 20, 25, 28, 30, 154, 173–74, 285
definition of the situation, 2–3
deviance: "death" of the study of, 276, 277–78; definitions of, 3–4, 85–90, 131n1, 132n4, 132n5, 132n6, 133n9, 133n10; as episodic notion, 193; feminist perspectives on, 85, 99–100, 115–24; as interactional conflict, 13, 99–100, 104–10, 132n7, 286; interactionist theories of, 13, 83–85, 98–124; key labeling questions of, 17–18; labeling, 1–5, 7–13, 16–18, 21, 30, 36, 38–39, 43, 46–49, 53, 78, 80n3, 83–85, 87–90, 275, 278–81, 285–86; labeling and conflict, 111; labeling and the Chicago School, 13, 99–104, 275, 279–80, 286; labeling and criticism, 92–97; as master status, 1, 6–8, 49, 121, 131, 284–85; and naturalism, 83–84, 89–92, 279–81; phenomenological conception of labeling, 85, 98–100, 111–15, 133n15; primary and secondary, 1, 89; and retrospective interpretation, 1, 280; and role engulfment, 1, 280; the social generation of, 8–10, 12–13, 40–41, 43, 85, 87, 102–3, 107, 110, 113–14, 124–28, 131; as stigmatization, 9–10, 12–13, 16–18, 75, 80n3, 83, 84, 87–90, 91, 95, 97, 99–104, 109–10, 114–15, 117–18, 121, 123, 125–26, 128–130, 131–32n2, 132n8, 225–28. *See also* rock music; scenario; stigma contest; stigma movie
deviant event, 16, 37–39, 41–43, 47–49; murder of Grace Brown, 226, 228–29, 231, 235, 236–38, 241–43, 250–51, 256, 260–61, 267–69
differential association, 99, 106–8, 133n13

ethnomethodology, 7, 79n1, 98–99, 111–12, 115, 133n9, 286
existential sociology, 98–99, 112, 115

feminism, 24, 133n14, 136; and criminology, 99, 116–17, 120; and deviance theory, 12–13, 85, 99–100, 115–24; and "matrix of domination," 162; polyvocal nature of criminology and, 118–24; and postmodernism, 24, 50n2, 140,

280, 286; and poststructuralism, 152, 158–63, 167. *See also* ideology

gender. *See* feminism; status as social construction

hyperreality, 20, 139, 179–80, 286

ideology, 5–6, 8–9, 11–13, 19–21, 99, 130, 136–37, 192–94, 211, 227, 234, 267–69; British cultural studies treatment of, 150–52, 185–86, 237–39; feminist critique of, 161–64; Foucault's discursive view of, 167–69; Frankfurt School conceptions of, 145–46; and hegemony, 140, 150–53; and "inferiorization," 123; and labeling, 121–23, 278–79; and "malestream" criminology, 116; media culture and, 19–20, 27, 30, 35–36, 39, 46–49, 152–53; and stigma, 89; of the "underdog" 96
implosion, 34, 40, 43, 179–80, 228
interpretive biography, 16, 23; and epiphany, 42–43; and multiple selves, 24–28; as textual method, 24–25, 259
interpretive interactionism, 7, 16, 276; characteristics of, 23–24

labeling theory. *See* deviance
linguistic turn: and neopragmatism, 54, 76–79; and poststructuralism, 149, 151–52, 159, 171, 279; and pragmatism, 13; and scenario, 20, 28, 46, 49, 279–80
literature (theory and criticism), 13, 76–78, 272n1, 279; and the linguistic turn, 242, 268; modernism, 239–40, 281; naturalism, 238–40, 261–63, 265, 272n1; realism, 238–39; and the scenario, 227, 277; and tragedy, 233–35
looking-glass self, 2–3

Marxism, 5, 11, 90, 95, 96, 99, 108, 111, 132n7, 140, 195, 197; and deconstruction, 175; importance for the Frankfurt School, 143–44, 146–48; influence on Baudrillard, 176, 178; influence on British cultural studies, 149–52, 183n9; and Mill's concept of class, 155–56
media culture. *See* cultural studies; scenario
modernism, 34, 39, 45–46, 54, 60–61, 72, 74–76, 148. *See also* literature; postmodernism; strategic postmodernism
moral panic, 39, 84, 233; and the history of rock music, 194–95, 203

naturalism. *See* deviance; literature
neopragmatism, 13, 21, 49, 54, 74–77; and post-philosophical culture, 77; as prophetic crisis, 74–75, 235

patriarchy, 5, 21, 48, 159, 161–64, 165; and the gender/race imaginary, 233
phenomenology, 13, 17, 45, 58, 286; Derrida's critique of, 171, 183n12; Foucault's articulation of, 167
A Place in the Sun (film), 13, 226, 242, 269–72, 282
popular culture. *See* cultural studies; scenario

SUBJECT INDEX

postmodern condition, 8, 136, 164, 166, 171, 181
postmodern social theory, 15–16, 48–49, 50n1, 76–77, 135, 140, 152, 156, 163, 176
postmodern turn, 8, 15, 31–32, 141, 165, 176, 181–82, 275–78, 281–82, 284–86
postmodernism, 28–48; and meaning crisis, 8, 29, 30, 45, 47, 49, 279, 285; and modernism, 76–78, 165–66, 183n5; and the poststructuralist critique, 5–6, 10, 13, 15–16, 18, 20, 28, 45–46, 279. *See also* cultural studies
poststructuralism. *See* cultural studies; postmodernism
pragmatism, 4–5, 10–11, 13, 50n9, 275, 278, 280; and feminism, 50n2; and Mead's behaviorism, 72; and modernism, 75; and neopragmatism, 74–78; as philosophical roots of interactionism, 53–56; as a philosophy of experience, 56–57, 59–61; as semiotics, 58, 81n11

race. *See* status as social construction
racism, 5–6, 35, 99, 237
realism. *See* literature
rock music: and deviance, 193–98, 281; and lifestyle deviance, 194; as media culture, 28–37, 193, 211–18, 221, 287n2; and political deviance, 194; as public drama, 198, 200–201, 208, 209; role of gender in, 191–92, 197; role of race in, 191, 223n1; as "seventh stream" of popular culture, 187, 220. *See also* aging rocker; The Who; Woodstock Music and Art Fair; youth subculture

scenario: characteristics of, 30–41; and cinematic society, 39–41, 48–49, 156; cultural consumption in, 176; cultural criminology and, 228–29; and deconstruction, 8–9, 30–31, 278–79; defined, 9, 28–29; and deviance-generation, 8, 38–39, 43–44, 78, 276–77; layers of, 41–44; and the linguistic turn, 20, 28, 46, 49; and meaning creation, 8–9, 16, 30–33, 240; and meaning crisis, 8, 29, 30, 45, 47, 49, 285; and popular culture, 21, 285; as stigma contest, 30, 37–41, 85, 128–29, 233, 250; as storytelling, 16, 41–43, 48, 276–77; and "symbolic studies," 276, 278, 284, 286, 287n1
self, 15, 47–48, 51n10; Blumer's conception of, 70–71; creative and ideological, 26, 209–12, 285; as literary product, 26–28; Mead's conception of, 61–67; narrative types of, 26–28; postmodern conception of, 138, 142, 157, 159, 164, 166, 219, 276, 280, 284–86; postmodern conception of and class consciousness, 155; postmodern conception of and *différance*, 154, 173–75; postmodern conception of and Foucault's subject, 24, 27, 170, 183n11. *See also* looking-glass self
sexism, 99, 237
social disorganization, 3, 99, 104–8
Social Gospel, 227, 269
sociological imagination, 16, 21–24, 28–29, 48, 275–76; and media culture, 155

spectacle, 32, 34, 36, 44, 157, 276, 283–84, 286
status as social construction, 4–9, 19–20, 26, 28, 32, 75, 78, 135, 137, 149, 154–58, 161, 181–82, 186–87, 189, 191–92, 276, 285; age, 118–20; biocultural, 115, 118–19, 121, 123, 154, 162; class, 22, 89, 96, 99, 120, 126, 147, 150–51, 153, 155, 163, 178; gender, 84, 89–90, 99, 115–19, 143; layered quality of, 118, 124, 130, 131n2; race, 89, 99, 115–23. *See also* rock music; youth subculture
stigma contest, 9–10, 12, 18, 30, 37, 39, 42, 85, 250, 284. *See also* deviance; scenario
stigma movie, 9, 16, 28, 39–44, 47–49, 227–28, 242, 261, 267, 271. *See also* scenario
strategic postmodernism, 31, 176, 279, 281
symbolic interactionism, 2–4, 79n7, 79n8, 275, 279; and Blumer's critique of science, 67–68, 72–74, 79n2; Blumer's root images of, 68–71; Chicago School of, 7, 10, 11, 12, 13, 53–54, 58–59, 67–68, 75, 78, 228; critiques of Chicago School of, 4–5; and dramaturgy, 79–80n3; modernism and Chicago School of, 263–64, 268; and pragmatism, 4, 75, 80n4; varieties of, 79n1. *See also* cultural studies; neopragmatism; pragmatism

teen subculture. *See* youth subculture
tragedy, 233–35
transgression, 3, 46, 78, 280, 285–86

The Who (rock band), 186, 200, 203; association with violence, 208; and Cincinnati concert deaths (1979), 203–7; *Quadrophenia* as mod history of, 204–5, 208
Woodstock Music and Art Fair, 13, 186, 198–203, 282; race and gender constructions and, 202

youth subculture, 13, 19, 49, 151, 158, 182, 186, 189, 192–95, 276, 281–82; fragmentation of, 198; as stigma contest, 194, 201; as stigma movie, 201–2, 208, 209, 216, 218, 222; and teenage subculture, 190–92; and youth culture, 196

ABOUT THE AUTHOR

Daniel Dotter is professor of criminal justice at Grambling State University in Louisiana. He received his Ph.D. from Virginia Polytechnic Institute and State University and does research in social deviance, youth subculture, and mass media and crime.